AF702653

Written by Giorgio Sacerdoti – with his decades of experience as both an investment arbitrator and a member of the WTO Appellate Body – and Niall Moran, this book does the nearly impossible: it reviews the origins, features, developments as well as current criticism and challenges to both the trade and investment dispute settlement systems. I have long struggled to find accurate and comprehensive materials to help my students understand the differences, similarities and complexities of international trade dispute resolution and investment arbitration. But with this book my search is over.

Jennifer Hillman, ***Georgetown University, former member of the WTO Appellate Body***

To date, scholars and lawyers have looked at the WTO and investor-state dispute settlement systems in separate silos – an ironic fact considering their shared prominence in international economic law. This text is fascinating and educational, taking a fresh approach by comparing the structure, procedure, evolution and future of these mechanisms, and evaluating their commonalities and differences. It invites the reader to think about how similar issues can be addressed differently, and the contribution each system can make to the other.

Meg Kinnear, ***Secretary-General of ICSID (2009-2024)***

The upholding of the rule of law in international economic law is fundamental to ensuring predictability, stability and security in international relations, both economic and beyond. At a time when rule-based adjudication is being challenged, and not just at the WTO, this book is a timely reminder of the value of this instrument in providing the certainty needed for cross-border trade and investment and in fostering an environment conducive to sustainable global economic growth. It represents an essential resource for anyone looking to understand these fields and the issues raised by their reform.

Pascal Lamy, ***Director-General of the WTO (2005-2013)***

The authors offer a unique and remarkable comparative study of the existing trade and investment dispute resolution frameworks, highlighting how both have developed and contributed to the formidable expansion of the global economy post-WWII, as well as the reasons why they have entered in a deep crisis. The book explores with remarkable clarity, for the benefit of all concerned, the commonalities of both and the possible ways to safeguard these indispensable tools to facilitate trade and investments worldwide.

Alexis Mourre, ***Arbitrator, Former President of the Court of Arbitration of the International Chamber of Commerce***

International Trade and Investment Dispute Settlement

This book provides a thorough comparative analysis of the trade dispute settlement system of the WTO, Regional Trade Agreements, and of Investor–State Dispute Settlement (ISDS).

Reviewing in parallel their origins, features, development, and current challenges, highlighting commonalities and differences, the book analyzes criticisms leveled against both regimes, explores current reform efforts at the WTO, ICSID, and UNCITRAL (including the controversial proposal to replace ISDS with a Multilateral Investment Court), and engages in the on-going debate by evaluating possible outcomes. As to trade, the book highlights the WTO system's successful operation for more than 20 years and its hobbling functioning since the paralysis of the Appellate Body in 2019. As to ISDS, the book details the procedural protection granted to foreign investors under Bilateral Investment Treaties (BITs), other International Investment Agreements and investment chapters of trade agreements such as NAFTA, USMCA, CETA, and the CPTPP, alongside the impact of case law on the regulatory space of states.

This authoritative book intends to serve as a fundamental reference for students and researchers in international investment and trade law, as well as for international lawyers, adjudicators, and diplomats involved in dispute settlement.

Giorgio Sacerdoti is an emeritus professor at Bocconi University in Milan, Italy, where he has taught international law for more than 30 years focusing his teaching, research and publications on international trade and investment law, economic cooperation and organizations, arbitration. He has been a member of the WTO Appellate Body (2001–2009) and its chairman (2006–2007). He is admitted to the Bar in Milan and has decades-long experience as an arbitrator in international trade, investment and commercial disputes, at ICSID, of whose roster he is a member, under the rules of a number of other arbitral institutions, and in ad hoc proceedings.

Niall Moran is a tenured assistant professor in Economic Law at Dublin City University, Ireland, where he is also Deputy Director of the Brexit Institute. He holds a PhD in International Economic Law from Bocconi University, and is also a law graduate of the University of Galway, and Université Toulouse 1 Capitole. Niall is a qualified barrister in Ireland and has been admitted as an Attorney in the State of New York. He previously worked for the Legal Service of the Council of the European Union and the Bilateral Relations with the Americas Unit at DG AGRI, European Commission.

Insights on International Economic Law

Series Editor: David Collins, Professor of International Economic Law at City, University of London.

International Economic Law is among the fastest growing and vibrant fields of international law, responding to the escalating tensions in global trade and investment which take on not only economic and legal but also social and geopolitical dimensions. In many respects the issues of International Economic Law are among the most important of our times, as captured for example in the ongoing fascination with the trade aspects of Brexit, the US-China trade war, security-related fears of foreign investment in critical infrastructure projects and the controversial elements of China's economic expansion into the developing world. The Routledge Insights on International Economic Law series an important conduit for the dissemination of crucial, socially valuable research, encompassing peer reviewed short-form style books which examine emerging hot topics in international economic law which have reached a pivotal stage of importance.

The Development Dimension: Special and Differential Treatment in Trade
James Bacchus and Inu Manak

International Insolvency and Finance Law: Legal Constants in Times of Crisis
Daniele D'Alvia

International Trade and Investment Dispute Settlement. From Rise to Crisis and Reform
Giorgio Sacerdoti and Niall Moran

https://www.routledge.com/law/series/IIEL

International Trade and Investment Dispute Settlement

From Rise to Crisis and Reform

Giorgio Sacerdoti and Niall Moran

Routledge
Taylor & Francis Group
LONDON AND NEW YORK

First published 2025
by Routledge
4 Park Square, Milton Park, Abingdon, Oxon OX14 4RN

and by Routledge
605 Third Avenue, New York, NY 10158

Routledge is an imprint of the Taylor & Francis Group, an informa business

© 2025 Giorgio Sacerdoti and Niall Moran

The content of this volume takes into account developments in international trade and investment relations until the end of April 2025, including the introduction of US additional tariffs on imports by the Trump administration until that date.

The right of Giorgio Sacerdoti and Niall Moran to be identified as authors of this work has been asserted in accordance with sections 77 and 78 of the Copyright, Designs and Patents Act 1988.

All rights reserved. No part of this book may be reprinted or reproduced or utilised in any form or by any electronic, mechanical, or other means, now known or hereafter invented, including photocopying and recording, or in any information storage or retrieval system, without permission in writing from the publishers.

Trademark notice: Product or corporate names may be trademarks or registered trademarks, and are used only for identification and explanation without intent to infringe.

British Library Cataloguing-in-Publication Data
A catalogue record for this book is available from the British Library

ISBN: 978-1-032-71061-7 (hbk)
ISBN: 978-1-032-74915-0 (pbk)
ISBN: 978-1-003-47150-9 (ebk)

DOI: 10.4324/9781003471509

Typeset in Times New Roman
by Deanta Global Publishing Services, Chennai, India

To my wife Liliana, in grateful appreciation of her life-long loving support.- Giorgio Sacerdoti

To my wife Alexandra, and our daughter Ailbhe Ivana, who arrived the day this book was completed.
- Niall Moran

To the 27 members of the WTO Appellate Body, coming from every corner and continent of the world, who provided their competent and professional services with dedication for a quarter of a century (1995-2020) to the WTO Members and all the stakeholders in international trade. They supported the smooth functioning of the multilateral trading system by ensuring, through consistent law-based interpretation of the WTO Agreements, legal security and the objective, impartial settlement of trade disputes, thereby advancing the role of international adjudication as an instrument of peaceful cooperation between nations.
- Giorgio Sacerdoti and Niall Moran

Contents

Abbreviations and Acronyms

1. Abbreviations (Publications)

Short citations of often referred to books:

- *A History*: G. Marceau (ed), *A History of Law and Lawyers in the GATT/WTO* (CUP 2015)
- *ICSID Commentary*: Schreuer's *Commentary on the ICSID Convention* (3rd ed. S. Schill, L. Malintoppi, A. Reinisch, C. Schreuer, I. Sinclair (eds), (2 voll. CUP 2022)
- *International Investment Law:* M. Bugenberg, J. Griebel, S. Hobe, A. Reinisch, Y. Kim (eds.), *International Investment Law. A Handbook* (Beck 2015)
- *Key Issues*: R. Yerxa, B. Wilson, *Key Issues in WTO Dispute Settlement* (CUP 2005)
- *Mavroidis:* P. Mavroidis, *The WTO Dispute Settlement System: How, Why and Where?* (Elgard 2022)
- *Merills:* J. Merills, E. de Brabandere, *Merill's International Dispute Settlement* (7th ed.) (CUP 2022)
- *Principles*: R. Dolzer, U. Kriebaum, C. Schreuer, *Principles of International Investment Law* (3rd ed.) (OUP 2022)
- *The WTO at Ten*: G. Sacerdoti, A. Yanovich, Jan Bohanes (eds.), *The WTO at Ten. The Contribution of the Dispute Settlement System* (CUP/WTO 2006)
- *Van den Bossche*: P. Van den Bossche, W. Zdouc, *The Law and Policy of the WTO* (5th ed) (CUP 2022)
- *WTO Handbook*: WTO Legal Affairs Division, *A Handbook on the WTO Dispute Settlement System* (2nd ed) CUP 2017

2. Abbreviations (Journals)

AJIL	American Journal of International Law
American Rev Int'l Arb	American Review of International Arbitration
Arb. Int.	Arbitration International
Arizona J. Int. Comp. L.	Arizona Journal of International and Comparative Law

BYIL	British Yearbook of International Law
Cal L Review	California Law Review
Chicago J Int L	Chicago Journal of International Law
CJIL	Cambridge International Law Journal
Columbia Un. Press	Columbia University Press
CJTL	Columbia Journal of Transnational Law
Cornell Int. L J	Cornell International Law Journal
CUP	Cambridge University Press
DCI	Diritto del Commercio Internazionale
Duke L. J.	Duke Law Journal
EJIL	European Journal of International Law
EJIR	European Journal of International Relations
Eur Law J	European Law Journal
EUI Working Papers	European University Institute Working Papers
EYIEL	European Yearbook of International Economic Law
FlaJIntlL	Florida Journal of International Law
Fordham Int. Law J.	Fordham International Law Journal
GaJIntl&Comp	Georgia Journal of International and Comparative Law
Harvard Un. Press	Harvard University Press
HILJ	Harvard International Law Journal
ICLQ	International & Comparative Law Quarterly
ICSID Rev	ICSID Review
IEEP	International Economics and Economic Policy
ILR	International Law Reports
Int. J. of Humanities and Social Sciences	International Journal of Humanities and Social Sciences
Int. Rev. Law and Economics	International Review of Law and Economics
IYIL	Italian Yearbook of International Law
J Int Trade Law Policy	Journal of International Trade Law and Policy
J. Int. Trade and Arbitration L	Journal of International Trade and Arbitration Law
JIDS	Journal of International Dispute Settlement
JIEL	Journal of International Economic Law
JWI	Journal of World Investment
JWIT	The Journal of World Investment and Trade
JWTL	Journal of World Trade Law
LJIL	Leiden Journal of International Law
Loy. L.A. Int'l & Comp. L. Rev.	Loyola of Los Angeles International and Comparative Law Review
LPICT	The Law and Practice of International Courts and Tribunals
MichJIntlL	Michigan Journal of International Law

MPEiPro	Max Planck Encyclopedia of International Procedural Law
MPEPIL	Max Planck Encyclopedia of Public International Law
Nw. J. Int'l L. & Bus.	Northwestern Journal of International Law and Business
NYU JILP	New York University Journal of International Law and Politics
Ohio State J of Dispute Resolution	Ohio State Journal on Dispute Resolution
OUP	Oxford University Press
Princeton Un. Press	Princeton University Press
RC	Recueil des cours (Hague Academy)
RDI	Rivista diritto internazionale
Rev. Arbitrage	Revue de l'arbitrage
RGDIP	Revue Générale de Droit International Public
Riv. Arbitrato	Rivista dell'Arbitrato
TDM	Transnational Dispute Management
TexIntlLJ	Texas International Law Journal
Trans. Corp. Rev.	Transnational Corporations Review
VaJIntlL	Virginia Journal of International Law
WM. & Mary L Rev	William and Mary Law Review
WSJ	Wall Street Journal
WTR	World Trade Review
Y.B.EUR.L.	Yearbook of European Law
YCA	Yearbook of Commercial Arbitration
YJIL	Yale Journal of International Law
ZEuS	Zeitschrift für Europarechtliche Studien

3. Acronyms

AA	Association Agreement
AANZFTA	Agreement establishing the ASEAN-Australia-New Zealand Free Trade Area
AB	WTO Appellate Body
ABMs	Appellate Body Members
AC	*Amicus/Amici Curiae*
ACWL	Advisory Centre on WTO Law
AD	Investigation and Determination
ADA	WTO Investigation and Determination Agreement
ADR	Alternative Dispute Resolution
AFA	Advanced Framework Agreement
AfCFTA	African Continental Free Trade Area
AR	ICSID Arbitration Rules

ARSIWA	Draft Articles on Responsibility of States for Internationally Wrongful Acts
ASEAN	Association of Southeast Asian Nations
BIICL	British Institute of International and Comparative Law
BIT	Bilateral Investment Treaty
CAS	Court of Arbitration for Sport
CEPS-CTR	Centre for European Policy Studies - Center for Transatlantic Relations
CCIAG	Corporate Counsel International Arbitration Group
CESifo	Center of Economic Studies Information und Forschung
CETA	Comprehensive Economic and Trade Agreement
CIGI	Centre for International Governance Innovation
CISG	United Nations Convention on Contracts for the International Sale of Goods
CJEU	Court of Justice of the European Union
CPTPP	Comprehensive and Progressive Agreement for Trans-Pacific Partnership
Ct	Court
DG	Director-General
DSB	WTO Dispute Settlement Body
DSM	WTO Dispute Settlement Mechanism
DSS	Dispute Settlement System(s)
DSU	WTO Dispute Settlement Understanding
EC	European Community
ECLI	European Case-Law Identifier
ECT	Energy Charter Treaty
ECtHR	European Court of Human Rights
EFTA	European Free Trade Association
EPA	Economic Partnership Agreement
ESG	Environmental, social and governance
EU	European Union
ECJ	European Court of Justice
EUSIPA	Investment Protection Agreement between European Union and its Member States and the Republic of Singapore
EWCA	Court of Appeal of England and Wales
EWHC	High Court of England and Wales
FATF	Financial Action Task Force
FCN	Friendship, Commerce and Navigation Treaties
FDI	Foreign Direct Investment
FET	Fair and Equitable Treatment
FOSFA	Federation of Oils, Seeds and Fats

FSB	Financial Stability Board
FSIA	US Foreign Sovereign Immunities Act
FTA	Free Trade Agreement
GAR	Global Arbitration Review
GAFTA	Grain and Feed Trade Association
GATS	General Agreement on Trade and Services
GATT	General Agreement on Tariffs and Trade
GC	WTO General Council
GDP	Gross Domestic Product
GSP	General System of Preferences
GVC	Global Value Chain
IBA	International Bar Association
IBRD	International Bank for Reconstruction and Development
ICC	International Chamber of Commerce
ICCPR	International Covenant on Civil and Political Rights
ICJ	International Court of Justice
ICS	Investment Court System
ICSID	International Center/Convention for the Settlement of Investment Disputes
ICTR	International Criminal Tribunal for Rwanda
ICTY	International Criminal Tribunal for the former Yugoslavia
IIA	International Investment Agreement
ICTSD	International Centre for Trade and Sustainable Development
IDB	Inter-American Development Bank
IDI	Institut de Droit International
IEHC	Irish High Court
IISD	International Institute for Sustainable Development
ILA	International Law Association
ILC	International Law Commission
IMF	International Monetary Fund
IPA	Investment Protection Agreement
IRA	US Inflation Reduction Act
ISDS	Investor-State Dispute Settlement
ITLOS	International Tribunal for the Law of the Sea
ITO	International Trade Organization
KORUS	US-Korea Free Trade Agreement
LCIA	London Court of International Arbitration
LDC	Least-Developed Country
MAI	Multilateral Convention on Investment
MC	WTO Ministerial Conference

MFN	Most-Favored Nation
MIC	Multilateral Investment Court
MIGA	Multilateral Investment Guarantee Agency
MPIA	Multi-Party Interim Appeal Arbitration Arrangement
NAFTA	North American Free Trade Agreement
NGO	Non-governmental organization
NIEO	New International Economic Order
NT	National Treatment
NYC	UN Convention on the Recognition and Enforcement of Foreign Arbitral Awards
OECD	Organization for Economic Co-operation and Development
OMC	Organisation Mondiale du Commerce
PCA	Permanent Court of Arbitration
PCIJ	Permanent Court of International Justice
PIIE	Peterson Institute for International Economics
PIL	Public International Law
PTA	Preferential Trade Agreement
PTIAs	Preferential Trade and Investment Agreements
RCEP	Regional Comprehensive Economic Partnership Agreement
RPT	Reasonable Period of Time
RTA	Regional Trade Agreement
RTIAs	Regional Trade and Investment Agreements
SACU	Southern Africa Customs Union
SADC	Southern Africa Development Community
SCC	Stockholm Chamber of Commerce
SCM	Agreement on Subsidies and Countervailing Measures
SIA	UK State Immunity Act
SIAC	Singapore International Arbitration Center
SMEs	Small and Medium Enterprises
SOE	State-owned Enterprise
SPS	Sanitary and Phytosanitary Measures
TEU	Treaty on the European Union
TPA	Trade Promotion Agreement (USA)
TBR	Trade Barriers Regulation
TBT	Technical Barriers to Trade
TFEU	Treaty on the Functioning of the European Union
TPP	Trans-Pacific Partnership
TRIMS	Agreement on Trade-Related Investment Measures
TRQ	Tariff Rate Quotas
TTIP	Transatlantic Trade and Investment Partnership

UK	United Kingdom
UN	United Nations
UNAT	United Nations Appeal Tribunal
UNCITRAL	United Nations Commission on International Trade Law
UNCLOS	United Nations Conventions on the Law of the Sea
UNCSI	United Nations Convention on Jurisdictional Immunities of States and Their Property
UNCTAD	United Nations Conference on Trade and Development
UNDT	United Nations Dispute Tribunal
UNGA	United Nations General Assembly
UNIDROIT	International Institute for the Unification of Private Law
US	United States of America
USD	United States Dollars
USMCA	United States-Mexico-Canada Agreement
USTR	United States Trade Representative
VCLT	Vienna Convention on the Law of Treaties
VER	Voluntary Export Restrictions
WB	World Bank
WG	Working Group
WP	Working Procedures/Working Paper
WTI	World Trade Institute
WTO	World Trade Organization
WWII	The Second World War

Table of Cases

Ad hoc investor–state arbitration

Aramco v Saudi Arabia, 23 August 1958 25
BP v Libya, 10 October 1973 and 1 August 1974 25
LIAMCO v Libya, 12 April 1977 25
Sapphire v NIOC, 15 March 1963 25
Texaco (TOPCO) v Libya, 19 January 1977 25

Court of Justice of the European Union

ANIE and others v Ministero Sviluppo Economico, C-798, 799/18 (2021) 194
Commission v UK, C-516/22 (2024) 165
Kadi v Council Cases C-402,415/05 (*Kadi I* 2008) and C-584, 593, 595/10 (*Kadi II* 2013) 34
Moldova v Komstroy C-741/19 (2021) 88, 116, 163, 165
Opinion 1/17 (2019) 238, 242
Opinion 2/15 (2017) 236
PL Holdings v Poland, C-109/20 (2021) 88
Portugal v Council, C-149/96 (1996) 47
Slovakia v Achmea BV C-284/16 (2018) 88, 116, 163, 165

Disputes under RTAs

CPTPP Panel Report, *Canada–Dairy Tariff Rate Quota Allocation Measures* (2023) 190
EU-Korea Free Trade Agreement, Panel Report, *Korea–Labor Commitments* (2021) 190
EU-SADC EPA, Panel Report, *SACU–Safeguards on Frozen Chicken Cuts* (2022) 190
EU-Ukraine Association Agreement, Panel Report, *Ukraine–Wood Export Ban* (2020) 189
USMCA Panel Report, *Canada–Tariff Rate Quotas (TRQ) Allocation Measures* (2021) 190

Investment Arbitration

National Courts

Permanent Court of International Justice/International Court of Justice

State-to-state arbitration under BITs, Permanent Court of Arbitration and Ad-hoc

WTO disputes

Introduction

Table of Contents

Introduction

1. The Comparative Approach of This Book

This book critically examines, from a comparative perspective, the basic features and functioning of the dispute settlement systems (DSS) applicable to international trade and investment relations, in light of the recent crisis affecting both and proposed reforms.

The novelty of our presentation of the two systems is that we follow a comparative approach in our analysis. We compare not only their general features, highlighting in context similarities and differences, but we also use a comparative approach in respect of the various specific elements that characterize them. We believe that this innovative approach is justified and fruitful for various reasons. First, in view of the interrelation between international trade and investment in today's globalized economy; secondly, because of the common function that trade and investment regulation perform in establishing the legal context for transborder economic intercourse since Wortld War II; thirdly because of the similarity of the challenges which both systems currently face. Their respective DSS, to which this volume is devoted, is an essential element of both rule-based regimes. These systems present similarities and differences that are worth exploring, especially at a time when their functioning is being reconsidered.

The trade and investment DSS aim at ensuring the respect of the substantive rights and obligations laid down in international agreements (WTO and RTAs, BITs and

DOI: 10.4324/9781003471509-1

other IIAs) governing the two regimes. They have been used to an unprecedented and unanticipated level, giving rise to an extensive body of case law, unparalleled in any other branch of international law and relations.[1] They have thus acquired a relevance that goes beyond their application to trade and investment relations or as a model in other sectors of international law and relations, attracting the attention of the broader public, beyond the circle of stakeholders directly involved (governments and business interests) and specialists (diplomats, academics and specialized lawyers). Notwithstanding the criticism addressed to both systems and the alleged backlash against international adjudication, which is however contrasted by the establishment of several new specialized and regional tribunals, the widespread recourse to the trade and investment DSS has not declined.[2]

The comparative approach adopted in this book is justified by the commonality of the economic principles underpinning the two systems, which are an expression of the capitalist, market economy system that characterizes most national economies and international economic intercourses post World War II. While first centred around "Western" countries, this system has expanded globally to include most post-colonial nations, and - after the demise of the Soviet state-economy system - most of the world. At the basis of the regulation of both trade and investment relations internationally are principles such as the opening of national markets to foreign goods, services, and competition; the reduction or elimination of customs barriers and discrimination against foreign products and economic operators; national and most-favoured-nation treatment; reciprocity; the protection of

1 Based the numbers, the WTO system has been very successful in settling trade disputes between its members for more than 20 years. The number of disputes notified to the WTO (consultations requests) from 1995 to the end of 2024 has numbered more than 600. Up to the end of 2024, 207 panel reports have been issued, while the AB has handed down 124 reports until it ceased operation in 2020 (counting as one the reports issued in disputes with multiple complainants, Article 9 DSU). In comparison, more than 1000 investment cases have been introduced at ICSID as of the end of 2024 since the first one in 1987, see ICSID, *2024 Year in Review*, News Release of 31 December 2024, www.icsid.worldbank.org. As to ISDS, see UNCTAD, *Investment Dispute Settlement Navigator* at http://investmentpolicyhub.unctad.org/IIA, accessed 3 January 2025, numbering 1332 known cases and 2221 IIAs in force as of the end of 2024. In contrast, a total of 170 cases, contentious and advisory opinions requests, have been introduced at the ICJ since the first one in 1948 to the end of 2023. The International Tribunal of the Law of the Sea has had 32 contentious cases since the first one introduced in 1997.

2 See D. Behn, O. Fauchald, M. Langford (eds) *The Legitimacy of international Arbitration* (CUP 2022); N. Grossman and others (eds), *Legitimacy and International Courts* (CUP 2018); J. Paine, "International Adjudication as a Global Public Good?" 29 EJIL (2018) 1223. On the "proliferation" of international tribunals in recent decades, which "is widely regarded as one of the most significant developments in international law in the last century" see G. Born, "A New Generation of International Adjudication" 61 Duke L.J. (2012) 775; A. von Bodgandy, I. Venkze (eds.), *International Judicial Lawmaking. On Public Authority and Democratic Legitimation in Global Governance* (Springer 2012). The *Newsletter* of the Interest Group on International Courts and Tribunals of the ASIL, at https://www.asil.org/search/node/type%3Ainterest_group%20international%20OR%20courts provides timely periodic information on the work and decisions of the many international adjudicatory bodies currently active.

competition against abusive or distortive practices by companies (dumping) or governments (subsidies).

Another common feature of the regulation of international trade and investment is that it accommodates different models of domestic political and economic systems, notably with respect of the role of the state. This approach is carried out through a variety of mechanisms, such as admitting recourse to national (but internationally-controlled) trade-restrictive defence measures and exemptions to reflect specific domestic sensitivities and non-economic values.

Examining jointly the key elements of the two DSS provides a better understanding of the overarching architecture of the systems, and their common purpose beyond their different features. It is thereby possible to capture more fully the underlying reasons for, and the merits and shortcomings of the solutions respectively adopted in the two fields and evaluate their respective "success" and their persistent usefulness in a changing environment.

Moreover, from an economic point of view, international trade and investment transactions perform complementary, and at times substitute, functions.[3] Some economic activities and governmental measures, notably direct investment in the service sector and trade-distortive incentives to inward investments, are covered both by WTO and investment rules.[4] Some basic principles, notably non-discrimination, MFN and national treatment, or key concepts, such as likeness (between products, services, sectors, situations) are common to the two systems.[5] Interpretation of these concepts by adjudicators in both sectors is a source of cross-fertilization.

Trade and investment have become more and more intertwined in the last decades due to the closer relations that have been established among national economies worldwide, thanks to the liberalization and growth of the transborder movement of goods, services, capital and know-how, fuelled in particular by multinational enterprises. Import-export trade opens foreign markets to producers located in different countries. This stimulates competition and technical progress allowing consumers

3 WTO *Trade Policy Review of the EU*, 6 November 2017, WT/TPR/M/357/Add.1, 24, reporting that the EU has referred to the need to strengthen policy coherence between trade and investment since they are "increasingly complementary, independent and intertwined in today's global economy".

4 GATS "mode 4" (Article I.3 (c)) GATS): trade in service "by a service supplier of one Member through commercial presence in the territory of another Member" covers direct foreign investment in the service sector. See also the TRIMs (Trade-Related Investment Measures) Agreement of the WTO. See F. Weiss, "Trade and Investment" in P. Muschlinski, F. Ortino, C. Schreuer (eds) *The Oxford Handbook of International Investment Law* (OUP 2008)182.

5 See J. Kurtz, *The WTO and International Investment Law: Converging Systems* (CUP 2016); A.I. Umar, "Making a Case for the Convergence of the Trade and Investment Regimes" 2 Int. J. of Humanities and Social Sciences (2018) 53; S. Puig, "The Merging of International Trade and Investment Law", 33 Berkeley J. Int'l L (2015) 1; S. Gáspár-Szilágyi, D. Behn, M. Langford (eds), *Adjudicating Trade and Investment Disputes: Convergence or Divergence?* (CUP 2020); N. Moran, *Engagement Between Trade and Investment –The Role of PTIAs* (Springer 2021); F. Baetens, "WTO Rules before Investment Tribunals: Facilitating Cross-Fertilization While Appreciating Particularities" 24 JWIT (2023) 1. This approach is however not shared by all observers. See N. DiMascio, J. Pauwelyn, "Non-Discrimination in Trade and Investment Law: Worlds Apart or Two Sides of the Same Coin" 102 AJIL (2008) 48.

to benefit from foreign products, thereby increasing their own and global welfare. Investment of capital and know-how in tangible and intangible assets (such as equipment or technology) by foreign companies promotes economic and technological development generally, besides specifically in the host state.

Complementarity is reinforced by the large share of import-export transactions occurring within multinational groups of companies, or between related enterprises, whose cross-border supply chains (GVCs) support the manufacturing, trading, and assembling of components in different countries.[6] Moreover, international regulation in both areas is inspired by the same approach that favours liberalization and non-discrimination between domestic and foreign actors in cross-border business activities, while preserving the ability of importing or host countries to regulate their economy and safeguard the general interest of their communities.

It is a fact, however, that the international trading system has come under pressure lately. There has been a growth of unilateral measures and "friend-shoring" of global value chains (GVC) for "economic security" concerns, coupled with promotion of industrial policies with protectionist overtones (including "green protectionism") in major countries which at times clash with the traditional objective of fostering open and competitive markets.[7] Foreign direct investment has decreased.[8] Patterns of trade do not indicate however that deglobalization is looming.[9] Interdependency between different markets remains crucial for sustaining welfare and development.[10]

It is not only the advent of regional agreements (RTAs/FTAs/PTAs) regulating both trade and investment relations (RTIAs/PTIAs) that warrants a study into the similarities and differences between the trade and investment DSS.[11] It is also the similarity of procedural issues that any adjudicatory and adversarial DSS has to address and resolve that justifies examining the similarities and differences in the systems and exploring the reasons behind them. This applies to all stages of

6 *Global Value Chains: Challenges, Opportunities, and Implications for Policy*, OECD, WTO and World Bank Group (2014) 7; OECD, Trade Policy Brief, *Trade Policy Implications of Global Value Chains* (February 2020).

7 See IMF, *Trade Disrupted*, Finance & Development (June 2023).

8 UNCTAD has registered a decrease of FDI of 2% in 2024 (- 7% in developing countries) to USD 1.3 trillion, see UNCTAD, *World Investment Report*, www.hbs.unctad.org, 2024.

9 In October 2024 the WTO (*Global Trade Outlook and Statistics*) projected world merchandise (goods) trade volumes to grow 2.7% and 3% in 2024 and 2025, respectively, after a significant decline in 2023, www.wto.org/english/res_e/booksp_e/stat_10oct24_e.pdf

10 WTO *Annual Report 2023*, 6: "Against a backdrop of diminished economic prospects facing people around the world, the case for multilateral cooperation on trade to combat fragmentation and bolster growth and productivity is stronger than ever".

11 Investment chapters of PTIAs tend, however, to be distinct from other chapters and have separate dispute settlement mechanisms. A breach of another provision of a RTIA or of another international agreement does not establish that there has been a breach of the minimum standard of treatment obligation. See to this effect. the NAFTA Commission Note of Interpretation of 31 July 2001 (at B.3), Article 14.3 USMCA, according to which in case of inconsistencies between the investment chapter and other chapters, the latter shall prevail. Similarly, Article 8.3 CETA ("Relations with other chapters") and CPTPP, Annex 9-A.

proceedings: the initiation of a case, jurisdictional prerequisites, pre-adjudication phases, the selection and qualifications of ad hoc adjudicators (panelists, arbitrators) in the absence of a permanent court, third-party intervention, due process in proceedings, rules of evidence, decision-making, the contents and requirements for decisions (reports, awards), finality and *res iudicata*, challenges (appeal or annulment), compliance, and enforcement.[12] In this respect, the commercial and interstate arbitration models also have to be taken into account since some of the issues mentioned are encountered in any type of adjudication and those models have inspired several features of the trade and investment DSS. A further similarity between trade and investment DSS is that both often involve the review of administrative domestic decisions concerning foreign interests on the basis of international standards.[13]

2. *Overview of the Content*

In pursuing the objective of offering an advanced comparative introduction of the subject, this volume is organized as follows.[14] After the present Introduction, we provide in Part I ("Trade and Investment Disputes Settlement Systems from Origins to Success ", Chapters I to VI) a detailed description of the current features of the two systems, their evolution, and functioning. In Part II, "From Success through Crisis to Reform" we analyse in Chapter VII the various criticisms that have been directed at both systems, and the crisis that has affected their functioning of late. Finally, in Chapter VIII we review reforms that have been made or are in progress and proposals for improvements and substantial revisions that are currently being discussed. A comparative analysis is particularly fruitful in this respect as many criticisms are addressed to both systems and reform proposals advanced in respect of one are inspired by features of the other one and vice-versa.[15]

12 The commonality of issues and approximation of solutions concern, in great part, also other international tribunals and courts, see C. Brown, *A Common Law of International Adjudication* (OUP 2007); E. De Brabandere, *International Procedure in Interstate Litigation and Arbitration: A Comparative Approach* (CUP 2021) and the contributions collected in the *Research Handbook on International Procedural Law* (Elgar 2024).

13 Based on this feature a number of observers have concluded for the emergence of a "global administrative law" as an international regulatory regime administered by international organizations. This regime would include besides adjudication the activity of various types of review boards and human rights bodies (which however mostly review actions taken by states towards their own nationals), see B. Kingsbury, N. Krisch, R. Stewart, "The Emergence of Global Administrative Law" 68 Law Contemporary Problems (2005) 15; B. Kingsbury, "The Concept of 'Law' in Global Administrative Law" 20 EJIL (2009) 23; S. Cassese, *Advanced Introduction to Global Administrative Law* (Elgar 2021).

14 The authors wish to thank Magdalena Greco, PhD candidate at Bocconi University, for her valuable research and editing assistance.

15 Thus, on one hand proposals have been made to introduce appeal in investment arbitration. On the other hand, proposals have been made to limit challenges of WTO panels reports to annulment for grave procedural breaches, as is the case for investment awards at ICSID; see Chapter VIII.B.4.

In more detail, this *Introduction* is devoted to an overall analysis of the origins and functions of the two regimes. It traces the connections existing between them within the broader context of international DSS that have taken on an increased role in international relations.

In *Part I* we devote a chapter to the salient features of each system, putting the trade (WTO) and investment (ICSID) systems alongside one another. Each chapter is concluded with a comparative evaluation where commonalities and differences are highlighted and analysed with a forward-looking perspective. Non-WTO trade dispute settlement in bilateral and regional trade agreements and non-ICSID investment arbitration are also considered and compared with their respective multilateral models.

Chapter I examines the historical evolution of the two systems, highlighting the various political and economic objectives at the root of their establishment and their evolution, which also explains basic differences in their setup. We highlight how, on the one hand, the trade dispute settlement system has evolved from the GATT (1947) to the WTO (1995), to become centralized, multilateral, intergovernmental, that is a rule-based DSS. This progression marks a shift from the loose, predominantly fact-finding and conciliatory panel system of the GATT. This evolution has been characterized by an increasing legalisation and judicialization, culminating in the establishment within the WTO of a two-tier binding DSS, where the legal findings of the *ad hoc* panels, a feature carried over from the GATT, are subject to appeal to a permanent Appellate Body (AB).

On the other hand, the investment DSS is geared towards the protection of foreign investors by empowering them, without the need for intervention from their national government, to access ad hoc arbitral tribunals to assert the rights granted to them by bilateral investment treaties (BITs) and other IIAs between home and host states against the state where they have invested. Procedurally, investment arbitration stems from the practice of international commercial arbitration of which it retains several features. The system is decentralized, notwithstanding the existence of the multilateral ICSID Convention (1965) which has established a Centre for administering investment arbitration proceedings (and which actively does so), whose effectiveness is ensured by it being an international mechanism based on the Convention's rules. In contrast to the WTO, since it lacks the institutional multilateral features of the trading system, the investment DSS can only be defined as a "system" from a conceptual and systemic perspective, based on the extensive network of comparable BITs including ISDS, the existence of ICSID, and in light of the (relatively) consistent case law of arbitral tribunals.

Chapter II covers the legal basis and basic features of the two systems. As to trade, the analysis is focused on the Dispute Settlement Understanding (DSU), the WTO agreement on dispute settlement, under which disputes between WTO members concerning the proper application of the WTO substantive provisions governing trade are adjudicated. The DSS of bilateral and regional trade agreements (RTAs) are also examined, analysing their innovative features compared to the DSU, in light of the increased usage of them by their parties in recent times.

As to investment, our analysis focuses on ICSID, as well as on the relevant provisions of BITs which complement those of ICSID as to the initiation and conduct of arbitration. Chapter II also examines the operation of investment arbitration outside of ICSID, especially when it takes place under the rules of permanent arbitral institutions and those of UNCITRAL.

Chapter III looks at how cases are initiated in both systems, focusing on pre-litigation requirements, such as compulsory consultations, as well as cooling-off periods and optional mediation and conciliation mechanisms. It examines the jurisdiction of WTO panels and investment arbitral tribunals, their constitution, the qualifications of their members – panelists and arbitrators – (notably the requirements for impartiality and independence, and challenges thereto) and applicable law.

Chapter IV is devoted to proceedings and decisions. Both systems contain procedural rules that typically characterize any adjudicatory rule-based system. These include rules of evidence, on the use of experts, the intervention of third parties, the role of the secretariat, costs, confidentiality and transparency. As to outcomes, we compare the binding effects of panels and AB reports after their adoption by the DSB with the *res judicata* effect of investment awards. The broader precedential effect that adopted reports at the WTO and investment awards may have for subsequent cases is discussed and compared.

Chapter V examines the features of the challenges that may be brought against panel reports (appeals at the WTO, and annulment proceedings before *ad hoc* committees at ICSID) comparing their respective setups, scope and effects within the two systems.

Chapter VI covers from a comparative perspective the post-decision phase focusing on compliance, implementation, and enforcement. A comparison is made as to how the two systems aim, with different methods, at ensuring that decisions are respected and implemented. This allows an analysis of how different instruments achieve the goal of effective enforcement of decisions in international law.

Part II (Chapters VII and VIII) deals with criticism, crisis and reform of the two systems. The fact that both systems, notwithstanding their structural differences, have been the target of considerable and at times blunt criticism, and are encountering serious problems in their ordinary functioning (especially the WTO) after decades of successful operation, once more justifies a comparative analysis of the causes of this discontent and possible remedies. At the same time, the two systems appear to be remarkably resilient. A strong majority of WTO members, as to trade relations, and home and host States as to investments, as well as traders and investors, trust the multilateral rules that protect market access and investments. The same can be said of BITs: exits from the system have been rare while initiatives to establish investment courts to replace arbitration are meant to reinforce, not undermine adjudication, and increase its legitimacy.

The availability of remedies to challenge, cure or compensate for breaches through the impartial application by independent adjudicators of agreed trade and investment rules is an essential feature of a global system that promotes welfare and development through trade and investment.

This requires that rules on trade and investment do not hinder but on the contrary are supportive of the overarching objectives of promoting development, safeguarding the environment and respecting human rights as expressed notably in the UN Sustainable Development Agenda.[16]

3. *The Progressive Legalization of the Trade and Investment Regimes and the Judicialization of their Dispute Settlement Systems*

International trade and investment relations have in recent decades experienced unprecedented growth, due also to the existence of a legal framework that supports the carrying out of cross-border trade and investment operations free of crippling protectionist barriers and origin-based discrimination.[17] Since the end of World War II, substantial free movement of goods, services, capital and direct investment has been progressively established and has expanded to cover most of the countries of the world. This has occurred under predictable rule-based multilateral, regional and bilateral frameworks,[18] forming the foundation of the economic globalisation that currently characterizes the world. It has brought a decisive contribution to the fight against poverty, especially in developing countries, though possibly leading to more inequality within developed economies and among different groups of countries.[19]

An essential common feature of the evolution of the trade and investment regimes has been and still is its "legalization": the progressive increase, through international agreements, of the rules governing trade and investment relations to ensure, based on reciprocity and the pursuit of mutual benefits, legal security for traders and investors and a predictable framework in which they may operate. A key element of this development has been the "judicialization" of dispute resolution methods, which have moved away from power-based solutions towards third

16 See www.un.org/sustainabledevelopment/development-agenda/. As to trade see WTO, *Mainstreaming Trade to Attain the Sustainable Development Goals* (2018); J. Bacchus, I. Manak, *The Development Dimension. Special and Differential Treatment in Trade* (Routledge 2021). As to investment see UNCTAD, *World Investment Report 2014. Investing in the SDGs* (UN 2014); G. Sacerdoti, "Investment Protection and Sustainable Development: Key Issues" in S. Hindelang, M. Krajewski (eds.) *Shifting Paradigms in International Investment Law* (OUP 2016) 19; C. De Stefano, "The Scrutiny of States' Climate Change Action under International Trade and Investment Agreements" 33 IYIL (2023) 153; A. Ipp, A. Magnusson (eds), *Investment Arbitration and Climate Change* (Kluwer 2024).

17 According to the WTO (*Evolution of Trade under the WTO: Handy Statistics*, www.wto.org, accessed 24 June 2024), compared with 1950 (index 100) world trade had increased in volume to 4.500 and in value to 25.000 as of 2022. The world's current MFN applied tariffs stand at an average of 9% (before the additional import tariffs introduced by the US in 2025).

18 Compared with the 193 members of the UN, the WTO as of 24 June 2024 had 166 members and its rules covered 98% of world trade in goods. ICSID has 158 contracting parties and BITs number more than 2200 in force, involving almost all states, see http://investmentpolicyhub.unctad.org/IIA, accessed 3 January 2025.

19 See WB, *Poverty and Shared Prosperity 2022. Correcting Course*. For critical views see D. Rodrick, *The Globalization Paradox* (OUP 2012); T. Picketty, *Capital in the Twenty-First Century* (Harvard University Press 2012).

party rule-based adjudication.[20] If the scope of rules and the import of rights and obligations stemming from them cannot be objectively determined and enforced in case of dispute, they will be of a reduced value. This is the prevailing situation in many sectors of international law where power-based relations prevail over rule-based relations. Such a situation does not accord with the requirement of legal certainty which is essential to sustaining the smooth conduct of business operations worldwide by private parties engaged in international trade and investment. From an academic perspective, this parallel progression of the trade and investment DSS justifies examining them as we do here, independently from their respective substantive provisions (trade obligations and investment standards). This is also the approach followed in the ongoing reform initiatives which focus on procedure, both as to trade (revision of the DSU at the WTO) and investment (within UNCITRAL WG III).[21]

The trend in the second part of the 20th century towards expanding adjudication and judicialization in order to resolve international disputes peacefully and justly is not limited to trade and investment.[22] It finds its underpinning in the obligation in the UN Charter to resolve disputes peacefully.[23] As to international criminal justice, the turning point has been the establishment of the International Criminal

20 The legalization process has affected the WTO beyond the DSS, see P. Lamy (at the time DG of the WTO) "La place et le role (du droit) de l'OMC dans l'ordre juridique international", Intervention devant la SFDI, 19 may 2006, available at wto.org/french/news_f/sppl_f/sppl94_f.htm; H. Ruiz-Fabri, "La juridictionnalisation du règlement des litiges économiques entre États" Rev. arbitrage (2003) 881; R. Howse, H. Ruiz-Fabri, G. Ulfstein, M. Zang (eds.), *The Legitimacy of International Trade Courts and Tribunals* (CUP 2018); C. Yu, *Dispute Settlement and the Reform of International Investment Law: Legalization through Adjudication* (Elgar 2023).

21 J. Jackson, *Sovereignty, the WTO and Changing Fundamentals of International Law* (CUP 2006). See, however, for caveats, A. Follesdal, G. Ulfstein (eds), *The Judicialization of International Law. A Mixed Blessing?* (OUP 2018). As to the "autonomy" of procedural mechanisms from substantive regulation see T. Meyer "Plurilateralism and the Future of International Investment Law" 26 JWIT (2025)219.

22 The initial movement in favour of adjudication dates from the end of the XIX century. It led first to the establishment in 1899 of the Permanent Court of Arbitration (PCA) as an intergovernmental organization. Membership of the 1899 and 1907 Conventions for the Pacific Settlement of International Disputes has reached 122 in 2023. In that year the PCA administered seven inter-state arbitrations, 122 treaty-based ISDS cases, 110 contract-based disputes with states or state-owned entities, in total 246 cases, PCA, *Annual Report 2023*, available at https://docs.pca-cpa.org/2024/06/0bd839f2-pca-annual-report-2023.pdf accessed 21 July 2024. In comparison ICSID administered 341 investment-only cases (58 new ones) in 2023-2024, ICSID, *Annual Report 2024*.

23 The various methods to be resorted to in order to peacefully settle international disputes are listed in Article 33 of the UN Charter, reflecting established practice. These methods ("negotiations, enquiry, mediation, conciliation, arbitration, judicial settlement, [and] resort to regional agencies or arrangements") are also available and used to resolve economic disputes between states. As opposed to "political" disputes, legal disputes, concerning points of law and involving the application and interpretation of existing rules, as well as the rights and obligations stemming therefrom, are typically amenable to third-party adjudication. This distinction is recognized in Article 36(3) UN Charter whereby "legal disputes should as a general rule be referred by the parties to the International Court of Justice" See *Merrills*, 8; C. Romano, K. Alter, Y. Shany (eds), *The Oxford Handbook of International Adjudication* (OUP 2013); L. Boisson de Chazourne, J. Vinuales, *(eds.), Diplomatic*

Court towards the end of the 20th century to prosecute individuals for grave international crimes. Among the most innovative judicial bodies are those that give standing to individuals (including business entities) and which protect fundamental rights at the international, mostly regional, level from encroachments by the parties to the relevant treaties, including their own state.[24] A substantial number of these mostly regional courts have been established for this purpose whose decisions, however, rarely have direct (self-executing) effects in domestic legal systems.[25] International law has thereby been transformed from a system where adjudication used to be a marginal feature, with tribunals' jurisdiction mostly being *ad hoc* and based on limited case-by-case acceptance by litigants, to a system where adjudication of interstate disputes is mostly based on advanced consent in treaties and exercised by permanent courts.[26] Notwithstanding several limitations to the basis of its jurisdiction and the scope of its acceptance by parties, the docket of the ICJ has boomed recently.[27]

A comparative approach is made more relevant by the natural tendency of international courts to adopt common approaches to questions of procedure and remedies. This leads to increasing commonalities in the resolution of procedural issues and, in turn, to a common law of international adjudication.[28] Within this evolution, the DSS applicable to trade and investment are the ones that have developed the

and Judicial Means of Dispute Settlement (Nijhoff 2013); Y. Tanaka, *The Peaceful Settlement of International Disputes* (CUP 2018).

24 This is the case of the European Court of Human Rights (ECtHR) of the Council of Europe in respect of the rights enshrined in the European Convention of Human Rights of 1950, and of the Court of Justice of the European Union (CJEU) ensuring individuals' and member states' rights based on the EU treaties and EU legislation. As to Latin America, see S. Caserta, *International Courts in Latin America and the Caribbean* (OUP 2020). As to Africa, J. Gathii (ed), *The Performance of Africa's International Courts: Using Litigation for Political, Legal, and Social Change* (OUP 2020).

25 The only international court extending its jurisdiction over inter-state disputes between a very large group of states is the Tribunal of the Law of the Sea established under the UNCLOS. The subject matter of the disputes that may be brought to it (or to connected arbitration) is however limited to a narrow set of maritime relations and conflicts. It has had 32 contentious cases since the first one was submitted to it in 1997, see *Merills*, 261 and the list of cases at www.itlos.org.

26 The traditional principle is that "it is well established in international law…that a State may not be compelled to submit its disputes to arbitration without its consent", ICJ *Ambatielos (Greece v UK)* Merits (1953) ICJ Rep. 10, 19.

27 The docket of the ICJ as of March 2025 included 25 pending cases, see www.icj-cij.org. In comparison in 2023, 45 new cases have been initiated at ICSID and 82 cases, of which 15 investment arbitrations, at PCA, see n 22.

28 See C. Brown, *A Common Law of International Adjudication* (OUP 2007); P. Webb, *International Judicial Integration and Fragmentation* (OUP 2013); K. Alter, E. Hafner-Burton, L. Helfer, "Theorizing the Judicialization of International Relations" 63 International Studies Quarterly (2019) 449; E. D Brabandere (ed), *International Procedure in Interstate Litigation and Arbitration: A Comparative Approach* (CUP 2021). This development has been the focus of the establishment at the University of Oslo of the Centre for the Study of the Legitimate Roles of the Judiciary in the Global Order - PluriCourts (2013-2023), funded by the Research Council of Norway, whose research results have been published by CUP in the often referred to here edited volumes of the series "Studies on International Courts and Tribunals".

most on a global scale, reflecting the certainty needed by the economic and commercial relations underlying these regimes. This development in the governance of economic relations has been facilitated by a relatively lower level of political sensitivity (at least in principle and until the coming in office of the second Trump presidency in the US in January 2025) compared to other fields. In other areas, great powers and other countries, are wary of removing dispute resolution from their political control by remitting them, especially, *ex ante,* to third party adjudication. [29]

4. *The WTO DSS and US President Trump's Tariff Increases (March-April 2025)*

The introduction in March-April 2025 by the second Trump Administration of a generalized tariff (customs duties) increase on US imports from all countries, differentiated in respect of different products and origins and scaled on the basis of the US bilateral trade deficit with targeted countries, is in plain disregard of the US' commitments under the WTO agreements.[30]

This development puts additional strain on the multilateral, until then rule-based, trading system. It is difficult to anticipate how the WTO DSS can cope with such a paradigm change in the set-up of international trade regulation. Moreover, it does not appear that the reactions (countermeasures) by affected WTO Members in turn respect the DSU procedural requirements.[31]

29 Even in such cases, challenges to courts' jurisdiction by respondents are frequent. See also the limited number of acceptances, often subject to severe restrictions, of the optional clause of compulsory jurisdiction under Article 36 ICJ (74 states of which 15 since 2010, of the 193 members of the UN). Finally, there have been high-profile disputes in which great powers as respondents have not even cared to participate, denying the adjudicators' jurisdiction from the "outside". This was notably the case of the US (ICJ *Nicaragua* case, 1984), Russia (*Greenpeace Arctic Sunrise ship* case, 2013) and, lastly, China (maritime arbitration *Philippines v. China,* Award 2016, PCA Case N° 2013-19). See generally C. McLachlan, "The Assault on International Adjudication and the Limits of Withdrawal" 68 ICLQ (2019)499.

30 See "US Trade Representative Issues Statement on President Trump's Declaration of a National Emergency," USTR Press release, media@ustr.eop.gov of 3 April 2025, defining the tariff measures as "urgent action to protect the national security and economy of the US. The current lack of reciprocity. demonstrated by our chronic trade deficit, has weakend our economic and national security." (...)

31 See P. Stoll,: "Reciprocity in Trade?: The Recent Initiative of the US President on "Reciprocal Trade and Tariffs"," VerfBlog, 2025/2/28, https://verfassungsblog.de/reciprocity-in-trade/, DOI: 10.59704/dc4fd99d64da494b

Annex: WTO and ICSID Disputes: Number of Cases Per Year

Table A.1: WTO Disputes

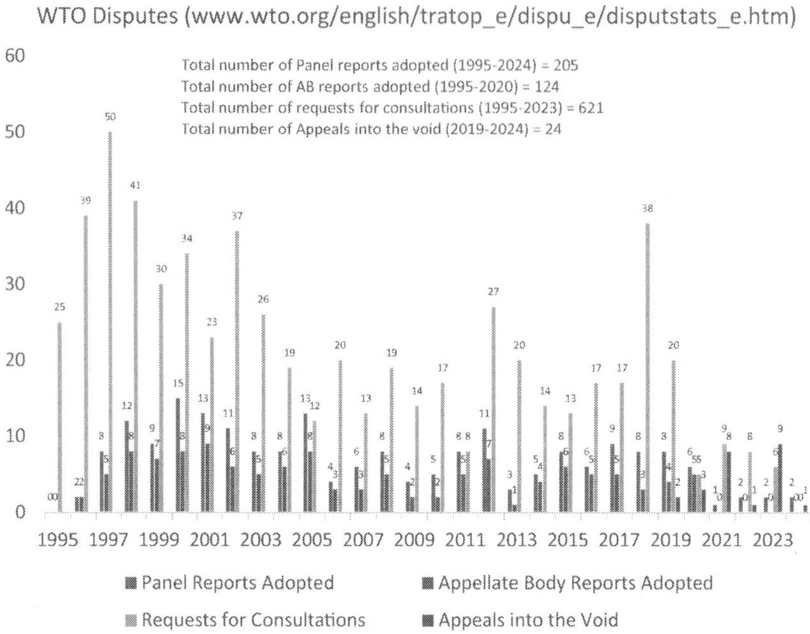

Table A.2: ICSID Disputes

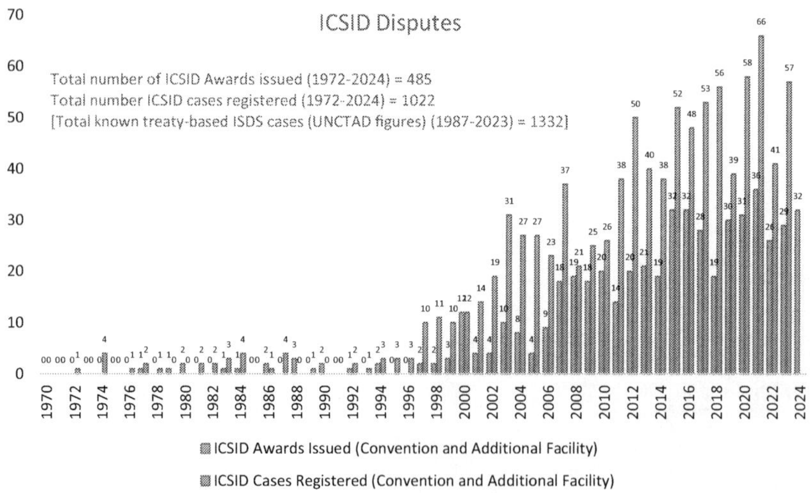

Part I

The Trade and Investment Dispute Settlement Systems from Origins to Success.

1 Historical Origins and Development

Table of Contents

Introduction

International trade and investment law has not developed in isolation from the general context of international law, which governs the relations between sovereign states and lays down the basic legal principles applicable to the life of the international community.

International economic law, of which trade and investment are two core pillars, is that part of public international law that deals with the legal regulation of

DOI: 10.4324/9781003471509-3

economic relations between states and their economies.[1] The sources of regulation, besides overarching customary principles, are found in relevant treaties (the WTO Agreements, bilateral and regional trade and investment agreements, ICSID, BITs, and other IIAs) which are to be interpreted and applied in conformity with relevant rules of international law, in light of their context, object, and purpose.[2]

Neither trade law (the WTO system and Regional Trade Agreements) nor investment law (ICSID and BITs) are "self-contained". They do not escape from the application of principles and disciplines that are generally applicable to relations between states as members of the international community.[3] In turn, relevant international treaties and the set-up and activity of international economic organizations reflect and are subject to the overarching principles of the post-World War II international legal order as enshrined in the UN Charter and subsequently developed through multilateral conventions and soft-law declarations of principles.

Hence, the applicability within trade and investment law of general principles of public international law (PIL) and the potential relevance of rules and principles developed in other areas of PIL for their regulation. Among these areas are sustainable development, environmental law, and climate change initiatives, as well as

1 International economic law in its various sub-sectors (trade, investment, monetary, and financial relations) has in recent decades been examined as a specific sub-sector of international law by a number of authors. See especially, in chronological order: A. Lowenfeld, *International Economic Law* (2nd ed. OUP 2008), which covers the WTO and GATT, international investment, sanctions, developing countries debt, competition and intellectual property international regulation; C. Picker, I. Bunn, D. Arner (eds.), *International Economic Law: The State and Future of the Discipline* (Hart 2008); S. Charnovitz, "What Is International Economic Law?" 14 JIEL (2011) 1; M. Herdegen, *Principles of International Economic Law* (2nd ed. OUP 2016) (also in German and Spanish); A.H. Qureshi, A. Ziegler, *International Economic Law* (4th ed. Sweet & Maxwell 2019); A. Mitchell, E. Sheargold, *Principles of International Trade and Investment Law* (Elgar 2021); E. Choukroune, J. Nedumpara, *International Economic Law. Text, Cases and Materials* (CUP 2022) covering in almost 800 pages trade and investment law, international monetary law and finance, development and aid, relations with human rights, digital trade, taxation and economic sanctions. D. Collins, *Foundations of International Economic Law* (2nd ed. Elgar 2025) includes, besides trade and investment law, International Monetary Law and Development. For treatises in other languages see, in French, D. Carreau, P. Juilliard, *Droit international économique* (6th ed. with R. Bismuth and A. Hamann, Dalloz 2017); in Italian, P. Picone, G. Sacerdoti, *Diritto Internazionale dell'economia* (2nd ed. F. Angeli 1986); E. Sciso, *Appunti di Diritto Internazionale dell'economia* (4th ed. Giappichelli 2021). In 2015, the 99 relevant entries of the *Max Planck Encyclopedia of International Law* have been collected, duly updated, in a single volume: *International Economic Law* (OUP 2015). See also the *Encyclopedia of International Economic Law*, T. Cottier, K. Nadakavukaren Schefer (eds.) (2nd ed.Elgar 2024), comprising more than 250 short entries. Settlement of disputes features prominently in these texts. Another specificity of international economic law is that an understanding (and a presentation) of the economic underpinning is required. See in this respect E. Posner, A. Sykes, *Economics Foundations of International Law* (Harvard University Press 2013); A. Sykes, *The Law and Economics of International Trade Agreements* (Elgar 2023).

2 See Articles 31–33 of the VCLT on the interpretation of treaties. For further developments, see E. Cannizzaro (ed.), *The Law of Treaties Beyond the Vienna Convention* (OUP 2011).

3 See "Fragmentation of International Law: Difficulties Arising from the Diversification and Expansion of International Law" Report of the Study Group of the International Law Commission finalized by M.Koskenniemi A/CN.4/L.682 (2006).

human – especially workers' – rights. In pursuing a variety of non-trade values of common concern to the international community, the regulation of international trade has thereby been impacted "from outside".[4] The same can be said in respect of investment law, taking into account, however, that investment law is more fragmented as it lacks a multilateral framework.[5]

In turn, the law applicable to trade relations, as well as dispute settlement under trade agreements, has made important contributions to the development of public international law.[6] This cross-fertilization has not been prevented by the fact that, within public international law, trade law may be viewed as *lex specialis*, whose specific rules derogate in part from the application of general rules of international law.[7] At the same time, given that trade and investment disciplines do not exist in "clinical isolation"[8] from the rest of public international law, the special principles that apply within international economic law can contribute to the development of the rules in other fields. This interaction reduces the risk of fragmentation in and of international law, a risk that is always present given the system's lack of a hierarchical structure and a coherent judicial system to ensure unity.[9]

4 D. McRae, 'The Contribution of International Trade Law to the Development of International Law' 99 RC (1996) 260; E. Petersmann, *International Economic Law in the 21st Century: Constitutional Pluralism and Multilevel Governance of Interdependent Public Goods* (Hart 2012).

5 PM Dupuy, F. Francioni, E. Petersmann (eds), *Human Rights in International Investment Law and Arbitration* (OUP 2009). F. Baetens (ed), *Investment Law within International Law: Integrationist Perspectives* (CUP 2013).

6 Specifically, the interpretation handed down by adjudicators (panels and the AB at the WTO, arbitral tribunals as to investment disputes) has contributed to the development of legal principles that go beyond the disciplines of trade and investment, notably the law of state responsibility at large. See Y. Zhang, "The Contribution of the WTO Appellate Body to Treaty Interpretation" *A History* 570; G. Sacerdoti, "La contribution de l'Organe d'Appel de l'OMC à la construction du droit international économique" 120 RGDIP (2016) 721; C. Tams, S. Schill, R. Hofmann (eds), *International Investment Law and General International Law: Radiating Effects?* (Elgar 2023). See also the various contributions appearing in the special issue of the ICSID Review on the 20th anniversary of ARSIWA, vol. 37, number 1–2 (2022), on the interpretation and application of the principles of state responsibility by investment tribunals.

7 See ARSIWA Article 55.

8 As famously stated in the first report of the AB *US–Gasoline* (DS2-1996), 17.

9 The risk of fragmentation by sectors and geographically (*rationae materiae* and *personae*) of the international legal system governing inter-state relations and the number of arbitral or judicial bodies created, which are not part of a coordinated or hierarchical structure, has given rise to concerns as to the unity of the system; see the "Fragmentation" ILC report (n 3). See, however, M. Andenas, E. Bjorge (eds) *A Farewell to Fragmentation: Reassertion and Convergence in International Law* (CUP 2015) emphasizing the role of the ICJ in the strengtheining of international law as a unitary legal system.

A. Trade

1. From the Havana Charter to the GATT (1947–1995)

In view of the massive development of the international regulation of trade since World War II, a historical perspective is essential when undertaking an examination of the origin and reasons for the current WTO-centred set-up. Previously, international treaties concerning trade were mostly bilateral and based on reciprocity and non-discrimination. They focused on regulating customs duties and other border barriers relating to the admission of goods and their treatment (market access, MFN, and national treatment). In the absence of such agreements, these matters were (and still are) unilaterally determined by the importing country as pertaining to its national sovereignty.[10] Export restrictions have historically been less prominent, but they have recently made a comeback for a variety of largely non-economic concerns.[11] Other matters of economic relevance, such as the treatment of foreigners, particularly merchants, which includes the protection of their property, were governed by customary rules on the treatment of aliens and their property, and by bilateral treaties with broader purposes. Typical agreements of this type were the treaties of amity and commerce, such as the US treaties of Friendship, Commerce and Navigation (FCN Treaties).[12] Provisions on compulsory dispute settlement mechanisms were not common in those agreements, but post-World War II FCN Treaties provided for the referral of disputes between the parties to existing institutions such as the International Court of Justice.[13]

The need for the multilateral regulation of trade became increasingly evident towards the end of World War II, in order to overcome restrictions on trade, protectionism, and beggar-thy-neighbour policies that had severely hampered trade between the two World Wars and had been among the causes of the conflict. A specialized UN agency, the International Trade Organisation (ITO), was devised to complete the post-war international economic framework after the two "Bretton Woods institutions", the International Monetary Fund (IMF) and the IBRD (WB) were established in 1944. Its broad ambitious objective was to facilitate the "solution of problems relating to trade in the fields of employment, economic development, commercial policy, business practices and commodity policy".[14] The Charter of the ITO was signed in Havana after two years of negotiations in March 1948

10 See M. Hoesch, "Commercial Treaties" *MPEPIL* (2014).

11 See generally I. Espa, *Export Restrictions on Critical Minerals and Metals: Testing the Adequacy of WTO Disciplines* (CUP 2015).

12 On these treaties, see K.G. Vandevelde, *The First Bilateral Investment Treaties, US Postwar FCN Treaties* (OUP 2017).

13 See, for instance, the US–Italy FCN treaty of 1948, which was invoked by the US in the ICJ *Elsi case,* Judgment, Merits (1989) ICJ Rep 15.

14 Article 1.6 of the Havana Charter. For more details, see C. Wilcox, *A Charter for World Trade* (Macmillan 1949); R. Gardner, *Sterling-dollar Diplomacy. Anglo-American Collaboration in the Reconstruction of Multilateral Trade* (Clarendon 1956); G. Sacerdoti, "Havana Charter (1948)" *MPEPIL* (2011).

by 54 countries (the "Havana Charter") but never entered into force because of the lack of ratification by the US. Its Chapter IV on Commercial Policy, however, became the basis for the General Agreement on Tariffs and Trade (GATT) which was negotiated and signed in 1947 as a provisional agreement (limited to trade in goods), pending the expected entry into force of the Havana Charter.[15]

The Havana Charter stipulated that Members should not have recourse to unilateral economic action in breach of the Charter's provisions and provided for proceedings by which Members could settle disputes.[16] They were available to any member which considered "that any benefit accruing to it directly or indirectly, implicitly or explicitly, under any of the provisions of this Charter other than Article 1, is being nullified or impaired".[17] There were several procedural avenues to settle such a dispute: first by recourse to the Executive Board that could decide the matter after an appropriate investigation; thereafter to the plenary Conference of the Members; and ultimately to the ICJ. It is worthwhile observing that these dispute settlement provisions of the Havana Charter were much more detailed and binding than those of GATT.

In the absence of an international organization governing trade, the GATT continued to be applied on a "provisional basis" until the entry into operation of the WTO in 1995.[18] In the geopolitical context of the time (the Cold War, the East–West divide, and differences in the structure of economies, with centralized, state-run systems in the East v market-based systems in the West), the expansion of the GATT was basically limited until the 1990s to market and mixed economies, including progressively developing countries.[19]

2. *The Main Features of the GATT Dispute Settlement System and Its Evolution Up to the WTO*

The scanty provisions on dispute settlement reflect the fact that the GATT was meant to be provisional. It was not even subject to parliamentary approval and formal ratification in most of the contracting parties. The GATT was a multilateral agreement (which did not intend to establish an international organization)

15 See J. Jackson, *World Trade and the Law of GATT* (Bobbs-Merrill 1969) 42.

16 Chapter VIII, Article 92.2 of the Charter.

17 Article 93.1.

18 The GATT was put in force by its contracting parties by a Protocol of Provisional Application (GATT Annex I) on 15 November 1947. The Protocol moreover included a "grandfathering clause" which limited the application of GATT's Part II "to the fullest extent not inconsistent" with the then-existing legislation of the parties. The effect of this clause was terminated only with the entry into force of the WTO Agreement which provides at Article XVI(4) that "Each Member shall ensure the conformity of its laws, regulations and administrative procedures with its obligations as provided in the annexed Agreements".

19 Part IV on "Trade and Development" was added to the GATT in 1964. In 1971, a waiver was agreed to authorize differential and more favourable treatment to developing parties. It was made permanent by the "Enabling Clause" in accordance with the UNCTAD Generalized System of Preferences (GSP) scheme as part of the Tokyo Round in 1979.

between an initially limited number of countries that undertook to act collectively in furthering the objective of liberalizing trade, primarily via the reduction of customs duties (tariffs), in a non-discriminatory manner, through periodic rounds of negotiations with the support of a small administrative and technical secretariat. The GATT had no institutional framework or bodies. Decisions were to be taken in principle by a simple majority of the votes cast by the parties (Article XXV(4)), although the practice of consensus immediately prevailed.

In view of the parties' pragmatic and flexible approach to the application of its provisions, the GATT was widely regarded as a "commercial agreement" rather than a treaty, aimed at satisfying the economic interests of its parties by "reciprocal and mutually advantageous arrangements".[20] The preservation of mutual advantages and upholding individual interests stemming from the GATT were preferred to the exact application in strict legal terms of its provisions. The text of Articles XXII and XXIII GATT on "consultation and dispute settlement" and their application, especially in the first years, fully reflected this practical approach. These Articles refer to "sympathetic" consideration of representations of other parties, consultation with a view "to the satisfactory adjustment of the matter", and, failing this, "investigation of the matter" so that the contracting parties acting collectively may make appropriate recommendations to the parties concerned, or give a ruling on the matter.

The focus of these provisions is clearly on the amicable settlement of any economic conflict concerning the application of the GATT, irrespective of the origin of the issue complained of by a party, be it due to treaty breach, the incorrect or questionable application of a measure by another party, or prejudice arising to the complaining party therefrom. The remedy provided by Article XXIII(2) GATT in cases of non-compliance is the recourse by the affected party to countermeasures, by way of the authorized suspension of previously negotiated concessions.[21]

Initially, disputes were submitted to the representatives of the contracting parties themselves, who established "working parties" of delegates, including those in dispute, to examine the matter and make recommendations. Subsequently (1955), this task was entrusted to five-member (later three-member) panels of governmental experts selected on an *ad hoc* basis, acting in their individual capacity. Panels would work confidentially with the parties in an attempt to find an amicable settlement. If this failed, the panel would issue a report addressed to the contracting parties, whose adoption by consensus would usually be based on an informal agreement between the parties involved.[22]

With the increase in the number of contracting parties and the expanded coverage of the GATT, especially following the Tokyo Round in 1979, this

20 As to the original design and its evolution besides J. Jackson, n 15, see R. Hudec, *The Evolution of the Modern GATT Legal System* (Butterworth 1993).

21 Suspension of obligations under this provision was authorized only once in 1953 in favour of the Netherlands vis-à-vis the US, but the suspension was never imposed. See R. Hudec "The GATT Legal System: A Diplomat's Jurisprudence" 4 JWTL (1970) 615.

22 J. Jackson, n 15, 137.

"similarly-minded members' club approach" required, in order to remain workable, a more "legalistic" framework for its proceedings and more attention to the correct application of the rules in order to work. The conciliatory approach declined, and the submission of "non-violation" complaints (where a loss of expected benefits was complained of notwithstanding the lack of a breach by the other party) was *de facto* abandoned. This development was enshrined in two decisions: first, the "Decision on Procedures under Article XXIII" of 1966, and second by the "Understanding regarding Notification, Consultation, Dispute Settlement and Surveillance", adopted in 1979 within the negotiation of the GATT Tokyo Round and modified in 1982.[23] Further changes were agreed during the Uruguay Round (the "Montreal Rules" of 1989).

On the other side, this more legalistic and contentious approach led to a situation whereby, as to sensitive matters, respondents resisted the establishment of a panel and, if they lost the case, blocked the consensus of all contracting parties required to adopt the panel's report and make it binding.[24] Of the 136 GATT reports issued, 40 were not adopted.[25] The credibility of the system was thus severely undermined, *de facto* encouraging recourse to unilateral action.[26] Finally, the GATT's provisions and practice were ineffective in monitoring and inducing compliance with adopted panel reports. Recourse to countermeasures in the form of the suspension of concessions, as permitted under Article XXIII(2), also required consensus under the GATT practice. Unilateral measures and widespread waivers (derogations) from the rules weakened the GATT system even further.

Over the course of the Uruguay Round (1986–1994), this situation led negotiators to envisage, going beyond the initial agenda, far-reaching reforms of the dispute settlement mechanisms through substantial changes (legalization) so as to improve the efficiency of proceedings and the effectiveness of results (compliance).[27]

Before concluding this section on the GATT dispute settlement system (DSS) and its operation, it must be underlined that its DS provisions are still of interest for various reasons: first, the WTO DSS has maintained several features of the GATT system, foremost among them the panel stage, though with substantial modifications. Second, the GATT remains in force as an annex to the WTO agreement, including its Articles XXII and XXIII which thus remain applicable within

23 GATT Doc. L5752, BISD 31 s/9.

24 This happened especially when non-trade interests were involved. See the GATT Panel reports *US—Restrictions on Imports of Tuna* (DS21-1991). and *US -Restrictions on Imports of Tuna* (DS29-1994).

25 See *Dispute Settlement Reports within the Framework of GATT 1947* (WTO 2018). All GATT panel reports can be accessed at www.wto.org.

26 See J. Bhagwati and H. Patrick, *Aggressive Unilateralism: Americas 301 Trade Policy and World Trading System* (University of Michigan Press 1990).

27 See J. Jackson, *Restructuring the GATT System* (Pinter 1990); D. Steger, "The Establishment of the Appellate Body" *A History*, 447; J. Hillman, "A Reset of the World Trade Organization's Appellate Body" (Council of Foreign Relations 2020), available at https://www.cfr.org/report/reset-world-trade-organizations-appellate-body, who recalls that the US was the "strongest proponent" of including an appellate mechanism within the DSU.

or alongside the DSU.[28] Third, within the current discussions on a reform of the Dispute Settlement Understanding, there are proposals in favour of reverting to a less constraining single-tier DSS, such as that of the GATT.[29]

B. Investment

1. The Commercial Arbitration Model for Investment Disputes before ICSID

Disputes concerning foreign investments have historically been very contentious. Investment disputes that have produced the most political conflicts have been those arising from acts of a host state that deprive foreign investors of their investment due to expropriation or broad nationalization measures. Disputes incidental to the normal carrying out of business operations, involving the breach of the standard of "fair and equitable treatment", have over time, however, outstripped cases involving expropriation.[30]

Since private investors are not primary subjects of international law, interstate dispute settlement methods are not available for settling these disputes. In the absence of specific agreements, disputes between foreign investors and host countries turned at times into highly sensitive political interstate controversies. However, only in a few cases was the investor's home state able and willing to bring the dispute for resolution before the ICJ based on the exercise of diplomatic protection.[31]

In view of this context, investment arbitration, and, in particular, ICSID arbitration, has been designed to accomplish two fundamental objectives. The first one is that of offering a neutral forum for the settlement of disputes directly between an aggrieved foreign investor and the host state. Arbitration is aimed at reconciling two divergent interests: on the one hand, that of foreign investors and their home states to access an effective impartial law-based determination of their rights, ensuring, irrespective of domestic law, the application of international law principles on the protection of foreign investment. On the other hand, the interest of host states to preserve their sovereignty by not having to defend before foreign courts

28 Article XXII and XXIII GATT are moreover specifically referred to in Article 4.11 DSU in the context of consultations.

29 See the article by the then USTR R. Lighthizer, "How to Set World Trade Straight" WSJ (20 August 2020), available at www.wsj.com accessed on 24 June 2024, advocating the replacement of the WTO two-tier DSS with "a single-stage process akin to commercial arbitration". For further details, see Chapter VIII.A.3(b) n 78.

30 According to UNCTAD, from 2010–2024 expropriation claims were raised in 400 disputes and allegations of breach of FET in 454 cases; see https://investmentpolicy.unctad.org.

31 See the ICJ *Anglo-Iranian Oil Co. (United Kingdom v Iran)* Preliminary Objection (1952) ICJ Rep, 93; *Barcelona Traction (Belgium v Spain)* (1970) ICJ Rep, 3; *Diallo (Guinea v Congo)* Preliminary Objections (2007) ICJ Rep, 1; Merits (2010) ICJ Rep, 1. See A. Pellet, "The Case Law of the ICJ in Investment Arbitration" 28 ICSID Rev (2013) 223. While in the cases above, claims made were based on customary international law, the *ELSI case (United States v Italy)* (1989) ICJ Rep, 15, concerned claims against Italy advanced by the US on behalf of US shareholders of an Italian company for alleged breaches of the US–Italy FCN Treaty of 1948.

(as opposed to arbitration in a neutral framework) their regulation of economic activity of foreigners in their territories.

The second objective was that of "de-politicizing" investor–state disputes, preventing them from escalating to the interstate level with a view to avoiding diplomatic, and possibly more radical, interventions by investors' home states.[32] Neutrality, effectiveness, and de-politicization have indeed been the main reasons for the success of investment arbitration.[33]

International arbitration for investment disputes was an innovative alternative, an additional protection for foreigners instead of subjecting themselves completely and exclusively to the jurisdiction of the host country once they have entered its market and established their investment there. The starting point is that, of course, local courts are in principle competent to adjudicate disputes involving the treatment of investments by the application of local laws, except if the parties have agreed otherwise through appropriate choice-of-law and choice-of-forum or arbitral clauses.[34] Investment contracts and concessions are in principle subject to the law of the host state, especially since host states usually refuse to subject themselves to foreign laws and jurisdictions, generally viewing this as being incompatible with their sovereignty. Accepting the competence of local courts may, however, be unsatisfactory for the foreign investor in respect of major investments, especially those involving large sunk costs and where the application of international law principles (typically those on expropriation) is at issue, especially in countries where political risks are considered to be high. Impartiality towards foreigners cannot be taken for granted in all domestic jurisdictions, nor can the local judiciary always be relied upon to be efficient and independent from political influence, especially when the host State is itself a party to the dispute. On the other hand, sovereign states are not likely to accept the jurisdiction of foreign courts for investment disputes with foreign parties.[35]

32 In order to prevent military intervention by home states, as was frequent at the time, Latin American countries successfully promoted the conclusion at the Hague in 1907 of the "Drago-Porter Convention", outlawing the employment of force for the recovery of contract debts, 36 Stat 2241 (US), see W. Benedek, "Drago-Porter Convention" *MPEPIL* (2007).

33 See I. Shihata (General Counsel of the WB at the time), "Towards a Greater Depoliticisation of Investment Disputes: The Roles of ICSID and MIGA" 1 ICSID Rev (1986) 4.

34 See G. Schwarzenberger, *Foreign Investment and International Law* (Stevens 1969); G. Sacerdoti, *Bilateral Treaties and Multilateral Instruments on Investment Protection* 269 RC (1997) 251. Article 4 of the UN GA Resolution on Permanent Sovereignty over Natural Resources of 1962, A/1803 (XVIII), adopted by consensus (differently from the subsequent resolutions voted within the NIEO), provided that "upon agreement by sovereign States and other parties concerned, settlement of the dispute should be made through arbitration or international adjudication" instead than be submitted to local courts. The ILA, "Seoul Declaration on the Progressive Development of Principles of Public International Law Relating to a New International Economic Order" ILA Report 62nd Conference, 1987, advocated "recourse to international adjudication, international or transnational arbitration, or other international procedures for the settlement of disputes" (para. 13.1).

35 See G. Kaufmann-Kohler, "Why Investment Arbitration and Not Domestic Courts? The Origins of the Modern Investment Dispute Resolution System, Criticism, and Future Outlook" European Yearbook of Int. Economic Law (2020) 7.

In contrast, developing states have for decades advanced in international fora the principles that (a) disputes with foreign investors should be settled exclusively by the host state's courts in accordance with its own local laws and regulations, and (b) foreign investors should receive treatment no better than nationals. Such principles, derived from the "Calvo Doctrine", have been advanced by Latin American countries from the end of the nineteenth century to prevent the abuse of weak nations by more powerful countries, and were advocated by developing countries in the 1970s at the United Nations.[36] According to the "Calvo Doctrine" foreign investors were also required to waive diplomatic protection by their home countries by signing a so-called "Calvo Clause" to this effect.[37] Home countries, however, have rejected these positions, sticking to the view that the exclusive competence of the host state courts over their investors and the waiver of diplomatic protection on their part cannot be invoked against them when international rights and obligations on foreign investment protection are at stake. This contrast was part of a broader conflict centred on the request of developing countries to rebalance the international economic order also in terms of its legal structure. The aim was to move its governance from specialized non-UN organizations to the United Nations General Assembly where they enjoyed, as the "Group of 77", an "automatic" majority with the support of the Soviet bloc.

Several economic and political conflicts arose between developed and developing countries following a number of nationalizations in the South of the world. While the overt use of force by home states has been banished since the beginning of the twentieth century and in any case under the UN Charter, amicable solutions have often taken years if not decades to be reached. Global settlements, via lump-sum agreements or through mixed commissions, have rarely satisfied (in any case not in full) foreign investors, while host states have on more than one occasion complained of improper pressures and encroachments upon their sovereignty by home states.[38]

In the pre-BIT and ICSID Convention era, *ad hoc* arbitration to settle investment disputes did occur, based on arbitral clauses in contracts or concessions agreed upon by host States and foreign investors.[39] Before the ICSID Convention came into force, major contracts, such as those in oil exploration and exploitation, sometimes included provisions on stabilization, to exempt them from future

36 Article 2.2(c) Charter of Economic Rights and Duties of States of 1974, UNGA Resolution 3281 (XXIX). On the NIEO, see G. Sacerdoti, "New International Economic Order (NIEO)" *MPEPIL* (2011).

37 See P. Juillard, "Calvo Doctrine/Calvo Clause" *MPEPIL* (2007).

38 S. Hobe, "The Development of the Law of Aliens and the Emergence of General Principles of Protection under Public International Law" *International Investment Law* 6.

39 On these developments from a historical perspective see generally A. Fatouros, *Government Guarantees to Foreign Investors* (Columbia University Press 1962); G. Sacerdoti, *I contratti tra Stati e stranieri nel diritto internazionale* (Giuffrè 1972); K. Böckstiegel, *Der Staat als Vertragspartner ausländischer Privatunternehmen* (Athenäum-Verlag 1974); I. Shihata, *The World Bank in a Changing World*, I, 237 (Nijhoff 1991); C. Leben, "La théorie du contrat d'Etat et l'évolution du droit international des investissements" 302 RC (2003) 197.

detrimental changes in legislation. Such contracts also included a choice of international law or principles of *lex mercatoria* (law merchant) as applicable to the merits ("delocalized contract") and provided for "autonomous" arbitration in case of dispute, disconnected from the *lex loci arbitratus* and patterned after interstate arbitration practice.[40]

Even these precautions at times proved to be ineffective in case of actual disputes.[41] When states have refused to participate in proceedings, difficulties in ensuring the carrying out of the arbitration have arisen. Even more difficult situations have materialized where a state party to an investment agreement annulled the contract or the arbitration clause, thus preventing the arbitration from taking place,[42] or where a state abusively annulled an international commercial award.[43] The "quasi-international" features of this type of arbitration, such as having been made subject to international law by contract, have not shielded these proceedings and their effectiveness from the abovementioned pitfalls.[44] The very fact that one of

40 See the *ad hoc* awards *Aramco v Saudi Arabia*, 23 August 1958, 27 ILR 117; *Sapphire v NIOC*, 15 March 1963, 35 ILR 136; *Texaco (TOPCO) v Libya*, 19 January 1977, YCA 1979, 177; *LIAMCO v Libya*, 12 April 1977, YCA 1981, 89; *BP v Libya*, 10 October 1973 and 1 August 1974, 53 ILR 297; on which see B. Stern, "Trois arbitrages, un même problème, trois solutions: les nationalisations pétrolières libyennes devant l'arbitrage international" Rev Arbitrage (1980) 3; R. von Mehren, N. Kourides, "International Arbitrations between States and Foreign Private Parties: The Libyan Nationalization Cases" 75 AJIL (1981) 476; C. Greenwood, "State Contracts in International Law – The Libyan Oil Arbitrations" 53 BYIL (1982) 27.

41 See A. Broches, "Awards Rendered Pursuant to the ICSID Convention: Binding Force, Finality, Recognition, Enforcement, Execution" 2 ICSID Rev (1987) 287; A. Van den Berg, "Recent Enforcement Problems under the New York and ICSID Conventions" 5 Arb. Int. (1989) 2; G. Delaume, "Contractual Waivers of Sovereign Immunity" 5 ICSID Rev (1990) 232; Id. "Enforcement of State Contract Awards: Jurisdictional Pitfalls and Remedies" 8 ICSID Rev (1993) 29.

42 In the *Anglo-Iranian Oil Co* case, n 31, the ICJ declined jurisdiction. Such a state action contrasts with and may (or should) be rendered ineffective by the principle that consent to arbitration cannot be revoked, not even by a subsequent statute of the state party that annuls the contract, given the universally recognized independence of arbitration clauses with respect of the rest of the contract, and the "competence–competence" principle (which confers on the arbitral tribunal jurisdiction to rule on its own jurisdiction). These principles have been codified in national arbitration laws, international conventions, and institutional rules. See Article 16 UNCITRAL Model Law on International Commercial Arbitration (1985, amended 2006); Article 6.3 ICC Arbitration Rules (2021); Article 21.2 UNCITRAL Arbitration Rules; Article V.3 of the European Convention on International Commercial Arbitration of 1961 (Geneva Convention); Article 41(2) ICSID.

43 Although, as highlighted in the preceding footnote, the principles of autonomy of arbitration agreements and of competence–competence of the tribunals are generally accepted nowadays (except in the US where courts assert their competence to ascertain arbitral tribunals' competence, US Supreme Court, *First Options of Chicago, Inc. v Kaplan*, 514 U.S. 938 (1995)), abusive interferences by host state's authorities with international arbitration proceedings based on international contracts with foreign investors still occur, as the investment arbitration case law indeed shows. See *Saipem v Bangladesh* ICSID ARB/05/07 Award (2009), holding that the Bangladeshi Supreme Court's decision declaring an ICC award "non-existent" amounted to an illegal expropriation under the Italy–Bangladesh BIT.

44 Starting from the celebrated *Anglo-Iranian Oil* case (n 42). In the literature of the time see G. Vedel, "Le problème de l'arbitrage entre gouvernements ou personnes de droit public et personnes de droit

the parties to proceedings is a sovereign state may prevent foreign investors from getting effective redress for breaches of the agreement. Recognition and enforcement of foreign or "international" awards in third countries when the defendant is a foreign state also gives rise to difficulties, first of all because of the obstacle of sovereign immunity from jurisdiction and execution. Thus, settling disputes between investors and foreign states by resorting to the instruments of commercial arbitration may encounter obstacles, particularly because the principles on which international commercial arbitration is based are not fully attuned and adapted to the additional constraints of state contracts.[45]

2. *The OECD Draft Multilateral Conventions on Investment Protection*

Capital exporting countries and business circles initially responded to the above problems by promoting the drafting of multilateral conventions on investments abroad to enhance their protection at a time when such protection was being challenged by developing countries at the UN. A Draft Convention on the Protection of Foreign Property was considered for some time at the OECD (1960–1967). Although the initiative was unsuccessful, its text became a model for subsequent BIT clauses, especially in relation to the Fair and Equitable Treatment standard and observance of undertakings ("umbrella clauses").[46] Subsequently, negotiations took place at the OECD on a "Multilateral Convention on Investment" (MAI) from 1995 to 1998, but this project was also abandoned after having been criticized for only reflecting the position of like-minded capital-exporting countries.[47] At the WTO Ministerial Conference in Singapore in 1996, it was decided to extend WTO agreements to include foreign direct investment, together with other subjects, such as competition policy, government procurement, and trade facilitation ("the

privé" Rev Arbitrage (1961) 116; P. Weil, "Problèmes relatifs aux contrats passés entre un Etat et un particulier" 128 RC (1969) 222; F. Mann, "State Contracts and International Arbitration" 42 BYIL (1967) 1; K.H. Böckstiegel, "Arbitration of Disputes between States and Private Enterprises in the ICC" 59 AJIL (1965) 579; G. Delaume, "State Contracts and Transnational Arbitration" 75 AIIL (1981) 809; F. Rigaux, "Souveraineté des Etats et arbitrage transnational" in P. Fouchard, P. Khan, A. Lyon-Caen (eds) *Le droit des relations économiques internationales. Etudes B. Goldman* (Litec 1982) 261; P Lalive, "Contrats entre Etats ou entreprises publiques et personnes privées" 181 RC (1983) 21; G. Sacerdoti, "State Contracts and International Law: A Reappraisal" 7 IYIL (1986–1987) 26.

45 See further on this issue in Chapter VI.B.1.2.

46 The text of the draft convention is available at https://investmentpolicy.unctad.org/international-investment-agreements/treaty-files/2812/download. It derived from the so-called "Abs-Shawcross" draft treaty (1959), named after the initiators, which had been endorsed by business organizations in Europe. The text is available at UNCTAD, *International Investment Instruments: A Compendium*, vol. V, 301, www.unctad.org. See generally F. Palombino, *Fair and Equitable Treatment and the Fabric of General Principles* (Springer 2018); F. Ortino, *The Origin and Evolution of Investment Treaty Standards: Stability, Value, and Reasonableness* (OUP 2019).

47 The text is available at https://web-archive.oecd.org/2012-11-16/72881-multilateralagreementoninvestment.htm; see J. Karl, "The Negotiations of the OECD Multilateral Agreement on Investment" in *International Investment Law* 342.

Singapore issues"). The work of the negotiating groups that had been established was, however, discontinued in 2004 after the inclusion of investment within the WTO appeared to be too controversial to be pursued.[48]

3. The ICSID Convention and BITs as a Turning Point

The ICSID multilateral convention represents a milestone in providing foreign investors with direct access to truly international arbitration with host States for advancing claims based on an alleged breach of international law standards, and, where successful, obtaining compensation for the damages suffered. Investment arbitration has advanced impressively since its beginnings based on contract clauses, thanks to an ever-growing network of BITs providing for international arbitration (specifically at ICSID) for investors of the contracting parties as the typical means of resolving investor–state disputes.[49]

The first BIT, between Germany and Pakistan, was concluded in 1959 although the first ICSID award under a BIT was issued as recently as 1990.[50] Since then, the network has expanded continuously, through the signing of BITs not only between capital-exporting (industrialized) and capital-importing (developing) countries but also within the "Global South" between developing countries *inter se*, and, under a few more recent IIAs, also between industrialized countries. Substantive protection standards are similar across BITs and have evolved over time.[51] Dispute settlement clauses are the provisions that present the highest degree of similarity across BITs, thus building a *de facto* multilateral system of access by investors to international arbitration with host states.

According to United Nations Conference on Trade and Development, almost 3000 IIAs have been concluded of which 2221 were in force at the end of 2024.[52] The impressive number of such treaties, alongside the "advanced consent" given by the state thereunder to being sued by any investor covered in accordance with the arbi-

48 See WTO, *Investment, Competition, Procurement, Simpler Procedures*, available at www.wto.org. Only work on trade facilitation continued, leading to an agreement at the Bali Ministerial Conference in 2013.

49 J. Crawford, "Continuity and Discontinuity in International Dispute Settlement" in C. Binder, U. Kriebaum, A. Reinisch, S. Wittich (eds) *International Investment Law for the 21st Century* (OUP 2009) 801, and 1 J International Dispute Settlement (2010) 3.

50 *Asian Agricultural Products Ltd (AAPL) v Sri Lanka* ICSID ARB/87/3, Final Award (1990), under the Sri Lanka–UK BIT of 1980.

51 See A. Newcombe, L. Paradell, *Law and Practice of Investment Tribunals: Standards of Treatment* (Kluwer 2009); T. St. John, *The Rise of Investor-State Arbitration: Politics, Law, and Unintended Consequences* (OUP 2018). According to the ICSID Annual Report for 2024, at 14, although the great majority of ICSID cases have been brought on the basis of BITs (83% in 2024), a number of cases have been brought under the ECT (14%), NAFTA and its successor USMCA (14%). Others are pending under the investment provisions of several bilateral trade agreements involving Latin American countries, including *inter se*. In 2023-2024 the first cases have been broungt to ICSID under the CPTPP.

52 See http://investmentpolicyhub.unctad.org/IIA accessed 3 January 2025..

tral rules referred to therein, are at the origin of investment treaty-based arbitration (also named as "arbitration without privity").[53] As reported by UNCTAD, as of the end of 2024, the total number of publicly known treaty-based cases had reached 1.332 of which 354 were pending.[54]

4. The Precedent of the Iran–US Claims Tribunal

An interesting example of the successful adjudication of economic disputes, which has been present in the minds of negotiators of BITs and the users of the system, is the Iran–US Claims Tribunal (1981). The Tribunal was established to resolve claims between nationals and governments of the two countries (mainly US investors against Iran) stemming from the nationalization of US property in Iran and the freezing of Iranian assets in the US as a consequence of the Islamic Revolution in Iran in 1979, thus enabling, by the use of the Iranian assets blocked in the US by the US government, the payment of US nationals' claims.[55] In this set-up (a contemporary version of the mixed claims commissions of the beginning of the twentieth century[56]), judges/arbitrators were appointed by the two state parties to hear all disputes by individuals against either party and, in a few cases, between the parties (Iran and the US) themselves, filed during their term of office. This experience has shown that it is possible, through the establishment of a permanent tribunal of limited duration (until all claims within its jurisdiction have been decided), to defuse a highly political conflict through arbitration. This has occurred by submitting to impartial arbitration economic claims of nationals of one party against the other by the application of principles of international law, notably those on state responsibility, expropriation and the calculation of damages.[57]

C. Comparative Evaluation

1. Commonalities and Differences

A comparative examination of the historical evolution of the two systems highlighted above shows substantial differences in their origins and institutional designs

53 This term was coined by Jan Paulsson in 1995 to identify international arbitration proceedings based on investment treaties thanks to which no previous specific agreement between the parties is required to trigger arbitration in case of dispute. See J. Paulsson, "Arbitration without Privity" 10 ICSID Rev (1995) 232.

54 See http:investmentpolicy.unctad.org Investment Dispute Settlement Navigator accessed 3 January 2025.

55 See S. Aldrich, *The Jurisprudence of the Iran–United States Claims Tribunal* (OUP 1996); C. Brower, J. Brueschke, *The Iran–US Claims Tribunal* (Nijhoff 1998); C. Drahozal, C. Gibson, *The Iran–U.S. Claims Tribunal at 25* (OUP 2007).

56 See R. Dolzer, "Mixed Claims Commissions" *MPEPIL* (2011); C. Giorgetti, P. Pearsall, H. Ruiz-Fabri (eds) *Research Handbook on Mixed Claims Commissions* (Elgar 2023).

57 R. Lillich, D. Magraw, D. Bederman, *The Iran–United States Claims Tribunal: Its Contribution to the Law of State Responsibility* (Nijhoff 1998).

but also certain common features and shared objectives that have been at the root of their development.

The starting points could not be more different. For trade, the GATT focused principally on non-discrimination rules and on the removal of import–export restrictions and the reduction of customs barriers through periodic rounds of negotiations, thereby facilitating commercial exchanges. Initially, and for about 20 years, the GATT's dispute settlement provisions were not at the forefront of the parties' concerns and were rarely used. Thereafter, from the mid-1970s, the movement towards more rule-based adjudication of trade disputes under the GATT gained momentum and inspired changes towards an adjudicative model, culminating in the establishment of a quasi-judicial two-tier system with the establishment of the WTO in 1995.

The DSS within investment law (ISDS) has also evolved in the direction of institutionalization, though attempts at multilateralization have failed to date. In order to protect investments abroad, the trend has been to move beyond the commercial model of contract-based arbitration to ensure by treaty the availability of investor–state arbitration and the effectiveness and enforceability of awards when sovereign states are involved. This has been achieved in two interconnected ways: first, by establishing an international organization, ICSID, within which investment disputes, initially predominantly based on contractual clauses, but also on domestic statutes and treaties, can be resolved through truly international arbitral proceedings, thus sidestepping the vagaries of municipal law and jurisdiction. Second, access to ICSID arbitration has been greatly facilitated and expanded by the network of BITs, which offer to aggrieved investors the option of taking to ICSID arbitral disputes under BITs, even in the absence of a prior specific agreement with the host state. They can invoke, in respect of their investment, the standards of protection laid down in BITs, which are higher than those afforded under the customary law on the rights of foreigners and which, depending on the host country's legal system, may be also higher than what is available domestically.

Both systems have thus evolved towards a rule-based system in the interest of security and predictability of relations for the participants and other stakeholders.[58] A substantial difference between them is that the trade DSS is multilateral. Adjudicators are appointed through a collective mechanism and are trustees of all the parties of the WTO: in adjudicating a dispute between specific litigants, they also act in the interest (as trustees) of the whole membership. In contrast, in the fragmented bilateral investment DSS, arbitrators are agents of the parties that appoint them and entrust them with the settlement of a specific dispute between

58 For definitions of the "rule of law", especially focused on the domestic dimension, see the conceptual and definitional work of the Venice Commission of the Council of Europe, www.venice.coe.int, and the eight elements elaborated by Lord (Judge) Bingham, *The Rule of Law* (Penguin 2011), the last one stating (at 130) that "The rule of law requires compliance by the state with its obligations in international law as in national law". See also E. Castellarin, "Investment Arbitration and the International Rule of Law" in M. Belov (ed), *Rule of Law at the Beginning of the Twenty-First Century* (Eleven, 2018) 211.

them.[59] Their accountability to a broader community by fostering the rule of law in international investment relations is at best indirect.[60]

In both settings, however, adjudicators are drawn from the social community of the addressees of their decisions and selected by them. Their independence, impartiality, and competence, ensured by appropriate provisions on their selection and activity, are key to the legitimacy of their decisions and ultimately of that of the respective adjudicatory systems.[61]

2. *International Trade and Investment Regime v International Commercial Law and Arbitration: Commonalities and Differences*

Investment arbitration stems from international commercial arbitration, from which it derives several key features (the choice of arbitrators by the parties, the organization of proceedings, and enforcement of the awards). Non-ICSID investment arbitration, as will be explored later, relies on the typical mechanisms of commercial arbitration in respect of its functioning and the implementation of awards. The commonalities and differences between the two systems therefore deserve a bespoke analysis.

As is well-known, commercial arbitration is the preferred means of settling through adjudication disputes arising from cross-border commercial transactions between business entities having their principal place of business (seat, residence) in different national jurisdictions.[62]

59 On the concept of trustees and agents in international dispute settlement, see especially K. Alter, "Agents or Trustees? International Courts in their Political Context" 14 EJIR (2008) 33; Id. *Global Judicialization Revisited, The New Terrain of International Law: Courts, Politics, Rights* (Princeton University Press, 2014).

60 See D. Desierto, "Public Policy in International and Investment Law: Community Expectations and Functional Decision-Making" 26 Florida JIL (2014) 52; S. Gáspár-Szilágyi, D. Behn, M. Langford (eds), *Adjudicating Trade and Investment Disputes: Convergence or Divergence?* (CUP 2020).

61 Independence and impartiality are also key for the legitimacy of international courts; see "Oslo Recommendations for Enhancing the Legitimacy of International Courts" (2018): "International Judges take a Stand on Current Challenges Facing the International Justice System", https://findingaids.brandeis.edu/repositories/2/resources/262. Politics however play a role with respect of international courts (as to appointments and constraints on decision-making) and may affect their independence ; see E. Posner and J. Yoo, "Judicial Independence in International Tribunals" 93 Cal L Rev 1 (2005); T. Ginsburg, "Political Constraints on International Courts" in *Oxford Handbook of International Adjudication* (OUP 2013) 483; Y. Shani, "International Courts in a Politicised World" in C. Brower and others (eds) *By Peaceful Means: International Adjudication and Arbitration. Essays in Honour of David D. Caron* (OUP 2021) 83. As to the ethical dimension, see C. Rogers, *Ethics in International Arbitration* (2nd ed. OUP 2025).

62 As to international commercial arbitration, see F. Fouchard, E. Gaillard, G. Goldman, *International Commercial Arbitration* (Kluwer 1999); G. Born, *International Arbitration: Law and Practice* (3rd ed. Wolters Kluwer 2021); F. Ferrari, F. Rosenfeld, F. Fellas, *International Commercial Arbitration* (Elgar 2022); A. Redfern & M. Hunter, *International Commercial Arbitration* (7th ed. OUP 2022); M. Moses, *The Principles and Practice of International Commercial Arbitration* (4th ed. CUP 2024).

In principle, international (cross-border) commercial dealings between parties of different nationalities are subject to domestic commercial law, and national jurisdictions have competence to handle disputes. However, the autonomy granted by state law to parties in international business operations allows them to minimize resulting conflicts of laws and between jurisdictions, by framing appropriately their transactions, choosing the applicable law and selecting the competent court (or arbitration as a preferred solution). Additionally, the harmonization of commonly used types of contracts across jurisdictions, based on treaties, soft-law instruments such as trade usages, model clauses and contracts developed by practice, business associations and institutions, and international organizations, tends to remove such transactions from domestic law.[63]

These transactions are moreover facilitated by the extensive network of multilateral, regional, and bilateral treaties and other arrangements on trade, commerce investment, and foreign exchange between the states concerned, along with regulations emanating from specialized international organizations.[64]

International (cross-border) business transactions pertain, however, factually, sociologically, and legally, to the realm of international (private commerce), which is different than that of the international regulation of trade between states by treaty at the WTO.[65] While international economic law is that part of public international

63 The extensive autonomy of international commercial arbitration from domestic law underpins the concept of international commercial relations as a system governed by a "non-national" *lex mercatoria*, emanating from the international traders' community, see E. Gaillard, *Legal Theory of International Arbitration* (Brill 2010); S. Schill, "Lex Mercatoria" *MPEPIL* (2014). Relations that the parties intend to remove from domestic legal constraints cannot, however, escape from the application of public order principles and imperative regulation in areas such as import–export, foreign exchange, taxation, anti-money laundering regulations, embargoes, and sanctions. Moreover, when one of the parties is a state or other public entity freedom of contract and of choice of law tends to be more limited because of the public interest pursued by the state party and the special regime to which its operations may be subject (such as administrative law).

64 The UN Commission on International Trade Law - UNCITRAL (www.uncitral.org), as the UN body devoted to furthering the progressive harmonization and modernization of the law of international trade, prepares and promotes the use and adoption of legislative and non-legislative instruments in a number of key areas of commercial law. The most relevant international instruments for the avoidance of conflicts and harmonization of the law of international commerce comprise multilateral treaties, such as the Convention on Contracts for the International Sale of Goods (CISG, Vienna 1980 https://uncitral.un.org/en/texts/salegoods), which calls for the application of trade usages in Article 9(2), and the NY Convention on the Recognition of Foreign Arbitral Awards of 1958, discussed in Chapter VI B.3. Among the most relevant non-binding texts, emanating from various sources, are the UNIDROIT Principles on International Commercial Contracts (2010), the UNCITRAL Arbitration Rules (2010, 2013), and the ICC Incoterms (2010).

65 The word *trade* is sometimes used also in respect of private commercial activity, especially since in many languages the English words *trade* and *commerce* are translated into the same term (such as *commerce* in French, *comercio* in Spanish, *Handel* in German). Thus, the book by C. Espluges Mota and others, *Derecho del Comercio Internacional* (10th ed. Tirant Lo Blanch 2022), covers international commercial contracts and dealings, whereas trade law is dealt with in works on "Derecho Economico Internacional". A comprehensive approach is also followed by F, Marrella, *Diritto del commercio internationale* (CEDAM 2023).

law dealing with relations between subjects of the international community, setting the framework and discipline for their relations in these fields, international commercial law, as a complex of rules and institutions from different sources governs transactions between private parties. There are too many fundamental differences between the legal regulation applicable to private parties' business transactions and that of public international law governing trade relations between States, including the WTO, to make a comprehensive analysis fruitful.[66]

The distinction between the two spheres as to parties and applicable legal regimes is confirmed by the lack of direct effect of international trade rules and decisions, typically those of the WTO, in domestic legal systems. As a consequence, private traders are prevented from invoking them before municipal courts except where and as far as they have been implemented in, and made part of domestic law.[67] Internationally, it is for the home state of producers and traders to invoke any treaty obligation of the importing state and to obtain redress either through negotiations and other diplomatic means, or through formal DSS procedures at the WTO.

As to investment, however, the above private–public and national–international divides are less clear. Although the underlying relations are subject to the domestic law chosen by the parties – usually that of the host state where the investment has been made, as often mandated by its imperative provisions – disputes between foreign investors and host states concerning the respect of BIT standards of treatment may be submitted to international arbitration at ICSID.[68] The connection with national legal systems is even closer in the case of investment disputes arising out of contracts or concessions. This private–public nature is confirmed by the fact that investment awards, even those of ICSID, which are international by nature, are recognized and ultimately enforced domestically if not complied with.[69]

The evolution of investment law and its DSS has thus not completely replaced the previous private domestic law framework but has rather supplemented it. A persistent interplay between private and public is thus a typical feature of investment law that calls for arbitrators, commentators, and lawyers with expertise in both fields. Contracts and the law of the host country, maintain a fundamental

66 Some authors in their work on international economic law also cover parts of "international business law". Thus M. Herdegen (n 1) deals in Part IV also with international sale and construction contracts, international companies, competition and tax law, and international accounting standards.

67 See C. Dordi (ed), *The Absence of Direct Effects of WTO in the EC and other Countries* (Giappichelli 2010); H. Ruiz-Fabri, 'Is There a Case – Legally and Politically – for Direct Effect of WTO Obligations?' 25 EJIL (2014) 151. The most notable case of domestic implementation of WTO agreements is that of the Antidumping Agreement, pursuant to an obligation to this effect in Article 18.4 of the ADA itself. See also generally J. Howley, *Overlapping Individual and Interstate Claims in International Law* (OUP 2024).

68 See references on state contracts at n 39 above.

69 See Chapter VI.B.1.2. In general, see Z. Douglas, "The Hybrid Foundations of Investment Treaty Arbitration" 74 BYIL (2003) 151; K-H Boecksiegel, "Commercial and Investment Arbitration: How Different Are They Today? 28 Arb.Int'l (2012) 577; B. Hess, *The Public-private Divide in International Dispute Resolution* 388 RC (2018) 71; C. Titi, "Investment Treaty Arbitration Caught in the Public-Private Law Divide" 45 Michigan J. Int. L. (2024) 441.

role in governing the rights and obligations of investors and the host state, but in applying them international tribunals have to take into account the requirements of international law.[70] Contractual disputes and those arising under BITs may be brought to local courts and to international commercial arbitration, especially when ICSID is not available (typically when either the home or the host state is not a party of the ICSID Convention). On the other hand, ICSID arbitration is a species of international public arbitration and is carried out under the rules of, and within, an international organization. ICSID awards have the nature of international decisions, though they settle disputes between a private party (a natural person or a legal entity organized under the municipal law of an ICSID contracting state) and another ICSID member state.

3. Dispute Settlement in Other Sectors of International Economic Law: Commonalities and Differences

Notwithstanding differences in regulation and in the set-ups of their respective DSS, trade and investment treaties share a common objective: adjudicating economic disputes arising under them impartially and bindingly based on due process and the application of pre-existing legal principles accepted by the parties.

This distinguishes trade and investment from most other sectors of international economic law, such as monetary and financial relations, anti-money laundering regulation, export credits, taxation, and economic sanctions.[71]

A basic reason for having an adversarial dispute settlement system in trade and investment relations, whereby individual rights (of states or business entities) can be directly or indirectly vindicated and breaches of applicable regulations sanctioned and remedied, is that private interests are directly (in investment) or indirectly (in trade) involved and affected. This is not considered to be relevant in the sphere of monetary relations, or in respect of foreign exchange and financial regulations (the supervision of banks to ensure the stability of the financial and payment systems, anti-money laundering), which govern relations between different economies, within the institutional framework of the IMF and through the adoption of common hard and soft-law standards and policy coordination.[72]

These regulations are agreed upon by states to govern their conduct as regulators within their borders in those areas, while private parties are subject to the respective domestic mandatory regimes put in place to implement them.[73] Although also in these sectors natural and legal persons may be affected by internationally agreed

70 As provided by Article 42.1 ICSID, see for more details in Chapter II.B.5.

71 As to sanctions, see A. Bultrini and others (eds) *International Sanctions in Practice: An Interdisciplinary Perspective* (Routledge-Giappichelli 2024).

72 M. Giovanoli (ed), *International Monetary Law: Issues for the New Millennium* (OUP 2000); A. Lowenfeld, "International Monetary Law" *MPEPIL* (2011); T. Cottier, R. Lastra, C. Tetje (eds) *The Rule of Law in Monetary Affairs* (CUP 2016); C. Tams and others (eds), *International Investment Law and the Global Financial Architecture* (Elgar 2017).

73 See F. Mann, *The Legal Aspect of Money* (6th ed. OUP 1992).

regulation impacting their transnational operations, they have no recourse against those rules except as available under the municipal law of participating countries on the basis of implementing legislation. In such a framework, the lack of, or incorrect implementation of international commitments is not subject to challenges by private parties.[74] States therefore maintain full authority over their participation in these schemes and how they adopt them domestically, including flexibility in derogating from them, in view of the prevailing collective interest in public goods such as monetary and financial stability. State-to-state dispute settlement proceedings are also uncommon in these areas since hard obligations are mostly only procedural.[75]

3.1. Monetary and Exchange Rate Regimes, Financial, and Anti-Money Laundering Regulation

Strict obligations concerning states' respective exchange rates, current payments regime, and capital movement controls under the supervision of the IMF were originally agreed upon in Bretton Woods in 1944 in conformity with the principles of the gold exchange standard. Since 1971, however, when the US decided to decouple the dollar from its gold peg and exchange rates were left to fluctuate, the direct supervisory function of the IMF has become looser, being based on flexible and variable monetary policy objectives.[76]

Freedom of movement of current payments under Article VIII IMF has progressively become the standard, while the reduction or elimination of controls on capital flows in respect of foreign direct investments (FDI) has become the rule, in any case between countries whose currency is freely convertible.[77] Trade and invest-

74 A well-known exception, however, is the *Kadi* Case, CJEU *Kadi v Council* Cases C-402,415/05 (*Kadi I* 2008) and C-584, 593, 595/10 (*Kadi II* 2013). Following these CJEU judgments affirming that the UN sanctions regime under UNSC Res. 1267 (1999) against Al-Qaeda and the Taliban did not adequately protect fundamental rights of those affected and could therefore not be applied in the EU, the UNSC reformed the UN scheme to allow individual recourses against blacklisting through the Ombudsperson (UNSC Res 1904 (2009) and 1989 (2011)), see M. Cremona, "EC Competence, 'Smart Sanctions', and the Kadi Case" 28 Y.B.EUR. L. (2009) 559.

75 Although these remedies are textually provided by Article XXIX IMF on decisions by the Executive Board and on referral by the Board of Governors on any "question" with or between members concerning the interpretation of the Articles of Agreement. See A. Viterbo "Dispute Settlement over Exchange Measures Affecting Trade and Investments: IMF, WTO, ICSID and Today's Relevance of Safeguard Clauses" 1 TDM (2009), available at www.transnational-dispute-management.com accessed 25 June 2024.

76 While under the original text of the IMF Articles of Agreement its members had to declare a parity in terms of gold (US dollar) for their currency, and changes could be introduced only after consultations with the Fund and its approval, following the amendment adopted in 1976, IMF members have the right to adopt a variety of exchange arrangements, including free floating, in consultation with the Fund. All relevant information is available at www.imf.org.

77 See in this respect the OECD Codes of Liberalisation of Current Invisible Operations and of Capital Movements (both first adopted in 1961), see B. Mercurio, *Capital Controls and International Economic Law* (CUP 2023).

ment flows could not have developed as massively as they have in the post-World War II period without these liberalizations.[78]

Other "expert" intergovernmental bodies (not established by treaty), such as the Financial Stability Board (FSB) or the Financial Action Task Force (FATF), which supplement the function of the IMF within their areas of competence, do not resort to hard law instruments. They focus on the coordination of national supervisory authorities to ensure the stability of banking systems and the fight against money laundering respectively, by laying down standards and policies to be implemented domestically by the participants.[79]

3.2. Export Credits, Taxation, and Regulatory Cooperation

Another area relating to trade where cooperation is not subject to formally binding commitments, but where agreed standards tend to be effectively observed, is governed by the "Arrangement on Officially Supported Export Credits". This Arrangement has been in place since 1978 among 11 major economies of the OECD in order "to provide a framework for the orderly use of officially supported export credits".[80]

In international tax matters, the jurisdiction of national authorities is usually subject to bilateral tax treaties, which are mostly patterned after OECD or UN models.[81] In the case of a conflict between competent authorities regarding the respective claims on the allocation of taxing rights, bilateral tax treaties provide for a mutual agreement procedure (similar in form to consultation). If the dispute

78 IMF members may use the flexibility recognized by the IMF in order to introduce or maintain capital movement restrictions and other measures for balance-of-payment reasons (Article XIV IMF). Domestic regulations are binding for private parties and are recognized as exceptions from commitments under the GATT (Article XII). As to BITs, see, for instance, the model clause on "Prudential Carve-Out" in the EU Commission's "non-paper" of 21 September 2023 on "Model Clauses for Negotiation or Re-negotiation of Member States' Bilateral Investment Agreements with Third Countries", available at https://policy.trade.ec.europa.eu accessed 25 June 2024. The clause is modelled after paragraph 2 of the GATS Annex on Financial Services. It allows parties to a BIA to adopt or maintain measures for prudential reasons, providing an indicative list. However, currently, more than 160 out of 184 IMF members have notified the Fund that they have accepted Article VIII's freedom of current payments obligations and no longer avail themselves of the transitional provisions of Article XIV.

79 See, respectively S. Gadinis, 'The Financial Stability Board: The New Politics of International Financial Regulation' 48 Texas International L.J. (2013) 157; L. Borlini, 'Regulating Criminal Finance in the EU in the Light of the International Instruments' 36 Y.B. EUR L. (2017) 553.

80 To this end, the Arrangement (defined as a "gentlemen's agreement") places limitations on the financing terms and conditions (repayment terms, minimum premium rate, minimum interest rates) to be applied when providing officially supported export credits as well as on the use of tied aid by the participants (Australia, Canada, EU, Japan, Korea, New Zealand, Norway, Switzerland, Turkey, UK, and US), see www.oecd.org/trade/topics/export-credits/arrangement-and-sector-understandings accessed 10 November 2023. Export credits under the OECD Arrangement are not considered prohibited export subsidies as per Annex I (k) of the WTO SCM Agreement.

81 See OECD, "Model Tax Convention on Income and on Capital" (2017), available at www.oecd.org; UN Model Double Taxation Convention between Developed and Developing Countries (UN 2017).

cannot be resolved, some treaties provide for arbitration between competent domestic authorities, which can be triggered by the taxpayer concerned.[82]

Intergovernmental cooperation in different areas where domestic regulation of national economies may collide is found in some recent Free Trade Agreements, while tax matters are explicitly excluded.[83] This development reflects the need to address the impact that divergent domestic regulations have on market access for foreign traders after customs duties have been substantially reduced through the periodic GATT rounds, thus ceasing to be an obstacle to trade.[84] However, chapters on regulatory cooperation have to date provided for relatively limited coordination between administrative bodies and other national authorities.

In areas such as the regulation of competition, treaty instruments and hard obligations are marginal compared to domestic regulation.[85] International cooperation in these areas is rather based on direct discretionary relations between national supervisory bodies, such as domestic antitrust authorities.[86] The fact that domestic regulation prevails in these areas is an indication that the international dimension of the sector is considered to be of minor importance.[87] However, as a consequence, market forces and private economic actors can more easily resort to "regulatory arbitrage". The absence of hard law obligations on the states involved makes it difficult to resort to more formalized methods of dispute settlement in these areas, in contrast to the international trade and investment regimes.

82 See Article 25 of the OECD Model. See also J. Chaisse, 'Arbitration in Tax Treaty Law and under BITs' in M. Lang and others (eds)., *International Arbitration in Tax Matters*, European and international tax law and policy series No. 2 (IBFD 2015).

83 For such an exclusion of taxation measures, also from dispute settlement, see Article 21 ECT.

84 See CETA Chapter 21 on "Regulatory Cooperation" and CPTPP Chapter 25 on "Regulatory Coherence".

85 See, for example, CETA Article 17.2.2: "The Parties shall take appropriate measures to proscribe anti-competitive business conduct. In this chapter, the EU and Canada agree to prohibit and sanction practices which distort competition and trade … They also recognize the importance of cooperation between their respective competition authorities".

86 See B. Kingsbury, Nico Krisch and Richard B Stewart, Introduction n 13.

87 Competition law, or the absence thereof in a given country, may take on an international dimension when, for example, goods become subject to anti-dumping or anti-subsidy measures, or investments are subject to foreign investment screening.

2 Basic Features of Trade and Investment Dispute Settlement

Table of Contents

DOI: 10.4324/9781003471509-4

Introduction

In this chapter, we give a general presentation of the trade and investment DSS, whose main aspects will be further discussed and highlighted in Chapters III to VI.

A. Trade

1. The WTO Dispute Settlement System

1.1. From the GATT to the WTO DSS: Continuity v Innovation

Two fundamental innovations characterize the "transformation" of the GATT into the WTO: first, the institutionalization of the trading system regime through the establishment of the WTO as a self-standing international organization comprising a fully fledged DSS; and second the extension of the coverage of the multilateral trade rules.

The first innovation has two aspects. The WTO is a fully-fledged international organization but its governance system is weak because it has no executive body (as is the case of councils with selective participation and executive powers at the UN, the WB, and the IMF) and its Director-General and secretariat have limited powers. Moreover, the efficiency of the negotiating function is hampered by the consensus principle that the organization has carried over from the GATT, and that its Members rigorously follow, although majority voting is provided for in the WTO Agreement.[1] This makes extending and updating the rule book almost impossible when Members are divided over the objectives of any development of the system, as is mostly the case nowadays. A major breakthrough during the Uruguay Round negotiations was the establishment of a rule-based DSS to deal with any and all disputes between Members under all of the WTO Agreements, including plurilateral agreements. Its creation and operation are fundamental, considering that the number of Members increased from fewer than 100 when the WTO entered into force to 166 today, with about 98% of world trade being subject to its rules. As to the second feature, multilateral trade agreements, annexed to the agreement establishing the WTO (the WTO Agreement) and representing with it a single inseparable treaty (the "single undertaking") expanded the WTO's coverage from just regulating trade in goods (GATT) to covering services (the GATS) and trade-related aspects of intellectual property rights (the TRIPS Agreement), with the addition of a number of other agreements that built on the provisions of the GATT as well as expand coverage into other areas.[2]

1 See Article XVI.1 of the Agreement Establishing the WTO ("WTO Agreement") according to which "the WTO shall be guided by the decisions, procedures and customary practices followed by the Contracting Parties to GATT 1947". As to the voting requirement see Article IX (Decision-Making) which provides however that "The WTO shall continue the practice of decision-making by consensus followed under GATT 1947" In general, see D. Bethlehem, D. McRae, R. Neufeld, I. Van Damme (eds), *The Oxford Handbook of International Trade Law* (2nd ed. Oxford 2021) Part VI.

2 Annex 1 of the Agreement establishing the WTO (the WTO Agreement). The term "Member(s)" is always officially used to indicate the parties to the WTO Agreement because also "separate custom

The Dispute Settlement Understanding (DSU) is part of the single undertaking and was agreed towards the end of the Uruguay Round negotiations.[3] Notwithstanding the substantial modifications introduced by the DSU, some key features of the previous non-binding GATT DSS were carried over. This approach, due to the Uruguay Round negotiators' desire to avoid the "over-legalization" of the system, resulted in the very title of the DSU ("understanding" rather than "agreement") and the use of intentionally imprecise or flexible terminology in many of its provisions. Moreover, with the GATT 1947, renamed GATT 1994, having remained part of the WTO, its Articles XXII and XXIII on disputes remain applicable, as stated in Article 3.1 DSU.[4]

Based on this approach, as to the core adjudication phase, the GATT dispute settlement system has not been replaced by a type of judicial system, such as establishing a "World Trade Court" as might have been envisaged but has rather been modified "incrementally", by adding key elements which are in any case typical of an adjudicatory system. As was the case under the GATT, at the WTO disputes are examined at first instance by a panel of trade experts that can be, and often are, delegates of other WTO Members.[5] Appeals may then be made to a permanent Appellate Body which in its composition, operation and functions is in substance akin to a permanent tribunal or court of appeal. Confidentiality characterizes most steps of the procedure. Direct settlement is encouraged both during the proceedings

territories possessing full autonomy in external commercial relations" which are not states can be Members of the WTO, following the GATT practice (Article XII of the WTO Agreement). Currently the WTO Members which are not states are Taiwan (called at the WTO Chinese Taipei), Hong-Kong and Macao. Both the EU and its member states are Members of the WTO pursuant to Article XI, but "Where the European Communities [since 2009 the European Union] exercise their right to vote, they shall have a number of votes equal to the number of their member States" (Article IX of the WTO Agreement).

3 The DSU constitutes Annex 2 of the Marrakesh Agreement establishing the WTO of 14 April 1994. The WTO agreements are thus, to be precise, just one treaty (signed and ratified as such) even if, for practical purposes, each agreement has distinct features. On the WTO DSS in general, see besides *Van den Bossche* 173–336; J. Jackson, *The World Trading System. Law and Policy of International Economic Relations* (2nd ed. MIT Press 1993); P. Mavroidis, *The WTO Dispute Settlement System: How, Why and Where?* (Elgar 2022); H. Gao, J. Hillman, N. Lamp, J. Pauwelyn, *International Trade Law: A Casebook for a System in Crisis* (2023), available at https://btn.genevatradeplatform.org accessed 25 June 2024.

4 "Members affirm their adherence to the principles for the management of disputes heretofore applied under Articles XXII and XXIII of GATT 1947, and the rules and procedures as further elaborated and modified herein". As a consequence, "non-violation complaints" are still possible (although they have hardly been brought) to address situations of frustration of legitimate expectations about the outcome of the operation of rules, even in the absence of a breach, provided this results in nullifying or impairing a benefit accruing directly or indirectly to the complaining Member under the GATT, as per Article XXIII (1) and Article XXIII (3) GATT. Generally, however, "there is normally a presumption that a breach of the rules has an adverse impact on other Members parties to that covered agreement" (Article 3.8 DSU).

5 As to the specific features of WTO panelists compared to investment arbitrators, see J Pauwelyn, 'The Rule of Law without the Rule of Lawyers? Why Investment Arbitrators are from Mars, Trade Adjudicators from Venus' 109 AJIL (2015) 761.

and after their conclusion since the "aim of the dispute settlement system is to secure a positive solution to a dispute" (Article 3.7 DSU). Finally, it is for the WTO Members, meeting within the Dispute Settlement Body (DSB), to adopt, and thereby render binding for the parties to the dispute, panel and AB reports. Their reports are nominally just recommendations to the DSB to, in turn, recommend to the Member found to be in breach to comply with its obligations, principally by withdrawing or adequately modifying the objectionable measure (Article 19.1 DSU). It is the DSB's adoption, that is their endorsement by the full membership, that makes reports binding.

The role of the DSB is emphasized by the provisions on the terms of reference of panels, determining their task, which is "to examine the matter … referred to the DSB … and to make such findings as will assist the DSB in making the recommendations or in giving the rulings provided for in that/those agreements" (Articles 7.1, 11 DSU). In reality, panels do not "assist" the DSB in making the rulings, they actually issue the rulings which the DSB then adopts. The negative (or reversed) consensus rule, which was considered necessary to avoid a recalcitrant party blocking adoption, as was the case under the GATT, has "completely nullified the supposed role of the DSB to make the final decision", to the point that *de facto* the DSB just "rubberstamps" the panel and AB decisions.[6] However, the involvement of the whole membership through the DSB, a distinct feature of the WTO system, is valuable because it encourages engagement by each WTO Member and "ownership" by all Members. This is reflected in Articles 16.5 and 17.14 DSU which provide that the "adoption procedure is without prejudice to the right of all Members to express their views' on a panel or AB report (a possibility that many of them use at the DSB session where reports come for adoption). Moreover, the adoption of the adjudicators' rulings by the DSB transforms what would be *per se* an adjudicatory (in substance arbitral or judicial) decision, that would only be binding upon the parties, into a decision of the WTO as an organization. As a result, such a decision is in principle endowed with more authority since the whole membership stands behind a panel or AB report, not just the adjudicators who issued it. This is the case instead for judgments of international courts and arbitration tribunals including investment tribunals which are final once issued and binding for the parties to the dispute.[7]

The solution is rule-based at all stages, since panels and the AB base their reports on a legal evaluation of the (in)consistency of the measures challenged with the WTO agreement invoked by the complainant.[8] The DSB recommendations and rulings, basically consisting of the adoption of the adjudicators' reports by negative consensus (thus almost "automatically"), "shall be aimed at achieving a satisfactory settlement of the matter" but "in accordance with the rights and obligations

6 A. Wolff, *Revitalizing the World Trading System* (CUP 2023) 239.

7 See Article 59 ICJ: "The decision of the Court has no binding force except between the parties and in respect of the particular case".

8 See Articles 4.4 ("the legal basis for the complaint"), 7, 17.13, 21.5, 22.2 DSU.

under this Understanding and under the covered agreements" (Article 3.5 DSU). The negative consensus rule (according to which consensus in the DSB is required not for adopting but in order to reject certain requests) is provided in the DSU for key decisions: the establishment of panels, the adoption of panel and appellate reports, and the authorization of countermeasures in case of non-compliance. It prevents individual WTO Members from blocking proceedings and their outcome based on the exercise of political discretion as was possible under the GATT.[9] This apparently small change from the GATT practice has had a major effect on the system, rendering the approval of reports by the DSB *de facto* automatic. In practice, as a result, although the binding decision is the one made by the DSB when adopting panel and AB reports, the obligation for Members to comply stems from the adjudicators' reports.[10]

In its operation, the system has adopted the rigour of adversarial legal proceedings with full respect for due process. Panels and the AB operate as arbitral tribunals and courts,[11] respectively, not as conciliation commissions. Moreover, their role as key elements of the system goes beyond their primary task of deciding specific cases. As spelled out in Article 3.2 DSU:

> The dispute settlement system of the WTO is a central element in providing security and predictability to the multilateral trading system. The Members recognize that it serves to preserve the rights and obligations of Members under the covered agreements, and to clarify the existing provisions of those agreements in accordance with customary rules of interpretation of public international law. Recommendations and rulings of the DSB cannot add to or diminish the rights and obligations provided in the covered agreements.[12]

The function of the WTO DSS thus goes beyond the settlement of individual disputes and serves the entire system for the benefit of each and all members, based on clarifying and interpreting the WTO Agreements "in accordance with customary rules of interpretation of public international law". Adjudicators serve as trustees for the whole membership, not as agents of the litigants as in arbitration.[13] A balance is thus struck between the settlement of individual disputes to serve the

9 See Articles 6.1, 16.4, 17.14, 22.6 DSU.

10 Negative consensus was not considered with respect of the appointment of the AB's Members (Article 17.2 DSU). This was an "oversight" that has enabled the US to block the filling of vacancies through the selection and appointment process starting in 2017 by objecting to the initiation of their selection and appointment process.

11 H. Ruiz-Fabri, 'Dispute Settlement in the WTO: On the Trail of a Court' in S. Charnovitz, D. Steger, P. Van den Bossche (eds), *Law in the Service of Human Dignity: Essays in Honour of F. Feliciano* (CUP 2005)136.

12 The AB has stated since its first report (*US–Gasoline* DS 2-1996) that those rules are to be found in Articles 31–33 VCLT on the interpretation of treaties.

13 For this distinction, see K. Alter, "Agents or Trustees? International Courts in their Political Context" 14 EJIR (2008) 33.

Members involved and the preservation of the system based on the respect of the rights and obligations of all Members thereunder (Article 3.3–3.5 DSU).

1.2. Key Procedural Features

First of all, the system is "single, comprehensive, integrated" (i.e. multilateral), in respect of all disputes between individual WTO Members (complainant(s) v a respondent) and for all provisions under all agreements.[14] It provides for (i) *compulsory*, (ii) *exclusive*, (iii) *law-based*, and (iv) *binding* settlement. *Compulsory,* because if a WTO Member decides to submit a dispute against another Member concerning an alleged breach of a WTO provision due to any "measure" (enactment, practice, omission) of such other Member, a panel to hear the dispute shall be established since the DSB accepts the request by negative consensus (Article 6 DSU). *Exclusive,* because Article 23.1 DSU provides that such disputes must be brought to proceedings under the DSU (and not to other *fora*). *Law-based,* because the panels and the AB, acting as impartial and independent adjudicators, resolve the disputes through the application of the principles on the interpretation of treaties within adversarial proceedings that respect procedural due process, as is the rule in any arbitral or judicial proceeding. *Binding,* as to the outcome, because the DSB, again by negative consensus, adopts panel and AB reports recommending the withdrawal of any measure found to be WTO-inconsistent. While the governance of the WTO is weak, having enforceable rules sets it apart from other international organizations.[15]

In addition to adjudication, the DSU provides for recourse to good offices, conciliation and mediation, by agreement of the parties in dispute, which may be offered by the Director-General (Article 5). It also provides for "expeditious" binding arbitration pursuant to Article 25 DSU. In contrast with regular proceedings, other WTO Members are not entitled to participate in these alternative proceedings and the DSB is not involved, except in respect of Articles 21 and 22 on implementation which are applicable to arbitral awards. As discussed in chapters VII and VIII, Article 25 arbitration was the basis for establishing the MPIA in 2019 by a sizeable group of WTO Members (27 as of the end of 2024 counting the EU as one) that intended to maintain appellate review for disputes among themselves, thus circumventing the blocking of the AB by the US.[16]

14 P. Van den Bossche, W. Zdouc, *The Law and Policy of the World Trade Organization. Text, Cases and Materials* (5th ed. CUP 2022) 196; D. Palmeter, P. Mavroidis, N. Meagher, *Dispute Settlement in the WTO. Practice and Procedure* (3rd ed. CUP 2022).

15 As stated by A. Wolff (n 6), 459, "Binding dispute settlement, meaning the ability to obtain a final judgment of whether a member has acted inconsistently with its WTO obligations, was the defining attribute" of the WTO in 1995 (and still is).

16 See Chapter VIII.A.2. *Ad hoc* arbitration outside the DSU is not unknown to the WTO. In 2005, arbitration was agreed and took place between the EU and the other parties of the "Banana case" (DS 27) to resolve a specific compliance dispute ("Banana Tariff Arbitration"), www.wto.org/english/tratop_e/dispu_e/cases_e/ds27_e.htm.

There are three distinct phases of dispute settlement proceedings at the WTO aimed at: (1) consultations aimed at an amicable settlement, (2) the impartial rule-based adjudication of the facts and the law, and (3) the effective implementation of any adjudicatory finding of non-compliance. Consultations are the first compulsory conciliatory phase of proceedings, in the course of which "Members should attempt to obtain satisfactory adjustment of the matter" (Article 4.5 DSU). These *consultations*, which last a minimum of 60 days, are initiated by a formal request identifying both the WTO provisions allegedly breached and the respondent's conduct (measure) that is in breach. If there is no agreement by the end of the period for consultations, the DSU provides for a two-level *adjudicatory phase*, the first of which is before an *ad hoc* panel, whose members are chosen by the parties with the support of the secretariat, entrusted with making "an objective assessment of the facts of the case and the applicability of and conformity with the relevant covered agreements" (Article 11 DSU).[17]

A peculiar feature carried over from the GATT is that the parties receive an advance confidential copy of the final report in draft form ("interim report", Article 15 DSU), which they can comment on also with a view to obtaining (minor) changes before its formal issuance and circulation to all Members.[18] In theory, this advance communication of the report should provide an opportunity for the panel to correct factual errors and facilitate last-minute direct settlement. But the addition of the appellate stage where a losing party can hope to overturn the outcome before the panel has reduced the utility of the interim report phase.[19]

1.3. Appellate Review

The WTO's system of appellate review is a rare feature in international adjudication.[20] It is meant to both allow review of legally erroneous panel decisions (panellists are not required to be professional lawyers and often are not) and ensure consistency in the interpretation of the WTO Agreements.

Appeal against panel decisions is provided for before the permanent AB only as to the correctness of the legal findings of the panel, and is one of the most notable innovations brought about by the DSU. At both stages, proceedings are predominantly written and confidential (Article 14, 17.10 DSU), although some Members publish their briefs. Public viewing of hearings is also possible (provided the parties agree) at both stages.

17 See Chapter III.A.2–5 for more details.

18 The final report is published on the WTO website, making it accessible to the general public worldwide even before its adoption by the DSB.

19 Hence calls to drop the interim phase so as to shorten the panel proceedings have been made. Since the demise of the AB, settlement negotiations between the parties in light of the interim report seem to have picked up, see Chapter VII.A.2.5.

20 See G. Sacerdoti, 'Appeal and Judicial Review in International Arbitration and Adjudication: The Case of the WTO Appellate Review' in E. Petersmann (ed), *International trade law and the GATT/WTO dispute settlement system* (Kluwer 1997) 245.

The appellate review by a standing body, competent to review (only) the legal reasoning and conclusions of a panel report, supports the aim of the DSS to contribute to providing "security and predictability to the multilateral trading system" for the benefit of all Members, notably by "clarifying" the provisions of the applicable WTO Agreements (Article 3(2) DSU). The AB is composed of seven Members, duly qualified and "unaffiliated with any government", and selected so as to be broadly representative of the WTO membership. They are appointed by the DSB by consensus for a relatively short four-year term, which is renewable only once.

The AB decides in divisions of three, randomly formed for each case, without any nationality bar.[21] It is empowered to address only those issues of law in the panel report that parties appeal and to "uphold, modify or reverse the legal findings and conclusions of the panel" (Article 17.13 DSU). The AB cannot decide *ex novo* the case if it considers that a panel made erroneous findings or conclusions. It may, however, modify the legal findings and conclusions of the panel by completing the legal analysis, provided the evidentiary factual record is sufficient. Its functions are thus comparable to those of a Court of Cassation, except that it has no power of remand. The AB's organization, working procedures, code of conduct for its members, and the fact that it has its own secretariat on which it relies (Article 17.7), make the AB akin to an international court and ensures, besides its competence, independence and impartiality for the benefit of all WTO Members (see Articles 17.9 DSU).

1.4. Third-Party Participation

Another notable feature of the system, in keeping with the idea that it operates for the benefit of all Members and not just the parties in dispute, is that all Members of the WTO are entitled (Article 10 DSU) to participate as third parties in any proceeding at all stages, though with more limited rights than the litigants. The procedural condition for joining consultations is that a third party has a "substantial trade interest" in ther matter. The respondent must agree to a third party participating in consultations pursuant to Article 4.11 DSU. Any interested Member can however join as a third party at the panel stage even if it was not a party at the consultations phase. A Member need only have a "substantial interest", also just a "systemic interest", to become a third party to panel proceedings (Article 10.2 DSU). Given the *de facto* precedential value that the interpretation of a given provision may have regarding guidance for its application by other Members or in subsequent cases, major economies almost always participate as third parties in disputes, exercising their right to make legal submissions and be heard by the panel and the AB.

21 The 27 Members of the AB (five of whom were women) from 1995 to 2020 came from 17 different countries (four members were from the US, three from EU member states (Germany, Italy, Belgium), three from Japan, two respectively from the Philippines, India, Korea, China, and Egypt, one each from South Africa, Brazil, Mexico, Uruguay, Australia, New Zealand, and Mauritius). Six AB Members have also occasionally acted as investment arbitrators, during or after their tenure.

1.5. Time Limits

A paramount objective of the DSU is that proceedings be expeditious. This starkly contrasts with practice before most international courts and tribunals and reflects the needs of commerce and the aim of promptly removing national barriers to trade introduced in breach of WTO obligations. Accordingly, the DSU provides that panel proceedings should not last more than nine months and that those on appeal shall not exceed 90 days (Articles 12.9 and 17.5 DSU). In the same vein, the deadline for the parties to compose a panel is just 20 days, otherwise the DG steps in upon the request of either party (Article 8.7 DSU); the deadline for the DSB to adopt a panel report in the absence of an appeal is 60 days (Article 16.4 DSU), while that for adopting an appellate report is 30 days (Article 17.14 DSU). Over the years, these short deadlines for panel and appellate proceedings have proved impossible to respect given the increased complexity of cases, the number of claims made before panels and on appeal, and the sheer number of concurrently pending cases that the secretariat has not always been able to handle.[22]

1.6. The Implementation Phase

An innovative feature of the system that distinguishes it from any other form of international adjudication is the regulation of the *implementation phase* when a breach has been ascertained. Implementation by a party found to have been in breach is not only compulsory, since adopted reports are binding for the parties, but should be induced by the surveillance entrusted to the DSB. It is typical of the non-strictly legal terminology of the DSU that the binding character (*res iudicata*) of adopted reports is spelled out through periphrasis in the DSU. Thus, Article 19.1 provides that "Where a panel or the AB concludes that a measure is inconsistent with a covered agreement, it shall recommend that the Member concerned bring the measure into conformity with that agreement". In turn, appellate reports "shall be adopted by the DSB and unconditionally accepted by the parties" unless the DSB decides by consensus not to adopt them (Article 17.14).

While "prompt compliance" with the DSB's recommendations is declared "essential in order to ensure effective resolution of disputes to the benefit of all Members" (Article 21.1), the same article provides for a reasonable period of time to be granted to Members "to implement Panel or AB recommendations … if it is impracticable to comply immediately" (Article 21.3). This period should not exceed 15 months (Article 21.4 DSU). This is coupled with recourse to arbitration to determine this period for compliance in case of disagreement between the parties, and recourse again to the original panel and the AB on appeal in case of

22 As of 2020, the average length was 539 days between panel establishment and DSB adoption, M. Wagner, "Panel: Dispute Settlement System of the World Trade Organization (WTO)" MPEiPro (2020). See also R. Ramirez, K. Castren, "Will the Increased Workload of the WTO Panels and the AB Change how WTO Disputes are Adjudicated?" in *A History* 616 (since their position is not full-time, AB members are allowed to engage in other non-conflicting activities).

disagreement as to whether proper compliance has been effected (Articles 21.3 and 21.5 DSU). Implementation, which is merely prospective (for the future), does not entail the payment of damages as is the rule in investment (and commercial) arbitration. Implementation at the WTO involves the withdrawal of the WTO-inconsistent measure, which can moreover be replaced by other forms of compensation agreed upon between the parties.[23] Prospective implementation is a *lex specialis* regulation which departs from the principles governing state responsibility in general international law where the duty to remove a breach and remedy its consequences is *ex tunc* (since then) rather than *ex nunc* (from now on).[24]

Finally, in the case of non-compliance, countermeasures in the form of the temporary suspension of concessions of an equivalent value (as temporary measures to induce compliance) are authorized by the DSB by reverse consensus (Article 22 DSU). This provision also takes into account the possibility that the countermeasures enacted are excessive: in this case, the original panel may be called to arbitrate whether they have exceeded the level of nullification of benefits caused by the breach. The DSU has thus laid down an innovative and complex system to ensure, or at least induce compliance that combines flexibility, mutual agreement between the parties concerned but also adjudication and strict procedural obligations.

1.7. The Inter-Governmental Set-Up and the Indirect Involvement of Private Parties Affected

A key feature of the system that was carried over from the GATT is that disputes are inter-governmental, that is state-to-state, even if the interests at stake are first and foremost those of private business, sometimes possibly (such as typically in case of anti-dumping) just those of a specific company.

An important "side effect" of this inter-governmental character is that it is up to governments to decide whether or not to initiate a dispute and how to conduct it, although in many cases the complaint originates from private parties such as exporters facing market access barriers abroad or the domestic industry affected by dumped or subsidized imports. These private parties and those with opposing interests in the country where these imports originate are on the other hand those mostly affected by the outcome of a dispute.[25]

Some countries have set-up procedures by which the domestic industry affected by an allegedly WTO-inconsistent measure abroad may petition their competent national authorities to take up a case. Thus, in the US, firms or industries may petition the USTR to initiate a WTO dispute against an allegedly adverse trade

23 Although Article 22.1 declares compensation to be only temporary, WTO Members have at times resorted to agreed compensation in lieu of compliance to settle a dispute, such as in *EC–Hormones* (DS 26-1998) and in *US–Clove Cigarettes* (DS 406-2012).

24 See ARSIWA Articles 31, 34, 36, 38 and Chapter VI.A.1 for more details.

25 G. Shaffer, *Defending Interests: Public-Private Partenerships in WTO Litigation* (Brookings 2003).

measure pursuant to Section 301 of the US Trade Act of 1974.[26] Similarly, the Trade Barriers Regulation (TBR) allows EU firms and industries to petition the European Commission to take action (including filing a WTO dispute) against foreign trade measures allegedly causing adverse effects.[27] In anti-dumping and subsidy cases, the initiation of a domestic procedure with a view to the possible application of anti-dumping and countervailing duties must, as a rule, be initiated at the behest of the domestic industry affected (Article 5.1 ADA; Article 11.1 SCM).

The WTO Agreement requires (Article XVI.4) that "Each Member shall ensure the conformity of its laws, regulations and administrative procedures with its obligations as provided in the Annexed Agreements" but does not require that they have "direct effect" domestically, that is that private parties may directly invoke them before national courts. The absence of direct effect both as to the agreements and as to the decisions (reports adopted by the DSB) has been formally spelled out in the US implementing legislation and has been affirmed in the EU by the European Court of Justice.[28] Private parties may, however, invoke domestic implementing legislation before competent national courts. This means, as happens frequently, that the same allegedly WTO-inconsistent practice is the object of parallel proceedings in the competent domestic courts of the country that adopted a restrictive trade measure (such as the Court of Justice in the EU and the Court of International Trade in the US) and at the WTO. Even if recourse by a government to dispute settlement at the WTO might be considered an exercise of diplomatic protection when the challenge is against a foreign measure specifically prejudicing a certain enterprise, there is no requirement that domestic remedies be previously exhausted. In contrast, the ICSID Convention enjoins contracting states from giving diplomatic protection or bringing an international claim in respect of a dispute which their nationals have consented to submit to ICSID arbitration with another contracting state "unless such other Contracting State shall have failed to abide by and comply with the award" (Article 27.1).

2. *Non-WTO Dispute Settlement*

Regional Trade Agreements (RTAs) feature bilateral dispute settlement systems that are generally patterned after the one of the WTO, the main differences being that the context is bilateral or regional, and there is no appellate review.[29] The

26 See A.Alemanno, Private Parties and WTO Dispute Settlement System, Cornell Law School LL.M Paper Series (2004) 1.

27 Regulation (EU) 2015/1843 of the European Parliament and of the Council of 6 October 2015 (repealing Reg. 3286/94) lays down Union procedures in the field of the common commercial policy in order to ensure the exercise of the Union's rights under international trade rules, in particular those established under the auspices of the WTO.

28 See, respectively, US Uruguay Round Agreements Act, 1994, Section 10; CJEU *Portugal v Council*, C-149/96 (1996) 34–46.

29 See G. Sacerdoti, "Resolution of International Trade Disputes in the WTO and Other Fora" 14 J Int Trade Law Policy (2015) 147; C. Furculiță, *The WTO and the New Generation EU FTA Dispute*

increased number of such RTAs and the first cases of referral of disputes to these mechanisms make an examination of their features appropriate. This is even more so the case, since in some RTAs additional features have been introduced to make the process more efficient and transparent, features that may one day be adopted at the WTO.[30]

2.1. Ad Hoc Arbitration to Resolve Trade Disputes

States also occasionally resort to *ad hoc* arbitration, both of a public international character and of the commercial type, to settle trade disputes. This shows that trade disputes can also be dealt with and resolved through traditional adjudication mechanisms, of both a public and private nature, especially in a purely bilateral context involving isolated disputes.

An example of a typical public international law *ad hoc* arbitration clause is found in Article 19 of the "Open Sky Agreement" between the US and the EU[31] of 2007/2010. According to this provision, any dispute not resolved by a meeting of the parties' Joint Committee shall be submitted to arbitration and decided by an arbitral tribunal of three members. Each party appoints one member, and the president is appointed by agreement between the two party-appointed arbitrators.[32] It is for the tribunal to determine its jurisdiction and to establish its procedural rules. The procedure is simple, with no hearing required. All deadlines for appointments and rendering the decision are quite short. If a decision determines the existence of a violation and the violation is not resolved or a mutually satisfactory solution is not reached within 40 days, the other party "may suspend the application of comparable benefits" arising under the Agreement until a resolution is agreed. Another example is the EU-UK arbitration of 2024 under the 2020 Trade and Cooperation Agreement (Brexit) challenging UK fishing restrictions.[33]

Resort to the international commercial arbitration model is also possible. Such an arbitration has taken place within the long-standing and recurrent dispute between the US and Canada concerning Canada's export of softwood lumber to

Settlement Mechanisms (Springer 2021); V. Beyer, "Dispute Settlement in Preferential Trade Agreements and the WTO: A Network Analysis of Idleness and Choice of Forum" 32 EJIL (2021) 433; see also the contributions featured in *The Oxford Handbook of International Trade Law* (2023), Part VI, "The Settlement of Trade Disputes in the WTO and Bilateral/Regional Trade Agreements".

30 Especially with respect of the pre-adjudication phase, including, for instance, mediation (see EU–Singapore FTA, Chapter 15), *amicus curiae* briefs, and public access to hearings.

31 The original agreement was concluded in 2007, while an amending Protocol was enacted in 2010, last accessed 19 July 2024.

32 Failing such agreement, the appointment is to be made by the president of the Council of ICAO.

33 See https://pca-cpa.org/en/cases/334. The "Sandel arbitration" was concluded by a "ruling" of the tribunal on 28 April 2025. In 2016, the EU Commission announced the initiation of such an arbitration against the US concerning the delay by the US in granting a licence to a European carrier, but the matter was resolved before proceedings were started. See https://www.reuters.com/article/business/exclusive-eu-to-seek-arbitration-in-dispute-with-u-s-over-norwegian-air-sources-idUSKCN10628B/ accessed 19 July 2024.

the US (a dispute that had resulted in several cases at the WTO as well as trade and ISDS disputes under NAFTA). The two countries agreed in their 2006 Softwood Lumber Agreement that any dispute concerning the application of this agreement, not resolved satisfactorily through consultation or mediation, would be submitted to arbitration under the rules of the LCIA. In fact, three such arbitrations were initiated by the US in 2007, 2008, and 2011 resulting in the issuance of awards.[34]

2.2. *The Main Features of Trade Dispute Settlement under RTAs*

2.2.1. *The Proliferation of RTAs*

There has been a proliferation of Regional Trade Agreements (RTAs/FTAs), both bilateral and among groups of countries, in recent decades. According to the WTO website, as of 1 December 2024, there were 373 Regional Trade Agreements in force involving all WTO Members[35] except Timor-Leste.[36] The parties' aims are, in conformity with Article XXIV GATT and Article V GATS, to encourage reciprocal trade, services, and investment through deeper liberalization, provided they do not raise barriers in relations with non-participating WTO Members. The aim is rarely that of establishing full integration, such as in customs (and monetary) unions of which the EU is the foremost example. More frequently, the objective is the reduction of customs barriers, mutual recognition, and harmonization of standards and qualifications, and other forms of "structured" cooperation or partnership.[37] In most RTAs, provisions on substantive rules and rights and obligations closely follow (or directly incorporate) the provisions of WTO Agreements in these areas, especially as to the GATT. A typical feature of recent RTAs has been their coverage of matters that go beyond the WTO Agreements (WTO-extra provisions) and their inclusion of investment chapters (RTIAs).[38] Some of these matters did not even exist when the WTO was established, or have been tackled unsuccessfully since in the multilateral framework, such as electronic (digital) trade, environmental and labour standards.

34 *US–Canada*, LCIA cases No. 7941, 81010, 91312, https://www.italaw.com/cases/1290

35 For up-to-date information on RTAs and the WTO, see the WTO RTA portal, https://rtais.wto.org. The terms Free Trade Agreement (FTA) or Preferential Trade Agreement (PTA) tend to be used interchangeably with RTA. The term "regional" is inacurate because trade agreements often go beyond any particular geographical region. The term PTA is at times preferred to FTA as it encompasses trade agreements that fall short of providing for fully free trading relations and the elimination of all customs duties on "substantially all the trade" between its members as required by Article XXIV GATT for free-trade areas to be compatible with the GATT.

36 See the WTO Regional Trade Agreements Database at https://rtais.wto.org.

37 See A. Dür, M. Elsig (eds), *Trade Cooperation: The Purpose, Design, and Effects of Preferential Trade Agreements* (CUP 2015).

38 This is the case of USMCA (and formerly of NAFTA), CETA, CPTPP, and the AANZFTA. See H. Horn, P. Mavroidis, A. Sapir, "Beyond the WTO? An Anatomy of EU and US Preferential Trade Agreements" 33 The World Economy (2010), 1565. In general, see also WTO, *The WTO and Preferential Trade Agreements: From Co-existence to Coherence. World Trade Report 2011,* available at www.wto.org.

2.2.2. *Dispute Settlement under RTAs*

Some agreements, typically those involving countries from East Asia, have "light" trade dispute settlement provisions in conformity with their minimalist institutional framework. Thus, the ASEAN Charter calls for Member States "to resolve peacefully all disputes in a timely manner through dialogue, consultation and negotiation" (Article 21). The Charter provides for good offices, conciliation and mediation (Article 22). It also envisages that the various specific ASEAN instruments contain their own dispute settlement mechanisms, and ultimately provides that "[w]hen a dispute remains unresolved [under these mechanisms] this dispute shall be referred to the ASEAN Summit, for its decision" (Article 26).[39]

Agreements involving the EU or the US contain more detailed provisions on trade dispute settlement mechanisms patterned closely after the WTO system, except for the lack of appeal and of collective monitoring on implementation as entrusted to the DSB at the WTO.[40] A notable difference in the practice has been the limited recourse to such mechanisms. Until recently WTO Members have tended to litigate at the WTO rather than under the dispute settlement mechanisms (DSMs) of RTAs for various reasons. These include the high levels of trust in the WTO dispute settlement system, its relative predictability, the enforceability of WTO decisions through the implementation mechanism, and the reputational damage the offending Member may suffer if it is seen to be violating its WTO commitments. Additionally, a likely factor is that in the context of Members who have concluded bilateral agreements amongst themselves, disputes may be more easily discussed and resolved informally by negotiations, and there may be less of an inclination to invoke formal mechanisms.[41] A point explored in Chapter VII Section A.2 is whether the current semi-paralysis of the WTO DSS due to the blocking of the AB will invigorate the dispute settlement mechanisms of RTAs. It appears that this may be the case in light of the increasing number of disputes that have been brought under RTAs in recent years, although several of them have involved the application of non-trade provisions (especially as to labour and environment) that have no parallel in the WTO agreements.

39 Under the Agreement on the Dispute Settlement Mechanism of the ASEAN–China FTA of 2004, however, binding arbitration is provided for where consultations fail to settle a dispute, with proceedings and implementation closely patterned after the WTO model (Articles 4–6).

40 L. Lebullenger, "Les mécanismes de règlement des litiges des accords externes de l'Unione Européenne et de l'ALENA", 118 RGDIP (2014) 241; G. Gáspár-Szilágyi, M.Usynin, "Investment Chapters in PTAs and Their Impact on Adjudicative Convergence" in S. Gáspár-Szilágyi, D. Behn, M. Langford (eds) *Adjudicating Trade and Investment Disputes: Convergence or Divergence?* (CUP 2020)

41 *Moran*, 24; G. Vidigal, "Why Is There So Little Litigation under Free Trade Agreements? Retaliation and Adjudication in International Dispute Settlement" 20 JIEL (2017) 927.

2.2.3. *RTA Dispute Settlement Provisions: Proceedings, Decision, Implementation*

Comparing proceedings under the DSU with those under RTAs, the latter also require initial consultations between the parties, but some also provide for previous recourse to mediation.[42] If the outcome is unsuccessful, the parties can request that an arbitration panel be convened.[43] As highlighted hereunder, the members of such panels are drawn from a previously agreed roster of individuals, some having the nationality of the parties and some being third-country nationals from which the president is chosen. The procedural aspects tend to be modelled on those of the WTO (with no appeal stage), while partially different regimes are envisaged in respect of the implementation stage.[44]

2.2.3.1 *European Union RTAs.*

The EU agreements with Canada (CETA 2017) and Japan (2018) are representative examples of the attention devoted to interstate trade dispute settlement in the EU's FTAs. Chapter 29 of the CETA regulates the settlement of trade disputes in great detail, building upon the provisions established in the EU's previous FTAs, such as the EU–South Korea FTA (2011). The scope of the dispute settlement mechanism under CETA covers any dispute concerning the interpretation or application of the provisions of the agreement, except as otherwise provided in the agreement for specific matters such as investments (Article 29.2). The arbitration panel shall present an interim report to the parties, which they can comment on, within 150 days from its establishment, and a final report should be issued within 30 days thereafter.

Article 29.17 CETA underlines the strong connection the parties intend to maintain with the WTO by providing that "The arbitration panel shall apply customary rules of interpretation of public international law, including those of the VCLT, and shall take into account relevant reports of WTO panels and the WTO AB".[45] The ruling of the arbitration panel in the final panel report is binding on the parties (Article 29.10). As to implementation, if immediate compliance is not possible, a reasonable period of time for compliance is to be agreed upon between the parties or determined by the panel. On the merits, compensation may be agreed upon as an alternative to compliance.[46] Otherwise, in cases of non-compliance within the reasonable period set, the affected party may suspend obligations to an equivalent

42 Chapter 15 of the EU–Singapore FTA. The EU–Chile AFA (Advanced Framework Agreement) also contains a Mediation Mechanism in Chapter 31, Section 4.

43 See R. McDougall, "Regional Trade Agreement Dispute Settlement Mechanisms: Modes, Challenges and Options for Effective Dispute Resolution," IDB & ICTSD Issue Paper (2018) 10, www.rtaexchange.org accessed 18 June 2024.

44 For instance, there is no surveillance mechanism to monitor implementation, see Chapter VI.A.1.

45 This provision takes on the practice of the AB in referring to the VCLT and in applying the principles of interpretation of public international law as prescribed by Article 3.2 DSU. Article 14.21 of the EU–Singapore FTA governs the choice by disputing parties between the WTO or under the FTA, so as to avoid duplication and replication of proceedings.

46 For further details on implementation mechanisms in RTAs, see Chapter VI.A.2.

level. As in the WTO, remedies are thus *ex nunc* (Article 29.14(1)(c) CETA). Any disagreement on compliance or the equivalence of the level of suspension with the nullification or impairment caused by the violation shall be referred to the arbitration panel (see Article 29.14.5 CETA). The suspension of obligations is temporary and only until the inconsistent measure has been withdrawn or amended, or until the parties have settled the dispute (Article 29.14.9 CETA).[47]

2.2.3.2. United States RTAs.

The DS provisions of the RTAs concluded by the US have been the first ones to be invoked since three interstate trade disputes were brought to Chapter 20 NAFTA panels in the 1990s, two by Mexico against the US and one by the US against Canada.[48] The US–Korea FTA of 2007 (KORUS) and USMCA, which has replaced NAFTA since 1 July 2020, contemplate several types of dispute procedures, including areas outside of those covered by WTO dispute settlement.[49] KORUS Chapter 22 regulates dispute settlement. It establishes a Joint Committee (Article 22.2), which can assist the parties to resolve the dispute after the consultations stage and before the establishment of a panel. Panels consist of three members: each party appoints one member and both parties should agree on a chair (Article 22.9.2).[50]

It is interesting to note that KORUS does not provide for a strict obligation to comply with the findings of the panel, thus expressing the cautious approach of the US in respect of binding adjudication. Article 22.12 provides that:

> 1. On receipt of the final report of a panel, the Parties shall agree on the resolution on the dispute, which normally shall conform with the determinations and recommendations, if any, of the panel. 2. If, in its final report, the panel determines that a Party has not conformed with its obligations under this Agreement or that a Party's measure is causing nullification or impairment in the sense of Article 22.4(c), the resolution, whenever possible, shall be to eliminate the non-conformity or the nullification or impairment.

If the parties are unable to agree on a resolution in light of the panel's determinations, they shall enter into negotiations with a view to setting a mutually acceptable level of compensation, with a temporary suspension of an equivalent value also being the permitted response. The pursuit of dispute settlement under the

47 Similarly, Article 21 EU–Japan EPA and Chapter 14 of the EU–Singapore FTA.

48 For further details on implementation mechanisms of RTAs see Chapter VI.A.2.

49 The US has sought review under the USMCA's Rapid Response Mechanism (a procedure concerning labour relations that has no parallel in the WTO Agreements) 22 times since 2021; see USTR, Fact Sheet, "The USMCA Rapid Response Mechanism Delivers for Workers" (10 April 2024), accessed 28 May 2024. See also Chapter VI.A.3.

50 If the parties do not agree, they select a chair by lot from the list of panelists established under the agreement (Article 22.9.2(e)). The USMCA Chapter 31 (trade disputes) presents the unique feature that a party in dispute has to select panelists from another party's list (the panel being made up of five persons, or of three if the parties so agree).

national law of one of the parties is prohibited and alternative dispute resolution is encouraged.[51]

Chapter 31 of the USMCA on state-to-state trade disputes takes on the provisions of Chapter 20 of NAFTA and is applicable to all three parties of the Agreement, while ISDS (Chapter 14) is limited to US–Mexico relations and applicable to certain industries only.[52] The scope of the dispute settlement chapter covers any dispute concerning the interpretation or application of the Agreement, or the nullification or impairment of benefits thereunder (Article 31.12.4). If the compulsory consultations are not successful within 30 days, a party may request the USMCA Free Trade Commission to establish a panel.[53] USMCA also encourages alternative dispute resolution including arbitration, mediation, online dispute resolution, and other procedures (see Article 31.22). The party to the USMCA not involved in the dispute may participate in the proceedings as a third party, as was the case under the NAFTA, in a position similar to that of third parties in WTO proceedings. Panels shall comprise five members, selected by agreement from the roster of individuals established by the parties by the date of the entry into force of the agreement and containing up to 30 individuals.[54]

As under the KORUS, USMCA panel reports are not automatically binding (a feature that the US might like to export to the WTO).[55] This is made clear by Article 31.18 providing that, if the report establishes that the measures challenged are inconsistent with the Agreement,

> the disputing Parties shall endeavour to agree on the resolution of the dispute. Resolution of the dispute can comprise elimination of the non-conformity or the nullification or impairment, if possible, the provision of mutually acceptable compensation, or another remedy the disputing Parties may agree.

51 Article 22.16 KORUS.

52 See K. Claussen,'Dispute Settlement Under Next Generation Free Trade Agreements' 46 Georgetown J Int'l L (2018) 611.

53 But see Article 31.3 Choice of Forum: "If a dispute regarding a matter arises under this Agreement and under another international trade agreement to which the disputing Parties are party, including the WTO Agreement, the complaining Party may select the forum in which to settle the dispute."

54 A peculiarity of the selection is that parties must select arbitrators from the list of the other party; see Annex IV, "Roster of Panelists for Chapter 31 Dispute Settlement Panels". A similar roster provided for by NAFTA Article 2009 was never established because the US did not appoint its nominees, in a manner reminiscent of the current stalemate at the WTO; see S. Lester, I. Manak, A. Arpas, "Access to Trade Justice: Fixing NAFTA's Flawed State-to-State Dispute Settlement Process" 18 WTR (2019) 63.

55 There is no reference to the finality of panels' reports in the US communication of 5 July 2023, WTO doc.JOB/DSB/4 "US Objectives for a Reformed Dispute Settlement System" which emphasizes, in general terms, that the US "supports a system that maximises the tools available under the DSU to assist WTO Members in resolving trade disputes", see Chapter VII. A.2.2. Some provisions, however, echo those of the DSU, such as Article 31.13.2: "The findings, determinations, and recommendations of the panel shall not add to or diminish the rights and obligations of the Parties under this Agreement" and Article 31.13.4: "The panel shall interpret this Agreement in accordance with customary rules of interpretation of public international law, as reflected in Articles 31 and 32 of the Vienna Convention on the Law of Treaties, done at Vienna on May 23, 1969".

If the parties are unable to agree on implementation, the complaining party may suspend benefits equivalent to those due to the non-conformity or nullification and impairment. The text also restates in peremptory terms the absence of direct effect of USMCA in domestic law in Article 31.21 on Private Rights: "No Party shall provide for a right of action under its law against another Party on the ground that a measure of that other Party is inconsistent with this Agreement".

2.2.3.3. Dispute Settlement in Other RTAs.

Aside from the FTAs involving the EU and the US, one can briefly mention the dispute settlement mechanism of the CPTPP signed by 11 Asia-Pacific countries in 2018, after the withdrawal of the US from the previously negotiated TPP, which had been signed in 2016. It incorporates most of the provisions of the TPP by reference, with the suspension of certain provisions (as provided for in Articles 1–2 of its introductory Articles[56]). The CPTPP provides for both state-to-state and investor–state dispute settlement. The latter applies only to alleged breaches of the provisions of its investment chapter (Chapter 9), but certain parties have fully excluded ISDS between them, while others have excluded compulsory ISDS.[57] If a trade dispute is amenable to both WTO and CPTPP dispute settlement, the claimant may choose either forum, and the choice is exclusive (Article 28.4.2).

Parties may request the establishment of an *ad hoc* dispute settlement panel (composed of three members) when mandatory consultations fail to resolve a dispute within 60 days (Article 28.5.6). Such consultations may also take place over proposed measures (Article 28.7.7). The CPTPP requires dispute settlement panels to present an initial or interim report to the disputing parties before issuing their final report (Article 28.17) in a manner similar to that of CETA, USMCA (Article 31.17), and the DSU. In case of non-implementation within a reasonable period (to be determined by the panel's chair in case of disagreement), the successful party is entitled to suspend benefits of an equivalent level. Some matters are excluded from the CPTPP's dispute settlement system, notably safeguards and antidumping measures, for which the rules and provisions of the WTO shall apply exclusively.

B. Investment

1. Basic Features of BITs

The primary focus of IIAs, BITs and others, is on the protection of investors through the laying down of standards as to their treatment by the host state. These commitments expand upon the more limited protections granted by customary law

56 See CPTPP, Annex II, List of Suspended Provisions, see www.international.gc.ca accessed 30 March 2024.The UK has joined the CPTPP in December 2024.

57 See, for example, Agreement Between Australia and New Zealand Regarding Investor–State Dispute Settlement, Trade Remedies and Transport Services (8 March 2018), see www.dfat.gov.au accessed 30 March 2024.

in relation to the economic rights of foreigners by way of diplomatic protection.[58] Typical standards found in IIAs include national and MFN treatment, compensation in case of expropriation for a public purpose, fair and equitable treatment, and freedom of transfers and divestment. The protection is afforded once an investment has been made, thus granting post-establishment rights. The right to make investments (market access) is generally not provided for, not even by the US which used to include it, though it was limited by a number of sectoral exceptions.[59]

By adopting broad definitions of covered investor and investment, IIAs extend their protection, also procedurally as to dispute settlement, to an open category of investors. This is neither limited to large corporations nor to certain sectors. Investments from SOEs and SMEs and in the service sectors are thus also protected. The right to have recourse to international arbitration for the protection of their investment operations in host states is granted regardless of whether or not such operations are based on a contract or a concession from a public authority. Recent IIAs, however, exclude specific sectors and measures (in respect of all or certain members only) from ISDS.[60]

Finally, IIAs also fill gaps in the customary law of foreign investment and the traditional law of claims (i.e. diplomatic protection) in relation to the international protection of local companies controlled by foreign shareholders. IIAs extend international protection to foreign shareholders (irrespective of whether they are minority or majority shareholders, or whether they directly or indirectly own and control their stake). This is a major breakthrough brought about by BITs, which reflects economic reality, considering that foreigners enjoy limited or no protection under customary law for losses suffered by a local enterprise in which they have invested.[61]

58 See J. Salacuse, *The Law of Investment Treaties* (3rd ed. OUP 2021). However, the Minimum Standard of Treatment obligation in the CPTPP (as also stated in other IIAs) does not go beyond the general international law standard and does not create any additional substantive rights beyond those required under general international law (Annex 9-A). A breach of another provision of the CPTPP or of another international agreement does not establish that there has been a breach of the Minimum Standard of Treatment obligation.

59 See G. Sacerdoti, "The Admission and Treatment of Foreign Investment under Recent Bilateral and Regional Treaties" 1 JWI (2000) 105.

60 Thus, USMCA limits ISDS in Mexico–US relations to selected sectors and in relation to certain governmental contracts (Annex 14-D). The CPTPP specifies that public tobacco control measures may be excluded from ISDS under Chapter 9 on investment if a party elects to do so, as Australia has done (Article 29.5).

61 The ICSID Convention also permits foreign-controlled companies having the nationality of the host state to access arbitration when they are foreign-controlled (Article 25 (2) (b)) if so agreed by the home and host states. According to the *Barcelona Traction* judgment of the ICJ, international law precludes shareholders' claims for losses resulting from injuries to their company whether the company is incorporated in a third state or is a local entity of the latter state, except in limited instances. See ICJ, *Barcelona Traction*, 47, 65–66, 92, and ICJ *Diallo* Preliminary Objections 61–67 (I.n 31). See P. Muchlinski, "Diplomatic Protection of Foreign Investors: A Tale of Judicial Caution" in C. Binder and others (eds) *International Investment Law for the 21st Century* (OUP 2009) 341. See also Article 11 ILC's Draft Articles on Diplomatic Protection (2006). On the issue of shareholders'

2. *ISDS in IIAs*

Dispute settlement provisions in the form of direct investor–state arbitration (ISDS) are an essential element of the protection offered by BITs. Investment treaties usually provide that an investor may submit its claim, aside from accessing the domestic courts of the host state, to dispute settlement under various sets of arbitration rules, among which it is for the claimant to choose. Most BITs and major trade and investment agreements such as CPTPP, USMCA, and ECT provide that a protected investor, besides accessing the municipal courts of the parties to the treaty, may submit a dispute against the host state under ICSID or UNCITRAL rules (specifically as administered by the PCA), and, depending upon the instrument, also in conformity with "any other" arbitration rules agreed by the parties, including commercial arbitration institutions.[62] ICSID is, however, the main forum for investment disputes, and the majority of investment cases are brought under the ICSID Convention.[63]

IIAs clauses on dispute settlement tend to include also procedural provisions that supplement arbitration regulations to which they refer, such as ICSID, as to how arbitration should be initiated (such as the obligation of pre-dispute attempts at amicable settlement) and conducted. Some IIAs are more detailed in this respect, for instance, by laying down provisions on the transparency of proceedings.[64] Through the investor–state dispute clauses of IIAs, contracting states give their "irrevocable" consent to submit investment disputes brought by investors of the other contracting state(s) to one of the arbitral *fora* listed therein where there is an alleged breach of the standards of treatment laid down in the treaty.[65]

("derivative") claims under BITs, see G. Bottini, *Admissibility of Shareholder Claims under Investment Treaties* (CUP 2020); G. Minervini, *Shareholder Claims in International Law* (Giappichelli 2024).

62 RCEP, on the other hand, includes investment protection but defers providing for the settlement of investment disputes to further discussions to be started within two years (Article 10.18). RCEP was concluded in 2020 between 15 countries in the East Asia-Pacific area (including China) and has been in force since 2022. See also D. Gantz, "Protecting Investment under NAFTA, the Trans-Pacific Partnership and the CPTPP" in J. Huerta-Goldman, D. Gantz (eds) *The Comprehensive and Progressive Trans-Pacific Partnership. Analysis and Commentary* (CUP 2021) 314.

63 Statistics show that ICSID had administered more than 1,000 cases by the end of 2024, with 325 pending, while PCA had administered 122 ISDS cases in 2023 (see Introduction, n 22).

64 See, for instance, Article 26.4 ECT giving the investor the possibility to choose to submit an investment dispute with another party to: ICSID arbitration, UNCITRAL arbitration, or arbitration proceedings under the SCC, besides the domestic courts of the host States (Article 26.2(a)). UNCITRAL Arbitration Rules (first issued in 1976, latest edition in 2021) provide a comprehensive set of procedural rules on which parties may agree for the conduct of arbitral proceedings arising out of their commercial (but also investment) relations and are widely used in *ad hoc* arbitrations as well as in some administered arbitrations, notably by the PCA. As to the differences, see G. Sacerdoti, "Investment Arbitration Under ICSID and UNCITRAL Rules: Prerequisites, Applicable Law, Review of Awards" 19 ICSID Rev. (2004) 1.

65 Contracting states can express such consent either explicitly or implicitly. For the first model, see Article 26.3(a) ECT ("Subject only to subparagraphs (b) and (c), each Contracting Party hereby gives its unconditional consent to the submission of a dispute to international arbitration or concili-

This general offer by the contracting parties to arbitrate disputes with each other's national investors in respect of all investments covered by the treaty is a key and innovative feature of BITs. In contrast, where parties consent to arbitration through contractual clauses, this is expressed by both parties simultaneously in the same instrument before any dispute has arisen. The consent through BITs or IIAs, on the other hand, becomes effective when the offer of the parties to the treaty to arbitrate is accepted by the investor of the other party. This usually occurs (at the latest) at the time of the institution of proceedings through the filing by the claimant/investor of a request for arbitration.

Investment protection extends beyond the termination of BITs to take into account the fact that investments are long-term operations. To this end, BITs generally include so-called sunset clauses, extending the treaty's application to investments made before the notice of termination of the treaty for a further period of time varying from five to 25 years.[66]

ISDS provisions have increased in complexity and detail from the "first generation" BITs of the 1980s and 1990s to recent texts ("second" or "last generation IIAs"[67]), as shown by the table at the end of this chapter comparing the dispute settlement clauses of a 1996 BIT with one of 2022.

As can be seen from these texts, the more recent provision contains additional details on the proceedings in "investment disputes", including in respect of pre-arbitration consultations, the possibility for the investor to choose non-ICSID arbitration, a compulsory waiver to pursue other methods after the submission of the dispute, the investor's right to seek interim injunctive relief, the possibility for the intervention in proceedings by the home country of the investor, the right to obtain restitution of property instead of monetary damages provided the respondent does not opt for the latter, publicity (transparency), and the enforcement of awards under the ICSID and New York conventions. On the other hand, recent BITs include more detailed, often restrictive, provisions on substantive protection aimed at safeguarding the pursuit by the host state of fundamental public interests, on eligible (protected) investments and investors, including obligations on them.

ation in accordance with the provisions of this Article"). Consent is implicit when a treaty gives the investor of each party the right to submit the investment dispute with the other party, at its choice, to the fora specified in the BIT. States' consent to ISDS can be also expressed in domestic legislation aimed at promoting foreign invesment in the country. See recently Argentina's Law 27.742 of 8 July 2024 and Regulatory Decree 749/2024 creating a new investment regime for large-scale investments in selected sectors of the economy.

66 See Article 9 of the Kuwait–Pakistan BIT (1983) which provides that the present agreement "shall remain applicable to the movement of investment and returns established while the agreement was in force until the rights related to it have been liquidated; provided that this period shall not exceed 25 years from the date of the termination of the present Agreement". A notable sunset clause is the 20-year clause provided for in Article 47.1.3 ECT. See Chapter VII.B.3.4.

67 See UNCTAD, *Trends in the Investment Treaty Regime and a Reform Toolbox for the Energy Transition*, IIA Issues Note (August 2023), www.unctad.org accessed 20 June 2024.

2.1. The ICSID Convention: General Features

The ICSID (Washington) Convention is a central element of the international investment regime and is its only multilateral instrument.[68] Concluded in 1965, it entered into force in 1969 and had been ratified by 158 states as of the end of 2024.[69] It established ICSID (the Centre) as a distinct international organization administering investment arbitration institutionally connected to the World Bank, which was instrumental in the elaboration of the Convention to promote private investment in developing countries.[70] ICSID established itself from the outset as the leading arbitration forum in the field, as one would expect, since it was created specifically to administer investment disputes. ICSID has administered more than 70% of all known international investment proceedings.[71] For this reason, the examination of the procedural features of investment arbitration will be primarily focused hereafter on ICSID arbitration.[72]

As recalled in Chapter I, the establishment of ICSID was aimed at overcoming the difficulties surrounding the use of commercial arbitration clauses in investment disputes with sovereign states. The drafters of the ICSID Convention envisaged various sources of consent to arbitration, such as domestic investment statutes of host states, besides arbitration clauses in contracts or *ad hoc* agreements.[73] At the time of the launching and drafting of the ICSID Convention, the drafters primarily had in mind the effectiveness problems concerning *ad hoc* arbitration contractual clauses that had been mostly negotiated by large corporations active in the extractive industry.[74] BITs also allow SMEs and natural persons to access ISDS since the

68 See generally, the contributions collected in M. Kinnear et al. (eds) *Building International Investment Law: The First 50 Years of ICSID* (Wolters Kluwer 2015). A more detailed analysis of ICSID and non-ICSID arbitration is found in Chapter III (procedure), Chapter IV (awards), V (challenges), and VI (enforcement).

69 In comparison, the WTO had 166 Members as of the end of February 2024. The ICSID Convention has signed by 165 states, of which 158 have ratified it. See ICSID List of Contracting States and Other Signatories of the Convention, available at https://icsid.worldbank.org accessed 28 May 2024.

70 See the *Official Report of the Executive Directors of the World Bank accompanying the text of the ICSID Convention*, available on the ICSID website www.icsid.worldbank.org; A. Broches, "The Convention on the Settlement of Investment Disputes between States and Nationals of Other States" 136 RC (1972) 331. The Centre has its offices at the premises of the World Bank in Washington, DC (USA).

71 ICSID 2024 Annual Report is available at www.icsid.worldbank.org

72 For a comparative view, see A. Stone Sweet, F. Grisel, *The Evolution of International Arbitration: Judicialization, Governance, Legitimacy* (OUP 2017).

73 See the *Official Report* (n 70), 24, observing that the Convention does not require the consent of the parties to be expressed simultaneously in a single instrument, and includes state consent expressed in investment promotion legislation.

74 See ICSID *The History of the ICSID Convention* II-I, Note by A. Broches, General Counsel, 1–3, www.icsid.worldbank.org. On the history of ICSID, see also A. Parra, *ICSID: An Introduction to the Convention and Centre* (CUP 2020).

provisions negotiated in such treaties by a home country benefit all of its investors 'who have invested' as previously instructed (investors who have invested in the other signatory's territory and vice versa).[75]

Aside from arbitration, the Convention also provides for conciliation as a form of resolution for who have invested–state disputes (though this has rarely been used until now).[76] While the first disputes were based on arbitral clauses in investment contracts or domestic legislation,[77] the source of consent in the great majority of ICSID cases is found in IIAs.[78]

The broad scope of the Convention is underlined by the fact that, while the dispute must have a "legal" character,[79] there is no definition of "investment" in the text. This was felt to be unnecessary since the consent of the parties (in their contract) would provide the decisive criterion, so that any type of investment, whatever its form, may qualify. That notwithstanding, the investment requirement has been contentious from the beginning, also because it has to be coupled with the more detailed definitions found in IIAs, as is examined in more detail in Chapter III.

The Centre does not arbitrate, but it performs a range of key administrative functions.[80] It operates as a registrar and provides administrative support in conciliation and arbitration proceedings. The Centre guarantees that proceedings may be conducted in all cases by intervening to remedy any party's obstruction, such as not participating in the appointment of arbitrators. The ICSID Secretary-General has been given the power to refuse the registration of a request for ICSID conciliation or arbitration when the Secretary-General "finds, on the basis of the information contained in the request, that the dispute is manifestly outside the jurisdiction of the Centre" (Article 36.3). This screening power, albeit limited, aims to avoid embar-

75 To facilitate access to proceedings by SMEs, the EU and Canada tentatively agreed in 2024 on an expedited procedure before a single judge of the CETA ICS when an SME is claimant, https://policy.trade.ec.europa.eu/news/commission-proposes-new-rules-help-smes-dispute-resolution-under-ceta-2024-04-26_en accessed 19 July 2024.

76 As of the end of 2022, there have been only 13 conciliation requests compared with 821 arbitrations under the Convention and 76 under the Additional Facility.

77 Initially, most cases were based on contracts, e.g. *Holiday Inns v Morocco* ICSID/ARB72/1, Decision on jurisdiction (1974); *Kaiser Bauxite v Jamaica* ICSID/ARB/74/3, Decision on jurisdiction (1975); *Alcoa v Jamaica* ICSID/ARB/74/2, Decision on jurisdiction (1975). Among the cases based on domestic investment laws, see *SPP v Egypt* /ICSID/ARB/84/3, Decision on jurisdiction (1988).

78 Only 7% of the cases filed in 2023 were contract-based; see ICSID, *The ICSID Caseload-Statistics (2024)*, https://icsid.worldbank.org.

79 As explained in the Report of the Executive Directors of the WB (n 70), 27, disputes falling within the jurisdiction of ICSID "must concern the existence or scope of a legal right or obligation, or the nature or extent of the reparation to be made for breach of a legal obligation".

80 The ICSID Administrative Council has adopted in 1979 an "Additional Facility", used in 76 cases up to mid-2023, which provides for a separate, but similar, set of rules to which parties can refer in order to have arbitration of investment disputes administered by ICSID when the conventional basis for its jurisdiction is lacking. This is the case when one or both host and home states are not parties to the ICSID Convention. This type of arbitration has been resorted to under Chapter 11 of NAFTA since Mexico and Canada were not parties when NAFTA entered into force. The resulting awards are domestic awards, subject to the law of the party where they have been rendered, including recourse to locally available challenges, and/or recognition proceedings under the NY Convention.

rassing the respondent state by preventing the institution of proceedings against it in disputes which it has clearly not consented to submit to the Centre.[81]

The Secretary-General's refusal to register a request constitutes an absolute bar to the institution of proceedings against which no appeal is possible, given that the screening function is administrative in nature (while registration is without prejudice to the competence of the tribunal to rule on its own competence) (Article 41(1)). A negative decision is only taken by the Secretary-General when it is obvious from the information contained in the request that the dispute is clearly outside of ICSID's jurisdiction. Examples of this may be where the home or host country is not a party to ICSID, or the investor is manifestly not a national of a party.[82] If the case proceeds, as an additional filter, the ICSID Arbitration Rules introduced in 2006 a preliminary procedure to dismiss a case, upon the request of a respondent, if the tribunal finds that it is "without legal merit" (AR 41.5).

ICSID arbitration and parties' consent thereto is exclusive of any other means of resolution, except if it has been otherwise agreed by the parties (Article 26) and once perfected, consent may not be unilaterally withdrawn (Article 25, para. 1). This is a key provision since it neutralizes any obstructive tactics by the respondent based on the alleged invalidity of the arbitral agreement or the unilateral cancellation or termination of the clause which is the basis of the ICSID jurisdiction. The Convention also prevents any disputing party from frustrating the proceedings by refusing to participate. According to Article 45, while non-participation or non-cooperation by a disputing party cannot be considered to be an admission of the counter-party's contentions, it does not prevent the tribunal from proceeding and rendering an award. Similarly, a disputing party's refusal to appoint arbitrators or engaging in similar dilatory tactics cannot prevent the constitution of a tribunal. If the tribunal is not constituted within 90 days after registration, the vacant position(s) will be filled by ICSID (Article 38).

Proceedings are governed by the relevant provisions of the Convention (Articles 41–47), as supplemented by the Arbitration Rules, last updated in 2022,[83] which allow a high degree of procedural flexibility based on the parties' consent in cooperation with the tribunal. This approach reflects the importance of party autonomy also in respect of procedural matters, provided that due process and equality of arms are respected. In contrast, domestic and international judicial proceedings are governed by the rules of the relevant court, which typically allows little flexibility. Also in this respect, one can observe the distinction between arbitration, which is based on consent, and judicial proceedings, which are based on authority.

81 Report of the Executive Directors (n 70) 20.

82 See *ICSID Commentary*, I, Article 36, 56.

83 Since amendments to the ICSID Convention are in practice impossible because unanimity of the contracting states is required by Article 66, amendments of the arbitration rules by the ICSID Administrative Council, which can be made with a two-thirds majority of the ICSID parties (amendments were adopted almost unanimously in 2006 and 2022 after protracted negotiations), are the only way in practice to introduce at least procedural changes.

ICSID awards "shall not be subject to any appeal or to any other remedy except those provided for in this Convention" (Article 53.1). Since ICSID arbitration is "self-contained", being it is based on an international treaty, and awards under it are international in nature, ICSID awards – in contrast with non-ICSID awards – are not open to attack on any ground in the courts of any contracting state.[84] The decision is binding on the parties, and "each party shall abide by and comply with the terms of the award" (Article 53.1).

As dealt with in more detail in Chapter VI, besides revision or corrections by the same tribunal in specific cases (Article 51), the only challenge admissible against an award is an annulment request on the limited grounds relating to alleged grave breaches of procedure listed in Article 52.1. An annulment requests is dealt with by an *ad hoc* committee of three persons appointed by the Chairman of the ICSID Administrative Council (the President of the World Bank) from the ICSID roster of arbitrators.[85] The procedure is exclusively governed by the provisions of the Convention and ICSID arbitration rules.

Arbitration proceedings at ICSID bar diplomatic protection and the bringing of an international claim in favour of a claimant investor by its home state (Article 27), except where the respondent state does not comply with the award. All contracting states must recognize awards as binding and must enforce the pecuniary obligations imposed by them within their territories, as if they were a final judgment of their own courts (Article 54.1). ICSID awards are not subject to any domestic *exequatur* procedure, thus allowing enforcement in case of non-compliance by the losing state in any of the 158 countries where the Convention is currently in force.[86]

The Convention thus provides a self-contained system of international arbitration between states and foreign parties for all types of legal relationships in matters of investment. These guarantees regarding the availability and non-frustration of the procedure and its exclusivity, as well as the execution and recognition of decisions, have been effective in the disputes resolved under the Convention so far except in rare instances. The objective has been attained (with occasional tensions) of "depoliticizing" investment disputes by providing an impartial dispute

84 This notwithstanding, attempts by host states to invalidate, terminate, or repudiate arbitral agreements with foreign investors still occur from time to time, as is shown by the *Saipem v Bangladesh* case, ICSID ARB/05/7, Award (2009). See also *ATA v Jordan* ICSID ARB/08/2, Award (2010), where the extinguishment of an arbitration agreement included in a construction contract between a foreign investor and a public entity of Jordan, due to the retroactive application by Jordan's state courts of a subsequent arbitration law, was found by the tribunal to be in breach of the Turkey–Jordan BIT.

85 There are two ICSID rosters: one of arbitrators and the other one of conciliators. Each ICSID Member State may designate up to four persons to each panel (Article 13.1), while the chairman of the Executive Council (the president of the World Bank) may (and does) designate ten persons to each of them.

86 According to Article 54.3, the execution of awards is governed by the domestic provisions on the execution of judgments in force in the State where the execution is sought, including those on sovereign immunity (Article 55).

settlement mechanism based on due process and the rule of law, thus avoiding the intervention of home countries on behalf of their investors.

This result has also been obtained thanks to the separation made by the Convention between procedural aspects, which are governed by its international framework, and substantive matters, which are left to the legal discipline governing the specific investment. The substantive investment relationship has, as a rule, a domestic (private or administrative) law character and is governed by the law of the contracting state party to the dispute (the host country), except where there is a different choice by the parties, and, as importantly stated in Article 42, taking into account also "such rules of international law as may be applicable".[87]

In whichever way the duty to also apply international law is interpreted (as complementary or supplementary to domestic law or to replace it when contrary to international law),[88] this provision in principle balances the application of the host state's law as a matter of sovereignty with the duty of international tribunals not to apply domestic law in breach of international norms, as well as with their duty to give effect to the international treaty obligations of treatment and protection undertaken by the host state.

2.2. Non-ICSID Investment Arbitration

Over the years, procedural changes and the recognition of the bespoke international nature of ICSID proceedings and awards have further removed investment arbitration at ICSID from its original commercial model. This is especially evident in relation to challenges to awards and their legal force, but links to commercial arbitration still remain.[89]

The most evident and persistent relevance of the private arbitration model concerns non-ICSID investment arbitrations, be they *ad hoc*, governed by the rules of private arbitration institutions, or managed by the PCA (which has been established by treaty[90]) because they are ultimately subject to the arbitration laws of the countries where the proceedings take place (seat), including supervision by the local courts and challenges made before them. This is the case whatever procedural rules

87 For more details, see Chapter III.B.5; *ICSID Commentary*, I, Article 42, 148–171.

88 On the matter, albeit putting forward different interpretations, see W.M. Reisman, "The Regime for Lacunae in the ICSID Choice of Law Provision and the Question of its Threshold", 15 ICSID Review (2000) 362; E. Gaillard and Y. Banifatemi, "The Meaning of 'and' in Article 42(1), Second Sentence, of the Washington Convention: The Role of International Law in the ICSID Choice of Law Process" 18 ICSID Rev. (2003) 375.

89 See Z. Douglas, 'The Hybrid Foundations of Investment Treaty Arbitration' 74 British Yearbook of International Law (2003) 151. B. Hess, 'The Private-Public Divide in International Dispute Resolution', 388 RC (2018) 49; C. Titi, "Investment Treaty Arbitration Caught in the Public-Private Law Divide" 45 Michigan JIL (2024) 3.

90 The PCA is an intergovernmental institution (see Introduction, n 22), but arbitration conducted under its rules (or UNCITRAL rules) is subject to domestic law and awards are challengeable under the law of the seat where they are rendered, which historically has been the Netherlands, see https://pca-cpa.org.

are adopted (UNCITRAL or those of the governing arbitral institution, including any specifically applicable to ISDS), regardless that, in view of the completeness of these arbitration rules, reference to domestic procedural provisions is in practice rarely required. They consequently result in an award that is governed by the domestic law of the country of the seat, which has a decisive role in cases of challenges. Recognition and challenges to an award in other countries are subject to the New York Convention of 1958, as is the case with any other commercial award.[91]

Depending on the options set down in the relevant BIT, proceedings may be administered by the PCA or commercial arbitral institutions such as the ICC (Paris), the SCC (Stockholm), LCIA (London), or SIAC (Singapore), based on the choice of the parties from the options set out in the relevant treaty. Some of these institutions have introduced special rules for investor-state arbitration.[92] Investment arbitration can also be conducted through *ad hoc* (non-institutional) arbitral proceedings and by arbitration institutions using the UNCITRAL Arbitration Rules.[93] In all these instances, which represent a sizeable share of cases,[94] ISDS takes place in accordance with the international commercial arbitration model, though taking into account any specific provision of the relevant IIA and other applicable instruments that recognize the public role of the state party.[95]

91 Many domestic laws on arbitration are nowadays shaped by the UNCITRAL Model Law on International Commercial Arbitration (1985), as amended in 2006. As is evident from the comparative table at the end of Chapter V, the Model Law provides grounds for the annulment of domestic awards that are substantially the same as those of the New York Convention, including on grounds of public policy (Article V.1 New York Convention). In some countries, arbitration which is considered international is subject to a more liberal regime than purely national arbitration, often by limiting the grounds for challenging awards. For instance, in France, this applies in respect of arbitration that involves international trade interests ("qui met en cause des intérêts du commerce international") (Articles 1504 ff of the Code of Civil Procedure).

92 The SCC Arbitration Rules of 2017 include specific provisions (Annex III) for investor–state disputes, such as with respect of submissions by other treaty parties and by non-disputing parties. SIAC has adopted, also in 2017, a distinct set of rules for investment disputes, https://siac.org.sg/siac-investment-rules-2017 (SIAC Investment Arbitration Rules) accessed 20 June 2024. These rules are designed to accommodate the special needs of states (which, for instance, may have to tender their legal representation and thus cannot react promptly to a request for arbitration) and requirements typical of public treaty-based litigation (such as transparency and third states and *amici curiae* participation).

93 *Principles*, 345.

94 Statistics are lacking on these often confidential proceedings. The SCC states that it is listed as an eligible forum in 121 BITs and that it has administered or acted as appointing authority over the past 20 years in more than 90 investment arbitrations in which 21% of the tribunals declined jurisdiction, 37% denied all of the investors' claims and 42% upheld their claim in part or in full, https://sccarbitrationinstitute.se accessed 20 June 2024.

95 See the UNCITRAL Rules on Transparency in Treaty-Based Investor–State Arbitration (2010, 2013), whose use has been recommended by UNGA resolution 68/109 (2014), and the UN Convention on Transparency in Treaty-Based Investor–State Arbitration (New York, 2014) (the "Mauritius Convention on Transparency") in force since 2017, currently binding at the end of 2024 only ten states and the EU, see D. Euler and others (eds) *Transparency in International Investment Arbitration* (CUP 2015).

3. *State-to-state Arbitration in BITs*

BITs also provide for state-to-state arbitration to settle disputes between the contracting parties concerning the interpretation or application of the treaty. This is a standard provision found in a variety of treaties. State-to-state arbitration can be resorted to by a home state where the other party fails to apply the treaty or disregards its obligations, to the prejudice of its investors. With reference to BITs, in the rare cases where this type of arbitration has been activated, both home and host states have used it to advance investment claims by their nationals or in connection with a specific ISDS case.[96]

Instances where a number of investors suffer damages or where the amount of individual investments and losses suffered is too small to render direct arbitration practicable can be the subject matter of such interstate proceedings, in the exercise of diplomatic protection, in their favor, as held by the arbitral tribunal in the *Italy v Cuba* dispute.[97] In fact, BITs do not limit diplomatic protection to cases where the defendant state obstructs direct arbitration or does not comply with adverse awards, as provided in Article 27 ICSID in respect of ISDS.

The only case where a home state used state-to-state arbitration to protect, exercising diplomatic protection, a number of its nationals that had made small investments in the other party (*Italy v Cuba*) shows, however, the hurdles that hamper such an action although the tribunal found it admissible.[98] Major obstacles that do not affect ISDS but may hinder an action by the home state include the requirement of pre-arbitration cooling-off periods, the previous exhaustion of local remedies, and limits concerning the nationality of the protected investors (if the investment has been made through a third-country company). It is no surprise that this mechanism has been so rarely used, also considering that in none of the three known cases did the claimant succeed.[99]

State-to-state arbitration is regulated differently and has a different role in BITs that do not provide for ISDS, as is the case of those of Brazil. According to the Brazil–Angola Agreement for Cooperation and Investment Facilitation of 2015 (Article 15 on the prevention and settlement of disputes), it is for a party to submit first to the Joint Committee of the parties a question of interest of an investor. The

96 See *Italy v Cuba*, Preliminary Award (2005); Final Award (2008), available at www.italaw.com accessed 22 June 2024; *Peru v Chile* (in connection with *Lucchetti v Peru*, ICSID ARB/03/4, Award (2005)), and *Ecuador v US* (PCA Case 2012-5) (2012), in relation to the *Chevron and Texaco v Ecuador* PCA Case No. 2007-2 (2010) concluding that there was no jurisdiction for lack of a dispute, available at www.italaw.com accessed 22 June 2024.

97 *Italy v Cuba*, Preliminary Award, 50.1.

98 For more details on this case, see G. Sacerdoti, M. Recanati, "Approaches to Investment Protection outside of Specific International Investment Agreements and Investor-State Settlement" *International Investment Law* 1839.

99 See M. Potestà, "State-to-State Dispute Settlement Pursuant to Bilateral Investment Treaties: Is There Potential?" in N. Boschiero and others (eds) *International Courts and the Development of International Law* (Asser Institute 2013) 753; N. Bernasconi-Osterwalder, *State–State Dispute Settlement in Investment Treaties* (IISD 2014), available at www.iisd.org accessed 22 June 2024.

Joint Committee shall attempt to resolve the matter amicably through bilateral consultations with the participation of the affected investor. Failing such a solution, the parties may initiate state-to-state arbitration, the format of which is not specified.[100]

The 2023 Draft Protocol on Investment to the Agreement Establishing the African Continental Free Trade Area (AfCFTA) does not currently provide for ISDS either. State-to-state arbitration is available to a party that intends "to submit a claim on behalf of its nationals through the exercise of diplomatic protection and in accordance with customary international law" (Article 44.2). Article 46.3 envisages an annex to the Protocol for regulating disputes between an investor of a party and a host state which should have been finalized within 12 months from the entry into force of the Protocol.[101]

C. Comparative Analysis

Arbitral features are common to the two systems but are fully developed in the investment system (ISDS). In the trade DSS, at the WTO or in RTA proceedings, the composition of panels is patterned after the arbitration model but diverges from it in respect of various key aspects. As will be evidenced in Chapters 3 and 4, nor has the trade DSS become judicial either in its transition from the GATT to the WTO. It has retained several features of the GATT, with panels being a kind of institutional arbitration, since each panel is made up of *ad hoc* selected panellists. Even the AB, with its part-time members, does not have all of the features one would expect from a court.

Summing-up, one could define the WTO DSS as a result of a "top-down" approach, due to its multilateral unitary basis and centralized setting and functioning. The ISDS system is "bottom-up", being the result of a multiplicity of essentially bilateral treaties, characterized by different features in the carrying out of actual disputes

1. Commonalities

(a) The two systems share several overarching common features. First, they both rely on impartial rule-based adjudication as the preferred way to settle disputes, contrary to the situation in other fields of international economic law and international relations in general.

(b) Secondly, they aim to depoliticize conflicts through the use of rule-based adjudication, notwithstanding differences in the two systems. As for the WTO, Article 3.10 DSU underlines this approach where it spells out that "It is understood that requests for conciliation and the use of dispute settlement procedures should not be intended or considered as contentious acts (...)".:

100 The agreement is available at the WTI's Electronic Database of Investment Treaties, available at https://edit.wti.org accessed 22 June 2024.

101 The Protocol is available at https://edit.wti.org accessed 22 June 2024.

(c) Both systems are two-tiered, though the WTO DSS provides for a comprehensive system of appeal on points of law rather than the limited grounds for annulment provided under the ICSID system. Consequently, appeal became a regular feature of the WTO system until the paralysis of its appellate stage in 2020, while the more limited annulment challenges available against ICSID awards have been lodged against a minority of awards.

2. *Differences*

(a) The two different models of DSS reflect their fundamental structural differences. The WTO DSS is institutionalized, inter-governmental (state-to-state), multilateral, and treaty-based; ISDS features a fragmented bilateral treaty-based system in relation to substantive provisions and dispute settlement mechanisms (though its procedure is centralized where the multilateral ICSID Convention is used for dispute settlement).

(b) Flexibility in proceedings and the role of the parties in organizing and conducting arbitral proceedings is greater in investment than in the trade DSS. Compared to the WTO DSS, ISDS is a decentralized and complex system, featuring multiple interactions and connections among adjudicators and across agreements. The role of precedent is less pronounced as a consequence in ISDS, although in both systems precedent is not binding.[102]

(c) The relationship between interested private parties and their home governments in respect to the "offending" state is different in the two systems. At the WTO, complaining states are free to initiate or not cases against another party under the DSU without formally coordinating their action with their business operators that have been prejudiced by the respondent Member's measure. The private party may carry on at the same time judicial actions in front of competent domestic courts of the respondent. At ICSID, instead, it is for the investor to initiate arbitration in order to take care of its interests, while its national state is prevented by Article 27 from extending to it its diplomatic protection.

102 For further details, see Chapter III.A.5 and B.5.; N. Ridi, "Approaches to External Precedent: The Invocation of International Jurisprudence in Investment Arbitration and WTO Dispute Settlement" in S. Gáspár-Szilágyi and others (eds) *Adjudicating Trade and Investment Disputes* 121.

Annex 1: Comparative Table of BITs Dispute Settlement Clauses (1996/2022)

Evolution of ISDS Clauses:
1. UK–Azerbaijan BIT (1996)
2. Japan–Bahrain BIT (2022)

****

1. UK–Azerbaijan BIT (1996)

https://investmentpolicy.unctad.org/international-investment-agreements/treaty-files/3598/download

Article 8

Reference to the International Centre for Settlement of Investment Disputes

(1) Each Contracting Party hereby consents to submit to the International Centre for the Settlement of Investment Disputes (hereinafter referred to as "the Centre") for settlement by conciliation or arbitration under the Convention on the Settlement of Investment Disputes between States and Nationals of Other States opened for signature at Washington on 18 March 1965 any legal dispute arising between that Contracting Party and a national or company of the other Contracting Party concerning an investment of the latter in the territory of the former.

(2) A company which is incorporated or constituted under the law in force in the territory of one Contracting Party and in which before such a dispute arises the majority of shares are owned by nationals or companies of the other Contracting Party shall in accordance with Article 25(2)(b) of the Convention be treated for the purposes of the Convention as a company of the other Contracting Party.

(3) If any such dispute should arise and agreement cannot be reached within three months between the parties to this dispute through pursuit of local remedies or otherwise, then, if the national or company affected also consents in writing to submit the dispute to the Centre for settlement by conciliation or arbitration under the Convention, either party may institute proceedings by addressing a request to that effect to the Secretary-General of the Centre as provided in Articles 28 and 36 of the Convention. In the event of disagreement as to whether conciliation or arbitration is the more appropriate procedure the national or company affected shall have the right to choose. The Contracting Party which is a party to the dispute shall not raise as an objection at any stage of the proceedings or enforcement of an award the fact that the national or company which is the other party to the dispute has received in pursuance of an insurance contract an indemnity in respect of some or all of his or its losses.

(4) Neither Contracting Party shall pursue through the diplomatic channel any dispute referred to the Centre unless:

(a) the Secretary-General of the Centre, or a conciliation commission or an arbitral tribunal constituted by it, decides that the dispute is not within the jurisdiction of the Centre, or
(b) the other Contracting Party should fail to abide by or to comply with any award rendered by an arbitral tribunal.

2. Japan–Bahrain BIT (2022)

https://investmentpolicy.unctad.org/international-investment-agreements/treaty-files/6431/download

Article 16

Settlement of Investment Disputes between a Contracting Party and an Investor of the Other Contracting Party

1. For the purposes of this Article, "investment dispute" is a dispute between a Contracting Party and an investor of the other Contracting Party that has incurred loss or damage by reason of, or arising out of, an alleged breach of any obligation of the former Contracting Party under this Agreement with respect to the investor of that other Contracting Party or its investments in the Area of the former Contracting Party.
2. Subject to subparagraph 7(b), nothing in this Article shall be construed so as to prevent an investor who is a party to an investment dispute (hereinafter referred to in this Article as "disputing investor") from seeking administrative or judicial settlement within the Area of the Contracting Party that is a party to the investment dispute (hereinafter referred to in this Article as "disputing Party").
3. Any investment dispute shall, as far as possible, be settled amicably through consultations between the disputing investor and the disputing Party (hereinafter referred to in this Article as "the disputing parties").
4. If the investment dispute cannot be settled through such consultations within six months from the date on which the disputing investor requested in writing the disputing Party for consultations, the disputing investor may, subject to paragraph 7, submit the investment dispute to one of the following international arbitrations: (a) arbitration in accordance with the Convention on the Settlement of Investment Disputes between States and Nationals of Other States, done at Washington, March 18, 1965 (hereinafter referred to in this Article as "ICSID Convention"), so long as the ICSID Convention is in force between the Contracting Parties; (b) arbitration under the Additional Facility Rules of the International Centre for Settlement of Investment Disputes, provided that either Contracting Party, but not both, is a party to the ICSID Convention; (c) arbitration under the Arbitration Rules of the United Nations Commission on International Trade Law; or (d) if agreed with the disputing Party, any arbitration in accordance with other arbitration rules.

5. Each Contracting Party hereby consents to the submission of an investment dispute by a disputing investor to arbitration set forth in paragraph 4 chosen by the disputing investor.
6. Notwithstanding paragraph 5, no investment disputes may be submitted to arbitration set forth in paragraph 4, if more than three years have elapsed since the date on which the disputing investor acquired or should have first acquired, whichever is the earlier, the knowledge that the disputing investor had incurred loss or damage referred to in paragraph 1.
7. No claim may be submitted to arbitration under this Article unless: (a) the disputing investor consents in writing to arbitration in accordance with the procedures set out in this Article; and (b) the disputing investor waives in writing any right to initiate or continue before any administrative tribunal or court of justice under the law of either Contracting Party, or other dispute settlement procedures, any proceedings with respect to any measure alleged to constitute a breach referred to in paragraph 1 before any judgment or award has been delivered on the subject matter of the dispute under the abovementioned mechanism.
8. The waiver provided pursuant to subparagraph 7(b) shall cease to apply where the arbitral tribunal rejects the claim on the basis of a failure to meet the requirements of paragraph 4, 6 or 7, or on any other procedural or jurisdictional grounds.
9. Notwithstanding subparagraph 7(b), the disputing investor may initiate or continue an action that seeks interim injunctive relief that does not involve the payment of monetary damages before an administrative tribunal or court of justice under the law of the disputing Party.
10. An arbitral tribunal established under paragraph 4 shall decide the issues in dispute in accordance with this Agreement and applicable rules of international law.
11. The disputing Party shall deliver to the other Contracting Party: (a) written notice of the investment dispute submitted to the arbitration no later than thirty days after the date on which the investment dispute was submitted; and (b) copies of all pleadings filed in the arbitration.
12. The Contracting Party which is not the disputing Party may, upon written notice to the disputing parties, make submissions to the arbitral tribunal on a question of interpretation of this Agreement.
13. In an arbitration under this Article, the disputing Party shall not assert, as a defence, counterclaim, right of setoff or otherwise, that the disputing investor has received or will receive indemnification or other compensation for all or part of the alleged damages pursuant to an insurance or guarantee contract.
14. The award rendered by the arbitral tribunal shall include: (a) a written decision whether or not there has been a breach by the disputing Party of any obligation under this Agreement with respect to the disputing investor and its investments; and (b) one or both of the following remedies, only if there has been such a breach: (i) payment of monetary damages and financial cost; and (ii) restitution of property, in which case the award shall provide that the disputing

Party may pay monetary damages and financial cost, in lieu of restitution. The arbitral tribunal may also award cost and attorney's fees in accordance with applicable arbitration rules.

15. The disputing Party may make available to the public in a timely manner all documents, including an award, submitted to, or issued by, an arbitral tribunal established under paragraph 4, except for: (a) confidential business information; (b) information which is privileged or otherwise protected from disclosure under the applicable laws and regulations of either Contracting Party; and (c) information which shall be withheld pursuant to the relevant arbitration rules.
16. Unless the disputing parties agree otherwise, the arbitration shall be held in a country that is a party to the Convention on the Recognition and Enforcement of Foreign Arbitral Awards, done at New York, June 10, 1958 (hereinafter referred to in this Article as "New York Convention").
17. The award rendered by the arbitral tribunal shall be final and binding upon the disputing parties. This award shall be executed in accordance with the applicable laws and regulations, as well as relevant international law including the ICSID Convention and the New York Convention, concerning the execution of award in force in the country where such execution is sought.

Annex 2: Proceedings Flow Chart: WTO/ICSID

Proceedings Flow Chart: WTO[103]

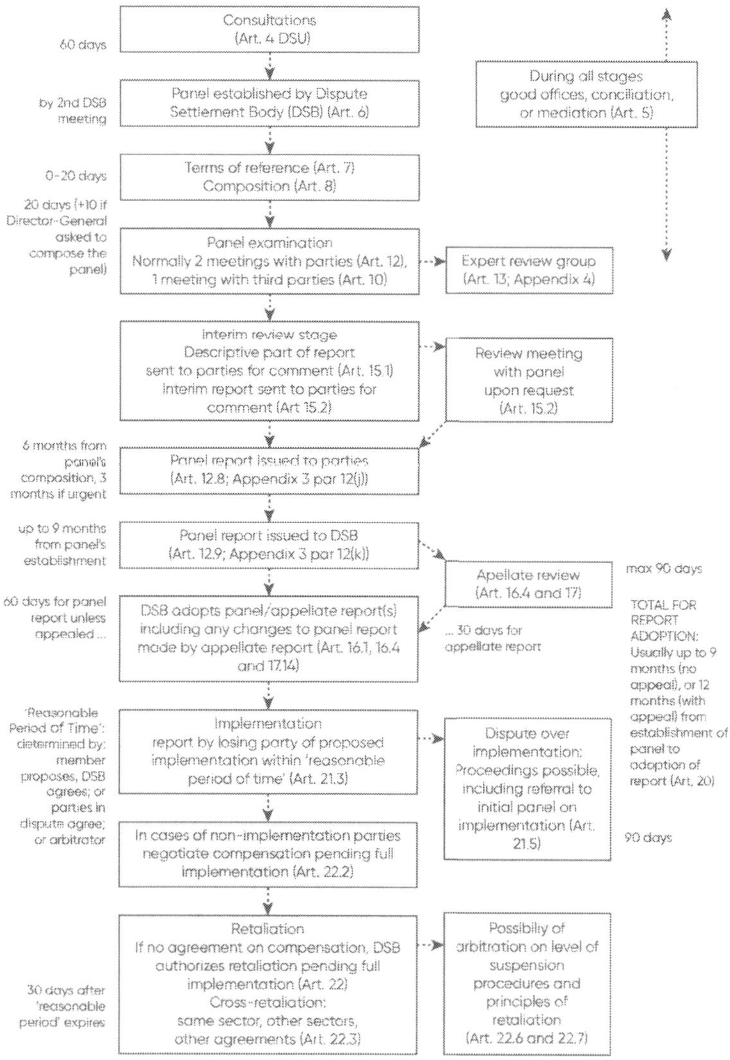

103 Available at https://www.wto.org/english/tratop_e/dispu_e/disp_settlement_cbt_e/c6s1p1_e.htm

Proceedings Flow Chart: ICSID[104]

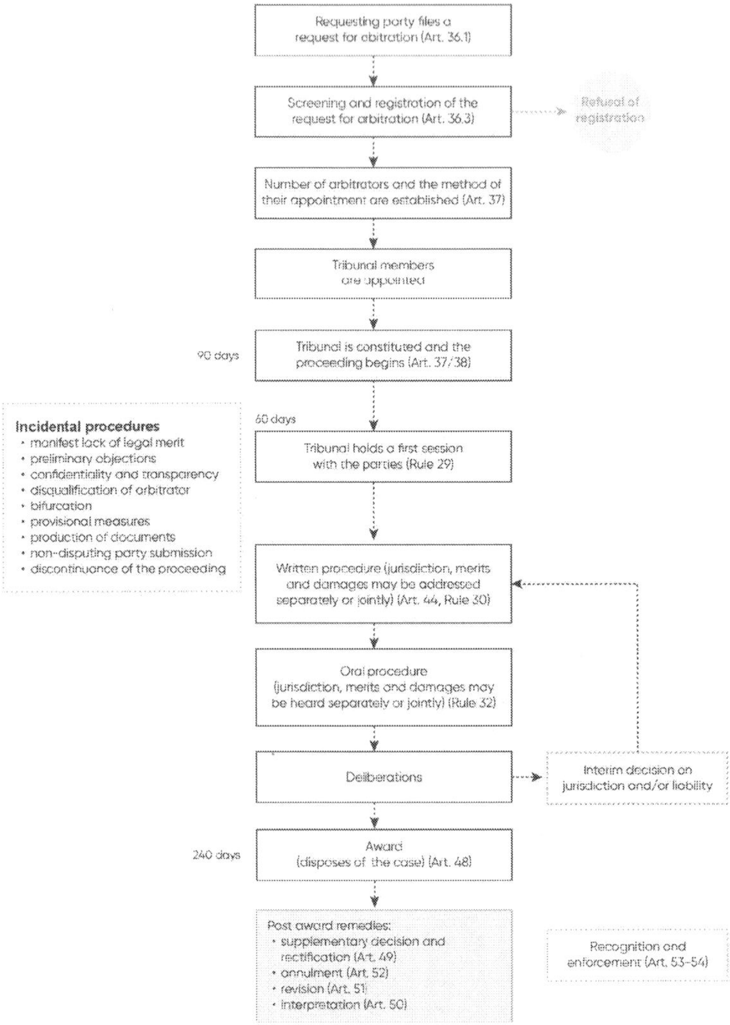

104 Available at https://icsid.worldbank.org/procedures/arbitration/convention/process/overview/2006#:~:text=The%20ICSID%20Convention%20provides%20the,required%20qualities%20of%20an%20arbitrator

3 Jurisdiction, Initiating Proceedings, and Applicable Law

Table of Contents

Introduction

The concept of the jurisdiction of an adjudicatory body (be it a permanent court, institutionalized or *ad hoc* arbitration) refers to the competence of the body or the system to decide in accordance with the law a category of disputes, or an individual dispute, with the power to issue a decision that is binding for the parties thereto.[1] Jurisdiction in international law is consensual and has several dimensions, the most important being: *ratione voluntatis* (consent and its limits); *ratione personae*

1 See A. Pellet, "Judicial Settlement of International Disputes" *MPEPIL* (2013). Certain courts, such as the ICJ and the Tribunal of the Law of the Sea, may also issue Advisory Opinions. This is not the case for trade and investment dispute settlement bodies, which are endowed only with contentious

DOI: 10.4324/9781003471509-5

(personal jurisdiction) as to which parties may or must subject their dispute to that adjudicatory body; *ratione materiae*, as to which subject matters can be brought to the body, reflecting the fact that international tribunals and courts, with the exception of the ICJ, are limited in their competence to a specific field (specialized courts); and *ratione temporis*, as to any time limit within which a dispute must have arisen or must thereafter be brought to the adjudicating body.[2]

The notion and extent of jurisdiction are especially important in international law because no court has a general pre-established jurisdiction over disputes between states in general. On the contrary, states tend to carefully calibrate the *matters* and the *parties* in respect of which they accept that a dispute may be resolved through third-party adjudication, the great powers being the most reluctant to do so.[3] In international law, the consent of the disputing parties to accept the jurisdiction is thus a fundamental requirement (jurisdiction *ratione voluntatis*), by which parties determine the competence of an adjudicatory body to decide certain disputes with certain parties (usually under the condition of reciprocity), thereby restricting the potential jurisdiction of a pre-established body (such as the ICJ) to those disputes to which they have explicitly consented.[4] The required consent can be given before a dispute arises (advance consent), either in the original agreement establishing the body or subsequently (*clause compromissoire*), or in respect of a specific dispute that has already arisen, submitting it to an existing body or establishing an *ad hoc* arbitral tribunal (*compromis*).[5]

These limitations explain why, in international disputes, objections to jurisdiction are frequent, with the respondent often submitting that the dispute is outside the mandate of the adjudicators, with a view to evading the authority of the body to pass judgment upon it. In turn, this often leads to a bifurcation in proceedings: in a preliminary phase, the existence of the body's jurisdiction is ascertained, and this is followed by a merits phase, if jurisdiction is established.[6]

As explained in more detail below, the procedural hurdles described above are frequent in investment arbitration since the jurisdiction of *ad hoc* arbitral tribunals to decide these disputes is limited to "investments" (as defined by the relevant treaty), made by "investors" (also defined in the treaty) of one contracting party of the relevant treaty in the territory of another contracting party.

jurisdiction to resolve disputes, that is a conflict on a point of law or fact (Article 36 ICJ) upon application of one party against another party.

2 See generally *Merills*, 1–35; C. Santulli, *Droit du contentieux international* (LGDJ 2015); C. Focarelli, *Giurisdizioni internazionali* (Wolters Kluwer 2017).

3 See Chapter 1, Section 3. *Merills*, 13.

4 See Article 36.2 ICJ Statute.

5 As an example of advance consent, see Article 26(3)(a) ECT: "Subject only to subparagraphs (b) and (c), each Contracting Party hereby gives its unconditional consent to the submission of a dispute to international arbitration or conciliation in accordance with the provisions of this Article".

6 See generally *Merills*, 198–204. As for ICSID, see Article 41.2 ICSID.

A. Trade

1. The Jurisdiction of Panels

Preliminary objections to jurisdiction have hardly any place at the WTO, as the DSU binds all Members to the jurisdiction of its DSS, that is of the panels and the AB (and ultimately of the DSB, which is, however, a political rather than an adjudicatory body) to entertain any dispute between WTO Members concerning any of the WTO agreements.[7] Personal jurisdiction and subject-matter jurisdiction are thus well defined.[8] It suffices that a Member alleges that another Member, through any "measure", has breached a provision of such an agreement, thereby nullifying or impairing any benefit accruing to that Member under it.[9] While before other courts any breach of a relevant obligation that is attributable to the respondent party may be challenged, the DSU textually limits jurisdiction to a "measure" of the respondent state.[10] This is so because trade is regulated in all countries by laws and regulations, which can be in breach of WTO obligations per se or in their application.[11] The reference to measures does not, however, exclude that a Member may commit a breach by omission or some other conduct, such as a consistent administrative practice in disregard of its obligations, even if the practice is not codified in a specific written provision.[12]

Although Article XXIII GATT requires a finding of impairment or nullification of a benefit as a basis for liability, this is implied when a breach of an obligation has been ascertained.[13] In this respect, the DSU does not require a complainant to have a specific interest in order to initiate proceedings, although where a party has

7 Only the TPRM, which establishes a periodic review of the trade policies of Members, is not covered by the DSU, while the additional (2013) Trade Facilitation Agreement is only partially subject to the DSU pursuant to its Article 18.5.

8 See generally J. Trachtman, "Jurisdiction in WTO Dispute Settlement" in *Key Issues* 132; G. Marceau, "Conflicts of Norm and Conflicts of Jurisdiction" 35 JWTL (2001) 1081.

9 See Article 3.8 DSU: "In cases where there is an infringement of the obligations assumed under a covered agreement, the action is considered prima facie to constitute a case of nullification or impairment". The measure must be attributable to the state so that the conduct of private parties is not covered, absent sufficient government involvement (as stated in Article 8 ARSIWA). This was specified by the (unappealed) panel in *Japan–Film* (DS 44-1998), 10.55–10.56, where the anticompetitive action of Fuji against US competitors was found not attributable to Japan.

10 See Article 4.2 DSU.

11 See *Van den Bossche*, 181.

12 See AB *US–CV Measures on Certain EU Products* (DS 212-2003), 151; AB, *US–Corrosion-Resistant Steel Sunset Review* (DS 244-2004): "any act or omission attributable to a WTO Member can be a measure of that Member for purposes of dispute settlement proceedings" (at 81). In *EC–Biotech Products* (DS 291-2006), 7.1272, the panel recognized that the EU's *de facto* moratorium on approvals could be challenged as a rule or norm of general and prospective application.

13 Article 3.8 DSU and Article XXIII GATT allowing a dispute to be brought because of nullification of a benefit (non-violation complaints) even without a breach reflect the "commercial", conciliatory original approach of the GATT, which the WTO has overcome through the legalization of the rules, although non-violation complaints under Article XXIII GATT (as restated in Article 26 DSU) are still possible.

not suffered any prejudice from a breach, it is unlikely that it would do so.[14] Any WTO Members may participate as a "third party" to a dispute that is already at the consultations stage, provided they allege a "substantial trade interest".[15]

Alternatively, they may opt to join as third parties to a dispute later on, once the DSB has established a panel, by just claiming a "substantial interest".[16]

Under the DSU, jurisdiction is *compulsory* because a WTO Member against which another Member initiates a dispute cannot escape DSS proceedings. It is also *exclusive* because, as stated in Article 23 DSU, parties to a WTO dispute "shall have recourse to, and abide by, the rules and procedures of this understanding".

On the other hand, the jurisdiction of panels is limited *ratione materiae* to disputes concerning one of the covered agreements. A party cannot bring to the DSS disputes concerning the interpretation and application of other treaties, nor can a panel decline jurisdiction once a WTO Member initiates proceedings alleging the infringement of a WTO provision.[17]

An important procedural requirement for a panel, which is better defined as pertaining to the admissibility of the complainant's request rather than to the panel's jurisdiction, is that consultations concerning the same dispute must have previously taken place with a view to resolving it. Over the years, this requirement has been interpreted more and more rigorously.[18] A request for consultations must identify exactly, in fact and law, the measure(s) challenged and the WTO provisions which have supposedly been breached. Furthermore, claims brought thereafter to the panel must coincide with those espoused in the previous consultations request.[19] As a consequence, panels lack jurisdiction to rule on claims that were not included in the panel request.[20]

2. *The Pre-Litigation Phase: Consultations and ADR*

Adjudication is but a means of settling disputes between WTO Members concerning the correct application of the WTO agreements according to the relevant legal

14 At the ICJ, instead, intervention in a pending case is limited to states that have "an interest of a legal nature which may be affected by the decision of the Court" (Article 62 ICJ).

15 Article 4.11 and 10.2 DSU.

16 For more details, see Chapter IV.A.6.

17 This matter was clarified in AB *Mexico–Taxes on Soft Drinks* (DS 308-2006) 41–57, where Mexico unsuccessfully raised a jurisdictional defence in respect of its own breach of the GATT by relying on the alleged non-compliance by the US with the NAFTA.

18 Though Articles 4 and 6 DSU do not require a precise and exact identity between the measure and claims of inconsistency made before the panel with those made in the consultations request, a panel lacks jurisdiction over a measure which has not been previously referred to in the consultations request, AB *US–Certain EC Products* (DS 165-2001) 70.

19 Requests for consultations are formal documents of the WTO, notified to the DSB (Article 4.4 DSU), circulated at the outset to the whole membership, and posted on the WTO website among the documents of the case.

20 A claim that a panel exceeded its jurisdiction by adjudicating issues not before it can be raised on appeal, AB *US–Offset Act (Byrd Amendment)* (DS 234-2003) 207–212.

principles. It is not an objective in and of itself but rather the traditional instrument to attain this end. In fact, according to the DSU, the DSS's aim is "to secure a positive solution to a dispute. A solution mutually acceptable to the parties to a dispute and consistent with the covered agreement is clearly to be preferred" (Article 3.7 DSU). This explains the importance attributed to reaching, first of all by non-adjudicatory means, such as negotiations and consultations, a satisfactory and "prompt settlement of any situation in which a Member considers that any benefits accruing to it directly or indirectly under the covered agreements are being impaired by measures taken by other Members". This is also "essential to the effective functioning of the WTO and the maintenance of a proper balance between the rights and obligations of Members" (Article 3.3 DSU). Any solution must however at the same time be "in accordance with the rights and obligations under this Understanding and under the covered agreement" (Article 3.4 DSU).

The consultations request initiates a WTO dispute and is a prerequisite for further submitting the case to adjudication by a panel. The regulation of consultations is fairly detailed in the DSU: a request for consultations must be accepted and given "sympathetic consideration" by the Member concerned in relation to any measure that is allegedly affecting the operation of a covered agreement to obtain the "satisfactory adjustment of the matter" (Article 4.5) before resorting to further action under the DSU. Only if consultations fail after 60 days may the complaining party request the establishment of a panel from the DSB.[21] Formal consultations, which are as a rule held by the respective delegations in Geneva and are confidential, may last longer and may be preceded by informal consultations between capitals. These often lead to the amicable resolution of the matter without the need for further proceedings. Of 631 disputes listed on the WTO website as of the end of 2024, 297 have not resulted in the establishment of a panel.[22] While the initiation of consultations and the request for the establishment of a panel are explicitly governed by the DSU, consultations themselves are confidential and are held in the manner that the parties see fit.[23]

In order to settle disputes, Article 5 DSU also provides for "Good Offices, Conciliation and Mediation", offered by the WTO Director-General acting *ex officio*. Any party may request one of these options at any time during a dispute, including during consultations and before proceeding to request a panel should consultations fail. Notwithstanding the current emphasis on ADR in the settlement

21 The 60-day deadline may be extended if the respondent is a developing country (Article 12.10 DSU). This is one of a number of procedural provisions aimed at facilitating the participation of developing and least-developed countries in the DSS (see also Articles 3.12, 4.10, 8.10, 24, 27.2, 27.3).

22 See www.wto.org/english/tratop_e/dispu_e/dispustats_e.htm.

23 If the requesting party has invoked Article XXII GATT as the basis for consultations (and not Article XXIII), other WTO Members can ask to join the consultations pursuant to Article 4.11 DSU, claiming that they have "a substantial trade interest" in them, but the request can be rejected by the complainant (as sometimes happens).

of international economic disputes (and in the current proposals of DSS reform), hardly any use has been made of these methods at the WTO.[24]

Even after a panel has been established, a complainant can withdraw a request, or the parties can settle their case as they see fit by negotiating outside of the formal WTO structures, in a manner similar to out-of-court settlements of private disputes. As a consequence, a panel once established might never be composed, or proceedings can be indefinitely suspended by agreement of the parties, leading to the lapsing of a panel's establishment.[25]

3. *The Initiation of Panel Proceedings: The Establishment and Composition of Panels*

If consultations are unsuccessful and a complainant intends to proceed to the panel stage, its request to the DSB for the establishment of a panel can be opposed by a respondent (as usually happens) at the first DSB meeting at which the request is submitted.[26] A request to establish a panel must include complete indications of the measure(s) challenged and the relevant WTO provisions that have allegedly been breached, corresponding to those previously included in the consultations request. When a complainant reiterates its request at a subsequent DSB meeting, the panel shall be established by reverse consensus notwithstanding any opposition from the respondent (Article 6.1 DSU).

Once the DSB has established a panel, a distinct phase concerning the panel's composition follows, for which there are (on paper) strict deadlines.[27] The procedure presents several peculiarities compared with interstate, commercial, and investment arbitration where each party nominates an arbitrator, and the chair is selected by agreement, and only failing such an agreement, by the institution that oversees the proceedings. Members of the WTO three-person panels must be "well-qualified governmental and/or non-governmental individuals, including persons … who taught or published on international trade law or policy, or served as

24 See *Van den Bossche*, 198.

25 Article 12.12 provides that if the work of a panel has been suspended for more than 12 months, "the authority for establishment of the panel shall lapse". This can also happen after the interim report has been confidentially circulated to the parties (as happened in, *EU–Price Comparison Methodologies (China)* (DS 516-2017), WT/DS516/14).

26 Article 6 DSU. More than one complainant may challenge a measure of a WTO Member. In such a case, a single panel may be established, or, if separate panels are established, "to the greatest extent possible the same persons shall serve as panelists on each of the separate panels and the timetable shall be harmonized" (Article 9.2 DSU). This explains why in some disputes more than one panel report is issued with substantially the same content, see Chapter IV.A.1.2. This result in variable figures for the number of panels established and panel and AB reports issued, depending on whether cases where a single panel is established to hear multiple complaints (Article 9 DSU) are counted as one or more.

27 Article 8 DSU.

senior trade policy official of a Member".[28] Since they "shall serve in their individual capacities", WTO Members "shall therefore not give them instructions nor seek to influence them as individuals with regard to a matter before the panel",[29] so as to ensure their independence and the impartiality of the decision.[30]

The requirement that citizens of parties to the dispute, including third parties, are not eligible to serve, unless the parties agree otherwise (a rare occurrence), restricts the pool of available panelists. This explains why nationals of major economies, which regularly participate in disputes at least as third parties, among whom many experts are to be found, are as a rule ineligible.[31] The active role of the Secretariat together with the parties in the selection of panelists also ensures that they do not have conflicts of interest that might undermine their effective and perceived impartiality and independence as required by the Rules of Conduct for the DSU that were adopted by the DSB at the beginning of the DSS operations in 1996.[32] As a consequence of this proactive approach, procedures for dealing with challenges to nominations are unknown at the WTO.

It is for the Secretariat to make proposals to the parties, who "shall not oppose nominations except for compelling reasons".[33] In practice, obtaining the agreement of the parties is not straightforward and rarely occurs within 20 days from the establishment of a panel as required by Article 8.7 DSU. As prescribed in this provision, it is then for the Director-General to choose the panelists (often after a considerable amount of time) looking at potential panelists' availability and expertise and, *de facto*, taking into account also the views of the parties.[34]

28 As provided for in Article 8.4 DSU, the Secretariat maintains an "indicative list" of potential panellists, whose names are supplied by WTO Members, but more than two-thirds of actual panellists have not been drawn from the list (see *Mavroidis*, 419). More than three-quarters of panellists are current or past governmental experts, a practice which is common as to members of inter-state arbitration tribunals and courts. On the possible upgrading of qualifications and responsibilities of panellists in current WTO reform proposals, see Chapter VIII.A.3.

29 Articles 8.1 and 8.9 DSU.

30 See WTO, *Rules of conduct for the understanding on rules and procedures governing the settlement of disputes*, WTO Doc. No WT/DSB/RC/1, https://www.wto.org/english/tratop_e/dispu_e/rc_e.htm> accessed 20 July 2024: Rules of Conduct for the DSU are "designed to maintain the integrity, impartiality and confidentiality of proceedings conducted under the DSU thereby enhancing confidence in the new dispute settlement mechanism", and are applicable to panellists, members of the AB, experts, and the staff of the Secretariat assisting them.

31 Article 8.3 DSU. For statistical detail, see *Mavroidis* 416, Table 9.3.

32 Section II of the Rules requires that panellists shall be "independent and impartial, shall avoid direct or indirect conflicts of interest and shall respect the confidentiality of proceedings". Panellists must disclose the existence "of any interest, relationship or matter that the person could reasonably be expected to know and that is likely to affect, or give rise to justifiable doubts as to, that person's independence or impartiality", Rules of Conduct, para. III.1. These Rules have been taken as a model for the similar (but more detailed) rules of RTAs. See, for instance, the EU–Ukraine AA (2014), Annex XXV "Code of Conduct for Members of Arbitration Panels and Mediators".

33 Article 8.6 DSU. As to the role of the WTO Secretariat in supporting panel procedures, see also Chapter IV.B.9.

34 See R. Malacrida, "WTO panel composition: searching far and wide for administrators of world trade justice" *A History* 311.

Panellists are appointed for a specific case and are not prevented from attending to their other ongoing activities, provided this does not generate conflicts. They are normally not all resident in Geneva so that panelists tend to meet in part in person and in part virtually. Most panelists are not professional jurists and are not necessarily experts in the subtleties of proceedings, in the intricacies of the provisions of the WTO agreements at issue, and the accumulated case law under them, even more so because repeat appointments are infrequent.[35] As a consequence, the role of the Secretariat in supporting them, including assisting panelists in drafting the lengthy reports, is fundamental. Notwithstanding Article 27 DSU that explicitly provides for such a support by the Secretariat, this role has been criticized by some as being excessive.[36] The prominent role of the organization through the Secretariat should however not lead to the conclusion that rather than the organization merely supporting the panels' work, the dispute settlement function is actually exercised by the WTO through the panels, which would serve almost an administrative function. It is on the contrary the panels who author the reports, just as the AB on appeal.[37]

4. *The Functions of WTO Panels*

The function, or mandate, of panels is in substance that of deciding the dispute submitted to them. However, in conformity with the approach of the DSU, it is the DSB that formally decides by adopting (by reversed consensus as provided by Article 16.4 DSU, thus in practice "automatically") panel reports. Nominally, panels are merely entrusted with the function of making findings that will assist the DSB "in discharging its responsibilities" under the DSU. As provided for in Article 11 DSU ("Function of Panels"), to this end, a panel "should make an objective assessment of the matter before it, including an objective assessment of the

35 According to the statistical data of *Mavroidis*, 417, only 20% of panellists have been appointed more than three times.

36 See J. Pauwelyn, K. Pelc, "WTO Rulings and the Veil of Anonymity" 33 EJIL (2022) 527, criticizing in particular the alleged "excessive" role of the Secretariat in the drafting reports. This position is not generally shared and has been in turn criticized, see D. Baker, G. Marceau, "The WTO" in F. Baetens (ed), *Legitimacy of Unseen Actors in International Adjudication* (CUP 2019) 70; G. Sacerdoti, www.ejiltalk.org&a-critical-reaction-to-joost-pauwelyn-and-krzystof-pelc-the-wto-secreatarias-open-secret-unpacking-the-controversy/ (5 September 2022). As to the broader functions of the WTO Secretariat, see Y. Renouf, "Legal Counsel to the Administration: a legal advisor who should not look like one" *A History*, 334. Panels established under FTAs do not benefit from the assistance of a permanent secretariat but may avail themselves of assistants of their choice. The rules of procedure of the EU–Ukraine AA (Annex XXIV, 13) specify that this notwithstanding, "The drafting of any ruling remains the exclusive responsibility of arbitrators and shall not be delegated". In 2024, for the first time an arbitral institution issued guidelines on the use of AI, see SCC, *Guide to the use of artificial intelligence in cases administered under the SCC Rules*, https://sccarbitrationinstitute.se (16 October 2024).

37 The economic press, however, tends to report on panel and AB reports with headlines such as "the WTO has decided …", whereas decisions by the ICJ or the CJEU are attributed directly to the court and not to the UN or the EU.

facts of the case and the applicability and conformity with the relevant covered agreements".

The subject matter of a dispute is defined by the "Terms of Reference" which in turn refer to the matter that the complainant has raised in consultations and therefore in its request for the establishment of the panel. These Terms of Reference identify, albeit indirectly, both the factual elements (the respondent's measure that is complained of as being in breach of the relevant WTO provisions) and the provisions challenged as WTO-inconsistent.

Panels are entrusted with ascertaining the facts of the case (the measure complained of and its application to the prejudice of the respondent) as well as determining whether the measure is in breach of a WTO provision by taking the appropriate procedural steps, as highlighted in Chapter IV. While "issues of law covered in the panel report and legal interpretations developed by the panel" are subject to appeal to and review by the AB, as provided for in Article 17.6 DSU, factual findings by panels are not subject to appeal.

Findings of fact by a panel are thus conclusive, provided that the "assessment of the facts of the case" has been carried out objectively as required under Article 11 DSU. Domestic law provisions of the respondent Member are often examined in detail, including their legal import, to determine their meaning and pinpoint the exact content of the challenged measure(s) in order to ascertain whether there has been any breach of a WTO obligation. This aligns with the approach generally followed by international courts in this respect, with the consequence that, as a matter of fact, the appreciation of domestic law in principle cannot be challenged before the AB.[38]

However, appellants have often challenged the assessment of facts by a panel before the AB, claiming that it had not been made objectively, thus complaining of a breach of Article 11 of the DSU by the panel. The AB has stated that "an allegation of violation of Article 11 is a very serious allegation"; thus, not just any error by a panel in the appreciation of evidence amounts to a breach of Article 11.[39] At the same time, the AB has held that the determination of the scope and content of municipal law by a panel for the purpose of ascertaining the Member's compliance with its WTO obligations is a question of law which the AB can review.[40]

A related question is that of the "standard of review", that is the nature and intensity of the review undertaken by panels to assess the compliance of domestic measures with WTO law. This issue is especially relevant when panels are called to

38 See T. Voon, A. Yanovich, "The Facts Aside: the Limitation of WTO Appeals to Matters of Law" 40 JWT (2006), 239; AB *EC–Hormones* (DS 26-1998) 132.

39 AB *China–Rare Earths* (DS 431-2014), 5.228; *US–COOL* (DS 384-2012), 299; *EC–Fasteners (China)* (Article 21.5) (DS 397-2016) 5.61.

40 AB *US–Section 211 Appropriations Act* (DS 176-2002), 104. The uncertain borderline between questions of fact and law encourages the invocation of Article 11 breaches by appellants and may circumvent the limitation of the AB's competence to review matters of law, thus expanding the complexity of appellate review. This has been one of the complaints of the US against the AB, and the MPIA has sought to discourage this practice (see Chapter VII.A.2.4).

examine the application by a WTO Member of the provisions of the covered agreements in domestic trade remedies proceedings, such as in matters of anti-dumping and countervailing duties. In this respect, the AB has held that panels are not called to re-examine all of the aspects of the determination made by national authorities in their investigations ("*de novo* review"), since panels are not an additional administrative level in trade remedies investigations. On the other hand, panels have to verify the compliance of national authorities with WTO requirements (which in these areas are fairly detailed) and cannot limit their review to the respect of procedural obligations without looking at the correct application on the merits of the WTO-prescribed standards by the domestic authorities.[41]

5. *Applicable Law and the Role of Precedent*

A distinction must be made between the provisions whose breach may be subject to a dispute, that is the WTO agreements on which the DSS has jurisdiction, and the legal principles based on which a finding of breach has to be made. The legal provisions that panels and the AB interpret and apply are those of the WTO Agreements, and what is at stake in each case is the precise meaning of obligations that apply to all WTO Members. Most disputes taken to the DSS focus on a small number of agreements, especially the GATT, ADA, TBT, and SPS agreements, as well as the DSU itself. In view of the fact that the WTO is a specialized subsystem of international law containing some unique provisions in terms of the consequences of breach and the remedies that can be granted where a breach is found, panels and the AB have been restrained in their references to customary law, other treaties, and the case law of other courts.[42]

As treaties, the WTO agreements are in any case, of course, part of and subject to public international law, and the principles applicable in this respect are to be followed. The DSU does not include a list of legal sources to be applied, as is found in Article 38.1 of the Statute of the ICJ, but has a specific, peculiar provision in this respect. According to Article 3.2 DSU, the DSS serves to preserve the rights and obligations of the WTO Members under these agreements but also "to clarify

41 As reaffirmed in AB *China–HP–SSST* (Japan/EU) (DS 454, 460-2015) 5.39. See S. Croley, J. Jackson, "WTO Dispute Procedures, Standard of Review, and Deference to National Governments" 90 AJIL (1996) 193, advocating the application of the "Chevron doctrine" which respects the discretion of administrative agencies, developped in the US (until its overuling by the US Supreme Court in 2024) as the standard of review of administrative action by courts, that would leave more discretion ("policy space") to national authorities in trade remedies investigations. Similarly, more discretion would have been granted to national authorities if the AB had adopted the "margin of appreciation" doctrine developed by the ECtHR. The issue of what deference international courts should extend to domestic authorities determinations when these are chellenged before them is an issue of generral interest beyond trade or investment disputes, see E. Shirlow, *Judging at the Interface. Deference to State Decision-Making Authority in International Adjudication* (CUP 2021); J Fahner, *Judicial Deference in International Adjudication. A Comparative Analysis* (Bloomsbury 2022).

42 In the whole of the AB's case law, there is just one reference to an ICSID award, in *US–Stainless Steel (Mexico)* (DS 344-2008) 160, n 313, in relation to the importance of consistency in case law.

the existing provisions of those agreements in accordance with customary rules of interpretation of public international law".

The AB has stated since its first report that those rules are found in the VCLT, whose provisions on the interpretation of treaties (Articles 31–33) have attained the status of customary rules.[43] Not only have these provisions been systematically relied upon by panels and the AB, but since the WTO agreements are not to be considered "in clinical isolation" from international law in general (as stated by the AB in contrast with the widespread approach under the GATT[44]), any rule of international law (such as those on conflicts between treaties) may be relevant to determine the meaning and import of WTO provisions. The AB's jurisprudence has been characterized by great care in rigorously applying the principles of interpretation of the VCLT: text (ordinary meaning), immediate and broader context (the entirety of the agreement in question as well as other WTO agreements), object and purpose in a "holistic exercise".

In view of the high number of cases that have come before the WTO DSS, panels and the AB have made an important contribution to treaty law interpretation in international law, although they have been restrained in referencing sources other than WTO agreements.[45] In this respect, the AB may be credited for having adopted a very systematic approach to interpretation, especially as to the use of the various criteria listed in Article 31–33 VCLT, possibly leaning excessively towards reliance on the ordinary (literal) meaning of the terms used.

The development of consistent case law by the AB has been key to the success of the DSS.[46] The AB approach to interpretation compares favourably with that of other courts and has been given attention by authors and other tribunals and courts.[47] The mandate to "clarify" the WTO rules in Article 3.2 DSU is quite unique, but does not result in the panels or the AB being entrusted with the task of giving opinions in the abstract ("advisory opinions") as to the meaning of WTO provisions, even if they appear ambiguous, giving rise to different interpretations

43 AB, *US–Gasoline* (DS 2-1996) 17.

44 AB, *US-Gasoline* (DS 2-1996) 17.

45 See Chapter I, n 4, and the contributions by J. Lockhart, P. Van den Bossche, G. Marceau, P. Mavroidis, D. McRae, B. Stern, V. Donaldson, A. Yanovich, J. Bohanes, and A. Sennekamp in Part IV "Ten Years and Sixty-three Cases Later: The Contribution of the Appellate Body to the Development of International Trade Law" in *The WTO at Ten* 285; A.H. Qureshi, *Interpreting WTO Agreements: Problems and Perspectives* (CUP 2006); I. van Damme, *Treaty Interpretation by the WTO Appellate Body* (OUP 2009); Y. Zhang, "Contribution of the WTO Appellate Body to Treaty Interpretation" in *A. History* 570. See also N. Meagher, "The Judicial Style of the Appellate Body", in Chang-fu Lo, J. Nakagawa, and Tsai-fang Chen (eds) *The Appellate Body of the WTO and its Reform* (Springer 2022) 141.

46 See G. Shaffer, M. Elsig, S. Puig, "The Extensive (But Fragile) Authority of the WTO Appellate Body" 79 Law and Contemporary Problems (2016) 237.

47 See the forum "Treaty Interpretation in International Law: Comparing the Appellate Body with the Courts in The Hague, Hamburg, and Luxembourg" in *WTO at Ten* 453, featuring contributions by prominent judges of those courts. See also J. Dunoff, "Benign neglect, anti-model or reverse learning? Tracking the ICJ's influence on WTO dispute settlement" in A. Skordas, L. Mardikian (eds) *Research Handbook on the ICJ* (Elgar 2025).

by different Members.[48] It is through individual decisions and interpretations on a case-by-case basis that "clarification" may emerge.[49]

The creation of a consistent case law is needed in a multilateral system, lest different parties be treated differently in cases involving the same provisions. It is the task of the AB, which was also established for this purpose, to resolve possible errors by panels and divergent interpretations. This does not mean that past cases become binding or that their legal effects go beyond being of (qualified) guidance for the future in similar contexts, especially for panels.[50] In this respect, the AB has stated that "It is well settled that Appellate Body reports are not binding, except with respect to resolving the particular dispute between the parties".[51] The AB has also said that for panels, following its conclusions in earlier disputes is not only appropriate, but is what would be expected from panels, especially where the issues are the same.[52]

48 On the other hand, panels and the AB cannot decline to rule due to the ambiguity of a provision, even if the prohibition of *non liquet* on the grounds of silence or obscurity of the law is not spelt out in the DSU (in contrast to Article 42.2 ICSID). Such a refusal to decide upon a claim would lead to its rejection and the upholding of the challenged measure of the respondent without any examination of the issue raised.

49 An interpretative power *erga omnes* is instead entrusted to the political bodies of the WTO (although it has never been used) by Article IX.2 of the WTO Agreement: "(t)he Ministerial Conference and the General Council shall have the exclusive authority to adopt interpretations of this Agreement and of the Multilateral Trade Agreements … The decision to adopt an interpretation shall be taken by a three-fourths majority of the Members. This paragraph shall not be used in a manner that would undermine the amendment provisions in Article X". Article 3.9 DSU states that the provisions of the DSU "are without prejudice to the rights of Members to seek authoritative interpretation of provisions of a covered agreement through decision-making under the WTO Agreement". See in general I. Venzke, "Authoritative Interpretation" *MPEiPro* (2018).

50 Any temptation to go beyond those limits and engage in judicial activism is constrained by the caveat in Article 3.2 and 19.2 DSU that the DSB, panels, or the AB "cannot add to or diminish the rights and obligations provided in the covered agreements", thereby pointing against the admissibility of extensive or analogical application of WTO or other provisions. This feature of the DSU may explain the heavy reliance by the AB on textual interpretation, with a first step often being to consult dictionary definitions of relevant terms. This prescription does not preclude evolutionary or dynamic interpretation in applying old language (such as the GATT of 1947) to new situations and needs reflecting technological change and concerns, as the AB did by including animal species in the definition of "exhaustible natural resources" under Article XX (g) GATT in *US–Shrimp* (DS 58-1998), Section 128–131. See G. Abi-Saab and others (eds) *Evolutionary Interpretation and International Law* (Hart 2019) 171.

51 AB *US–Stainless Steel (Mexico)* (DS 344-2008) 158, referring to Article 59 ICJ, which states: "The decision of the Court has no binding force except between the parties and in respect of that particular case".

52 AB *US–Stainless Steel (Mexico)* (DS 344-2008) 159–160, quoting *US–Oil Country Tubular Goods Sunset Reviews* (DS 268-2004) 188. Para 160 states: "Ensuring 'security and predictability' in the dispute settlement system, as contemplated in Article 3.2 of the DSU, implies that, absent cogent reasons, an adjudicatory body will resolve the same legal question in the same way in a subsequent case", especially in "the hierarchical structure contemplated by the DSU", AB *US–Stainless Steel* (Mexico) 161. On the issue, see G. Sacerdoti, "The Authority of 'Precedent' in International Adjudication: The Contentious Case of the WTO Appellate Body's Practice" 19 LPICT (2020) 497. The AB has at time changed its interpretation albeit without proclaing it, following the approach of other

B. Investment

1. The Jurisdiction of Arbitral Tribunals

In stark contrast with trade disputes, objections to jurisdiction frequently occur in investment disputes by respondent home states and are facilitated by the fact that tribunals are *ad hoc* and endowed with the competence to resolve only those disputes defined in the relevant treaty.[53]

The jurisdiction of tribunals is therefore limited in respect of the parties (*ratione personae*), depending on how the treaty defines the protected investors who are entitled to initiate arbitration; the subject matter (*ratione materiae*), with respect to the definition of protected investments; and possibly *ratione temporis*,[54] provided in any case that there is a valid consent by both parties in dispute (*ratione voluntatis*).[55]

All these criteria involve the substantive definitions laid down in BITs and cannot be dealt with in detail here, beyond introductory remarks. Starting with the personal requirement, the *consent* of a Member state and a foreign investor to subject a specific dispute to ICSID arbitration is a precondition (as stated in Article 25 ICSID), which can be expressed in a contract, domestic legislation, or in a BIT. In the two latter instances, the case of BITs being by now the more frequent, the consent of the two parties in dispute is split both in time and form ("consent without privity"[56]). The state gives its advance consent through the BIT, by accepting *a priori* to subject itself to arbitration, as provided for in the treaty, with any investor entitled to do so in respect of any dispute that falls under the BIT. The investor as a

courts in this respect, see F. Roessler "Changes in the Jurisprudence of the WTO Appellate Body during the Past Twenty Years" 14 JITLP (2015) 129.

53 Chapter II (Articles 25–27) of the ICSID Convention is titled "Jurisdiction of the Centre", thus implying that jurisdiction pertains to ICSID as a whole. However, it is up to each tribunal to determine whether a dispute falls within ICSID's jurisdiction and any stricter jurisdictional limits that a BIT or a contract may establish (cf. Article 41.1 ICSID "The Tribunal shall be judge of its own competence"). Article 25 ICSID thus determines the outer limit of the organization's competence to settle investment disputes. It is doubtful that parties could extend ICSID's jurisdiction to purely commercial disputes. Article 46 further empowers a tribunal to adjudicate any incidental or additional claims or counterclaims arising directly out of the subject matter of the dispute "provided that they are within the scope of the consent of the parties and are otherwise within the jurisdiction of the Centre". The possibility of extending a tribunal's jurisdiction under a BIT by using the MFN clause to import from an other BIT a further jurisdictional basis has been met with criticism and has been explicitly excluded in recent IIAs, see Z. Douglas, "The MFN Clause in Investment Arbitration: Treaty Interpretation Off the Rails" 2 JIEL (2011) 97.

54 Time limitations may concern the date when the dispute has arisen, such as if the dispute predates the entry into force of the treaty, or if the arbitration was initiated after the termination of an IIA and after the expiry of a treaty's sunset clause. It may also concern the time remoteness of a claim if, according to the treaty, arbitration must be initiated within a certain deadline from when the dispute arose (most commonly three years in recent IIAs).

55 A further requirement is that the dispute be "a legal dispute" that is capable of being solved based on law, thus echoing Article 36.3 of the UN Charter.

56 As famously defined by J. Paulsson, "Arbitration without Privity" 10 ICSID Rev. (1995) 232.

rule accepts the offer, making it binding and irrevocable for the state, by submitting the dispute to ICSID or another arbitral forum listed in the BIT.[57]

On *nationality*, the requirement that the investor, be it a natural person, a corporation, or another legal entity, must have the nationality of the home state under the BIT and ICSID often opens up the possibility of various challenges, depending on the precise text of the BIT and on the relevant provisions of domestic law on the matter.[58] These may concern the effectiveness of the nationality of a natural person, the relevance of the investor having more than one nationality (which may be problematic if one of them is that of the host state[59]), the admissibility under the treaty of investments made, indirectly, through a third-country entity.

A further restriction to jurisdiction may derive from the exclusion of portfolio investment or the possible exclusion of a claim under a "denial of benefits" clause, which may apply to companies that do not have a substantial connection with the home country ("mail-box companies").[60]

The most extensive discussions concern the notion of investment, which the ICSID Convention purportedly does not define with a view to offering the broadest possible coverage, but for which BITs have more precise definitions that must also be taken into account by tribunals.[61] A typical "asset-based" definition is found in Article 1.6 ECT, according to which "Investment means every kind of asset, owned directly or indirectly by an investor". The provision contains, in addition a broad list of assets such as tangible and intangible, movable and immovable property, companies, business enterprises, shares, bonds "and other debts of a company", as well as "claims to money and claims to performance pursuant to contract having an economic value and associated with an investment". Even here doubts may arise as to the borderline with commercial operations (such as a sales contract).[62] States looking to avoid broad interpretations of what constitutes an investment under their BITs may prefer an "enterprise-based" to an asset-based definition.[63]

57 *ICSID Commentary*, I, Article 25, 825–862. 1057–1110.

58 *ICSID Commentary*, I, Article 25, 598–610.

59 Article 25.2(a) ICSID precludes access to arbitration by natural persons having also the nationality of the respondent (host) state. According to Article 25.2(b), foreign-controlled companies having the nationality of the host state can also access ICSID if the parties have so consented, *Principles* 61.

60 Jurisdiction can be further circumscribed in BITs by the exclusion of certain matters (e.g. measures taken for the "protection of essential security interests" as in the US–Argentina BIT 1991, Article XI), tax measures (as provided in Article 21 ECT), prudential measures in the banking sector, or other types of measures (such as with tobacco control measures with Australia under the CPTPP), or in relation to specific types of investments such as bonds issued abroad.

61 See Article 25 ICSID: "The jurisdiction of the Centre shall extend to any legal dispute arising directly out of an investment, between a contracting State … and a national of another Contracting State, which the parties in dispute consent to in writing to submit to Centre": See *Report of the Executive Directors*, Chapter II, n 71, 27.

62 In the *Komstroy* case (n 69) the CJEU held that the operation at issue in the underlying arbitration was a commercial operation and not an investment covered by the ECT.

63 Though the enterprise-based definition is much rarer, only featuring in about 1% of IIAs. See UNCTAD Investment Policy Hub, Mapping of IIA clauses, www.investmentpolicy.unctad.org accessed 27 June 2024.

There have been two main jurisprudential approaches in this respect. Under the subjective approach, the ICSID Convention would leave the definition of investment mainly to the parties and, in particular, to the discretion of states through BIT clauses.[64] As a result, broad BIT definitions of covered investments, such as asset-based ones, would require a tribunal to endorse a more liberal attitude, extending its jurisdiction *ratione materiae* essentially to any kind of economic operation covered by the treaty, except for mere contracts for the sale of goods. Under the objective approach instead, although the ICSID Convention contains no definition, investment must be defined objectively, as was decided in *Salini v Morocco* in 2001.[65] Therefore, if the investment in question does not meet such criteria, the tribunal should dismiss the case for lack of subject-matter jurisdiction.

According to the widely applied "Salini test", an investment requires four distinctive elements: (a) a contribution from the investor, (b) a certain duration over which the project is implemented, (c) sharing of the operational risks, and (d) a contribution to the host state's development.[66] These jurisprudentially developed requirements have not been unchallenged, especially in respect of the last element.[67] A further requirement, which is explicitly laid down in certain BITs but is implicit by nature, is that the investment be and has been carried out legally (such as not being tainted by corruption). This has been considered to be a jurisdictional precondition by some tribunals and by others as an issue pertaining to the merits.[68]

Another jurisdictional issue that has attracted considerable interest recently, in view of the many cases where it has been raised, is whether intra-EU BITs and the ECT dispute settlement provisions are inapplicable to arbitrations initiated by investors of one EU Member state against another Member state. It is argued that this is the case on the grounds that such arbitration would be incompatible with

64 See, inter alia, *Middle East Cement v Egypt* ICSID ARB/99/6 Award (2002), paras 134–136; and *Ambiente Ufficio v Argentina*, ICSID ARB/08/9 Decision on Jurisdiction and Admissibility (2013), paras. 441–474, 479, endorsing "the view that the term 'investment' in Article 25.1 of the ICSID Convention should not be subjected to an unduly restrictive interpretation. Hence, the *Salini* criteria, if useful at all, must not be conceived of as expressing jurisdictional requirements stricto sensu". See C. Brower, A. Goetz-Charlier, "International Investment Arbitration and the Global Financial System: Are They 'Yin' and 'Yang' or like Oil and Water?" in C. Tams, S. Schill, R. Hofmann (eds.) *International Investment Law and the Global Financial Architecture* (Elgar 2017) 23, 35, observing that "the subjective or traditional approach still dominates arbitral practice".

65 *Salini v Kingdom of Morocco* ICSID ARB/00/04 Decision on Jurisdiction (2001), 44, 52.

66 Based on these criteria, the tribunal in *Salini* concluded that highway construction works pursuant to a contract constituted an investment under the Italy–Morocco BIT.

67 See *ICSID Commentary* I, Article 25, 258; Z. Douglas, *The International Law of Investment Claims* (2009) 190.

68 See R. Lorz, R. Busch, "Investment in Accordance with the Law – Specifically Corruption" in *International Investment Law* 577; A. Tussupov, "Corruption and Fraud in Investment Arbitration Procedural and Substantive Challenges" 22 EYIEL (2023) 28; G. Cordero-Moss, "Corruption and Arbitration: Arbitrability, Jurisdiction, Admissibility or Merits" in A. Crivellaro, M. Benedettelli, M. Deli, A. Carlevaris (eds) *Arbitration as Balanced Administration of Justice, Essays in Honour of Piero Bernardini* (Brill 2024) 194; Y. Krivoi, "Corruption and Foreign Investments; Empirical Lessons from Treaties and Arbitration Cases" 22 Int'l J Constitutional Law (2024) 585.

EU law and the primacy of EU law over international commitments given between Member states. This position has been firmly adhered to by the CJEU in *Achmea* and subsequent cases.[69] In *Komstroy*, the CJEU found that ISDS under Article 26 of the ECT was not applicable to intra-EU disputes due to the autonomy and primacy of EU law, while these principles do not preclude arbitral mechanisms in relation to investors from third states. As a consequence, Member states' courts have set aside non-ICSID intra-EU awards, starting in Sweden in *Novenergia II v Spain*.[70] The EU position has, however, been consistently rejected by ICSID tribunals. They have affirmed their jurisdiction over such disputes, denying that EU treaties prevail over the ICSID Convention under the VCLT. Additionally, they have relied on Article 25.1 ICSID to assert that consent, once given, cannot be withdrawn by invoking EU law.[71]

Whether the claimant failed to satisfy a condition precedent to arbitration (e.g. mediation or litigation for a set period of time) is instead generally regarded as a matter of admissibility also for the tribunal to decide.[72]

2. *The Pre-Litigation Phase: Consultations and ADR*

Amicable settlements are encouraged under BITs: most treaties contain a waiting or cooling-off period which must be observed as a pre-requisite for an investor to initiate arbitration.[73] In this time span, usually three or six months, amicable settlement must at least be attempted, although investment agreements, at least first-generation BITs, do not provide for procedural requirements or recourse to specific ADR methods. In those BITs, there is usually no requirement, such as at the WTO, that attempts at amicable settlement have been actively pursued and that the legal challenges later brought to arbitration have previously been raised in the pre-litigation phases.

69 CJEU *Slovakia v Achmea BV* C-284/16 (2018) ECLI:EU:C:2018:158 (with reference to an intra-EU BIT); CJEU *Moldova v Komstroy* C-741/19 (2021) ECLI:EU:C:2021:655; CJEU *PL Holdings v Poland*, C-109/20 (2021) ECLI:EU:C:2021:875 (under the ECT).

70 Supreme Court of Sweden, *Novenergia II v Spain*, SCC Case No. 2015/063 (2023), available at www.italaw.com, followed by further annulments of SCC awards against Spain and Italy by the Court of appeal of Stockholm.

71 The first such case being *Eastern Sugar v Czech Republic*, UNCITRAL, SCC Case No 088/2004, Partial Award (2007), para 172, 185; more recently among many *Vattenfall v Germany* ICSID ARB/12/12 (2018), 159, 164; *S. Beheer v Spain* ICSID ARB/16/2 (2022), 7 (in respect of the ECT). For a critical view, see G. Sacerdoti, "After Komstroy. Have the EU Member States Withdrawn by the Lisbon Treaty, as an Inter-se Agreement under Article 41 VCLT, their Consent to ICSID Jurisdiction on ECT Intra-EU Investment Disputes?" *Arbitration as Balanced Administration of Justice* (n 68) 471.

72 The US Supreme Court *BG Group v Argentina* 572 U.S. 25 (2014) considered, however, that the matter is jurisdictional and as such reviewable by courts "with deference" to the interpretation of the (*in casu* UNCITRAL) arbitrators.

73 For other methods, see G. Sacerdoti, M. Recanati, "Approaches to Investment Protection outside of specific International Investment Agreements and Investor-State Settlement" *International Investment Law* 1839.

The ICSID Convention provides for conciliation as well as arbitration, but this route has historically represented just a small fraction of cases.[74] Initiatives to promote mediation in respect of investment disputes have been undertaken by the IBA (2012) and more recently by ICSID (2022) and UNCITRAL (2023), but no information is available as to their use, possibly also due to the confidential nature of such proceedings.[75]

The requirement of previous recourse to litigation in front of domestic courts before engaging in arbitration cannot be properly categorized as a pre-litigation requirement meant to avoid formal arbitration since it is a traditional requirement in international law, which however BITs intend to avoid by providing ISDS. Recourse to domestic courts, which is in principle always available in the host state, is often referred to in BITs as an alternative to arbitration. An example of such a provision is a "fork-in-the-road" clause, typically stating that "The investor's choice of the court or arbitral tribunal is final and binding".[76] The international arbitration of investment disputes has been conceived as an alternative to the claims of foreign investors being taken against the host state by means of diplomatic protection by their home states, a context in which the requirement of the previous exhaustion of domestic remedies is customary. It is not by chance that the default rule under the ICSID Convention is that consent to ICSID arbitration is exclusive, and that no diplomatic protection is admitted unless an award has not been complied with.[77]

Certain BITs impose as a precondition for arbitration that the investor pursues its claim in front of the host state's courts for a certain period (such as 180 days), and be allowed to initiate arbitration only if no final domestic decision has been made during that period.[78] This requirement is rather a condition of admissibility, which tribunals have sometimes declared to be futile and dispensed with, in view

74 As of the end of 2022, there have only been 13 conciliation requests compared with 821 arbitrations under the Convention and 76 under the Additional Facility. See more generally C. Tomutschat, M. Kohen (eds.) *Flexibility in International Dispute Settlement. Conciliation Revisited* (Brill 2020).

75 See, respectively, IBA, *Rules for Investor-State Mediation* (2012) on www.ibanet.org; ICSID, *The ICSID Mediation Rules* on https://icsid.worldbank.org; UNGA, *Draft UNCITRAL Guidelines on Investment Mediation, Note by the Secretariat* UN Doc. A/CN.9/1151 of 23 April 2023 on https://uncitral.un.org.

76 This clause is found in a number of BITs (see, for instance, Article 8.2 of the France-Argentina BIT of 1991). The most frequent issue in this respect is what features domestic proceedings must have in order to preclude subsequent arbitration. Generally, there is no preclusion if the two proceedings do not involve identical parties (for instance, because the claimant in the domestic proceedings was a local subsidiary and not the foreign parent company which initiated the arbitration), as well as an identical cause of action and object, see, for instance, *LG&E v Argentina* ICSID Case No. ARB/02/1, Decision on Jurisdiction (2004), 75–76. See generally K. Hober, *Res Judicata and Lis Pendens in International Arbitration*, 366 RC (2014) 109; G. Zarra, *Parallel Proceedings in Investment Arbitration* (Eleven International Publishing and Giappichelli, 2017).

77 See Articles 26 and 27 ICSID.

78 This clause is present in several first-generation BITs between European and Latin American nations, such as Article 10.2 of the Argentina–Germany BIT (1991).

of the impossibility of obtaining a decision on an investment dispute in such a limited timeframe.[79]

3. *The Initiation of Arbitral Proceedings: The Constitution of the Tribunal*

The relevant provisions are found in the ICSID Convention and Rules and in other applicable arbitration rules. BITs are usually silent on arbitration proceedings, making them subject to the procedural rules of the institution which a claimant investor has selected among those listed in the BIT.[80]

Arbitration starts with a formal request filed with the secretariat of the institution selected by the claimant, which must contain all of the relevant identification data, including the basis of the parties' consent, a summary of the facts and legal principles invoked, and an indication of the remedy sought.[81] The typical arbitration tribunal consists of three arbitrators, two of whom are appointed by the parties, with each party appointing one. The third arbitrator, who presides over the tribunal, is either directly agreed to by the parties, or is agreed to by the two party-appointed arbitrators if the parties have entrusted them with the selection.[82]

Qualification requirements apply, and restrictions on nationality usually result in no arbitrator having the nationality of either party.[83] While the appointment, particularly by investors, of well-known commercial arbitration practitioners, mostly from developed countries, used to prevail, public international lawyers are now frequently appointed.[84] If difficulties arise in the prompt composition of a tribunal (because of a party not participating in proceedings, not appointing an arbitrator, or the parties being unable to agree on the president), it is for the institution to step in upon the request of a party and to complete the tribunal respecting any selection criteria set forth in its rules.[85] While parties are free to appoint to the tribunal

79 See, for instance, *Urbaser v Argentina* ICSID ARB/07/26, Decision on Jurisdiction (2012), 106–202.

80 Recent ("second generation") IIAs often contain specific provisions on arbitral procedure, notably on the transparency of proceedings (the publication of exhibits, briefs, decisions, and the award, the opening of the hearing to the public, and *amicus curiae* submissions).

81 See Article 36.1 and 36.2 ICSID. As to the screening power of the Secretary-General under Article 36.3 ICSID, see Chapter II. B.2.1.

82 Article 37 ICSID.

83 Article 39 ICSID.

84 See J. Pauwelyn, "The Rule of Law without the Rule of Lawyers? Why Investment Arbitrators Are from Mars, Trade Adjudicators from Venus" 109 AJIL (2015) 761. The lack of diversity among arbitrators also concerns the paucity of women. See R. Chen, "The Substantial Value of Diversity in International Investment Arbitration" 31 VJIL (2021) 61, https://ssrn.com See also W. Byrne, "The Influence of Legal Scholars on the Development of International Investment Law" 27(2) JIEL (2024) 278.

85 Article 38 ICSID (after 90 days). Article 12.5 ICC provides for a shorter deadline (30 days) and the institution steps in without the need for a request by one of the parties. In ICC arbitration, party-nominated arbitrators must be confirmed by the ICC (Article 13), also to verify the candidate's ability to conduct the arbitration, and their suitability also in respect of nationality. In 2018, the ICJ decided to make the position of judge incompatible with appointments as investment arbitra-

any person of their choice endowed with the required qualifications, appointments made by ICSID are restricted to persons included on the list (defined as a roster or panel) of arbitrators kept by ICSID.[86]

A typical feature of both commercial and investment arbitration is the right for either party to challenge arbitrators for a lack of the required qualities, especially alleging that an arbitrator should be disqualified because of a conflict of interest that may prejudice or appear to prejudice the person's independence or impartiality.[87] According to Article 57 ICSID, a party to a dispute may propose the disqualification of an arbitrator for a "manifest" lack of the qualities required by Article 14, such as competence and the ability "to exercise independent judgment". To reduce instances where parties "strategically" challenge the appointment of an arbitrator by the other party – often to remove an arbitrator perceived to be unfavourable, even though the great majority of such challenges fail – the obligation for arbitrators to disclose any potential conflicts of interest has recently been made more stringent.[88] A peculiarity of the ICSID disqualification procedure, compared with the rules of commercial arbitration institutions, is that the challenge is not decided by the institution but by the other arbitrators. It is only if they are not in a position to decide on a disqualification request (or if they prefer not to decide in order to avoid embarrassment) that the Chairman of the ICSID Administrative Council (i.e. the President of the World Bank) decides.

While the general impartiality of investment tribunals is not seriously in doubt, the "private" selection method and the resulting limited diversity of the selected

tors, www.icj-cij.org/files/press-releases/0/000-20181025-PRE-02-00-EN.pdf. This choice prevents (unlikely) conflicts but deprives investment arbitration of the competence of ICJ judges and the potential for cross-fertilization and learning between the two fields. For a different view see "IISD Welcomes ICJ Judges' Decision to No Longer Participate in Investor–State Arbitration" 18 October 2018, available at www.iisd.org/articles/press-release/iisd-welcomes-icj-judges-decision-no-longer-participate-investor-state> accessed 17 July 2024.

86 Each contracting state may designate four persons to the roster (who may be, but need not be, its nationals) and the Chairman may designate ten persons, each of a different nationality, paying due regard "to the importance of assuring representation on the Panels of the principal legal systems of the world and the main forms of economic activity" (Articles 12–16 ICSID). A similarly constituted roster of conciliators is also provided for by the same articles.

87 See Article 57 ICSID; Article 14 ICC ("for an alleged lack of impartiality or independence"). According to ICSID data concerning Decisions on Disqualification, of over 100 challenges only six have been successful <https://icsid.worldbank.org/cases/content/tables-of-decisions/disqualification> accessed on 17 July 2024.

88 See for more details in Chapter VIII.B.5.2.2.2(b). See IBA, *Guidelines on Conflict of Interest in International Arbitration* (latest edition 2024) on www.ibanet.org, which are also applicable to commercial arbitration; UNCITRAL Code of Conduct for Arbitrators in International Investment Disputes (2023), available on https://uncitral.un.org, drafted in cooperation with ICSID, includes a prohibition against "double hatting" (i.e. the practice of sitting as an arbitrator in one case and a party representative or expert in another involving one of the parties or the same issue) and lists specific disclosure requirements. Other matters that are also addressed include obligations related to the confidentiality of proceedings, reasonable fees and expenses, and the role and duties of tribunal assistants. See generally C. Giorgetti (ed), *Challenges and Recusals of Judges and Arbitrators in International Courts and Tribunals* (Brill 2015).

arbitrators (as to cultural background, geographical origin, gender, etc.) has been criticized for not reflecting the public nature of investment arbitration, which deals with states' public interests, in contrast to international commercial disputes.[89] Nevertheless, a common opinion is that, thanks to the parties' participation in the selection process, by and large "arbitrators sitting on investment treaty cases are among the most experienced and respected professionals in the arbitration community".[90]

4. *The Functions of Investment Tribunals*

Section 3 of the ICSID Convention, titled "Powers and Functions of the Tribunal" comprises Articles 41–47. These articles, in relatively few sentences, cover the applicable law, the conduct of proceedings in accordance with Section 3, the tribunal's power to rule on its jurisdiction, decide incidental or additional claims and counterclaims, and recommend provisional measures in order "to preserve the respective rights of either party" during proceedings. The overall function of tribunals – that of deciding impartially the disputes submitted to them in accordance with the law, by addressing jurisdiction and the merits, facts, and law – is not spelled out as such but results from the totality of the applicable provisions dealing with proceedings and the award, which becomes binding on the parties once issued (Article 48, 53 ICSID).[91]

5. *Applicable Law and the Role of Precedent*

According to Article 42.1 ICSID,

89 See Chapter VII.B.3.2 for more details, and in general, Y. Shany, "Squaring the Circle? Independence and Impartiality of Party-Appointed Adjudicators in International Legal Proceedings" 30 Loy. L.A. Int'l & Comp. L. Rev. (2008) 473; S. Brevoulaikis, "Systemic Bias and the Institutions of International Arbitration" 4 JIDS (2013) 553–585; D. Behn, K. Fauchild, M. Langford (eds.) *The Legitimacy of Investment Arbitration* (CUP 2022); M. Waibel et al., *The Backlash against Investment Arbitration* (Kluwer 2010). Specifically, as to the appointment process and party-appointed arbitrators, C. Rogers, "Reconceptualizing the Party-Appointed Arbitrator and the Meaning of Impartiality" 64 HILJ (2023) 129–202, argues that the sharing by party-appointed arbitrators of their appointers' vision is not incompatible with impartiality and may increase the legitimacy of *ad hoc* tribunals. S. Brevoulakis, A. Howard, "Impartiality and the Construction of Trust in ISDS" 39 ICSID Rev. 644 (2023), concluding that "The empirical findings show that the parties' choice of a predisposed arbitrator is generally considered compatible with the understanding of impartiality in ISDS". Ultimately, however, the reputation and competence of an arbitrator should be the paramount factors in an appointment decision.

90 Global Arbitration Review, T.H. Cheng & S.N. González, "Advocacy in Investment Treaty Arbitration" (18 August 2023), <https://globalarbitrationreview.com/guide/the-guide-advocacy/sixth-edition/article/advocacy-in-investment-treaty-arbitration> accessed 21 July 2024.

91 Disputes may be decided *ex aequo et bono* only in the unlikely case that parties empower the tribunal to do so (Article 42.3 ICSID).

> The Tribunal shall decide a dispute in accordance with such rules of law as may be agreed by the parties. In the absence of such agreement, the Tribunal shall apply the law of the Contracting State party to the dispute (including its rules on the conflict of laws) and such rules of international law as may be applicable.

While many BITs are silent on this issue, some BITs have their own provisions on applicable law, referring to both domestic and international law,[92] or just to the latter, as is the case with Article 26.6 ECT: "A tribunal established under paragraph (4) shall decide the issues in dispute in accordance with this Treaty and applicable rules and principles of international law". A related development in IIAs is the establishment of joint committees of the parties, empowered *inter alia* to render binding opinions on the interpretation of the relevant treaty, as a way of affirming the "parties' control" over the interpretation of the treaty.[93] Investment tribunals may (or under some treaties must) request their interpretations in cases of doubt, which are binding upon them.[94]

The exact relationship between the domestic law of the host state and international law has given rise to considerable debate, but ICSID case law has been consistent that in case of a conflict international law shall prevail.[95] Since foreign investments are made and operated in a given country, the law of that country, the host state, will normally govern all matters pertaining to the making and operation of that investment. A conflict arises when it is alleged that domestic law or the conduct of state authorities breaches international law, most frequently the relevant BIT, entailing the responsibility of the host state. While claims based on

92 See Argentina–France BIT (1991), Article 8.4. "The arbitration panel shall decide on the basis of the provisions of this Agreement, the law of the Contracting Party party to the dispute, including the rules relating to conflicts of law, of the terms of any specific agreement which may have been entered into regarding the investment as well as the principles of international Law" (UN translation, available at the WTI's Electronic Database of Investment Treaties https://edit.wti.org/document/show/14ba629b-6d59-45ed-8c77-196e3d23cc46 accessed 21 July 2024). Article 8 of the BIT between the Netherlands and Slovakia (1991), which was at issue in the *Achmea* case, states as follows: "The arbitral tribunal shall decide on the basis of the law, taking into account in particular though not exclusively: the law in force of the Contracting Party concerned; the provisions of this Agreement, and other relevant agreements between the Contracting Parties; the provisions of special agreements relating to the investment; the general principles of international law".

93 See generally A. Roberts, "Power and Persuasion in Investment Treaty Interpretation: The Dual Role of States" 104 AJIL (2010) 179.

94 See Article 14.D.9.2 USMCA on Governing Law: "A decision of the Commission on the interpretation of a provision of this Agreement under Article 30.2 (Functions of the Commission) shall be binding on a tribunal, and any decision or award issued by a tribunal must be consistent with that decision".

95 See W. Reisman, "The Regime for Lacunae in the ICSID Choice of Law Provision and the Question of the Threshold" 15 ICSID Rev 362 (2000) 380; E. Gaillard, Y. Banifatemi, "The Meaning of 'and' in Article 42.1 Second Sentence of the Washington Convention: The Role of International Law in the ICSID Choice of Law Process" 18 ICSID Rev. 375, (2003) 378–381; *Principles*, 416–424; M. Benedettelli, "Determining the Applicable Law in Commercial and Investment Arbitration: Two Intertwined Road Maps for Conflict-Solving" 37 ICSID Rev. (2022) 687.

a contract may just raise domestic law issues, claims under BITs by definition involve an alleged breach of international law through the host country's conduct (by the legislative, executive, judiciary, or another body) irrespective of the fact that such conduct may be compliant with domestic law.[96] Since ICSID tribunals are international tribunals established under an international convention, they are required to apply international law in case of conflict, first the relevant BIT, and, as context and instrument of interpretation, any other applicable and relevant norm and principle. [97]

Otherwise than is the case at the WTO, arbitration tribunals look extensively to general international law and the case law of international courts when interpreting and applying the relevant BIT, especially in relation to attribution, responsibility (liability), causation, and damages.[98] Even if, looked at comprehensively, investment treaties may be considered to be a system, each BIT must be considered on its own terms. Aside from ICSID, there is no multilateral investment law framework for dispute settlement and procedure. Even in the instances where a given BIT or other IIA has been interpreted and applied repeatedly (such as has recently been the case with the ECT), previous decisions (precedents) are not controlling for subsequent tribunals.[99] Among different BITs, provisions on the same matter, whether

96 The enmeshment of domestic and international law issues before arbitration tribunals is epitomized by the issue of their competence to adjudicate breaches of BITs' "umbrella clauses". These clauses enable investors to escalate contract breach claims, arising from the exercise of sovereign authority or power, to treaty violation claims, thus making international arbitration a possible route for dispute resolution. On this issue, to which investment tribunals have given conflicting answers, see A. De Luca, "Umbrella Clauses and Transfer Provisions in the (Invisible) EU Model BIT, 15 JWIT (2014) 506; J. Chaisse, "Rethinking umbrella clauses in international investment agreements", Columbia FDI Perspectives, No. 368 (2023), available at https://ccsi.columbia.edu.

97 Among several statements to this effect, see *Santa Elena v Costa Rica* ICSID ARB/96/1, Award (2000), 60–68; *Maffezzini v Spain* ICSID ARB/97/7, Award (2000), 92; *LG&E v Argentina* ICSID ARB/02/1, Decision on Liability (2006), 94. Cf. Article 27 VCLT: Internal law and observance of treaties – "A party may not invoke the provisions of its internal law as justification for its failure to perform a treaty", and Article 32 ARSIWA: *Irrelevance of internal law* – "The responsible State may not rely on the provisions of its internal law as justification for failure to comply with its obligations under this part". The issue of the standard of review under which investment tribunals should evaluate the correctness (fairness) of host states' actions affecting investments arises also in ISDS as in WTO disputes, see J. Paine "Standard of Review (Investment Arbitration)" *MPEiPro* (2018).

98 See A. Reinisch, "The Interpretation of International Investment Agreements" in *International Investment Law*, 372; I. Marboe, *Calculation of Compensation and Damages in International Investment Law* (2nd ed OUP 2017); B. Sabahi, *Compensation and Restitution in Investor-state Arbitration* (OUP 2011); F. Baetens (ed) *Investment Law within International Law. Integrationist Perspectives* (CUP 2013); J. Viñuales, "Customary Law in Investment Regulation" 23 IYIL (2015) 23; C. de Stefano, *Attribution in International Law and Arbitration* (OUP 2020); A. Culick, M. Waibel (eds) *International Law in International Investment Law: A Commentary* (OUP 2024). See also the contributions in the special issue of the ICSID Review (vol. 37, n 1–2) on the extensive application of ARSIWA by ICSID tribunals, published in 2002 on the occasion of the 20th anniversary of the ARSIWA, vol. 37, 1–2, 2022.

99 See *ICSID Commentary*, I, Article 42, 251; see also Chapter VII. B.3.3; F. Gélinas, "Investment Tribunals and the Commercial Arbitration Model: Mixed Procedures and Creeping Institutionalisation"

substantive or procedural, tend to be similar but are rarely identical. Previous decisions involving different parties and different BITs, although often extensively cited, may be persuasive depending on their thoroughness and serve as guidance but cannot be defined strictly as precedent for subsequent tribunals.[100] Hence the reliance on other sources (such as the ARSIWA for attribution and causation) and other case law, especially from the PCIJ and the ICJ in matters of damages.[101] The value of developing as far as possible consistency in case law ("aiming at a *jurisprudence constante*"[102]) is however advocated for reasons of predictability for parties and has been more than once praised by tribunals.[103]

C. Comparative Evaluation

There are marked differences between the trade and investment frameworks due to their different multilateral v bilateral settings and the different types of parties involved in each: states v states in the trade regime and private parties v states in the investment regime. However, at the initial stage of the adjudicatory phase, parties and adjudicators do face some similar issues.

in M. Gehring, M. Cordonier Segger (eds) *Sustainable Development in World Trade Law* (Kluwer 2005) 577.

100 See *ICSID Commentary*, II, Article 53, 21.

101 See B. Simma, D. Pulkowski, "Two Worlds but Not Apart: International Investment Law and General International Law" in *International Investment Law* 361. In respect of the international law principle of full reparation for damages stemming from an illegal act, PCIJ *Chorzów Factory*, PCIJ Reports Series A No. 17, Merits (1928) ("Chorzów") is often referred to. See, for instance, *Quiborax v Bolivia* ICSID ARB 06/2, Award 16 (2015) and Partially Dissenting Opinion of B. Stern (2015).

102 For more detail,see Chapter VII.B.3.3.

103 See *Saipem v Bangladesh* ICSID ARB/05/7, Award (2009) 90, where the tribunal famously stated, "The Tribunal considers that it is not bound by previous decisions. At the same time, it is of the opinion that it must pay due consideration to earlier decisions of international tribunals. It believes that, subject to compelling contrary grounds, it has a duty to adopt solutions established in a series of consistent cases. It also believes that, subject to the specifics of a given treaty and of the circumstances of the actual case, it has a duty to seek to contribute to the harmonious development of investment law and thereby to meet the legitimate expectations of the community of States and investors towards certainty of the rule of law". This statement has been cited with approval by the AB report in *US–Stainless Steel (Mexico)* (DS 344-2008) 161, n 313. According to *Encavis v Italy* ICSID ARB/20/39, Award (2024), 607: "the Tribunal is not bound by prior awards. There is no system of stare decisis in investment arbitration, and the Tribunal is free to reach a conclusion different from those of other tribunals. That said, legal certainty is enhanced when subsequent tribunals, applying the same treaty and confronted with an analogous factual situation, strive to reach the same conclusions already established by their predecessors. Unnecessarily contradictory decisions only cause confusion, increase the risk for investors and thus operate contrary to the very purpose of investment treaties".

1. Commonalities

(a) The definition of the jurisdiction of adjudicators is a threshold question in both systems, as indeed it is for all international courts and tribunals. Both the WTO and the investment regime under ICSID are systems of dispute settlement, within which individual panels or tribunals adjudicate specific disputes.
(b) Jurisdiction is therefore an inherent feature of both systems (the jurisdiction of the WTO DSS under the DSU, or the jurisdiction of ICSID and of specific tribunals under the applicable IIA) and decisions on this issue are within the competence of the adjudicators and should be decided as preliminary (threshold) issues. Since investment arbitration is fragmented and arbitration proceedings are held on the basis of different treaties, the competence of a given tribunal must be checked with reference to the consent of the parties to arbitration, personal and subject-matter jurisdiction requirements, and comparing the criteria laid down in the BIT with the facts of the case. At the WTO, which is a centralized system of dispute settlement, no such problems arise. Any WTO Member may have recourse to the DSS against another Member, alleging that a measure taken by the Member has breached an obligation included in the WTO agreements towards the complainant. Jurisdictional issues are mostly procedural and can be better considered as pertaining to admissibility, such as compliance with the consultations requirement before bringing the dispute to a panel.
(c) As to access to adjudication, neither system permits the immediate initiation of proceedings before attempts at an amicable settlement have been pursued for a given period of time, albeit limited (60 days in trade, three to six months in investment disputes). In both systems, the conduct of consultations or negotiations, though a formal prerequisite for pursuing adjudication thereafter, is left to the discretion of the parties to the dispute, with no support or intervention from outside.
(d) Recourse to ADR is possible, and instruments have been developed to facilitate it, but they do not seem to have been used often, notwithstanding encouragement to do so and the underlining of the advantages of these methods in order to avoid the inevitable tensions, time, and costs implied by formal proceedings.
(e) As to the applicable law, each system is called to apply the specific treaties that are the basis of the challenges before them: the relevant WTO Agreement under the DSU, and BITs/IIAs by arbitration tribunals. Both apply the same interpretative criteria that are set forth in the VCLT, but ICSID tribunals are less constrained by precedent and tap more extensively into the case law of other international jurisdictions.

2. Differences

(a) On the establishment of a panel or an arbitral tribunal in case of dispute, both systems give precedence to the choice and agreement of the parties in the selection of adjudicators (a typical feature of adjudication by non-permanent bodies in international law). At the WTO, however, there is a previous intervention of the Membership at the DSB in "establishing" panels, in view of the collective interest in the operation of the DSS. Moreover, where there is no agreement between the parties, the composition of panels is actively managed by the WTO Secretariat to ensure, besides the acceptance by the parties of prospective panelists, their competence and availability, so that the process may get underway in a speedy manner.

(b) In contrast, in investment arbitration, the traditional commercial arbitration model prevails: each party is free to select an arbitrator of its choice (and the president is selected jointly), provided the persons chosen are endowed with the qualifications required (hence the practice of challenges), while the institution only steps in at the parties' request when they are unable to agree.

(c) The profiles of adjudicators in the two systems are quite different, but this does not affect the quality and impartiality of decisions, although there are recurrent criticisms of the "private" selection process in ISDS as undermining its legitimacy as an instrument to resolve public matters.[104]

(d) The role of the Secretariat in the selection of panellists and thereafter in supporting the work of adjudicators, including with assistance in drafting, is much more pronounced at the WTO than at ICSID (even more in comparison with the support provided by other arbitral institutions).

(e) Procedurally, both systems ensure equal treatment of the parties and due process in general (the right to be heard and to submit evidence), although the WTO DSS is more institution-run than investment arbitration, which is based on ad hoc tribunals, and where parties have more freedom to agree among themselves on the organization of the proceedings.

(f) The duties and approaches of the two systems diverge in respect of the relevance of the domestic law of the respondent state. Investment tribunals have to apply it not just as fact, as panels and the AB under the DSU do, following the principles of public international law, but as part of the law applicable to the investment at issue. This evidences the mixed nature – private and public – of investment arbitration, especially in the case of non-ICSID arbitrations.

(g) Panels (and the AB, which is akin to a permanent high tribunal also in respect of the authority of its legal statements) systematically interpret and apply between WTO Members a defined set of interconnected agreements, those of the WTO, and a body of case law that grows year on year creating a generally coherent jurisprudence.

(h) *Ad hoc* investment tribunals instead deal with disputes in a more decentralized context, between wholly different parties (especially in view of the variety of claimant investors), concerning mostly different and unconnected investment

104 For more details, see Chapter VII.B.3.2.

treaties. They rely much more, somehow by necessity, on a variety of international legal sources, referring to the case law of other ISDS tribunals and international courts more often than WTO adjudicators. The investment regime is a conceptual construction; it does not represent a unitary system, connected to a specialized organization as is the case with the DSS in respect of the WTO.[105]

105 For a comparative view, see J. Huerta-Goldman, A. Romanetti, F. Stirziman (eds) *WTO Litigation, Investment Arbitration and Commercial Arbitration* (Wolters Kluwer 2013); F. Palombino (ed), *Introduction to International Economic Law* (Giappichelli 2025).

4 Procedural Features and the Final Decision

Table of Contents

DOI: 10.4324/9781003471509-6

Introduction

The rules governing proceedings at both the WTO and in respect of investment disputes are inspired by a common overarching principle, which is typical of adversarial proceedings for settling disputes in accordance with the law: that of ensuring fairness to each party and equality of arms between them in deciding the dispute.[1] This principle serves as the basis for procedural justice and due process, which are essential for rendering substantive justice. This requirement is common to other forms of international adversarial rule-based dispute settling proceedings, be they judicial or arbitral, between states or private parties, including international commercial arbitration.[2]

Other considerations also play a role in shaping proceedings, including efficiency, the fact that states and hence public collective interests are involved, and the existence of a community interest that goes beyond the interest of the litigating parties. This community interest necessitates systems in which the correct administration of proceedings and the correctness of the outcome are ensured in order to establish trust in the system and its legitimacy in the eyes of stakeholders. On the other hand, the two systems provide different solutions to similar procedural issues which are rooted in the different origins and set-ups of the two regimes: state-to-state and centralized at the WTO; private investors versus states, decentralized and *ad hoc*, in ISDS. The WTO model, originating from the GATT where

1 S. Forlati, "Due Process and Protection of the Parties' Rights" *Research Handbook* 375.

2 See R. Kolb, "General Principles of Procedural Law" in A. Zimmermann and others (eds) *The Statute of the ICJ: A Commentary* (OUP 2006) 830; the entries on various aspects of proceedings in *MPEiPro* (online, OUP 2019) and in *Research Handbook*.

panel proceedings resembled expert commissions rather than judicial bodies, is also reflected in the DSU's unique and non-strictly legal terminology. This terminology differs from that found in the rules of procedure of international tribunals and courts, as is highlighted hereafter. Thus, the standard term "judgment" for the final decision of a dispute, both domestic and international, is replaced by that of "report" (to be adopted by the DSB) at the WTO, and by that of "award" in commercial and investment arbitration.[3]

1. The Organization of Proceedings: WTO Panels and Investment Arbitration

1. Working Procedures for WTO Panels/ICSID Procedural Rules

A. Trade

The DSU rules on the organization of panel proceedings (Article 12 DSU) and on the basic applicable principles to ensure due process are rather scant as to how panels should proceed in deciding disputes in accordance with due process. As discussed in Chapter III, the basic provisions in this respect are found in Article 11 DSU ("Function of Panels") according to which, in the typical non-legalistic terminology of the DSU, a panel "should make an objective assessment of the matter before it, including an objective assessment of the facts of the case and the applicability and conformity with the relevant covered agreements". Thanks to the jurisprudence of the AB, this generic provision has been given substance as the basis on which panels conduct proceedings in accordance with due process principles.[4]

One of the first tasks of a panel is to draw up, in consultation with the disputing parties, its "working procedures" and a timetable, based on the model of Appendix 3 of the DSU.[5] The practice of panel proceedings under the WTO has further developed this template with appropriate adaptation in individual cases.[6] Additional matters addressed in the working procedures of individual cases, which are not covered by the template of Appendix 3, typically include preliminary ruling requests (such as when a respondent challenges a claim because it was allegedly not included in the consultations request), consultations with experts (if any), the redaction of business or confidential information in the public report, and the panel's preliminary agreement with the parties on the length of their briefs and their executive summaries (which the panels incorporate into their report).

The procedure is both written and oral, starting with a submission (brief) by the "complaining party" (claimant), followed by that of the "party complained against"

3 See D. Costelloe, "Judgments and the Termination of Proceedings" *Research Handbook* 475.

4 See *Van den Bossche*, 290.

5 See Article 12 DSU.

6 The *WTO Handbook* includes examples of working procedures which have been adopted in different cases, by original and compliance panels.

(respondent), and thereafter by a second round of written exchanges.[7] The briefs are typically lengthy and are usually accompanied by a high number of factual and legal exhibits, which almost invariably include evidence of the respondent's challenged measures and how they have been applied. As a consequence, the procedure is tilted in favour of written submissions. Moreover, there are no hearings in the usual sense; instead, the panels hold "meetings" with the parties, which are preceded by an exchange of briefs. There are typically two such "substantive meetings", where the parties respond to the detailed, usually numerous questions the panel has drafted and transmitted to them in advance, concerning the factual and legal aspects of the case. At these meetings, the parties answer or present and summarize their previously filed written responses.

B. *Investment*

The few provisions of the ICSID Convention devoted to procedure (Section 3, "Powers and Functions of the Tribunal", Articles 41–47) are supplemented by the ICSID Arbitration Rules, adopted by the Administrative Council under Article 6.1(c) ICSID. By successive amendments of the whole set of arbitration rules, they have become an increasingly detailed body of procedural prescriptions, containing, after the 2022 updating, no fewer than 86 provisions.[8] The arbitration rules of the various international arbitration institutions, mostly dealing with commercial cases but also open to investment disputes, perform the same functions.[9]

Similar to the DSU, where the working procedures adopted in each case follow a standard model, one of the first tasks of an ICSID tribunal is to determine the most important procedural matters, drawing up a sort of "road map" for the proceedings together with a procedural calendar (which may be, and are in fact often revised as proceedings unfold) in conformity with the guiding principle of "efficient management of arbitration".[10] The tribunal determines these matters in a

7 See Article 12 DSU "Panel Procedures". Proceedings could be held in any of the WTO official languages (English, French, Spanish) but in practice most proceedings are conducted in English. Since the English, French and Spanish texts of the WTO Agreements are equally authentic, as stated in the last clause of the Final Act of the Uruguay Round (Marrakesh 15 April 1994), irrespective of the fact that negotiations and drafting were essentially in English, all texts must be taken into account for interpreting their provisions. In case of difference of meaning " the meaning that best reconciles the texts, having regard to the object and purpose of the treaty, shall be adopted" (Article 33.4 VCLT), see B.Condon "Lost in Translation: Plurilingual Interpretation of WTO Law" 1 JIDS (2010) 191.

8 The ICSID Convention is effectively unchangeable because amendments require ratification by all its Members (Article 66.1). As a result, amending its AR has become an important tool for updating the rule book since decisions of the Administrative Council, where all parties are represented and by which AR can be amended (Article 6(c) ICSID) require only a majority of the votes cast, provided a quorum of a majority of its members convenes (Article 7).

9 Some institutions, notably the SCC and SIAC, have adopted special specific rules applicable when a party is a state or state entity; see Chapter II, n 92.

10 This is done at ICSID with Procedural Order nr. 1, which is drafted by the tribunal with the parties, mostly via a video-hearing, following a standard template. The equivalent at the ICC is the Terms of Reference (Article 33 of the Rules), which are to be drawn up within 30 days from the transmission

procedural order or decision as soon as it is duly constituted and after hearing from the parties (normally in agreement with them), in a "first session" (which tends to be held remotely).

Procedural decisions are, as a rule, made in agreement with the parties, which have a substantial role in the actual conduct of proceedings.[11] Matters typically covered in the first order are the confirmation by the parties that the tribunal is regularly constituted, the obligation of the parties to make in equal shares advances for costs to ICSID (as the Secretariat determines and requests periodically), the arbitrators' fees (those uniformly fixed by ICSID for all tribunals on an hourly basis), the power of the tribunal to issue procedural rulings and fix time limits, the secretary of the tribunal (a dedicated official of the ICSID secretariat), the place of the hearings (while all proceedings are nominally seated at the offices of ICSID in Washington, DC, US[12]), the representation of the parties (that is the lawyers appointed by them before the tribunal), the procedural language(s),[13] the number and sequence of pleadings, and the production of documents, including witness statements and expert reports. Other matters to be agreed and that are the subject of a procedural decision of a tribunal include the organization of the hearings, post-hearing briefs, the treatment of confidential information, and the publication of orders, decisions, and the award.[14]

Arbitration proceedings are often complicated and made lengthier than anticipated by incidental requests made by the parties that may require separate proceedings for their resolution. ICSID admits preliminary objections to the jurisdiction of the Centre or to that of the tribunal on various grounds, as mentioned in Chapter III. Objections to jurisdiction may be joined to the merits or decided preliminarily by the tribunal.[15] The second option entails the bifurcation of the proceedings and the suspension of the examination of the merits and is preferred when it is likely that the case may be resolved, in whole or in part, through a finding that

of the file to the arbitrators, and which include a summary of the parties' claims, the relief sought, and the issues to be decided. See the ICC, *Effective Management of Arbitration: A Guide for In-House Counsel and Other Party Representatives* (2017), available at https://iccwbo.org

11 This is reflected in the provision (ICSID AR 31) on "case management conferences" (a requirement also introduced in the most recent regulations of commercial arbitral institutions), to be held by the tribunal with the parties with a view "to concluding expeditious and cost-effective" proceedings.

12 The seat of the arbitration (chosen by the parties or determined by the tribunal or the institution) may be different from the place where the actual hearings take place. The location of the seat is crucial for private (commercial) arbitration since it determines the domestic procedural law subsidiarily applicable to the proceedings and the domestic legal system competent for challenges against the award. See Article 18 ICC Rules and Article I.1; Article V.1(d) New York Convention; for more detail, see Chapter VI.B.1.2.

13 The language of proceedings may be fixed in advance or decided by the parties in agreement with the tribunal. Arbitration under BITs drafted in more than one language are often conducted in both languages, with or without translation and interpretation; see ICSID AR 7.

14 See Rule 29.4.

15 Under USMCA Chapter 14, Article D.7.4 on Mexico–US investment disputes, objections to jurisdiction must be decided as a preliminary question.

the tribunal lacks jurisdiction.[16] A summary preliminary proceeding is provided for by Arbitration Rule 41.5 to deal with an objection by the respondent that "a claim is manifestly without legal merits", either as to jurisdiction or on the merits. This proceeding, introduced in the arbitration rules in 2006, is aimed at expediting such cases and avoiding for respondent states the nuisance of being dragged into cases that appear *prima facie* to be frivolous, unmeritorious, or abusive.[17] The 2022 Arbitration Rules provide moreover for an "expedited procedure", meant for dealing with smaller or simpler disputes, where this is agreed to by the parties, with the possibility of having a sole arbitrator and with shorter time limits.[18] On the other hand, the complexity and length of proceedings may be increased by requests for provisional measures "for the preservation of the rights of a party" while proceedings are ongoing. This is an important instrument in order to maintain or restore the status quo, prevent action that is likely to cause current or imminent harm to the party requesting the provisional measure or aggravate the dispute while the case is pending.[19]

Usually, after an exchange of several briefs with documents and experts' opinions (commonly on quantum), there is typically just one substantive hearing on the merits, often extending over several days, once all briefs have been exchanged and the evidence has been submitted.[20] Subsequently, post-hearing briefs summarizing each party's arguments are common. This explains why the record of a case often exceeds 1,000 pages.

16 See AR 42–45 on the procedure applicable to preliminary requests for bifurcation of proceedings.

17 See *ICSID Commentary*, I, Article 41, 128–150; C. Brown, S. Puig, "The Power of ICSID Tribunals to Dismiss Proceedings Summarily" 10 LPICT (2011) 227. CETA provides for preliminary decisions on claims that are "manifestly without legal merit" (Article 8.32) and of those "unfounded as a matter of law" (Article 8.33).

18 AR 75–86. This 2022 addition to the AR is in line with the similar recent practice of arbitral institutions such as the ICC (Article 30 of the 2021 Rules). It is meant to facilitate the arbitration of small cases (where up to USD 3/5 million are in dispute) and to reduce costs by having them decided by a sole arbitrator.

19 Article 47 ICSID and Rule 47, E. Gaillard, *Interim and Emergency Measures of Protection* (Kluwer 2017); F. Palombino, G. Zarra, R. Virzo (eds) *Provisional Measures issued by International Courts and Tribunals* (Asser Press 2021). Despite Article 47 ICSID stating that tribunals may "recommend" provisional measures, "tribunals have developed a doctrine under which provisional measures have binding effects" (following the practice of the ICJ under Article 41 of the Statute), *ICSID Commentary*, II, Article 47, 21. For data on the practice, see BIICL and White & Case, *Empirical Study: Provisional Measures in Investor–State Arbitration* (2023), available athttps://www.whitecase.com/insight-our-thinking/empirical-study-provisional-measures-investor-state-arbitration-2023 accessed 22 July 2024.

20 ICSID AR 32. Tribunals' orders on procedure often refer as a guideline, in respect to the submission and evaluation of evidence, to the *IBA Rules on Taking Evidence in International Arbitration* (3rd revised ed. 2020), available at https://www.ibanet.org

2. *The Consolidation of Proceedings*

A. *Trade*

Both systems provide mechanisms to consolidate or coordinate separate proceedings against the same respondent concerning the same or related measures. They are provided for reasons of judicial economy, to avoid the duplication of costs, and to prevent contradictory or conflicting decisions. At the same time, consolidation should not make proceedings more cumbersome. The premises and modalities for activating this process are, however, different in trade and investment disputes.

At the WTO, trade measures of a Member often affect several other Members, such as when an import restriction that applies across the board injures the exports of various countries to that market. Historically, this has led to more than one Member initiating proceedings against the Member that enacted such a measure, claiming a breach of a WTO obligation.[21] Compared to the option of participating as a third party in a dispute initiated by another Member, acting as a complainant allows a member to fully articulate its grievances and be in control of proceedings. Article 9 DSU regulates this situation of "multiple complainants" by providing for the establishment of a single panel for judicial economy and the avoidance of possibly conflicting decisions "whenever feasible". This more efficient solution is not always possible, such as when proceedings are initiated on different dates. In such a case, a different format is offered by Article 9.2 with distinct panels established for each complainant. These panels should, however, be composed of the same persons and the proceedings should be harmonized, especially regarding the timetables. In both cases, an additional complexity may arise from the fact that different claims of WTO-inconsistency may be made by different complainants, leading to separate reports with partially different content concerning the same measure of a given respondent.[22]

B. *Investment*

Parallel proceedings pitching different investors against the same home states in proceedings involving the same subject matter (challenges against the same measures), sometimes brought in substance by the same investor, even if the claimants are formally different, are a problem in the uncoordinated ISDS system (where estoppel based on *lis pendens* is difficult to conceive). They can lead to conflicting decisions, increased costs, and "double jeopardy" for a host state, while an investor may thereby have "two bites at the same cake".[23]

21 See *WTO Handbook*, 61.

22 This situation explains the difference in numbers between the panel reports and the proceedings in case statistics.

23 See the well-known cases of the two PCA–UNCITRAL arbitrations against the Czech Republic, challenging the same measure by substantially the same investor: the first by R. Lauder under the US–Czech Republic BIT (2001) was lost by the investor; the second case by CME, a Dutch company controlled by Mr. Lauder, under the Netherlands–Czech Republic BIT (2003), was won by the

The consolidation of separate arbitration proceedings is a device to resolve this conundrum, at least in part, because the agreement of both parties may be necessary. Consolidation leading to a single award by one tribunal was introduced for the first time in investment arbitration under NAFTA in order to respond to the increased costs and burden, especially for a respondent NAFTA Member when faced with a multiplicity of claims in different proceedings started by different investors in relation to the same or related measures affecting them. NAFTA, followed by USMCA, has a unique mechanism for consolidation. In case of a consolidation request by either party where "the claims have a question of law or fact in common and arise out of the same events or circumstances", a new tribunal replaces the existing tribunals and decides whether to order consolidation. If the new tribunal grants consolidation "in the interest of fair and efficient resolution of the claims", the new tribunal replaces the original ones.[24]

At ICSID, "consolidation" and "coordination" of pending arbitrations have been introduced with the 2022 Arbitration Rules. In the case of consolidation, "all aspects" of the arbitrations concerned are joined (leading to a single award), while in the case of coordination, only specific procedural aspects are aligned. Both procedures require a request from the parties to ICSID and hence their agreement once proceedings have been instituted. The Secretariat proposes the appropriate terms thereafter, but, otherwise than under NAFTA and USMCA, the existing tribunals are not replaced by a single, different tribunal.[25]

3. *Parties' Representation*

A. *Trade*

In international judicial proceedings, a traditional distinction is made between the "agents" of governments, who legally represent them before the court, and counsel who plead on behalf of the parties.[26] No such distinction exists at the WTO and in ISDS. While in ISDS, duly empowered lawyers represent the parties in all respects, whether they are investors or states, the GATT tradition was that governments were represented by their officials.

Shortly after governments began employing specialized lawyers for WTO disputes, due to their complexity and the lack of internal resources, especially among small states, the objection was raised that representing states in WTO proceedings

investor with a sizeable award of damages. In general, see K. Hober, *Res Judicata and Lis Pendens in International Arbitration*, 366 RC (2014) 109; G. Zarra, *Parallel Proceedings in Investment Arbitration* (Giappichelli–Eleven 2017).

24 See Article 1126 NAFTA, Article 14.D.12 USMCA. ICSID chooses all the arbitrators of the consolidation tribunal which must include as side-arbitrators a national of the home and the host state nominated by them in the ICSID roster.

25 See AR 46.

26 See Article 42 ICJ Statute, which distinguishes agents who represent the parties from counsels (advocates) who may assist them and plead on their behalf before the ICJ.

was limited to governmental officials.[27] This position was, however, rejected by the AB, which ruled that under customary law, and given the absence of any specific WTO provision to the contrary, nothing prevents a WTO Member from including external legal counsel in its delegation in dispute settlement proceedings.[28] On the contrary, recourse to private counsel enables governments, especially those of developing countries which may lack the necessary human resources within their ministries, to fully participate in dispute settlement proceedings. Aside from participating in meetings with panels, lawyers and law firms are regularly entrusted with assisting delegations in preparing a government's position in respect of a case and with drafting written submissions. As with hearings, their role here is less overt and somewhat hidden, in sharp contrast with the explicit and prominent role that law firms and individual lawyers assume in ISDS and in international commercial arbitration.[29] The modalities of proceedings, where there is no witness testimony with examination and cross-examination as is the case of adversarial judicial and arbitral hearings, makes the role of intervening lawyers less prominent although not less important.[30]

WTO Members may also have recourse to legal assistance in disputes (as in other trade matters) from the Advisory Centre on WTO Law (ACWL), an independent inter-governmental organization established for that purpose in 2001. Services to developing countries (especially to least developed countries) are provided at much lower rates than those normally charged by private law firms as a means of enabling them to fully participate in the WTO's DSS, both as claimants and as respondents.[31]

B. *Investment*

In commercial and international arbitration, the practice is that parties are represented by counsel, that is private lawyers of their choice.[32] while representation by "agents" and reliance on counsel from internal legal offices is common in disputes

27 Only a handful of WTO Members have adequate internal legal departments (such as the EU Legal Service and the USTR) to enable them to represent themselves without external counsel.

28 AB *EC–Bananas III* (DS 27-1997), 10, reversing the contrary holding of the panel, 7.10–7.12.

29 Panels and AB reports do not indicate the names of those appearing before them for the parties, contrary to the practice of international courts and investment awards.

30 See G. Sacerdoti, "The Role of Lawyers in the WTO Dispute Settlement System" in *Key Issues*, 125. On the origin of the ever-increasing role of private lawyers in international proceedings see C. Romano, "The Americanization of International Litigation" 19 Ohio State J of Dispute Resolution (2003) 89.

31 For more detail, see www.acwl.ch

32 See IBA, *Guidelines on Party Representation in International Arbitration* (2013), available at https://www.ibanet.org, which makes no distinction between representatives that are employees of a party, whether or not they have been admitted to a domestic bar, and outside counsel both being permitted to represent a party.

between states.[33] The need for specialized advice on the highly complex matters usually raised in ISDS and the legal resources required makes reliance on specialized lawyers common also for respondent states in investment disputes. Lawyers are so crucial that the major international law firms to which parties often turn are credited with having a decisive say in some of the most important choices made by the parties, such as the selection of the forum (when several are available under the applicable IIA) and of the arbitrators, the decision to settle a case, or to challenge an award. Specialized lawyers have displaced academics in this respect, while academics still compete with lawyers for appointments as arbitrators. Additionally, in view of the role of pleadings at the hearings, advocacy, that is the ability of a lawyer to persuasively convince a tribunal on the merits of the client's case, is of great importance in investment treaty arbitration. A persistent issue is, however, that of the ethical standards of counsel and conflicts of interest since there is no international bar to which lawyers appearing before international courts and tribunals (not just investment tribunals) would belong and to whose ethical rules they would all uniformly be subject. The different rules of their home countries' bars may be inapplicable, contradictory, or insufficient in this respect. The Code of Conduct for investment arbitrators, drafted by UNCITRAL WG III in 2023 in cooperation with the ICSID Secretariat, is meant precisely to introduce high uniform standards.[34]

With a view to easing the burden on developing countries, especially least-developed countries, in obtaining quality legal assistance when faced with investment cases, a project to establish an Advisory Centre on International Investment Dispute Resolution, patterned after the one on trade law (the ACWL), has been pursued at UNCITRAL WG III, has been finalized in spring 2024 and has been approved "in principle" by the UNCTAD Commission in its July 2024 session.[35] The draft provides for the establishment of the Advisory Centre as an independent body, preferably within an existing UN institution, to provide assistance to developing countries not just in disputes but possibly also with an advisory function, at concessional financial terms. The Centre's lawyers, besides advising a party, could also represent it in proceedings, including hearings, as is the case for the ACWL.[36] The availability of competent and independent legal assistance from the Advisory Centre should rebalance any existing inequality, also due to financial constraints,

33 See AR 2.2. Since the names of counsel representing parties in proceedings are listed in awards, it is possible to verify that several countries are represented by their own internal legal services.

34 The *IBA Guidelines on Party Representation in International Arbitration* (2013) are meant to fill this vacuum on a voluntary basis in relation to any person appearing for a party as its representative, be it an employee of such a party or another person, whether admitted to a domestic bar or not. For details on the UNCITRAL Code of Conduct, see Chapter VII.B.5.2.2(b).

35 See A/CN.9/WG.III/WP.238 – Possible Reform of Investor–State Dispute Settlement (ISDS): Draft Statute of an Advisory Centre on International Investment Dispute Resolution (2024) adopted in principle by the UNCITRAL Commission in July 2024, A/79/17, para.167; for more details, see Chapter VIII.B.5.2.2(c).

36 As to the ACWL, see www.acwl.ch.

in the respective abilities of private investors as claimants and developing states as respondents to obtain an effective legal defence.[37]

4. *Rules of Evidence, Witnesses, Experts*

A. *Trade*

The apportionment of the burden of proof between the parties to a dispute is a fundamental issue to ensure the fairness of adversarial proceedings. The principle is that it is for each party to give evidence of the facts it invokes to substantiate its claim or defence and to convince the adjudicator of its legal arguments. In this respect, both WTO and ISDS proceedings are akin to civil or commercial domestic disputes, where the judge will decide upon being convinced by the preponderance of the evidence in favour of one of the parties.[38] In criminal trials, instead, it is for the prosecutor (representing domestically the state and at international criminal courts the institution involved) to indict an accused and gather full evidence to prove guilt.[39]

The text of the DSU is wanting also in this respect, since it does not contain any rule on the burden or standard of proof. The practice of dispute settlement has brought clarity in this respect thanks to multiple contributions of the AB which has stressed, since its first decisions, that mere assertion of a claim does not amount to proof. In accordance with accepted practice of international tribunals,

> the party who asserts a fact, whether the claimant or the respondent, is responsible for providing the proof thereof … If that party adduces evidence sufficient to raise a presumption that what is claimed is true, the burden then shifts to the other party, who will fail unless it adduces sufficient evidence to rebut the presumption.[40]

The task of a panel is to balance all of the evidence that is on the record. In order for a claimant bearing the burden of proof to prevail, it must convince the panel of the validity of its claim; otherwise, its claim of breach will be factually rejected.[41]

It is also for the party claiming that another party's laws are inconsistent with relevant WTO obligations to support its claim with relevant evidence, such as the text of municipal laws and the pronouncements of domestic courts.[42] In contrast, with respect to applicable WTO law, the principle *iura novit curia* applies, as is

37 For more detail, see Chapter VIII. B.5.2.2 (c).

38 See A. Mitchell, "Due Process in WTO Disputes" in *Key Issues* 144; J. Devaney, "Evidence, Fact-finding and Experts" *Research Handbook* 1395.

39 The standard of proof for a conviction is also higher in criminal proceedings, usually set at the level of "beyond a reasonable doubt" with some variations such as "intime conviction" in France. See G. Cook, "Defining the Standard of Proof in WTO Dispute Settlement Proceedings: Jurists' Prudence and Jurisprudence" 1 J. Int. Trade and Arbitration L (2012) 50.

40 AB *US–Wool Shirts and Blouses* (DS 33-1997), 14.

41 Panel *US–Section 301 Trade Act* (DS 152-2000), 7.14.

42 AB *US–Carbon Steel* (DS 213-2002), 157.

generally the case before international courts. A panel will be aided by the arguments of the parties, but it is for an adjudicator - panels and the AB - to determine the correct interpretation of the applicable provisions in accordance with the customary rules of treaty interpretation as prescribed by Article 3.2 DSU.[43]

Since breaches of WTO obligations typically involve general or specific state measures, such as laws or their application in specific instances, customs duties above negotiated levels, or the imposition of trade remedies in breach of WTO requirements, panel proceedings involve "almost exclusively documentary evidence".[44] As to the determination of facts and matters that require technical or scientific expertise, typically in respect of sanitary and technical standards under the SPS or TBT agreements, Article 13 DSU ("Right to seek information") deals with the fundamental issue of gathering and evaluating evidence. This provision allows a panel, very broadly, and in a discretionary manner, "to seek information and technical advice from any individual or body which it deems appropriate" (including specialized international organizations), to "consult experts to obtain their opinion on certain aspects of the matter", or to request an advisory report from an "expert review group".[45] This "ex officio' experts" appointment model is different from the one followed in the application of adversarial principles before international courts and arbitral tribunals. It is rather for the parties there to submit evidence, including experts' opinions, to them, or to propose court-appointed experts. According to the practice that has developed at the WTO, parties do have a role in the selection of experts by the panel, but the process is fully in the hands of the latter.[46] This has given rise to appeals on the correctness of the process (independence and impartiality of the experts selected) and the weight given by the panel to their conclusions (especially when they are in conflict).[47]

B. *Investment*

The fundamental principle that each party has the burden to submit evidence in support of its case and to convince, in fact and law, the tribunal to rule in its favour is fully applicable in arbitration, including investment arbitration. ICSID Rules

43 AB *EC–Tariff Preferences* (DS 242-2004), 105. As to the principle in general, see L. Fumagalli, *Iura Novit Curia, MPEPIL* (2018).

44 *WTO Handbook*, 95, although parties do submit individual statements and affidavits as evidence. See also K. Connolly, M. Dossche, "Testing Witnesses in International Dispute Settlement. WTO versus other International Courts and Tribunals" in E. De Brabandere (ed) *International Procedure in Interstate Litigation and Arbitration* (CUP 2021) 263.

45 Article 11.2 SPS provides more specifically that "in a dispute under this Agreement involving scientific or technical issues, a panel *should* seek advice from experts chosen by the panel in consultation with the parties to the dispute" (italics added).

46 See the example of panel working procedures, with expert consultation, *WTO Handbook* 250; M. Cossy, "Panel's Consultations with Scientific Experts" in *Key Issues* 204.

47 See *Van den Bossche*, 245; L. Gruszczynski, "The Role of Experts in Environmental and Health-related Trade Disputes in the WTO" in M. Ambrus and others (eds) *The Role of "Experts" in International and European Decision-Making Processes* (CUP 2014) 216.

dedicate specific provisions to the evidentiary phase of the proceedings: each party has the burden of proving the facts relied on to support its claim or defence, while it is for the tribunal to determine the admissibility and probative value of the evidence adduced.[48]

The Rules also take into account the widespread practice, patterned after common law judicial procedure (discovery), that parties can ask the other party for the production of documents, in a process that often gives rise to reciprocal objections (relevance of documents, the scope of the discovery, etc.) that are for the tribunal to decide upon. Another typical feature of arbitral procedure is that witnesses are examined and cross-examined at hearings based on written testimony drafted by the witness with the assistance of the parties' lawyers, or rather vice versa (another source of discussions), in advance of the hearing.[49] Furthermore, expert reports (typically on the quantum of damages), as well as legal opinions mostly on the content of relevant domestic law, are submitted by the parties, with the experts being subject, possibly together, to examination and cross-examination and questioning by the tribunal at the hearing. The civil law practice, reflected in the DSU, of the tribunal appointing experts and determining the questions for them, is permitted but not followed in practice.[50]

It thus appears that the adversarial model, predominantly that patterened after the common law tradition, is generally applied in investment arbitration practice, including in matters of evidence.[51]

48 AR 36. However, according to para. 4, "The Tribunal may call upon a party to produce documents or other evidence if it deems it necessary at any stage of the proceeding".

49 This practice, which in many civil law jurisdictions would render the testimony inadmissible, is recognized as proper by the *IBA Rules on The Taking of Evidence,* 4.1.3. In accordance with ICSID AR 9.1, it is in any case for the tribunal to determine the admissibility, relevance, materiality, and weight of any evidence.

50 ICSID AR 39 allows tribunals to appoint experts "unless the parties agree otherwise". This is an example of the freedom that the parties have to frame, by agreement, the actual procedure of any case. See M. Sassoon, "Is there a Usable 'Civil Law Approach' to Document Production in International Arbitration?" 37 DCI (2023) 845.

51 Tribunals often refer to the *IBA Rules on The Taking of Evidence in International Arbitration* (3rd revised ed. 2020) as a guideline with respect to the submission and evaluation of evidence. These rules are a soft law instrument defined as combining "both civil and common law practices for the taking of evidence ... Their aim is to provide an efficient evidence-gathering process by supplementing laws, as well as institutional and ad hoc rules applicable in international arbitration, which are normally not specific enough to capture the breadth of issues that may arise during the evidence-gathering process", see www.ibanet.org. As an alternative to the IBA Rules, in 2018 civil lawyers, mostly from Central and Eastern Europe, approved the "Prague Rules" on the taking of evidence in international arbitration (see www.praguerules.com) based on an "inquisitorial" approach typical of the civil law tradition, generally giving the tribunal a more proactive role in the evidential phase of proceedings.

5. *Counterclaims*

A. Trade

The concept of "counterclaims", which are claims brought by a respondent against a complainant in the same case and arising from the same or a related matter, does not apply in WTO proceedings. This is because, in a dispute under the DSU, a complainant alleges a breach of a treaty obligation by a respondent and seeks the withdrawal of the challenged measure. In contrast, counterclaims by respondents in commercial or investment disputes are premised on the claimant being (also or solely) in breach of the same or a closely connected obligation. A counterclaim by a respondent aims at offsetting the claimant's request for monetary damages or to have the claimant sentenced to pay higher damages to the respondent.

At the WTO, a different scenario can be envisaged which, however, presents some similarities to that of a counterclaim. A respondent may be tempted to react to the filing of a case by another Member challenging a measure it has adopted as WTO-inconsistent, by challenging, in turn, a different measure of the claimant by introducing a separate dispute against the latter. The DSU intends to discourage such conduct by stating in Article 3.10 DSU that "It is also understood that complaint and counter-complaints in regard to distinct matters should not be linked". A similar situation has occurred when a Member hit by another Member's restriction against its exports responds not only by filing a complaint in accordance with the DSU, but also by introducing some restriction of its own against the other Member's exports to its territory, without awaiting the outcome of the dispute. This was the case in the US–China "Trade War" in 2018 (and again starting with Donald Trump's reelecton in 2025), when the US increased customs duties on China's exports to the US worth USD 300 billion and China reacted by imposing additional customs duties on US exports to China. Separate panels were established to evaluate these measures, with both concluding that these measures were inconsistent with the GATT.[52]

B. Investment

The issue of counterclaims in investment arbitration has been controversial at ICSID since only the investor in practice initiates proceedings. Respondent host states often complain that the conduct by the claimant investor has not been in conformity with the treaty requirements or that the investor in turn has breached some domestic regulation in making its investment. Counterclaims thus appear to be an instrument to rebalance the situation and ensure equality of the parties' substantive positions. However, counterclaims in ICSID proceedings are constrained by the requirement that they be "within the scope of consent of the parties and …

52 For more details on the matter and the cases filed by China (DS 513) and the US (DS 558), see Chapter VIII n 22. Both parties appealed "into the void" the panel reports which had declared their measures WTO-inconsistent, and the respective measures have been left in place. See also A. Ligustro and M. Buccarella, "The WTO Condemns Trump's Tariffs on Steel and Aluminium, but Biden Condemns the WTO" 58 JWT (2024) 131.

otherwise within the jurisdiction of the Centre".[53] Counterclaims based, as it often occurs, on alleged wrongdoings of the claimant in the carrying out of its investment do not usually present the close connection required by the provision and hence are most of the time found inadmissible or out of the jurisdiction of the tribunal.[54]

6. *Third Parties*

A. *Trade*

Although disputes at the WTO pit one or more claimants against a respondent, giving rise to a bilateral dispute, a peculiar feature of the DSS is that any WTO Member may become a participant in a dispute at the panel stage by requesting to intervene as a third party.[55] In order to do so, a Member has to notify the DSB that it has a "substantial interest" in a dispute, without the disputing parties having a right to object.[56] The interest can be merely "systemic". This is an important feature, since it allows any WTO Member which, although not interested in the outcome of the dispute, may have an interest in the interpretation of the WTO provision under consideration, to make its position known by filing an individual submission. The procedural rights of third parties are more limited than those enjoyed by the disputing parties since their intervention is primarily geared towards influencing the interpretation of the legal issues before the panel rather than aiming at challenging the respondent's measure at issue. Third parties do not participate in the meetings of the disputing parties with the panel but are heard in a separate session which is devoted to the legal rather than the factual aspects of the dispute.

The right of third states to intervene in proceedings is not unknown before international courts but tends to be more limited, with the exception of those operating under regional treaties with a limited number of parties.[57] The right to intervene reflects the common interest of all WTO Members in the functioning of the DSS, especially in respect of the development of its case law, which may acquire de

53 Article 46 ICSID.

54 See A. Hoffmann, "Counterclaims" in M. Kinnear and others (ed) *Building International Investment Law: the First 50 Years of the ICSID Convention* (Kluwer 2015) 505; T. Ishikawa, "A New Approach in Determining Jurisdiction over Counterclaims in ICSID Arbitration" 32 ICSID Rev (2017) 721; E. Guntrip *Countercliams in Investment Arbitration: Holding Foreign Investors Accountable for Violations of International Law* (Brill 2024)."

55 Article 10 DSU. For data on the participation of WTO Members as third parties, see *Mavroidis* 186.

56 Alternatively, to intervene as a third party already at the consultations stage, another WTO Member must claim to have a "substantial trade interest", but the respondent can object to this (Article 4.11 DSU), in *WTO Handbook* 55, see Chapter III.A.1.4.

57 This is the case of proceedings at the CJEU and the ECtHR where all Member States may intervene in all cases. At the ICJ (Article 62 Statute), intervention in proceedings is limited to states that can show "an interest of a legal nature which may be affected by the decision of the case". Under Article 63, however, when "the construction of convention to which states other than those concerned in the case is in question", these other states have a right to intervene. If they do so, "the construction given by the judgment will be equally binding" upon them. The same rules are applicable in disputes before the Tribunal of the Law of the Sea (Articles 31 and 32 of its statute, Annex VI to UNCLOS).

facto precedential value. Major economic actors among the WTO Members tend to intervene as third parties in most cases since their potential interests concerning the interpretation and application of WTO provisions are broad.[58] In RTAs with more than two parties, a party that is not a disputing party may fully participate in the proceedings in view of the interest of all of the parties (as is the case at the WTO) to contribute to the interpretation of the RTA.[59]

B. *Investment*

Under a BIT the home state of a claiming investor may have a systemic interest in participating in a dispute as a "non-disputing party" because of its institutional role as a contracting party and the potential fallout from the interpretation of the treaty that the tribunal will lay down. In RTIAs, which have more than two parties, non-disputing parties include parties other than the home country of the claimant. These treaties (such as USMCA and CPTPP) allow non-disputing parties to the treaty to intervene in all proceedings.[60] Arbitration rules admit such an intervention irrespective of the text of the relevant IIA.[61] Thus, under ICSID AR 68, a tribunal shall permit such a third party to file a submission on the interpretation of the treaty at issue and may invite such a submission after having consulted the parties, provided this does not disrupt the course of proceedings or unfairly burden either party.

7. Amici Curiae

A. *Trade*

The DSU is silent on whether panels and the AB may accept and consider unsolicited submissions from non-WTO Members, such as NGOs and trade associations, as *Amicus/Amici Curiae* (AC), that is "friend(s) of the court". The purpose of these submissions is to make known to the adjudicators the views of stakeholders, which the parties may not put forward, thus assisting them in their decision by providing further information and perspectives. The inter-governmental, confidential mechanism of the WTO DSS does not appear on paper to be open to such a possibility, which is, in fact not mentioned by the DSU. On the other hand, the widespread recognition that the WTO's purpose extends beyond merely regulating trade between

58 A typical instance is that of the US which, in Panel *Russia–Traffic in Transit* (DS 511-2019) 7.52, took the same position as Russia as a third party in favour of the self-judging nature of the Security Exception of Article XXI GATT (a position which the US also later took as respondent in cases brought against measures the US had sought to justify under Article XXI; see Chapter VIII.A.1.2).

59 Article 28.14 CPTPP on Third Party Participation typically provides: "A Party that is not a disputing Party and that considers it has an interest in the matter before the panel shall, on delivery of a written notice to the disputing Parties, be entitled to attend all hearings, make written submissions, present views orally to the panel, and receive written submissions of the disputing Parties".

60 See USMCA Article 14.D.7.42 ("The non-disputing Annex Party may make oral and written submissions to the tribunal regarding the interpretation of this Agreement") and CPTPP Article 9.23.2.

61 See UNCITRAL Transparency Rules (2014), Article 5; see also ICSID AR 68.

Members and settling their bilateral disputes, as stated in the preamble of the WTO Agreement, and that its operation concerns and may affect a broad range of stakeholders and non-trade interests and values, militates in favour of such an opening. In any case, the marginal position of AC in international proceedings, even where admitted, which is limited to the filing of a brief, ensures that their participation in no way encumbers the disposition of the case.

At the WTO, this issue has been contentious since it was first raised in *US–Shrimp*, where the claimants denied that the panel could accept unsolicited briefs from NGOs, while the US urged the panel to do so.[62] The panel rejected this request as being inadmissible under the DSU (except if such a brief is included by a party in its filing), but the AB on appeal held that a panel may admit AC submissions if it considers them to be relevant. In so opining, the AB relied on panels' authority under Article 13 DSU to seek information from any source, which allows them to accept even unsolicited information.[63] In *US–Lead and Bismuth II*, the Appellate Body found that the DSU contains no explicit prohibition on the acceptance of such briefs and that panels have broad authority to adopt their own procedural rules so long as they are consistent with the DSU and the covered agreements.[64] The AB has confirmed its position that AC briefs are admissible in subsequent cases involving the protection of health and natural resources, although it has never ultimately found it to be useful to rely on them in deciding a dispute before it.[65] A number of developing countries have, however, criticized the position of the AB on this issue, arguing that the admission of AC briefs is contrary to the state-to-state nature of the WTO DSS and might influence a panel or the AB in breach of their duty of impartiality.[66]

Recent RTAs explicitly allow the submission of AC briefs, without admitting AC to intervene further in the proceedings, such as participating in hearings (in contrast to third-party Members in some RTAs with more than two Members that are allowed to participate).[67]

62 See generally B. Stern, "The emergence of non-state actors in international commercial disputes through the WTO Appellate Body case-law" in *The WTO at Ten* 372. For data on AC filings, see *Mavroidis* 196.

63 AB *US–Shrimp* (DS 58-1998) 105–108.

64 AB *US–Lead and Bismuth II* (DS 138-2000) 39.

65 See *EC–Asbestos* (DS 135-2001), 52–55. In fact, the issues that are dealt with in AC briefs filed by NGOs tend to focus on the impact that the measures at issue may have on non-trade values (such as the environment), while the dispute concerns their conformity with specific WTO provisions.

66 A special meeting of the GC was convened to discuss the matter in relation to the *EC–Asbestos* case on the initiative of India and other developing countries concerned. See Minutes of the GC meeting of 22 November 2000, WT/GC/M/60. No shared conclusions were reached due to the divergent views of Members on the admissibility of AC submissions.

67 See Article 28.13 (e) CPTPP: "the panel shall consider requests from non-governmental entities located in the territory of a disputing Party to provide written views regarding the dispute that may assist the panel in evaluating the submissions and arguments of the disputing Parties". The AA between the EU and Ukraine (2014), Annex XXIV, Rules of procedure for dispute settlement, Articles 37–39, regulate the submission of AC briefs in trade disputes, facilitating them through the transparency of the proceedings. Unsolicited AC submissions can be received from natural and legal

B. Investment

As investment arbitration is patterned after the commercial model, initially ISDS procedural rules did not admit the intervention of third parties that wished to draw the attention of the tribunal to some collective interest that may be affected by the outcome of the dispute and that should, in their view, be considered in deciding the case.[68] This approach has, however, been modified by the progressive recognition that investment disputes are not limited to protecting the interests of investors but may affect the general interest in the respondent state as well as common goods (such as human rights, the environment, local indigenous communities), so that those representing such interests or groups should be allowed to participate in proceedings. It is by now recognized that opening proceedings to such non-disputing parties enhances the legitimacy of investment arbitration in the eyes of the public and the credibility of the system.[69]

Current arbitration rules leave this possibility for third persons to file submissions to the discretion of the tribunal, after having consulted with the parties, in light of relevant information supplied by the third party (the *Amicus*) in a specific application.[70] Thus, since their amendment in 2006, ICSID Arbitration Rules have granted tribunals the discretionary power to allow persons or entities that are not a party to the dispute, upon their request, to file a written submission subject to various conditions, including that: 1) the submission would address a matter within the scope of the dispute; 2) it would assist the tribunal "to determine a factual or legal issue related to the proceedings by bringing a perspective, particular knowledge or insight that is different from that of the parties"; and 3) the non-disputing party has a significant interest in the proceedings.[71]

persons established in the territories of the parties, must be concise, and must be "directly relevant to the factual and legal issues under consideration before the arbitration panel".

68 Amicus submissions have traditionally been admitted at the US Supreme Court and in a few international courts, but this is not the case in most civil law jurisdictions. See P. Sands, R. MacKenzie, "Amicus Curiae, International Courts and Tribunals" *MPEPIL* (2008).

69 NAFTA Free Commission Statement on Non-Disputing Party Participation, 7 October 2003, first recognized Amici submissions under the following terms which have been replicated in subsequent IIAs: "[T]he Tribunal will consider, among other things, the extent to which: (a) the non-disputing party submission would assist the Tribunal in the determination of a factual or legal issue related to the arbitration by bringing a perspective, particular knowledge or insight that is different from that of the disputing parties; (b) the non-disputing party submission would address matters within the scope of the dispute; (c) the non-disputing party has a significant interest in the arbitration; and (d) there is a public interest in the subject-matter of the arbitration".

70 See UNCITRAL Transparency Rules (2014), Article 4. The EU Commission has systematically asked and, in most cases obtained to be admitted to file an AC brief in intra-EU investment arbitration. The main purpose of the EU Commission intervention has been to support the respondent EU Member state in arguing that investment tribunals lack jurisdiction on such disputes under BITs and the ECT, because of the exclusive jurisdiction of domestic courts under the principle of primacy of EU law affirmed by the CJEU in *Achmea* and *Komstroy*; see Chapter III fn 71.

71 See currently ICSID Arbitration Rule 67 (2022). Moreover, according to para. 4, "The Tribunal shall ensure that non-disputing party participation does not disrupt the proceeding or unduly burden or unfairly prejudice either party".

8. Confidentiality, Transparency and Third-Party Funding

A. Trade

An overarching principle of the WTO DSS is that confidentiality is the rule from consultations to the end of panel and AB proceedings. The work of the panel, and in any case its deliberations, are confidential; panels meet in "closed session".[72] The confidentiality of proceedings, beyond the secrecy of deliberations (the latter being a general feature of the decision-making of adjudicatory bodies), is a typical feature of the practice of expert committees that the WTO "inherited" from the GATT. In contrast with most judicial proceedings, hearings (meetings of the panel with the parties) are also not public. However, subject to the consent of the disputing parties, more publicity has been injected into the process over the years. Thus, the AB has ruled that, with their consent, hearings may be viewed by the public via closed-circuit broadcast from within the WTO.[73] In any case, parties may publish their own submissions on their websites or otherwise.[74] Both possibilities have only been used by a limited number of WTO Members, in particular by those where publicity of domestic judicial and other proceedings is common and whose governments do not fear negative reactions from the public as a consequence of disclosing the positions they take and the arguments they make in international proceedings.

The major procedural and substantive steps are, in any case public and published on the WTO website. This is the case for the initiation of proceedings (consultations, the establishment of panels and their composition), the extension of the deadline to issue their reports, the text of panel and AB reports when issued, notices of appeal, DSB-related activities, as well as major steps in the implementation phase that follows.

B. Investment

In commercial arbitration, confidentiality is the rule and is often regarded as one of its key advantages. Confidentiality can make arbitration more attractive than litigation in court for settling business disputes, as it ensures that the the very existence and details of the dispute, including the parties, subject matter, and outcome remain private. In contrast, investment arbitration, especially treaty-based, involves public interests. This, in principle, justifies disclosing key information and documents to the public, allowing access to hearings and public knowledge and hence scrutiny of awards. Public hearings, moreover, contribute to the accountability of parties, counsel, and arbitrators, while the publication of awards helps increase the

72 See Article 4.6, 14.1, 17.10, 18.2 DSU.

73 In contrast, the EU-Ukraine AA provides that the hearings of the panel shall be open to the public (Annex XXIV, para. 26). On this development see L. Ehring, "Public Access to Dispute Settlement Hearings in the World Trade Organization" 11 JIEL (2008) 1021; see in general G. Kaufmann-Kohler, 'Transparency in Trade and Investment Disputes" *Encyclopaedia of International Economic Law* (2nd ed. Elgar 2024), Section 1.3.1.

74 Article 18.2 DSU.

consistency of case law as a source of information on previous interpretations and how frequently invoked provisions have been applied.[75]

In recommending the use of the "Rules on Transparency in Treaty-Based Investor–State Arbitration" adopted by UNCITRAL in 2013, the UNGA recognized "the need for provisions on transparency in the settlement of such treaty-based investor-State disputes to take account of the public interest involved in such arbitrations, … increase transparency and accountability and promote good governance".[76] Shortly thereafter, the Mauritius Convention on Transparency of 2015,[77] also drafted under the auspices of UNCITRAL, was meant to supplement existing investment treaties with respect to transparency-related obligations by reinforcing the commitment to apply the UNCITRAL Transparency Rules.

The principle of transparency, which has inspired these instruments, has not, however, been fully embraced in investment treaty and arbitration practice. Parties to disputes, including states, have often shown reluctance to make proceedings transparent. As of the end of 2023, the Mauritius Convention had been ratified by fewer than ten countries. An important development occurred in June 2024 when the EU signed the Mauritius Convention, thus paving the way to the EU Member States becoming individually a party to it.[78] Within the process of modifying and updating the ICSID Arbitration Rules of 2006 (which took six years and was concluded in 2022), the Secretariat proposed to make the publication of awards the default rule, but a sizeable number of Members objected. Rule 62 confirms Article 48(5) of the Convention, stating that awards may be published only with the consent of the parties (if requested by either of them, in a redacted form); otherwise, ICSID may only publish excerpts after consulting the parties.

A contentious issue that involves the transparency of proceedings but also the integrity of the arbitral process is that of *third-party funding*. Claimants can overcome a shortage of financial means, possibly due to the harm caused to them by the actions of host states against their investments that they challenge as unlawful in the arbitration, by arranging funding from third parties (most of the time financial entities professionally engaged in such activity). Thanks to this kind of arrangement, an investor secures the commitment of a funder to finance the costs of the proceedings against the assignment to the funder of a share of the proceeds

75 ICSID Arbitration Rule 65 admits "observation of the hearings by third persons unless either party objects", subject to appropriate procedures.

76 Preamble of the UNGA Resolution 68/109 of 16 December 2013.

77 UN Convention on Transparency in Treaty-Based Investor–State Arbitration adopted pursuant to UNGA Resolution 69/116 of 10 December 2014 and opened to signature in Mauritius on 17 March 2015, see D. Euler, M. Gehring, M. Scherer (eds) *Transparency in International Investment Arbitration* (CUP 2015).

78 See European Commission, "Council Approves EU Signature of Convention on transparency for dispute settlement" 25 June 2024, available at https://policy.trade.ec.europa.eu/news/council-approves-eu-signature-convention-transparency-dispute-settlement-2024-06-25_en accessed 22 July 2024. Signature by the EU followed on 2 July 2024.

expected from the arbitration. This scheme frees claimants from financial constraints that might otherwise deter them from initiating cases against host states, especially when a favourable outcome is doubtful. This is one of the reasons for which third-party funding is facing opposition, given its potential to increase the number of investment cases, some of which may be speculative. On the other hand, its proponents argue that third-party funding, where professional funders also assist their clients in arranging their legal defence and in conducting the case, advances the cause of justice. This is because professional funders typically do not finance overly speculative actions.

The middle ground which currently receives the most support in this respect is that of transparency. The reform of the ICSID Arbitration Rules in 2022 followed this path. Rule 14 requires that any party receiving third-party funding to finance its defence disclose the fact that it is backed by a funder along with the funder's identity. Additionally, the tribunal may ask for further information on the funding agreement and the identity of the funder. This requirement is not due to transparency concerns in the abstract but aims at identifying potential conflicts of interest involving the funder and providing a basis for ordering security for costs upon unpecuniary claimants, should they lose their case and be liable for legal costs of the respondent.[79]

9. *The Secretariat*

A. *Trade*

As mentioned in Chapter III regarding the composition of panels, the fundamental role of the WTO Secretariat in supporting panels and assisting in drafting their lengthy reports is recognized in Article 27 DSU.[80] The system could not work effectively without such support, given that panelists are appointed on an *ad hoc* basis for specific disputes, are part-time, and may have a limited knowledge of the subtleties of the WTO agreements and of precedents.[81] Repeat appointments, which would be a way for panelists to acquire more experience, are moreover rare. Notwithstanding these shortcomings, proposals to draw panelists from a

79 Reliance on third-party funding by a claimant may indicate that the claimant would have difficulties in paying an adverse decision on costs in case its action were to be rejected. This, in turn, may prompt a respondent to ask for security for costs under AR 53(1). For a similar disclosure obligation, see ICC Rules, Article 11.7. See generally ICC Dossier *Third Party Funding in International Arbitration* (2013); G. Lampo *Il finanziamento da parte di terzi nell'arbitrato commerciale e d'investimenti* (ESI 2024)

80 See Chapter III.A.3. Parties exchange their briefs and correspond through the Secretariat, Article 12.6 DSB.

81 Article 27 (Responsibilities of the Secretariat) entrusts it with "the responsibility of assisting panels, especially on the legal, historical and procedural aspects of the matters dealt with, and of providing secretarial and technical support".

semi-permanent group, thereby enhancing their experience and availability, have never met with the approval of WTO Members.[82]

The role of the WTO Secretariat is similar to those of permanent courts; it goes beyond administration and communications (typical of commercial arbitral institutions) extending to assistance in research and drafting.[83] The Secretariat also has another important role in the functioning of the DSS, namely that of assisting the DG in the selection of panelists under Article 4 DSU. However, this does not mean that the Secretariat "controls" the panelists as some academics have hinted at.[84] Rather, it reflects the set-up of the WTO DSS, where panels are "embedded" in the organization and the Secretariat under the DG has the overall responsibility of ensuring the proper functioning of the DSS.

B. *Invesment*

The support that secretariats of arbitral institutions give to tribunals established and operating under their rules varies, but in any case, is considerably more limited than that extended by the WTO Secretariat in support of its panels.[85] As a rule, secretariats of commercial arbitration institutions, including their governing organs such as the ICC Court of Arbitration (which despite its name, is an administrative and not a judicial body), limit their activity in both commercial and investment cases to registering and administering proceedings. This includes intervening when needed, in accordance with relevant rules, including having a role in appointing or replacing arbitrators when required under the rules and deciding challenges. They monitor tribunals' respect for deadlines and other procedural requirements, take care of financial aspects of cases (requesting down payments from the parties, holding funds, paying arbitrators, settling final accounts), certify awards, and take responsibility for issuing them.[86] The ICSID Secretariat performs additional functions such as assisting individual tribunals in the management of cases, maintaining communications with the parties on behalf of tribunals, taking care of hearings and transcripts, and editing the final text of decisions and awards. In addition, the

82 The "Molina proposal" presented at MC 13 in February 2024, which covers the reform of the panel phase, does however move in this direction; see Chapter VIII.A.3.1(a).

83 See K. Claussen "Gatekeeper Secretariats" in F. Baetens (ed) *Legitimacy of Unseen Actors in International Adjudication* (CUP 2019) 139.

84 See J. Pauwelyn, K. Pelc, "WTO Rulings and the Veil of Anonymity" 33 EJIL (2022) 527. On this issue see also Chapter III n 36.

85 We do not deal here with the more general function of the secretariats of the WTO and ICSID as secretariats of their respective international organizations, performing the functions which the respective treaties entrust to them (ICSID Convention Articles 9–11). As to ICSID, see specifically the Administrative and Financial Regulations adopted by its Administrative Council pursuant to ICSID Convention Article 6.1(a).

86 See ICC Arbitration Rule 35. This practice is not followed by all institutions. Thus, under the SCC rules, it is for the tribunal to deliver the award to the parties (Rule 42.4).

ICSID Secretariat assigns a staff member to act as secretary for each tribunal.[87] The ICSID Secretariat's functions and support to tribunals are thus more extensive than that of other arbitral institutions, though its support also does not approach the level provided by the WTO Secretariat to panels, such as assisting them in research and drafting.[88]

10. The Time-frame for Proceedings

A. Trade

The importance of the prompt resolution of disputes at the WTO is reflected in several provisions of the DSU, first of all in Articles 12.8 and 12.9 (for panels) and Article 17.5 (for the AB). Panels "should" issue their reports within six months from the date of their composition (extendable to six months) while AB proceedings "shall" not exceed 60 or 90 days. Other deadlines, such as for the composition of panels, are quite short, reflecting this same concern.[89] The calendar annexed to the working procedures of each panel also reflects this time constraint when fixing intermediate deadlines for submissions and the dates for the meetings.

In practice, the completion of dispute settlement under the DSU has, in many cases required a considerable extension of the set deadlines for various reasons, such as the complexity of many matters, the part-time availability of panelists, the limited resources of the Secretariat relative to the high number of panel proceedings pending at certain times, and the requirement that reports be issued in all three official languages of the WTO.[90] The date announced for the issuance of reports has often been postponed for reasons such as these. Thus, proceedings have taken much longer than the set deadlines notwithstanding the recent introduction of various procedural devices (such as limiting the number of pages of submissions). In recent years, panel proceedings have lasted on average more than two years and sometimes much longer, due to the factors listed above, as well as the postponement or pausing of proceedings at the request of the parties.[91]

87 The ICC Court, however, decides the arbitrators' fees (which are scaled according to the value of the claims and counterclaims) and must approve draft awards before they may be rendered, a power which the ICSID does not have. According to Article 34 of the ICC Arbitration Rules, the court may correct the form and "without affecting the tribunal's liberty of decision, may also draw [the tribunal's] attention to points of substance".

88 Moreover, it is for the Secretary-General of ICSID to act as registrar, to reject arbitration requests that are "manifestly outside the jurisdiction of the Centre and authenticate arbitral awards" (Articles 11, 36.3 and 49.1 ICSID, respectively).

89 See Chapter II.A.1.5. On the issue in general, see A. Gattini (ed) *The Temporal Factor in Proceedings before International Courts and Tribunals* (Brill 2025).

90 For more detail, see Chapter VII, A.2.1.1.

91 Also the interim review stage (Article 15 DSU), besides translations in the other two official languages of the WTO contributes to delays to the submission of panels' reports to the DSB for adoption and their circulation to the whole membership and the public.

B. Investment

Repeated mantras such as "justice delayed is justice denied" and "time is of the essence" point towards a commitment from all concerned (the parties, institutions, and tribunals) to ensure that arbitration is conducted as speedily as possible, without prejudicing the right of the parties to fairness and equal treatment in proceedings by constraining the parties' ability to prepare and present their case. Arbitration rules, especially after recent amendments, contain provisions that encourage all actors concerned to deal promptly with cases. Thus, the current 2022 ICSID Arbitration Rules provide that the first procedural session, where the most important procedural matters are decided and a case calendar is established, shall be held within 60 days of the constitution of the tribunal;[92] that one or more case management conferences of the tribunal with the parties be held "with a view to conducting an expeditious and cost-effective proceeding"; and that an award must be issued within 240 days from the last submission.[93] As mentioned above, arbitral institutions have also introduced in their rules the possibility of expedited arbitration, such as by a sole arbitrator to settle small claims,[94] for the prompt disposal of claims that are allegedly "manifestly without legal merit", as well as bifurcation in order to deal with jurisdictional objections separately from the merits when they may lead to resolving the dispute without entering into the merit.[95]

However, in practice, complex arbitral proceedings may take years from the request for arbitration to the issuance of the award. Delays may, first of all, be due to extensions of deadlines at the request of the parties, incidental proceedings, as well as scheduling difficulties arising from the lawyers' and arbitrators' diverse locations and busy schedules.[96] Further delays before the final disposition of a case may occur because of subsequent annulment and enforcement procedures. It can also be said that states tend to move more slowly, or at least more formalistically, than private parties when participating in proceedings.[97]

92 AR 29.

93 See, respectively, AR 29, 31, 58. Previously, the only deadline was that of 120 days from the closing of the proceedings for the tribunal to issue the award (2006 AR 46). Since the formal closing under AR 38 (2006) was usually postponed until the award was ready to be issued, this limit was more apparent than real. As to the ICC, see ICC, *Note to the Parties and Arbitral Tribunals on the Conduct of the Arbitration* (2021), available at https://iccwbo.org/news-publications/arbitration-adr-rules-and-tools/note-parties-arbitral-tribunals-conduct-arbitration/ accessed 22 July 2024.

94 See ICSID AR 75, Article 30 ICC Rules.

95 See respectively ICSID AR 41 and 42, see Chapter IV.B.1.

96 See as an example: *Total v Argentina* (ICSID 04/1): arbitration request: January 2004; decision on jurisdiction: 2006; decision on liability: 2010; award: 2013; annulment proceedings (rejection) concluded in 2016. A simpler "smaller" case such as *Gavazzi v Romania* (ICSID 12/15) lasted from August 2012 to April 2017.

97 For instance, the selection of their lawyers may be subject to public tendering.

11. Costs

A. Trade

Arbitral, judicial, and similar dispute settlement proceedings entail substantial internal and external costs for the parties (first of all, their lawyers' and experts' fees) and for the institution organizing them. In domestic civil proceedings, costs for representation are covered by each party, who may moreover be called upon to pay, in advance or subsequently, a part of the cost of the overall proceedings (institution, secretariat), as well as at least a part of the other party's costs if they are on the losing side. This approach is followed in commercial and investment arbitration, where the parties also have to cover arbitrators' fees and expenses.

This is not the case before international courts, where parties are not required to make advance payments to the institution or cover case-specific costs because the court's expenses, including the secretariat's and translation services, and judges' compensation are included in its budget.[98] Likewise, at the WTO the parties incur no costs payable to the organization for any case, whether as complainants or respondents, nor do reports apportion such costs based on the outcome. All WTO Members, rather than the litigants themselves, thus cover the costs incurred by the WTO for maintaining a functioning DSS.[99] The widespread practice of relying on private law firms in WTO dispute settlement proceedings results in any case in sizeable costs for the parties involved in disputes as complainants or respondents if they avail themselves of outside counsel. These costs may be reduced through recourse to the ACWL, a service available to, and used by many developing and least developed countries.[100]

B. Investment

One of the features – and possible disadvantages – of arbitration compared to litigation in court is that all costs are entirely borne by the parties. Moreover, if the respondent does not pay its share of the advance, which the institution requires in equal parts from the parties, the claimant has to advance the whole amount. Advances are meant to cover the institution's costs for the proceedings, including the arbitrators' fees, while it is for the tribunal to decide at the end of the case the apportionment of all costs between the parties (including reasonable attorney's fees, the institution's administrative costs, and the tribunal's fees and costs) whose amount is determined or vetted by the arbitral institution. In civil and commercial

98 In *ad hoc* arbitration, however, while there are no institutional costs for the parties, they have to fully finance the costs of the proceedings, including arbitrators' fees.

99 In 2019, at the instigation of the US, which threatened otherwise to vote against the budget for the year 2020, the WTO cancelled the AB costs item from its yearly budget.

100 See generally S. Dezalay, "Law Firms and International Adjudication", *MPEiPro* (2016). When a WTO Member challenges another Member's measure solely for the benefit of one of its enterprises, the practice of some Members is to request the interested company to bear the costs of the proceedings.

matters, including commercial arbitration, the principle "costs follow the event" is generally applied in this respect. This means that as a rule the losing party is ordered in the final decision to pay "reasonable" legal costs incurred by the successful party, as well as that share of the costs of the institution which, according to its rules, are to be paid by the parties.[101]

In investment arbitration, tribunals enjoy greater flexibility in the absence of strict prescriptions in arbitration rules.[102] According to the ICSID Arbitration Rules, when allocating the costs of the proceedings, a tribunal shall consider all relevant circumstances, including the outcome of the proceedings, the conduct of the parties, the complexity of the issues, and the reasonableness of the costs claimed.[103] In any case, by far the largest share of the costs of arbitral proceedings is represented by the fees and other costs of the parties' lawyers, who are often specialists from large international law firms.[104] In complex investment arbitrations involving large sums of money, lawyers' and experts' fees can run into the millions of dollars. Such amounts do not, however, seem to be out of proportion with the amounts that may be at stake, which may run into the billions.[105]

B. The Decision: Panel Reports and ISDS Awards

1. Deliberations, Content and Issuance of Decisions

1.1. Deliberations

A. Trade

The DSU directs panels to draft their reports in stages and envisages the parties to be involved in the process. After all procedural steps have been exhausted, the panel sends the "descriptive part" of the report to the parties for their comments, which contains a description of the case, the factual findings, and a summary of the

101 Article 42 UNCITRAL Arbitration Rules (2010) provides that "the costs of the arbitration shall in principle be borne by the unsuccessful party or parties", see also ICC, *ICC Arbitration and ADR Commission Report on Decisions on Costs in International Arbitration* (2016), available onhttps://iccwbo.org; G. Born, *International Commercial Arbitration* (3rd ed. Wolters Kluwer 2021) 23.08.

102 According to Article 61.2 ICSID in its award, the tribunal "shall, except as the parties otherwise agree, assess the expenses incurred by the parties in connection with the proceedings, and shall decide how and by whom those expenses, the fees and expenses of the members of the Tribunal and the charges for the use of the facilities of the Centre shall be paid". At the ICC (Article 38), it is for the Secretariat (the ICC court) to assess the amount of costs.

103 See Article 59–61 ICSID; AR 50–53, *Principles*, 431.

104 According to an ICC Report (2015), 83% of the overall costs of an arbitration are accounted for by the costs directly incurred by the parties (including the costs of counsel, experts, etc.), with arbitrators' fees accounting for 15% and the administrative costs of arbitration for about 2%. See *ICC Commission Report: Decisions on Costs in International Arbitration*, Offprint from ICC Dispute Resolution Bulletin 2015, Issue 2, available on https://iccwbo.org/, accessed 16 June 2024.

105 The Advisory Centre on international investment disputes approved by UNCITRAL in 2024 (see Chapter VIII.B.5.2.2(c)) is also meant to reduce the costs of defence for developing and least developed countries by providing to them advice and legal representation at concessionary terms.

parties' and third parties' legal arguments. Thereafter, the panel will send to the parties in strict confidence (to avoid leakages) the full text as an "interim report"; the parties may comment on it in writing and ask for a meeting to discuss it in person. Following this phase, the panel will finalize the report, including a section on the interim review stage.[106]

The preliminary communication to the parties of the report before its formal and final issuance is a continuation of the GATT practice and reflects the non-contentious and non-judicial approach to proceedings there, which were initially more akin to those of a commission of inquiry or conciliation by experts. The parties are able to remedy factual errors in the report at the interim stage and can make a last-minute attempt at conciliation (settlement) in light of the panel's tentative decision. They may also try to convince the panel to change its findings in their favour (an objective which is practically never achieved). Doubts have been raised as to the utility of the interim review stage at the WTO in view of the existence of an appellate stage.[107] If a party detects what it believes to be a legal error in a report that affects the panel's conclusions to its detriment, usually it will not raise the matter before the panel at the interim stage, but will rather invoke it as a legal challenge on appeal. Considering the sensitivity surrounding the (excessive) length of the panel stage, the abolition of the interim review would make a positive contribution to the shortening of the process.

B. *Investment*

A final award contains the final and complete resolution of a case, states the holdings in fact and law, the reliefs granted, and the reasons supporting the tribunal's conclusions and findings. The determination of the costs and their apportionment must also be included in the final award.[108] Partial decisions that do not conclude proceedings, such as those on jurisdiction, liability, and some of the claims, may take the form of decisions or partial awards depending on arbitral regulations, international conventions and applicable domestic law. Depending on the applicable national law, international commercial partial awards may be challenged separately, before competent domestic courts upon their issuance. At ICSID, such non-final determinations are named "decisions" and not awards and are annexed to

106 See Article 15 DSU ("Interim Review Stage"). Article 14 DSU on "Confidentiality" states that "Panel deliberations shall be confidential" and that panel reports "shall be drafted without the presence of the parties", thereby implicitly admitting that members of the Secretariat assisting a panel may be present.

107 See *Van den Bossche* 296. In the absence of a functioning appellate stage, as has been the case since 2020, or should such a stage not be restored (see Chapters VII.A.3 and VIII.A.3.1(b)), the function of the interim review might be reinvigorated. Interim review patterned after the DSU is found in some RTAs where no appeal stage is provided. For a lengthy discussion of interim review in a final report, see the panel report (2020) in the dispute between the EU and Ukraine under their bilateral AA, https://policy.trade.ec.europa.eu/enforcement-and-protection/dispute-settlement/bilateral-disputes/ukraine-wood-export-ban_en accessed 22 July 2024.

108 See Article 61.2 ICSID, Article 38.4 ICC.

the final award. They may be subject to an annulment challenge only as part of a challenge against the final award.[109]

An award is the result of the confidential deliberations of the members of a tribunal, in which all arbitrators must participate.[110] Decisions, including the award, may be made by majority vote, and individual (dissenting) opinions indicating the name of the dissenter are admitted.[111] Arbitration rules list the formal and substantive content of awards, requiring that all relevant data of the dispute be articulated (such as the parties, the relevant arbitral clause in the contract or treaty, the main procedural steps, the arguments of the parties, the reasons on which the decision is based, costs etc.).[112] Lack of the most important requirements, such as adequate reasoning and the indication of the arbitration clause on which jurisdiction is based (for commercial arbitration), are grounds for annulment.[113]

1.2. Content and Remedies

A. Trade

The DSU provides that where a breach by a party of its WTO obligations is established, the primary obligation for the wrongdoer is to bring the measure in breach into compliance. This implies withdrawing or correcting the objectionable measure.[114] The objective is to re-establish the *status quo ante*, the balance of rights and obligations between the parties stemming from the rules, and the reciprocal concessions undertaken within the periodic multilateral negotiation rounds.[115] Panel reports therefore invariably conclude, as provided in Article 19(1) DSU, with the recommendation that the party found in breach, if this is the case, brings the measure into conformity with the relevant WTO agreement.

The obligation to eliminate the breach conforms with the general international law principle that the first obligation of a state responsible for an internationally

109 For more detail see Chapter V.B.2; G. Sacerdoti, C. de Stefano, "The Award on Jurisdiction and Merits" in K. Fach Gómez and C. Titi (eds) *The Award in International Investment Arbitration* (OUP 2024) 20.

110 ICSID AR 33 provides for a majority of the tribunal to constitute a valid quorum. The tribunal may be assisted by a secretary in its deliberations (AR 34.3).

111 Article 48 ICSID, AR 35, 59.3; Article 32 ICC Rules. In investment arbitration, dissenting opinions are frequent, mostly by side-arbitrators supporting the arguments of the party which has appointed them, reflecting their sympathetic attitude towards the position of that party. Such an attitude is not necessarily at odds with the requirement of impartiality required from all Members of an arbitral tribunal (see on this issue Chapter III.B.3 n 89). Differences of opinion within a tribunal reflect the uncertain import of several key provisions in IIAs and different approaches to the determination of states' obligations towards investors, depending on the arbitrators' legal, cultural, and political background. Hence the importance of diversity in a tribunal's composition, see Chapter VII.B.3.2.

112 ICSID AR 59. See generally H. Ruiz-Fabri, M. Sorel (eds), *La motivation des sentences internationales* (Pedone 2008).

113 For more detail see Chapter V.B.1.

114 Article 3.7 DSU.

115 See Article 3.2 and 3.3 DSU.

wrongful act is to cease its conduct, if it is of a continuous nature.[116] However, at the WTO not all of the adverse consequences of the breach are remedied through compliance, since under Article 21.3 DSU, the obligation to comply is prospective (forward-looking) rather than retrospective from the date of the breach. The wrongdoer has the advantage of not having to comply with its obligations as long as the dispute is pending and even beyond, since the DSU grants a "reasonable period" of time to comply if immediate compliance with the DSB recommendations and ruling is "impracticable".[117] Since the effect of past breaches can normally only be cured by monetary damages, the fact that the DSU does not contemplate such a remedy confirms the political choice made by WTO Members, in line with the GATT, of granting flexibility to Members at the expense of legality, in order to induce compliance.[118]

B. *Investment*

Investors' claims are almost invariably aimed at obtaining monetary compensation for the loss they have suffered due to the breach, so that the damages (quantum) phase is the culmination of the findings of awards, if the respondent is found to have been in breach of its obligations. In order to avoid excessively encroaching upon states' policies, some IIAs go so far as to expressly preclude tribunals from ordering the withdrawal or correction of the measure found to be in breach and always allow the state to pay monetary compensation instead.[119] Investment law thus derogates from the basic principle in public international law that the first consequence of the obligation of full reparation stemming from a wrongful act is restitution in kind, that is to re-establish the situation that existed before the

116 Article 30 ARSIWA.

117 According to Article 31 ARSIWA (Reparation), the responsible state is under an obligation to make full reparation for the injury caused by an internationally wrongful act. Injury includes any damage, whether material or moral, caused by the internationally wrongful act of a state. Full reparation entails, when possible, restitution, that is to re-establish the situation that existed before the wrongful act and the obligation to compensate for the damages caused, insofar as such damage is not made good by restitution. "Compensation shall cover any financially assessable damage including loss of profits insofar as it is established" (Articles 35 and 36 ARSIWA). Article 3.7 DSU provides instead for agreed temporary "compensation" as an alternative to withdrawal "only if the immediate withdrawal of the measure is impractical" (although in practice, compensation as an alternative method of final compliance has often been agreed). By compensation, at least in practice, the granting of equivalent trade concessions rather than monetary payments is meant, although in at least one instance a monetary payment by the US to the EU was agreed (*US–Section 110.5 Copyright Act* (DS 160-2000)). See also Chapter VI.B.A.1.

118 This "commercial" approach is further confirmed by Article 3.8 DSU, which is focused on the elimination of the prejudice caused by non-compliant measures. This provision lays down the presumption that "where there is an infringement of the obligation assumed under a covered agreement, the action is considered prima facie to constitute a case of nullification or impairment. This means that there is normally a presumption that a breach of the rules has an adverse impact on other Members parties", and not just on the complainant.

119 See Article 14.D.13 UMSCA, Article 8.39 CETA.

wrongful act. If damages have been thereby caused to the investor, "Compensation shall cover any financially assessable damage including loss of profits insofar as it is established" (as stated in Article 36 ARSIWA). Tribunals have emphasized the limitation to "non-speculative profits" that have been proven when applying this principle.[120]

We just recall here – since it is a matter of substance not covered in this book – that the determination of the amount of damages due to a foreign investor, in the case of expropriation or unfair and inequitable treatment by the host state, is a hotly disputed issue because of the indeterminate or contentious valuation and accounting criteria by which they are to be measured, especially in respect of loss of future profits (*lucrum cessans*).[121]

Once signed by the arbitrators, the award is typically issued to the parties by the institution to which the original signed award has been submitted by the tribunal.[122] Contrary to judicial practice and in compliance with the requirement of confidentiality, there is no public proclamation of the decision.[123]

120 See *Amco Asia v Indonesia* ICSID ARB/81/1, Award in Resubmitted Proceeding (1990) 178; see also ARSIWA, Commentaries, Article 36, para 27.

121 See as a guide in this respect the International Valuation Standards of the International Valuation Standards Council (IVSC – www.ivsc.org). It is sometimes reported in the press that investors can sue states if they take decisions that "reduce their future profits". It is not possible to sue merely for lost profits; tribunals only consider profits at the damages stage, once responsibility for a breach has been established, based on widely used (but not uncontested) valuation techniques such as Discounted Cash Flow. See, for example, Irish Examiner, "Q&A: What is the CETA deal?" 16 December 2020 on https://www.irishexaminer.com/. On damages in ISDS, see generally B. Sabahi, *Compensation and Restitution in Investor-State Arbitration. Principles and Practice* (OUP 2011); U. Kriebaum, *Damages in Investor-State Arbitration* (Brill 2018). See also the ICCA-ASIL, "Damages in International Arbitration" web tool ()https://icca-asil-damages.com/; UNCTAD, IIA Issue Note, *Compensation and Damages in Investor-State Dispute Settlement Proceedings* (2024), available at https://unctad.org/system/files/official-document/diaepcbinf2024d3_en.pdf

122 ICSID Rule 60 on the rendering of the award provides that it be dispatched to the parties by the Secretary-General of ICSID. As mentioned above, at the ICC, the draft award is subject to a formal control by the ICC before being sent by the Secretariat to the parties in its final form (Articles 34, 35 ICC Rules). Under the SCC Arbitration Rules (Article 43.2, 2023), it is for the tribunal to deliver the award to the parties.

123 In investment arbitration, just as in commercial arbitration, there is no "interim" phase, as is provided for in the DSU, where the draft award is sent to the parties for their comments before being signed and issued. USMCA is an exception - patterened after the DSU provision - in providing at Article 14.D.7.12 that "at the request of a disputing party, a tribunal shall, before issuing a decision or award on liability, transmit its proposed decision or award to the disputing parties. Within 60 days after the tribunal transmits its proposed decision or award, the disputing parties may submit written comments to the tribunal concerning any aspect of its proposed decision or award. The tribunal shall consider any comments and issue its decision or award no later than 45 days after the expiration of the 60 day comment period".

2. *The Finalization of the Decisions and Their Effects*

A. *Trade*

Panel reports are very detailed and lengthy. They are required to set out "the findings of fact, the applicability of relevant provisions, and the basic rationale behind any findings and recommendations they make" (Article 12.7 DSU).[124] The final report is issued to the disputing parties following the interim review phase and then, following translation, circulated to all the WTO membership and made available to the public through the WTO website in the three official languages of the WTO.[125]

If the panel finds, either by majority or unanimously,[126] that the challenged measure is inconsistent with a covered agreement, the report will conclude with a recommendation that the respondent bring the measure into conformity with the relevant agreement. As to its formal nature and effects, a panel report may be distinguished on several counts from an international judgment of a court or an award of an arbitral tribunal (be it state-to-state, investment, or commercial). While judgments are binding for the parties *per se* once issued and become *res iudicata*,[127] any finding of a breach in a panel report is formally merely a recommendation to remedy the breach found.[128] The subsequent steps provided by the DSU render, however, a non-appealed panel (and an AB report) comparable to a final judgment.

124 Panel reports often run into the hundreds of pages, with three of them having gone beyond a thousand: *EC–Approval and Marketing of Biotech products* (DS 291, 292, 293-2006), *EC-Large Civil Aircraft* (DS 316-2011), *Australia–Tobacco Plain Packaging* (DS 435, 441, 458, 467-2020).

125 Translation, which is done in-house, adds a considerable amount of time to the issuance of reports.

126 In prescribing that "Opinions expressed in the panel report by individual panelists shall be anonymous", Article 14.1 DSU links this anonymity to the confidentiality of proceedings. Allowing for individual concurring or dissenting opinions is a standard feature of international courts and tribunals, inspired by the tradition of common law countries, where the name of the dissenting author is public. The contrary DSU rule (applicable also to the AB, Article 17.11) may be due to the intent to reinforce the authority of the decisions and dissuade this very practice; see E. Kim, P. Mavroidis, "Dissenting Opinions in the WTO Appellate Body" EUI Working Papers 2018/51, available at https://scholarship.law.columbia.edu. This 2018 paper states that there had been eight separate opinions at the AB up to 2018 (and 14 in panel reports). Since then, three more were included in AB Reports, *US–Countervailing Measures (China) – Recourse to Article 21.5 of the DSU by China* (DS 437), where there was more than one separate opinion; *US–Supercalendered Paper* (DS505); and *Australia–Tobacco Plain Packaging (Honduras)* (DS435). NAFTA also provides for the publication of anonymous separate opinions in Article 2017, and a similar provision is included in USMCA Article 31.13.8.

127 See hereunder Chapter IV.B.2.2.

128 It has been observed (*Mavroidis*, 180) that in the great majority of cases the respondent has been found to be in breach of at least some of the WTO obligations invoked by the claimant. This is all but natural because (a) cases are normally initiated only when there is a reasonable chance that a breach by another party will be found, and (b) the complexity of many WTO rules makes it the difficult to fully and correctly comply with all WTO obligations.

The panel report must be adopted by the DSB to become final, which occurs "automatically" due to the rule of reverse consensus.[129] The DSB thereby confirms the panel's recommendation that the respondent comply if it is found to have been in breach.[130] The DSU does not spell out clearly that the adoption of a report triggers an obligation for the party in breach to remedy its non-compliance.[131] However, this obligation is inferred from the cumulative effect of various provisions. These include references to "ways in which the Member concerned could implement the recommendation" (Article 19.2 DSU), a declaration that "Prompt compliance with recommendation or rulings of the DSB essential in order to ensure effective resolution of disputes to the benefit of all Members" (Article 21.1 DSU), and a provision granting WTO Members a reasonable period of time to comply "If it is impracticable to comply immediately with the recommendation" (Article 21.3).

B. Investment

Final awards in investment and commercial arbitration alike are binding for the parties, and only for them, thus excluding third persons.[132] Except for any remedies provided for by arbitration rules or applicable legal provisions, such as appeal or annulment proceedings, parties are under an immediate obligation to comply with it and implement its prescriptions. The award precludes submitting the same dispute again for adjudication because of its effects as "res iudicata".[133]

There is a fundamental divide between ICSID awards and those of all other arbitral institutions with respect of the applicable regime. ICSID awards are international judgments subject only to the ICSID regime, whereas awards issued under the aegis of other arbitral institutions, even if labelled "international", are ultimately subject to the domestic law of the state where or according to whose law they have been rendered. This is especially relevant when it comes to challenges to

129 The time limit for adoption is 60 days (Article 16.4 DSU), provided there is no appeal in the meantime to the AB by the losing party. Cross-appeals ("other appeals") by an appellee are frequent since it is rare that a winner prevails on all claims (and vice-versa).

130 Article 16 DSU. All WTO Members can express their views on the report at the relevant DSB meeting. Lengthy comments, favourable or critical, may be found in the summary minutes of meetings, which are published on the WTO website. This practice confirms that the relevance of reports' findings extends to the whole membership.

131 This is only clearly stated in respect of adopted AB reports at Article 17.14 DSU: "An Appellate Body report shall be adopted by the DSB and unconditionally accepted by the parties to the dispute".

132 See Article 59 ICJ: "The decision of the Court has no binding force except between the parties and in respect of that particular case".

133 *Res iudicata* means that the decision being final, the dispute cannot be rejudged by the same tribunal between the same parties and precludes other tribunals from doing so, provided that the subsequent dispute is identical as to the parties, subject matter, and object of the claim. See ICJ *Effect of Awards of Compensation Made by the UN Administrative Tribunal* Advisory Opinion (1954) ICJ Rep, 47; Y. Shany, *The Competing Jurisdictions of International Courts and Tribunals* (OUP 2003) 299; G. Sacerdoti, "The Proliferation of BITs: Conflict of Treaties, Proceedings and Awards" in K. Sauvant (ed) *Appeals Mechanism in International Investment Disputes* (OUP 2008) 127.

awards which, for ICSID awards, are exclusively governed by the ICSID convention. Other awards, though "international" in certain respects (such as the types of institutions administering them, such as the PCA or the ICC, as well as the different locations or nationalities of the parties, and the subject matter pertaining to international commerce or investment), may be challenged in accordance with the remedies provided for under the competent domestic legal system.[134]

C. Comparative Evaluation

The above analysis shows that there are substantial differences, but also similarities, between dispute settlement proceedings before WTO panels and in ISDS. The main differences are due to the fact that the first one is inter-governmental, and the other patterned after the traditional commercial arbitration model between private investors. The peculiar set-up of proceedings under the DSU owes much to the initial investigatory model of the GATT commission of experts. This model was predominantly inquisitorial and several of its features have been carried over into the DSU. The organization itself plays a prominent role in supporting the settlement of trade disputes between Members by panels, a system that is "embedded" in the WTO. In contrast, ISDS evolved from commercial arbitration, retaining many of its procedural features under ICSID and almost all of them in non-ICSID arbitration.

1.1. Commonalities

(a) Proceedings are subject to the due process principles of fairness and equality of arms in the evidentiary and pleading phases. In both DSS adjudicators apply international law, passing upon alleged breaches of the WTO agreements and the relevant IIAs in treaty-based investment arbitration, respectively;
(b) Proceedings are party-driven: it is for an aggrieved party to decide to start a case and put forth its claims; it is incumbent upon each party to submit sufficient evidence to meet the standard of proof and support its case in conformity with basic due process requirements;
(c) Amici curiae have a limited possibility to make submissions, which at the WTO has been recognized by practice and in ISDS has been codified in IIAs and arbitral regulations;
(d) Avoiding the excessive length of proceedings is a common concern, but its realization in practice is hampered by multiple obstacles, such as the factual and legal complexity of disputes, safeguarding the rights of the parties and ensuring fair and equal treatment, and the part-time availability of adjudicators;
(e) Transparency is praised, but confidentiality still prevails.

134 Article 35.6 ICC aims at limiting recourse to domestic remedies, where it states that parties are "deemed to have waived their right to any form of recourse insofar as such waiver can validly be made".

1.2. Differences

(a) Any WTO Member may initiate DSU panel proceedings, whereas in investment arbitration, only investors can sue host state parties to IIAs in accordance with the dispute settlement provisions of these agreements;

(b) In the selection of panellists for WTO panels (which are made up predominantly of former and actual governmental experts), the WTO Secretariat has an important role under the DSU. This can be contrasted with the unfettered right of parties to select tribunal members in ISDS. They are chosen either directly or indirectly by the parties, usually among highly qualified lawyers specializing in investment law, with the institution intervening only to remedy blockages in the appointment mechanism;

(c) The WTO Secretariat is fully involved in all aspects of panel proceedings. This is in contrast with the more limited administrative role of arbitral institutions in ISDS, albeit more pronounced at ICSID in comparison with private arbitral institutions;

(d) The organization and unfolding of the proceedings are more predetermined under the DSU, as compared with the more flexible arbitration practice where many aspects of proceedings are left to the agreement of the parties;

(e) Under the DSU, the role of adjudicators is dominant in evidence-gathering. While the type of dispute does not usually require factual evidence-gathering through witness testimony, experts are selected directly by the panels. In ISDS, the overwhelming practice is for each party to select and submit the reports of witnesses and experts (both technical and legal) who are then cross-examined by the other party in hearings;

(f) The full right for other interested WTO Members to intervene as third parties contrasts with the more limited right for non-disputing third states to take part (under recent IIAs only) in investor–state arbitration under agreements to which they are a party;

(g) Panel reports become binding on the parties, with some spill-over (de facto precedential) effect for other WTO Members, only after having been approved by the WTO Members collectively in the DSB. In contrast, once issued, arbitral awards are final and binding, for the parties only. Investment awards have a more limited effect as precedent than WTO reports;

(h) The costs of proceedings are borne by the WTO under the DSU, while the parties to ISDS proceedings have to finance the proceedings themselves, with the apportionment among them ultimately decided by the tribunal;

(i) Remedies in case of breach under the WTO agreements aim to re-establish the status quo ante (the withdrawal of objectionable measures) and are prospective. In ISDS, monetary damages are, in practice or legally, the sole remedy for past and future damages caused to the claimant investor by the respondent state.

5 Reviewing Decisions: Appeal and Annulment

Table of Contents

Introduction

Two-tier adjudication, whereby a judgment or an award of an arbitral tribunal or a court may be challenged before another adjudicatory body, used to be, and in part still is exceptional in international law.[1] In domestic legal systems, on the other hand, the right to appeal against an unfavourable judicial decision on its merits

1 See generally G. Sacerdoti, "Appeal and Judicial Review in International Arbitration and Adjudication: The Case of the WTO Appellate Review" in E. Petersmann (ed) *International Trade Law and the GATT/WTO Dispute Settlement System* (Kluwer 1997) 245; K. Sauvant (ed) *Appeals Mechanisms in International Investment Disputes* (OUP 2008); M. Dupuy and J. Viñuales, "The Challenge of 'Proliferation': An Anatomy of the Debate" in C. Romano, K. Alter, Y. Shany (eds) *Oxford Handbook of International Adjudication* (OUP 2014) 135.

DOI: 10.4324/9781003471509-7

is a standard feature. The purpose is to afford the parties (in civil litigation) or an accused (in a criminal trial) the right to have such a decision re-examined as to its correctness in fact and in law by judges who are, in principle, more senior and competent. Legal systems thereby aim, especially through an ultimate level of review by a national supreme court, not only to reduce the likelihood of judicial errors but also to enhance consistency in the interpretation and application of the law.[2]

In international law instead, the emphasis in interstate disputes is on the finality of any decision settling a dispute. The consensual underpinning of third-party binding adjudication in international law justifies the absence in principle of further remedies against such decisions and their *res judicata* (finality) character. Proposals to introduce a review of interstate awards have envisaged annulment for serious procedural defects, rather than review of the merits, even if limited to legal errors.[3]

The situation has changed with the institution of a number of international jurisdictions that have been entrusted with competence over individuals. This is the case of international criminal courts, entrusted with the competence of judging individuals accused of international crimes,[4] human rights courts,[5] administrative or employment tribunals,[6] and arbitral tribunals which individuals or companies

2 Appeal is considered so fundamental that it has been made a basic human right in criminal matters. According to Article 14.5 UN ICCPR "everyone convicted of a crime shall have the right to his conviction and sentence being reviewed by a higher tribunal according to law", a principle that has been applied within international criminal tribunals and courts.

3 The Model Rules on Arbitral Procedure for interstate disputes adopted by the ILC in 1958, available at https://legal.un.org, reprinted hereunder, provide at Article 35 that: "The validity of an award may be challenged by either party on one or more of the following grounds: (a) That the tribunal has exceeded its powers; (b) That there was corruption on the part of a Member of the tribunal; (c) That there has been a failure to state the reasons for the award or a serious departure from a fundamental rule of procedure; (d) That the undertaking to arbitrate or the *compromis* is a nullity". Article 36 provides that absent a different agreement by the parties, the ICJ "shall be competent to declare the total or partial nullity of the award on the application of either party" to be made within six months.

4 The ICTY and ICTR both provided for an appeal chamber. At the International Criminal Court, Trial Chambers' decisions of acquittal or conviction of an accused can be appealed to the appeal chamber by both the Prosecutor and the Defence (Article 81 of the Statute) on grounds of (i) Procedural error, (ii) Error of fact, (iii) Error of law, or (iv) Any other ground that affects the fairness or reliability of the proceedings or decision, or on the ground of disproportion between the crime and the sentence.

5 The ECtHR Grand Chamber, under Article 43 of the ECHR can hear cases (a) where a Chamber relinquishes jurisdiction because a case raises a serious question affecting the interpretation of the Convention or there is a risk of inconsistency with a previous decision of the Court (Relinquishment), or (b) by a request of a party within three months of delivery of a Chamber's judgment for re-examination, subject to a favourable decision of a panel of judges (Referral).

6 The UN features a first-instance UN Dispute Tribunal (UNDT) and a UN Appeals Tribunal (UNAT) for employment disputes. Judgments on first instance, besides correction of clerical or arithmetical mistakes, or interpretations by the tribunal having issued them, are subject to appeal before the UNAT when it is asserted that the UNDT (a) exceeded its jurisdiction or competence; (b) failed to exercise jurisdiction vested in it; (c) erred on a question of law; (d) committed an error in procedure, such as to affect the decision of the case; or (e) erred on a question of fact, resulting in a manifestly unreasonable decision, see O. Elias and M. Thomas, "Administrative Tribunals of International Organizations" in C. Giorgetti (ed) *The Rules, Practice and Jurisprudence of International Courts and Tribunals*

can access to protect their rights against states or organizations (such as investors in ISDS, international civil servants to administrative tribunals of international organizations, or enterprises directly affected by acts of EU institutions to the CJEU).[7] A two-tier system is justified by the same due process and fundamental rights protection concerns that are at the basis of the review of first-instance judgments in domestic legal systems when private rights are, at least indirectly, at stake, as is the case at the WTO. The review of decisions of *ad hoc* panels by a single second-level adjudicator (such as the AB) is further justified by the objective of consistency in decisions, especially where the number of disputes makes divergence among them more likely.

There is, however, a substantial difference as to the type and standards of review provided, depending on the nature of the regimes, with regard to the parties (states, individuals, enterprises) and the rights involved. There is also a need to balance the finality of decisions with the review of their correctness, as well as considerations of delays in rendering a final decision and the additional costs entailed by any review process. In this respect, different types of review may be distinguished as to competence, scope and effects. At the outset, a distinction should be made between two types of re-examination of an arbitral or judicial decision. On the one side (a) the correction of errors (including curing omissions (ICSID Article 49.2) and (b) the interpretation of a decision (to clarify its meaning) which complete the decision (ICSID Article 50.1) and are functions usually entrusted to the same tribunal that has issued such a decision. On the other side substantive review by which the decision challenged can be quashed entirely or in part (Article 17.13 DSU; Article 52.1 ICSID), with or without remand, and, depending upon the rules, be replaced by the review decision. This is the case of (c) appeal on the merits (full or limited to legal issues as under Article 17 DSU) and (d) annulment or revision due to serious procedural (due process) errors (Article 52.66 ICSID). Functions under (c) and (d) are entrusted to distinct, often "superior", bodies, preferably of a permanent nature.

The table provided in the Annex below compares the type of admissible challenges against various types of awards and international decisions, setting out the different intensity of controls in annulment and appeals in different settings.

A. Trade

1. The Introduction of Appeal against Panel Reports at the WTO

The GATT did not provide any mechanism to challenge a panel report. This was logical since the opposition of the losing party could anyhow block its adoption.

(Nijhoff 2012), 159; S. Villalpando, "International Administrative Tribunals" in J. Katz Cogan, I. Hurd, I. Johnston (eds) *The Oxford Handbook of International Organizations* (2016) 1085.

7 Established in 1989, the EU General Court (a part of the CJEU) is competent to deal, *inter alia*, with recourses by individuals or companies against acts of EU institutions that are addressed to them or that affect them directly and individually, including in respect of employment relations. Its decisions can be appealed to the Court of Justice on points of law only (Article 256.1 TFEU).

This context changed with the advent of the WTO, as the reverse consensus rule under which the DSB adopts panel reports makes them almost automatically binding. This warrants giving losing parties a chance to have reports re-examined to check the correctness of their findings and conclusions, as well in view, from a systemic point of view, of ensuring correctness and consistency in the interpretation and application of WTO law.

The institution of appellate review by a permanent ("standing") body endowed with the necessary competence and authority was not however of concern until the final phase of the Uruguay Round negotiations, and came almost as an "afterthought".[8] It was only then that the institution of an appeal mechanism of a standing nature was deemed to be necessary. The main reasons therefore were, first, that panels are *ad hoc* and mostly made up of trade diplomats, who may not necessarily have extensive experience and expertise adjudicating such disputes. Secondly, it was felt that an appeal review by a permanent group of mostly legal experts would increase the consistency and quality of the case law and thus be beneficial to the whole membership in terms of the predictability and stability of the system.

Having opted for a full legal review of panel reports, the negotiators believed that appeals would only be "occasional" against some "bad reports" by some unlikely "rogue panels". Accordingly, the AB was not endowed with all the features of a regular international court, beginning with its very name.[9] Accordingly, although the AB was conceived as a permanent organ and an integral part of the WTO, it was set up with a limited number of part-time members (not defined as judges, though entrusted in substance with judicial functions), providing their services under contract to the WTO, an arrangement more akin to that of panelists or arbitrators than to that of a permanent court. The carrying on of the GATT model of the contracting parties ultimately deciding disputes by approving panel reports, albeit restricted in its effectiveness at the WTO by the reverse consensus rule, shows that negotiators did not intend to upend the existing system by creating a fully judicial mechanism by establishing a kind of "World Trade Court".

Both premises quickly turned out to be incorrect. The existence of a review mechanism has encouraged losing parties to systematically appeal unfavourable panel reports, resulting in a ratio of appeals as high as around 70%. The AB as a permanent adjudicatory body inevitably assumed the role of a court and became the centre of gravity of the DSS. The sustained and increasing activity of the

8 See D. Steger, "The founding of the Appellate Body" in *A History* 447 (D. Steger was a negotiator for Canada at the Uruguay Round and the first head of the AB Secretariat); J. Lacarte Muro, "Launching the Appellate Body" in *A History* 476. J. Lacarte Muro was the chairman of the negotiating group on dispute settlement in the Uruguay Round and thereafter the first chairman of the AB. He had extensive experience in diplomacy and trade matters having represented Uruguay at the Havana Conference in 1947–1948 (and before that at the San Francisco Conference in 1945). P Van den Bossche, "Appellate Body (WTO)" *MPEiPro* (2019).

9 This is textually reflected in the fact that the whole regulation of the AB set-up and function is included in just one article of the DSU (Article 17).

AB (which issued 124 reports between 1996 and 2020), without organizational improvements to the DSS, brought stress to the functioning of the DSS, which over time led to substantial delays in the issuance of its reports (as has been the case for panels).[10]

2. The Composition and Functioning of the Appellate Body

The AB is a distinct branch within the WTO whose role is set forth in the DSU. It is endowed accordingly with a separate administrative and legal Secretariat to ensure its independence from the other branches of the WTO.[11] It is not, however, separate from the rest of the organization (including as to its location which is within the premises of the WTO in Geneva), as is the case, even geographically, of the ICJ within the UN or the CJEU within the EU.

The AB consists of seven members appointed by the DSB after a selection process among candidates proposed by WTO Members, in order that the AB's membership be "broadly representative of the membership in the WTO" also in terms of its geographical balance.[12] Their term of office is just four years, renewable only once: this is a small number and a rather short term in office compared with other, sometimes plethoric international courts where tenures tend to be considerably longer.[13] AB Members must be "of recognized authority, with demonstrated expertise in law, international trade and the subject matter of the covered agreement generally".[14] They must be "unaffiliated with any government", and must avoid any direct or indirect conflict of interest to ensure their complete independence and impartiality.[15]

Appeals are decided by divisions of three AB members, serving randomly and in rotation, with no constraints on nationality, contrary to the requirements for the composition of panels.[16] The AB Working Procedures, however, provide for an "exchange of views" in respect of each case among all AB members "to ensure

10 For more detail, see Chapter VII.A.2.1.

11 See Article 17.7 DSU.

12 The 27 Members of the AB (1995–2020) came from 17 different countries.. They featured a variety of cultural, legal, and professional backgrounds, as former diplomats, academics, practicing lawyers and public officials.

13 The term of the 15 ICJ judges is nine years, as is the term of the 21 judges of ITLOS (both terms are renewable). For more details see J. Dunoff "Selection of WTO Appellate Body Members" *MPEiPro* (2018).

14 These qualifications are significantly different from those required for members of courts, who must typically possess "the qualifications required in their respective countries for appointment to the highest judicial offices, or are jurisconsults of recognized competence in international law" (Article 2 ICJ Statute).

15 See Article 17.3 and the AB Working Procedures (WP) WTO Doc. No. WT/AB/WP/6 (www.wto.org/english/tratop_e/dispu_e/ab_e.htm), that were drawn up by the AB in consultation with the chairman of the DSB and the DG pursuant to Article 17.9 DS (last revised in 2010), with the Code of Conduct, Annex II, available at www.wto.org/english/tratop_e/dispu_e/ab_e.htm

16 Article 8.3 DSU.

consistency and coherence in decision-making", though the responsibility of any report rests exclusively with the division assigned to it.[17] All AB members are thereby informed of all issues raised on appeal, thus favouring uniformity in the interpretation and application of procedural and substantive provisions by the AB.[18] Finally, as is the case with panels, individual anonymous opinions are allowed.[19] As with panels, AB proceedings are confidential, so that (video-)observation of hearings by the public has been permitted only with the parties' consent.[20] Amicus briefs have also been allowed by the AB, though under strict conditions.[21] WTO Members who have participated as third parties at the panel stage cannot appeal the panel report but may intervene once more during appeal proceedings, in writing and addressing the division at the hearing.[22]

As already mentioned, AB proceedings are supposed to be swift: appeals should be disposed of within 60 days, with a possible (de facto regular) extension to 90.[23] However, from 2010 onwards the AB has generally been unable to respect the short 90-days limit due to the complexity of cases, the number of appeals and of claims made, often by both parties.[24]

3. *The Scope of Appellate Review*

According to Article 17.6 DSU, "[a]n appeal shall be limited to issues of law covered in the panel report and legal interpretations developed by the panel". This means that the AB may review the correct interpretation and application of legal provisions made by the panel but not enter into its factual determinations. Such a

17 WP Rules 4.2 and 4.3.

18 This practice can be compared to that of courts comprising several chambers, such as the ECtHR and the CJEU, where sensitive cases are remitted to their Grand Chambers, which have a larger composition and whose members are selected from the various chambers.

19 Article 17.11 DSU. This possibility has been used sparingly, as for the panels, leading to only 11 individual (dissenting) opinions in the history of the AB. See Chapter IV n 126; N. Meagher "The Judicial Style of the Appellate Body" in Chang-fa Lo, J. Nakagawa, Tsai-fang Cen (eds) *The Appellate Body of the WTO and its Reform* (Springer 2019) 141.

20 A complete set of individual AB members' files covering all cases from 1995 to 2009 can be accessed under conditions of confidentiality at the WTI library in Bern to which they were donated in 2022 ("Feliciano-Sacerdoti papers").

21 See Chapter IV.A.7.

22 Article 17.4.

23 Article 17.5. Upon the filing of an appeal, the AB Secretariat draws up a calendar for the case which usually provides for one brief from each disputing party (appellant and appellee, who may also have filed a cross-appeal), a short brief by each third party, and one hearing. In the practice of the AB, after brief introductory statements by the parties, most of the hearing is devoted to the parties answering questions from the members of the division aimed at clarifying outstanding doubts about the parties' positions.

24 An unexpected side effect of the long duration of many appeals (and the reduced number of AB members from 2017 to 2020) has been that resort to WP Rule 15, according to which an AB member whose term is expiring may complete the disposition of a pending appeal (as provided by many courts' rules), has been more frequent. This has resulted in the extension of the term of office of AB members in the last years of functioning of the AB for periods that were longer than anticipated.

limitation is common in many domestic legal systems as to the review of lower courts' decisions by supreme courts, such as *Cour de cassation* in France.[25]

The dividing line between law and facts is somewhat blurred before international tribunals, especially when the existence of a breach of an international obligation depends on the content and effect of domestic law. Appeals against a panel's application of Article 11 DSU, which requires that a panel "make an objective assessment of the matter before it, including an objective assessment of the facts of the case and the application of and conformity with the relevant covered agreements" have often been invoked by appellants to adduce an alleged erroneous assessment of domestic law by a panel as a legal error to be reviewed by the AB.[26] The AB has held that a claim of breach by the panel of its duty to make an objective assessment is a serious claim; only those errors that are so material that "taken together or singly" undermine the objectivity of the panel assessment can lead to a violation of Article 11.[27]

As stated in Article 17.13, the AB "may uphold, modify or reverse the legal finding and conclusions of the panel". Since appellants often raise multiple claims of error in their appeals, in most cases at least some panel conclusions are modified on appeal by the AB.[28] As the AB has no power to remand a case to the panel, appeal may leave disputes unresolved. This gives rise to the possibility of the same dispute being resubmitted before a different panel though this has never occurred in practice.[29] The AB has, however, used the method referred to as "completing the analysis" in order to resolve a dispute when the evidentiary record of the panel report enabled it to apply the proper interpretation or the correct provision based on the undisputed facts ascertained by the panel.

As is the case with panel reports, after they have been issued to the parties appellate reports are circulated to the WTO membership and made public. Also AB reports need to be adopted by the DSB to become binding, following the same procedure (negative consensus) that is applicable to panel reports.[30] When the AB has upheld or modified a panel report, the DSB adopts both of them together.

25 This is also the case for appeal from the EU General Court to the CJEU, see above n 7.

26 See Chapter III.A.4.

27 AB *Russia–Railway Equipment* (DS 499-2020), 5.68; *Van den Bossche*, 259.

28 Based on the provisions of Articles 17.6 and 17.12 that mandate the AB to address each of the legal issues raised on appeal, parties tend to appeal not just the legal findings underpinning the conclusions but also intermediate legal considerations by panels, thereby overburdening appeals (though the AB may dismiss claims as moot, based on judicial economy), see AB *Australia–Salmon* (DS 18-1998), 223; A. Alvarez-Jimenez, "The WTO Appellate Body's Exercise of Judicial Economy" 12 JIEL (2009) 393; S. Friess "Judicial Economy (WTO)" *MPEiPro* (2017).

29 See however the dispute concerning the implementation of the report in *EC–Hormones* (DS 26-1998) which was the object of Panel/AB reports in *US–Continued Suspension* (DS 320-2008),

30 Article 17.14 DSU.

4. The Operation of the DSS in the Absence of a Functioning AB

The AB quickly acquired a central place in the WTO DSS in view of its functions, abundant case law, the recognized quality of its legal reasoning and the contribution it has made to the legal interpretation of the WTO agreements, specifically in respect of several key provisions that have been repeatedly the object of disputes in the DSS.[31] It has thereby decisively contributed to the functioning of dispute settlement, described in Article 3.2 DSU as being "a central element in providing security and predictability to the multilateral trading system". As stated there, the DSS serves "to preserve the rights and obligations of Members under the covered agreements, and to clarify the existing provisions of those agreements in accordance with customary rules of interpretation of public international law".

The AB's reputation has extended beyond the WTO as a model adjudicatory institution that has dealt with difficult methodological and substantive questions of interpretation under the VCLT with competence and restraint.[32] The AB has had a heavy caseload, issuing up to ten decisions per year, which is more than other international courts have issued over longer periods. The respect that the AB has gained from WTO Members and experts in the field has enhanced the authority of its decisions and its role as the judge of last resort in relation to the compliance of WTO Members with their commitments. Hence the label of "jewel of the crown" that has been bestowed upon it by WTO Directors-Generals since its early days.

The current paralysis of the appellate stage must be briefly addressed in this chapter covering appeals and other reviews, although this matter will be covered in more details in Chapter VII. The reasons that have motivated the US to be dissatisfied with the AB's activity are political more than legal.[33] The US, alone among WTO Members, has accused the AB of "overreach" and "judicial activism", leading it to the extreme step of blocking the appointment of its members (which requires positive consensus at the DSB) from 2017 on, to the point of making it non-operational by the end of 2019 - beginning of 2020 because of lack of Members. It is necessary at this point to briefly present the current situation, highlighting the impact of the paralysis of the appellate stage on the operation of

31 See *Merills*, 328.

32 See Chapter VII.A.2.2. This includes questions with importance beyond the WTO context, such as the relevance of soft-law declarations of international organizations (AB *EC–Tariff Preferences* (DS 246-2004), 163), the relationship between different treaties, including between different parties (Panel *EC–Chicken Cuts* (DS 269, 286-2005) 7.181–7.189), bilateral derogations from multilateral treaties (AB *Peru–Agricultural Products*, (DS 457-2015) 5.81–5.119), the conditions making subsequent practice relevant for treaty interpretation (*EC–Chicken Cuts* cit.) 251–276.

33 See FT (Editorial), "Fears of Destructive Protectionism Are Overdone" (26 April 2024), asserting that the WTO's rule book "is inadequate to constrain China's state capitalist model, and the US is keener on subverting the institution by crippling its dispute settlement system than on truly reforming it", available at https://www.ft.com/content/c8d841ec-8f78-47b7-b016-52dad74c4bff accessed 23 July 2024; see also Y. Fukunaga "Interpretative Authority of the AB. Replies to the Criticism by the US" in *The Appellate Body of the WTO and its Reform,* cit n 19, 167, arguing that "the US wrongly or deliberately alters what the AB in fact stated in the past decisions in view to discrediting the AB".

the DSS, especially since the reinstatement of a functioning AB appears far from imminent.

The panel stage of WTO dispute settlement remains fully functioning. Claims of non-compliance with the WTO agreements may be brought by Members against one another in line with the DSU. Panels are established at the request of a complainant where consultations have failed to resolve the matter. If, however, the panel phase concludes with a finding that the respondent is in breach of one of its WTO obligations, and no satisfactory settlement is achieved by the parties, the respondent may exercise its right to appeal by filing it "into the void", which is a proper description as there is no AB in place to examine it. As a consequence, the panel report cannot be adopted by the DSB and the case remains indefinitely pending and unresolved, as has been the case for about 25 proceedings by the end of 2024.[34] A respondent can thus keep its non-compliant measure in place, which *de facto* encourages the other party to react with countermeasures without any authorization by the DSB, thus leading to a further breach of the DSU procedural requirements, weakening of the rule of law base of the DSS and trust in the system.[35]

As a consequence, the DSS, and more broadly the WTO, is seemingly back to the set-up of the GATT where a losing party could unilaterally block the adoption of a panel report. This is a step back from the WTO's rule-based system to the GATT's power-based system where a powerful losing party could either pressure a weaker winning party to accept an unfavourable settlement or indefinitely defy its obligations to comply. Even more, the blockage by the US does not exempt only the US from any final decision against its measures, it blocks all the membership.

The MPIA, launched by the EU with other Members in 2019, as an alternative voluntary system of appeal based on arbitration under Article 25 DSU will be examined in detail in Chapters VII and VIII. While the MPIA is capable of overcoming the AB blockage, of course it only works among those Members that have signed up to it. This is the case of 27 WTO Members (counting the EU as one), including a number of large economies and frequent users of the DSS (such as Australia, Brazil, Canada, China, the EU, Japan, and Switzerland). Aside from the US, however, several other frequent parties to WTO disputes (such as India, Indonesia, and South Africa) have not subscribed to it, availing themselves of the possibility of appealing adverse panel reports into the void. A further consequence

34 See Chapter VII.A.2.5.

35 This is what has happened in respect of US additional duties on steel and aluminium imports, to which some of the WTO Members affected have reacted by introducing duties against US exports, besides challenging them before panels, see the critical comments of J. Weiler, "Black Lies, White Lies and Some Uncomfortable Truths in and of the International Trading System" Editorial, 29 Eur. J. Int'l L. (2018) 339. In turn, the US has challenged these duties before panels but none of the disputes have been resolved (though panels have found that both actions were WTO-inconsistent) due to appeals into the void. See Chapter VII.A.2.5. See generally R. Polanco and S. Stacy "Process Failure: What does the Lack of Appellate Review Mean for Due Process of Law in WTO Disputes?" 27 ZEuS 539 (2024). This stalemate has amplified in respect of the US unilateral tariff increases in 2025.

affecting the functioning of the WTO as a whole is that trust in the usefulness of having recourse to the DSS as the principal avenue for upholding Members' rights has dropped, as evidenced by the decrease in new cases after 2019.[36]

B. Investment

1. Annulment Against International Arbitral Awards

One of the typical and key features of arbitration as a consent-based alternative to accessing the judiciary is that it consists of a one-stage process for deciding disputes. The lack of review by national courts of the merits of awards is justified by the consensual basis of arbitration, including as to the choice of format and selection of arbitrators. The limitation of review to annulment (defined as the "setting aside" of an award in some jurisdictions and in the 2006 UNCITRAL Model Law on International Commercial Arbitration[37]) in case of grave breaches of due process in proceedings rests on several justifications. Foremost, because recourse to arbitration as an alternative to normal courts' competence is limited to business (commercial) relations where parties are presumed to be capable of evaluating where their best interest lies, and hence the pros and cons of such a choice.[38]

The reasons are even more evident in respect of international commercial arbitration which, as recalled in Chapter I, is a standard way of settling disputes that may arise in commercial intercourses pertaining to cross-border dealings between parties having their place of business in different countries. In comparison with any purely domestic context, international arbitration has the additional advantage of avoiding conflict of laws and jurisdictions. It allows parties to choose important elements that facilitate the resolution of a transnational dispute, such as adjudicators, the applicable law, language, seat, and rules of proceedings. Arbitration is favoured by domestic law and international conventions, as it enhances the legal security of these transactions and relieves overloaded domestic jurisdictions from having to entertain complex, time- and resource-demanding cases. The absence, as a rule, of appeal even for legal errors against international commercial awards is a logical consequence of those features, with the same rationale being true for investment awards.[39]

36 See Chapter VIIA.2.5 for statistical data.

37 See UNCITRAL, *Model Law on International Commercial Arbitration* (1985), with amendments as adopted in 2006 available at https://uncitral.un.org, accessed 18 July 2024.

38 See generally A. Mourre, "La légitimité de l'arbitrage" 427 RC (2022) 211. This consensual underpinning is not found in all types of arbitration; Hence the Conclusions of AG Capeta (16 January 2025), in case C-600/23 before the CJEU that CAS awards in sports arbitration should be always subject to full review by national courts in the EU, www.curia.europa.eu.

39 For a limited appeal to a court on a point of law see, however, Section 69 of the UK Arbitration Act (1996) available at www.legislation.gov.uk. Appeal to a review board against awards is provided for by some trade associations, such as GAFTA (which is specialized in agricultural commodities, see https://www.gafta.com/Arbitration) and the Federation of Oils, Seeds and Fats Associations (FOSFA, see https://www.fosfa.org/). From time to time, there are calls for a right of appeal as a

This does not mean that states involved, including where such awards are issued or where their recognition is sought, renounce all checks on them. Limited controls are exercised by those jurisdictions through annulment proceedings (in the place of arbitration) or denial of recognition in other countries, with the aim of ensuring the respect for fundamental due process principles in the arbitral process and the absence of conflicts with local public policy. While non-ICSID awards are subject to those controls, ICSID provides for a self-contained international arbitral system which is distinct also as to its internal exclusive system of review of awards.[40]

2. *The Annulment of Awards under the ICSID Convention*

The ICSID Convention follows the typical arbitration model in providing for annulment but not appeal against its awards. As international decisions, ICSID awards are subject only to the Convention's regime. As stated in Article 53.1 of the ICSID Convention, "The award shall be binding on the parties and shall not be subject to any appeal or to any other remedy except those provided for in this Convention". Annulment is provided by Article 52:

> Either party may request annulment of the award by an application in writing addressed to the Secretary-General on one or more of the following grounds: (a) that the Tribunal was not properly constituted; (b) that the Tribunal has manifestly exceeded its powers; (c) that there was corruption on the part of a member of the Tribunal; (d) that there has been a serious departure from a fundamental rule of procedure; or (e) that the award has failed to state the reasons on which it is based.[41]

remedy against legal errors in the application of the law against international commercial awards, but these efforts have not been successful. For a discussion, see W. Knull III, N. Rubins, "Betting the Farm on International Commercial Arbitration: Is it Time to Offer an Appeal Option?" 11 American Rev Int'l Arb (2000) 531. Introducing appeal in ISDS, as a possible alternative or an addition to the EU proposal of a MIC, is, however, an option currently envisaged in the works of UNCITRAL WG III, see Chapter VIII.B.5.2.

40 For a comparison see G. Sacerdoti, "Appeal and Judicial Review in International Arbitration and Adjudication: The Case of the WTO Appellate Review" (n 1); V. Pratan Singh et al, "Annulment and Vacatur: ICSID and non-ICSID" (GAR, 21 December 2023) <https://globalarbitrationreview.com/guide/the-guide-investment-treaty-protection-and-enforcement/second-edition/article/annulment-and-vacatur> accessed 23 July 2024.

41 The ICSID Convention at Articles 49–50 provides also for *rectification* of awards by the same tribunal in respect of "any question it has omitted to decide" or of any "clerical, arithmetical or similar error"; *interpretation* (in case of dispute "between the parties as to the meaning or scope of the award". *Revision* may be requested by either party (Article 51) "on the ground of discovery of some fact of such a nature as decisively to affect the award, provided that when the award was rendered that fact was unknown to the Tribunal and to the applicant and that the applicant's ignorance of that fact was not due to negligence". This provision, which has been rarely resorted to and is rarely found in arbitration rules, is patterned on Article 61 ICJ Statute.

No other ground is admitted, although the ones listed "do not constitute neatly distinguishable categories" and each of them covers a rather broad number of possible defects.[42]

As is apparent from the above list and the comparative table annexed to this chapter, remedies against an award provided at ICSID are patterned after those listed in the ILC Model Rules on Arbitral Procedure (for interstate disputes) and those available against international commercial awards under the NY Convention, both of which were adopted in 1958. They relate to the correct conduct of proceedings, in order to remedy serious breaches affecting the integrity of an arbitration, but do not include, except in the most extreme cases (such as where an award lacks reasoning), a review of the substance (merit) of decisions of arbitral tribunals. Specifically, there is no review of the appreciation of evidence nor of the choice, interpretation and application of legal principles as is instead typical of appeals.[43]

Annulment requests by either party are to be submitted within 120 days after the issuance of an award. These applications are heard by *ad hoc* committees of three persons chosen from the roster of arbitrators by the Chairman of the Administrative Council (i.e. the president of the World Bank). Committees are in substance panels of arbitrators that are drawn from the same roster from which arbitrators may be drawn. Committees are in no sense "superior" to tribunals; their role as reviewers does not give them a higher hierarchical position. This is consistent with committees, like arbitral tribunals, being *ad hoc*, with their members however being chosen by the institution, rather than by the parties. Committees do not lay down jurisprudence that tribunals are supposed to follow, although their interpretation and application of the requirements that proceedings and awards must comply with under Article 52 represent guidance for tribunals in this respect. The procedure follows for the relevant parts the provisions that are laid down for tribunals, with the caveat that the record to be examined is that of the tribunal and no new evidence can be submitted. While annulment proceedings are pending, a committee has the power to stay the enforcement of the award, with or without imposing conditions such as the posting of a guarantee.[44]

A committee may reject the request for annulment, as has occurred in the great majority of cases, or may annul the award partially or in whole. As stated in Article 53.2 ICSID, a committee's decision is final and binding in the same way as an award. Annulment committees have no power to amend an award or to remand cases.[45] In case of annulment, either party has the option of resubmitting the dispute

42 *ICSID Commentary* II, Article 52, 119.

43 Applicants have sometimes argued that a breach of Article 42.1 on the applicable law may amount to an excess of power or a failure to state reasons, *ICSID Commentary* II, Article 52, 1258, 116.

44 See Article 53.5 ICSID and AR 73.

45 However, after having partially annulled the award challenged, the Committee in *Occidental v Ecuador* ICSID ARB/06/11, Decision on Annulment (2015), proportionately reduced the compensation that the tribunal had granted.

to a new tribunal in accordance with the Convention as explicitly provided for in Article 52(6).[46]

Annulment requests have for a long time been rare under the Convention but the pace has increased while the standard of review has over time become more rigorous.[47] Until 2000, there had been just five annulment decisions. The number increased to 21 by the end of the 2000s, 63 by the end of the 2010s.[48] By mid-2024, there have been 125 annulment decisions in total, leading to 23 partial or total annulments of awards.[49]

The high ratio of unsuccessful annulment requests is due both to the care with which tribunals deal with procedural due process issues, and the high bar set by the text and its application by committees for finding a violation of Article 52. This is in line with the "extraordinary" nature of annulment in the ICSID system.[50] In this respect committees, though *ad hoc* and mostly composed of different members from case to case, have developed a remarkably consistent (and abundant) jurisprudence "after an uncertain start".[51]

Looking now briefly at the practice of the application of each ground listed in Article 52 ICSID, the improper constitution of the tribunal in subparagraph 1(a) relates to the qualifications of arbitrators required by Article 14.1 and their alleged lack of independence and impartiality, provided that the lack of these qualities could have had a material effect on the award.[52]

A tribunal may manifestly exceed its powers (Article 52.1(b)) when it decides the case in a way that goes beyond the submissions of the parties (or refrains from deciding an issue submitted to it),[53] notably if it exercises jurisdiction and rules on the merits without a proper basis. The term "manifest" points to an excess of pow-

46 Resubmission under Article 53.6 has been rare, leading to further annulment proceedings in five cases.

47 For an analysis see A. Crivellaro, "Annulment of ICSID Awards. Back to the 'First Generation'" in L Levy, Y. Derains (eds) *Liber Amicorum S. Lazareff* (Pedone 2011) 145.

48 Moreover, during the same period, 42 annulment proceedings were discontinued. See *The ICSID Caseload – Statistics (Issue 2024–2)* available at https://icsid.worldbank.org accessed 18 January 2025; ICSID, *Background Paper on Annulment* (3rd ed. 2024), available at https://icsid.worldbank.org accessed 18 July 2024.

49 The ratio of annulments to the number of requests decided has varied over the years: initially, the number was substantial, thereafter for many years annulments were isolated (in correspondence with a decrease in the ratio of requests) and thereafter both numbers have been increasing again.

50 Thus, Article 52 (b) requires as a ground for annulment that the tribunal has "manifestly" exceeded its powers, while under Article 52 (d) the departure from a rule of procedure must be "serious" and concern a "fundamental" rule.

51 See *ICSID Commentary* II, Article 52, 1230–1240, quoting, at 1235, the Committee Decision on Annulment *MTD v Chile* ICSID ARB 01/7 (2007) 54.

52 See the Decisions on Annulment *Azurix v Argentina* ICSID ARB/01/12 (2009), and *Eisner v Spain* ICSID ARB/13/36 (2020), annulling the awards because of a conflict of interest of an arbitrator due to his close relationship with a party's expert. On the qualifications and duties of investment and commercial arbitrators in general see Y. Derains *The Conduct of International Arbitration Proceedings* (Elgar 2024).

53 That is *infra* or *ultra petita*.

ers that is both obvious and substantial, thus limiting the permissible reassessment of tribunals' decisions, especially in matters of jurisdiction. This limitation has not prevented committees, when requested by a party, from re-examining several of the complex jurisdictional bases required by Article 25 ICSID.[54] Failure to apply the proper law (including international law), as distinguished from alleged errors in its application, has also been recognized as a possible excess of powers.[55] The awkward result of this inherent limitation is that a committee may detect errors in the application of the law by the tribunal which may well have led to a wrong outcome, without being able to rectify the award challenged before it.[56]

Corruption of a tribunal member (subparagraph 1(c)) has never been successfully raised in annulment proceedings.[57] The text of Article 52(d), requiring as a ground for annulment "a serious departure from a fundamental rule of procedure", is further evidence that annulment is only warranted in cases of breach of basic due process principles which ensure the fairness of proceedings, the right to a defence and the equal treatment of the parties.[58] The case law on annulment indicates that tribunals enjoy reasonable discretion as to the admissibility and probative value of the evidence and the use of inferences, as recognized by AR 36, as long as they "remain within the legal framework established by the parties", that is the Convention and the relevant BIT.[59]

The failure to state reasons (subparagraph 1(e)) is the most frequently invoked ground for annulment. Such failure does not solely arise where there is a total absence of reasons, a failure that is unheard of in the practice of international

54 See V. Djani, S. Schill, "Article 52(1)(b)" in J. Fouret and others (eds) *The ICSID Convention: A Practical Commentary* (Elgar 2019) 4.1007; *Soufraki v UAE* ICSID ARB/02/7, Decision on Annulment (2007), 118.

55 See the many decisions referred to in *ICSID Commentary* II, Article 52, 1290–1295. Although the distinction is not always easy to make, it is fundamental in order for annulment not to be turned into appeal.

56 This is what happened in *CMS v Argentina* ICSID ARB/01/8, Decision on Annulment (2007), 130–136. Generally, as to the distinction between appeal and annulment, see K. Sauvant (ed) *Appeals Mechanism in International Investment Disputes* (OUP 2008).

57 A different issue concerns the treatment by arbitral tribunals of allegations that the investment has been obtained or maintained due to corruption, which might lead to the dismissal of a claim for lack of jurisdiction (because the investment was not "legal") or rejection of the claim on the merits, see Y. Yan, "Corruption and the (Un)Clean Hands Doctrine in Investor–State Arbitration: Definitional and Reciprocity Challenges" 39 ICSID Rev (2024); G. Cordero-Moss, "Corruption and Arbitration: Arbitrability, Jurisdiction, Admissibility or Merits?" in M. Benedettelli and others (eds) *Arbitration as Balanced Administration of Justice* (Brill 2024) 194.

58 On the crucial importance of equality of the parties as a general principle of law applicable to the procedure of international courts and tribunals, see the IDI Resolution on the Equality of Parties before International Investment Tribunals (2019) available at https://www.idi-iil.org and commentary by C. McLachlan, *The Institute of International Law's Resolution on the Equality of Parties Before International Investment Tribunals. Introduction, Text and Commentaries* (CUP 2021)

59 See *Caratube v Kazakhstan* ICSID ARB/08/12, Decision on Annulment (2014), 93–94. Under AR 28 (*Waiver*) a party that does not react to a violation of the correct procedure of which it is aware will be considered to have waived its right to subsequently object to that irregularity.

arbitration.[60] This requirement refers rather to the need for the operative part of the award (*decisum*), in its various findings or conclusions, to be sustained by pertinent, non-contradictory legal arguments, logically capable of explaining how the tribunal has come to its decision. This does not however mean that the correctness of such reasons (its quality) is reviewable, thus maintaining the distinction between annulment and appeal.

The grounds for annulment in Article 52 are limited and closed. Nullity will only be declared where the existence of one of the listed grounds is convincingly found to have affected the substance of an award. However, the mere existence of such a review has a "self-disciplinary" effect on tribunals, mandating completeness and accuracy in their examination of parties' arguments and submissions, lest their decisions be set aside.

3. *Annulment and the Denial of Recognition of Non-ICSID Investment Awards*

As mentioned above, arbitration awards are, as a rule, not subject to appeal on the merits. International commercial awards are not subject to public international law as interstate awards are. This is the case also for non-ICSID investment awards, both when they are issued by treaty-based organizations, as the PCA, and by private-commercial institutions, such as the ICC, LCIA, SCC, or SIAC.[61] On the contrary, since even international commercial awards (those settling an international commercial dispute) are ultimately connected to a domestic jurisdiction, controls on the respect for basic principles are provided in the jurisdiction where proceedings were seated (through annulment or other proceedings to set the award aside), or by the judiciary of other countries as a condition for granting recognition when sought there. Investment awards rendered in such contexts are indistinguishable as to their form and legal regime from other awards dealing with commercial disputes between business entities and are thus subject to the same challenges.

3.1. *Annulment in the Country of the Seat of Arbitration*

As explained above, arbitral proceedings and investment awards issued pursuant to non-ICSID rules or on an *ad hoc* basis are subject to the municipal law of some jurisdiction, in principle that of the seat of the tribunal. This is true even if, in practice, due to the extensive use of arbitration administered by arbitral institutions, application of local procedural law and recourse to local courts before and during proceedings is residual and rare.[62] An award may be challenged at the seat even if the parties are all based abroad and the seat was chosen as a "neutral" place unconnected with the subject matter and the parties. Often the seat (which as a legal

60 *Vivendi v Argentina (I)* ICSID ARB/97/3, Decision on Annulment (2002), 64–65; *ICSID Commentary* II, Article 52, 1344.

61 See Chapter II.B.2.2.

62 According to its Article I.1, the NYC also applies "to arbitral awards not considered as domestic awards in the State where their recognition and enforcement are sought" even if made there.

concept usually, but not necessarily, coincides with the place where proceedings have taken place and the award has been issued) is chosen precisely because of the reputation of the judiciary as to efficiency and impartiality in respect of challenges of awards. Recognition of an award in other countries is usually sought by the winning party in order to enforce the judgment against the assets located there of a non-complying losing party. In turn, the latter may oppose recognition and challenge such an award in order that its recognition be denied and its enforcement prevented. As a rule, while annulment of an award in the place of the seat affects in principle its validity in all other countries, non-recognition in another jurisdiction has no extra-territorial effects.[63]

Awards are subject to annulment for serious breaches of fundamental procedural principles, but review on the merits is typically excluded. This is the approach adopted by the UNCITRAL Model Law on International Commercial Arbitration whose text has been accepted, with or without modifications, by most countries when enacting or updating their legislation. As advocated by UNCITRAL, awards settling domestic disputes are mostly subject to the same rules, although in some jurisdictions controls over awards concerning international disputes are more limited.[64]

The Model Law does not spell out the binding effect of awards for the parties, an inherent feature of final arbitral decisions that is provided in arbitration rules and relevant domestic statutes on arbitration.[65] It is for such statutes to specify whether an award is final and binding upon its rendering or whether it must be filed in court or another public office, for enforceability. Historically, such requirements often included a preliminary court examination of local awards (*exequatur*), making recourse to arbitration more burdensome than accessing the courts. These kinds of requirements have however been progressively reduced. The prevailing situation currently is rather that national awards are equated to local courts' judgments.[66]

According to Article 34 of the Model Law, application for setting aside (annulment) is the exclusive recourse against arbitral awards, based on the six grounds listed there, namely (a) if the party making the application furnishes proof that: (i) a party to the arbitration agreement was under some incapacity; or the said agreement is not valid under the law to which the parties have subjected it or, failing

63 See for more detail, see Chapter VI.B.1.2. Article V.1 (e) NY Convention lists as a possible ground for non-recognition that "(e) the award has not yet become binding on the parties, or has been set aside or suspended by a competent authority of the country in which, or under the law of which, that award was made".

64 See n 68.

65 See, for instance, Article 35.6 ICC: "Every award shall be binding on the parties. By submitting the dispute to arbitration under the Rules, the parties undertake to carry out any award without delay and shall be deemed to have waived their right to any form of recourse insofar as such waiver can validly be made".

66 See G. Born, *International Commercial Arbitration* (3rd ed. Wolters Kluwer 2021), Chapter 22.03. See typically Article 804-bis Italian code civil procedure: "An award has the same effect as a court judgment from the date of the last arbitrators' signature" and must be deposited at the local tribunal only if enforcement is sought in Italy.

any indication thereon, under the law of this state; or (ii) the party making the application was not given proper notice of the appointment of an arbitrator or of the arbitral proceedings or was otherwise unable to present its case; or (iii) the award deals, in whole or in part, with a dispute not contemplated by or not falling within the terms of the submission to arbitration, or contains decisions on matters beyond the scope of the submission to arbitration; or (iv) the composition of the arbitral tribunal or the arbitral procedure was not in accordance with the agreement of the parties. An award may also be set aside if (b) the court finds that: (i) the subject matter of the dispute is not capable of settlement by arbitration under the law of this state; or (ii) the award is in conflict with the public policy of this state.

The Model Law "presents a special legal regime tailored to international commercial arbitration … as a response to the inadequacies and disparities of national laws", although "it offers a set of basic rules that are not, in and of themselves, unsuitable to any other type of arbitration", specifically in respect of domestic disputes.[67] Some jurisdictions distinguish between "purely domestic" proceedings and awards (between local parties and having as their object domestic matters) and those between parties of different nationalities involving international business matters. The latter are subject to a different regime as to proceedings (with greater autonomy granted to the parties) and more limited review of awards, also as to public policy.[68]

3.2. Denial of Recognition in Other Countries

The recognition of foreign awards is governed in most countries by the New York Convention of 1958 on the Recognition and Enforcement of Foreign Arbitral Awards (NY Convention) which was in force in 172 parties as of the end of 2024.[69] The limited checks on foreign awards permitted by the Convention, in conformity with the *favor arbitratus* which inspires it, make the international circulation of awards easier than that of foreign judgments.[70] The general rule of Article III is

67 See UNCITRAL Secretariat, *UNCITRAL Model Law on International Commercial Arbitration*, Explanatory Note <https://uncitral.un.org/sites/uncitral.un.org/files/media-documents/uncitral/en/19-09955_e_ebook.pdf> 26.

68 See respectively Articles 1492–1497 of the French Civil Code, introduced in 1981, and Chapter 12 of the Swiss Law on private international law, Articles 176–193. Article 192 allows parties, if none has its domicile, habitual residence or seat in Switzerland, to exclude almost all recourses against arbitral awards. A similar provision is that of Article 1718 of the Belgian Judicial Code.

69 The Convention also includes, importantly, at Article II, the obligation upon contracting states to "recognize" arbitration agreements, that is to deny access to their courts at the request of one of the parties and to refer them to arbitration if arbitration has been agreed, unless the competent court finds the arbitration agreement (clause) "null and void, inoperative or incapable of being performed".

70 See generally A.J. Van den Berg, *The New York Convention of 1958* (Kluwer 1981); H. Kronke and others (eds) *Recognition and Enforcement of Foreign Arbitral Awards. A Global Commentary on the New York Convention* (Kluwer 2010); G. Born n 66; F. Ferrari, F. Rosenfeld, F. Fellas, *International Commercial Arbitration. A Comparative Introduction* (Elgar 2021); M. Moses, *The Principles and Practice of International Commercial Arbitration* (4th ed. CUP 2024). Up-to-date information

that each contracting state undertakes to recognize foreign arbitral awards as binding and to enforce them in accordance with its applicable procedural rules subject to a simple procedure. The party applying for recognition and enforcement must only supply the original award, or a duly certified copy thereof, and the arbitration agreement. It is for the other party to oppose the request for recognition.

The grounds for objection under the NYC are similar to those provided for in the UNCITRAL Model Law against locally issued awards. According to Article V(1), recognition and enforcement *may* be refused, at the request of the party against whom it is invoked, only if that party furnishes to the competent authority proof that: (a) the arbitration agreement is invalid because of some incapacity of a party, or under the law applicable to it; or (b) the party against whom the award is invoked was not given proper notice of the proceedings or was otherwise unable to present his case; or (c) the award deals with a subject matter not falling within the terms of the arbitration agreement; or (d) the composition of the arbitral authority or the arbitral procedure was not in accordance with the agreement of the parties, or the law of the country where the arbitration took place; or (e) the award has not yet become binding on the parties, or has been set aside or suspended by a competent authority of the country in which, or under the law of which, that award was made. Two additional grounds for non-recognition, listed in Article V (2), concern the relation between the foreign award and the local legal system: if (a) the subject matter of the dispute is not capable of settlement by arbitration under the law of that country; or (b) the recognition or enforcement of the award would is contrary to the public policy of that country. The first five grounds must be raised by the party against whom the award has been invoked, while the last two may be raised by the court *ex officio* since they protect general interests of the country where recognition is sought.[71]

This list is broader than that of Article 52 ICSID. This is but natural considering that the NY Convention is applicable to all sorts of awards in commercial matters between the most diverse parties, rendered in any context, normally based on a contractual arbitration clause. In contrast, ICSID governs a specific type of proceedings against member states, carried out within the framework of its procedural rules and under the supervision of its international Secretariat.

Inevitably, the NY Convention's standards are applied somehow differently in different countries. This can be observed especially in the context of public policy, which in international arbitration should be limited to "truly" accepted international principles, such as those concerning fundamental human rights and international crimes, rather than local regulations.[72]

on the NYC's application is available at www.newyorkconvention.org/english and through www.wolterskluwer.com/en/solutions/kluwerarbitration

71 See A. Maurer, *The Public Policy Exception Under the New York Convention. History, Interpretation and Application* (2nd ed. Juris 2022). On the effect in other countries of annulment in the country of the seat and denial of recognition under the NY Convention, see Chapter VI.B. 1.2.

72 As famously advocated by P. Lalive, "Ordre public transnational (ou réellement international) et arbitrage international" Rev. Arbitrage (1986) 329. See also L. Radicati di Brozolo, "Arbitrage com-

C. Comparative Evaluation

1. Commonalities

(a) Both systems, trade disputes under the WTO DSU and ISDS at ICSID, provide for two-tier adjudication whereby the decisions of panels and investment tribunals are subject to review within the respective systems at the initiative of the losing party. The commonalities end here however, since the WTO DSS features an almost unique system of appeal in law to a permanent court-type body, whereas ICSID has adopted the commercial arbitration model whereby there is a limited review of awards, entrusting this to *ad hoc* arbitral committees, which may annul the challenged award based on a limited number of grounds.

(b) In both systems if a decision (panel report, award) is annulled (set aside, reversed) the review jurisdiction may neither re-judge the case nor remand it to a WTO panel or arbitration tribunal respectively. The winning party, if interested, must restart the case.

(c) In the multilateral trade system, in the current situation of a non-functioning AB, a provisional partial solution has been found replacing it by an *ad hoc* arbitration mechanism (the MPIA), which is only binding for the subset of WTO Members that have agreed to it. This structure brings the review of trade decisions closer to that of annulment review of investment awards at ICSID, not as to the substance but as to the structure. It evidences the usefulness, albeit as a fallback, of the flexibility of arbitration as a means of maintaining the integrity of any international binding DSS. On the other hand, the MPIA is a second-best solution in the context of trade, while annulment works satisfactorily for investment disputes under IIAs. Calls for it be supplemented or replaced by appeal to a permanent appeal tribunal have not gained momentum in the past although the issue is again under examination at UNCITRAL WG III.[73]

2. Differences

The salient differences may be summarized as follows:

(a) The WTO DSS includes the right to an appeal in law to a permanent institution, the AB (functioning as a court), while ICSID awards are subject to more limited annulment review by *ad hoc* committees. Moreover the AB at the

mercial international et lois de police: considérations sur les conflits de juridictions dans le commerce international" 315 RC (2005) 267.

73 See B. Legum, "Options to establish an appellate mechanism for investment disputes" in K. Sauvant (ed) *Appeals Mechanism in International Investment Disputes* (OUP 2008) 231. As to the discussion of the issue at UNCITRAL WG III in 2024, see Chapter VIII.B.5.3. A different, more radical approach is that of replacing ISDS altogether with investment tribunals (ICS) or a multilateral court (MIC), as advocated by the EU, and analysed in Chapter VIII.B.3–4, including an appeal stage.

WTO is a central feature of the system; it has been called to review a substantial majority of panel reports, ensuring consistency in the interpretation and application of the WTO multilateral trade agreements by all WTO Members beyond the dispute context. Annulment in ISDS is an eventuality, used on a case-by-case basis; it does not contribute to the interpretation of the substantive standards of protections of IIAs, but only - at ICSID - to due process in arbitration.

(b) Recourse against panel reports at the WTO is allowed for any legal reason, principally concerning the merits, whereas annulment at ICSID (and by domestic jurisdictions in respect of non-ICSID awards) may be requested only based on specific grounds relating to the integrity of proceedings.

(c) The AB reviews all of the legal findings of panels that have been challenged, especially where they relate to the interpretation and application of the substantive provisions of the WTO agreements that govern the conduct of its Members in international trade matters. The limited annulment powers of ICSID committees do not include reviewing the correct application by tribunals of the standards of treatment of foreign investment laid down in applicable IIAs. It is limited to the review of the correct application by the tribunal of fundamental requirements of due process disputed by the applicant.

(d) As a consequence, while the AB ensures consistency in the interpretation of the substantive rules of the WTO for the benefit of all participants, review at ICSID does not contribute to the interpretation of the substantive provisions (standards of protection) of IIAs.

(e) Non-ICSID investment awards are subject to annulment only for serious procedural defects and breach of public order principles, as generally provided for international commercial awards under domestic law. Annulment may be requested at the place of arbitration according to the local regulation of annulment of (international) commercial awards rendered there. If granted, annulment, in principle, renders the award null and void and unenforceable also in other countries. Denial of recognition pursuant to the NY Convention in other states may be granted for similar due process and public order reasons, with effects limited however to the jurisdiction denying recognition.

Annex

Comparative table of appeal/annulment provisions in international instruments (WTO, UN Model Rules on Arbitral Procedure, ICSID Convention, UNCITRAL Model Arbitration Law, and the New York Convention)

WTO DSU Article 17 DSU *Appeal*	*UN Model Rules on Arbitral Procedure ILC 1958* *Invalidity*	*ICSID Convention Article 52* *Annulment*	*UNCITRAL Model Arbitration Law (2006) Article 34* *Set Aside*	*UN Convention on the Recognition and Enforcement of Foreign Arbitral Awards (New York 1958)* *Annulment*
Article 17 *Appellate Review Standing Appellate Body* 17.6. An appeal shall be limited to issues of law covered in the panel report and legal interpretations developed by the panel. 17.12. The Appellate Body shall address each of the issues raised in accordance with paragraph 6 during the appellate proceeding.	**Article 35** *Validity and Annulment of the Award* The validity of an award may be challenged by either party on one or more of the following grounds: (a) That the tribunal has exceeded its powers; (b) That there was corruption on the part of a Member of the tribunal; (c) That there has been a failure to state the reasons for the award or a serious departure from a fundamental rule of procedure;	**Article 52** (1) Either party may request annulment of the award by an application in writing addressed to the Secretary-General on one or more of the following grounds: (a) that the tribunal was not properly constituted; (b) that the tribunal has manifestly exceeded its powers; (c) that there was corruption on the part of a Member of the tribunal; (d) that there has been a serious departure from a fundamental rule of procedure; or (e) that the award has failed to state the reasons on which it is based. (6) If the award is annulled the dispute shall, at the request of either party, be submitted to a new tribunal constituted in accordance with Section 2 of this chapter	**Article 34.** *Application for setting aside as exclusive recourse against arbitral award* (1) Recourse to a court against an arbitral award may be made only by an application for setting aside in accordance with paragraphs (2) and (3) of this article. (2) An arbitral award may be set aside by the court specified in Article 6 only if: (a) the party making the application furnishes proof that: (i) a party to the arbitration agreement referred to in Article 7 was under some incapacity; or the said agreement is not valid under the law to which the parties have subjected it or, failing any indication thereon, under the law of this state; or (ii) the party making the application was not given proper notice of the appointment of an arbitrator or of the arbitral proceedings or was otherwise unable to present his case; or	**Article V** 1. Recognition and enforcement of the award may be refused, at the request of the party against whom it is invoked, only if that party furnishes to the competent authority where the recognition and enforcement is sought, proof that: (a) The parties to the agreement referred to in Article II were, under the law applicable to them, under some incapacity, or the said agreement is not valid under the law to which the parties have subjected it or, failing any indication thereon, under the law of the country where the award was made; or (b) The party against whom the award is invoked was not given proper notice of the appointment of the arbitrator or of the arbitration proceedings or was otherwise unable to present his case; or

WTO DSU *Article 17 DSU* *Appeal*	*UN Model Rules on Arbitral Procedure ILC 1958* *Invalidity*	*ICSID Convention Article 52* *Annulment*	*UNCITRAL Model Arbitration Law (2006) Article 34* *Set Aside*	*UN Convention on the Recognition and Enforcement of Foreign Arbitral Awards (New York 1958)* *Annulment*
17.13. The Appellate Body may uphold, modify or reverse the legal findings and conclusions of the panel	(d) That the undertaking to arbitrate or the *compromis* is a nullity. *Article 37* If the award is declared invalid by the International Court of Justice, the dispute shall be submitted to a new tribunal constituted by agreement between the parties, or, failing such agreement, in the manner provided by Article 3		(iii) the award deals with a dispute not contemplated by or not falling within the terms of the submission to arbitration, or contains decisions on matters beyond the scope of the submission to arbitration, provided that, if the decisions on matters submitted to arbitration can be separated from those not so submitted, only that part of the award which contains decisions on matters not submitted to arbitration may be set aside; or (iv) the composition of the arbitral tribunal or the arbitral procedure was not in accordance with the agreement of the parties, unless such agreement was in conflict with a provision of this law from which the parties cannot derogate, or, failing such agreement, was not in accordance with this law; or (b) the court finds that: (i) the subject matter of the dispute is not capable of settlement by arbitration under the law of this state; or (ii) the award is in conflict with the public policy of this state	(c) The award deals with a difference not contemplated by or not falling within the terms of the submission to arbitration, or it contains decisions on matters beyond the scope of the submission to arbitration, provided that, if the decisions on matters submitted to arbitration can be separated from those not so submitted, that part of the award which contains decisions on matters submitted to arbitration may be recognized and enforced; or (d) The composition of the arbitral authority or the arbitral procedure was not in accordance with the agreement of the parties, or, failing such agreement, was not in accordance with the law of the country where the arbitration took place; or (e) The award has not yet become binding on the parties, or has been set aside or suspended by a competent authority of the country in which, or under the law of which, that award was made. 2. Recognition and enforcement of an arbitral award may also be refused if the competent authority in the country where recognition and enforcement is sought finds that: (a) The subject matter of the difference is not capable of settlement by arbitration under the law of that country; or (b) The recognition or enforcement of the award would be contrary to the public policy of that country

6 Compliance and Enforcement

Table of Contents

Introduction

This chapter sets out the differing regimes for the implementation of decisions in trade and investment law by voluntary compliance or enforcement.[1] Compliance has tended to be robust across the two systems ever since the two DSS began operating. Records indicate that decisions requiring respondents to comply with their treaty obligations and remedy ascertained breaches (in the trade system) and pay monetary compensation in case of breach if so ordered (in the investment system), have generally been complied with.[2] Enforcement mechanisms have ensured com-

1 One can define "compliance" as the end-result of implementing an unfavourable international decision, with enforcement being the process through which compliance is pursued in the case of lack of voluntary implementation. Non-compliance with binding international adjudicatory decisions is a problem across all sectors of international law and imperils its effectiveness (see *Merills*, 423). As to the difference between recognition, enforcement, and execution of ICSID awards, see *ICSID Commentary* II, Article 54, 78–87.

2 According to the latest data from ICSID, "Notably, looking at all 151 Awards in the study that awarded damages to a party ('Damages Awards'), award creditors obtained satisfaction through vol-

DOI: 10.4324/9781003471509-8

pliance when implementation of an unfavourable decision has not been voluntary. However, the recent crisis in the trade regime and disenchantment with the investment regime have resulted in challenges against existing regulation and may have contributed to the resistance to compliance observed recently. While Chapters VII and VIII chart this regression, its causes, and the likely future direction for compliance and enforcement in the trade and investment regimes, this chapter focuses on the law as it currently stands in this respect. Accordingly, in this chapter, we focus on the legal framework and institutional structures governing the post-decision phase, providing an overview of the outcomes in terms of achieving effective compliance with trade and investment decisions.

A. The Trade Regime

1. Implementation of WTO Panel and AB Reports

Articles 19–23 of the DSU comprehensively regulate the follow-up to panel or AB reports where they have concluded that a challenged measure is WTO-inconsistent, once they have been adopted by the DSB.[3]

The timeframe for DSB decisions adopting panel and AB reports, thus making them binding for the parties, is laid down in Article 20 DSU. Article 16 DSU (Adoption of Panel Reports) and Article 17.14 on the adoption of AB reports provide for a time limit of 60 and 30 days, respectively, from their circulation for the DSB to adopt them.[4] The basic principle stated in Article 21.1 is that recommendations and rulings of the DSB should be promptly complied with, this being

untary compliance or post-award settlements in 66% of cases, while 31% went to enforcement and in 3% enforcement was not pursued". ICSID Background Paper "Compliance with and Enforcement of ICSID Awards" (June 2024) 11, available at https://icsid.worldbank.org. As to trade, see G. Horlick and J. Cleman, "The Compliance Problem of the WTO" 1 Arizona J. Int. Comp. L. (2007) 21. According to W. Davey (a former director of the WTO Legal Division), in the first ten years of operation the compliance rate under the DSU was 83%, see W. Davey, "The WTO Dispute Settlement System: The First Ten Years" 8 JIEL (2005) 17. See also Id, "Compliance Problems in WTO Dispute Settlement" 42 Cornell Int. L. J. (2009) 19, referring to T. Ginsburg, R. McAdams, "Adjudicating in Anarchy: An Expressive Theory of International Dispute Resolution" 45 WM. & Mary L. Rev. (2004) 1229 for the proposition that "The success rate in the WTO system is clearly better than the success rate in the ICJ" (estimated at 68%).

3 According to Article 19.1 DSU, panels and the AB "may suggest ways in which the Member concerned could implement the recommendations". However, they have generally refrained from doing so, first because they are ill-equipped to make such suggestions (which would have to take into account the political and legal domestic context) and, secondly, since their (in any case non-binding) suggestions could be considered to be an encroachment on the Member's freedom to choose how to comply with its implementation obligation (such as by modifying a measure in one way or another rather than withdrawing it).

4 A panel stated that this time limit was "indicative only", Panel *US–Sections 301 Trade Act* (DS 152-1999), 7.31, but the DSB is convened regularly and in a timely manner in order to respect these deadlines. Footnote 7 at Article 16 DSU provides that: "If a meeting of the DSB is not scheduled within this period at a time that enables the requirements of paragraphs 1 and 4 of Article 16 to be met, a meeting of the DSB shall be held for this purpose."

"essential in order to ensure effective resolution of disputes to the benefit of all Members". Articles 21 and 22 DSU provide for a series of procedural steps involving DSB surveillance, parties' initiatives, resort to the original panel, the AB, and ad hoc arbitration in order to ensure full implementation in a "reasonable period of time" (RPT). The provision of detailed bilateral and collective procedures and obligations to ensure compliance is unique to the WTO DSS.

This objective conforms with the principle spelled out in Article 35 ARSIWA (*Restitution*) that "A State responsible for an internationally wrongful act is under an obligation to make restitution, that is, to re-establish the situation which existed before the wrongful act was committed". What is instead distinctive about the legal consequences of a breach under the WTO is that the obligation is prospective, focusing on future obligations, and does not entail an obligation to remedy past uncompliance, such as paying compensation for past and ongoing damages. Additionally, compliance with these obligations need not be immediate where this is "impracticable".[5]

Within 30 days from the adoption of a panel or AB report, the Member which has been found to be in breach of its WTO obligations (the losing respondent) must inform the DSB of its intentions in relation to implementation (Article 21.3 DSU). Where immediate compliance is impracticable (as respondents always tend to claim), the Member is given a "reasonable period of time" (RPT) to comply.[6] Such a period of time may be (i) proposed by the Member concerned and approved by the DSB, (ii) mutually agreed between the parties, or (iii) determined through binding arbitration within 90 days of the date of the report's adoption. The reasonable period of time should not exceed 15 months from the date of adoption of the report.[7]

5 According to Article 31 ARSIWA (Reparation): "1. The responsible State is under an obligation to make full reparation for the injury caused by the internationally wrongful act. 2. Injury includes any damage, whether material or moral, caused by the internationally wrongful act of a State". According to Article 36 (Compensation): "1. The State responsible for an internationally wrongful act is under an obligation to compensate for the damage caused thereby, insofar as such damage is not made good by restitution. 2. The compensation shall cover any financially assessable damage including loss of profits insofar as it is established". In general, as to the differences between the general international regime of reparation and the *lex specialis* (Article 55 ARSIWA) of the WTO DSS, see C. Brown, *A Common Law of International Adjudication* (OUP 2007) 189, 217.

6 There is no definition of "impracticable", which may refer to the practical implications of amending a legislative provision (when found non-compliant "as such") or of replacing an administrative act (such as re-doing an AD investigation and determination). The time needed in the first case is generally seen as warranting a longer RPT, due to the necessity of potentially overcoming political and business opposition and obtaining parliamentary (legislative) approval for the new measure.

7 However, as specified in Article 21.3 (c) DSU, "that time may be shorter or longer, depending upon the particular circumstances". Statistics show that until the end of 2023 there have been 38 cases where the RPT has been set by arbitration. The length of the RPT granted by arbitrators has varied from 6 months to 15 months and 1 week. If the parties cannot agree on an arbitrator (in practice, this is always a single arbitrator), the DG appoints the arbitrator (as has happened in 18 cases), who has, in most cases, been chosen among acting or past AB Members.

Where the parties disagree as to the existence or conformity of measures taken to comply with recommendations and rulings, the implementing measures may be challenged under Article 21.5 DSU in new panel proceedings (compliance proceedings) by resorting "whenever possible" to the original panel.[8] Questions of compliance in Article 21.5 proceedings may relate to the consistency of the measures, that is whether a measure has been correctly modified or withdrawn. The Article 21.5 panel's findings may be appealed to the AB.[9] Until the party responsible for implementing a panel or AB recommendation notifies the DSB that it has fully complied with that recommendation, or the parties inform the DSB that the dispute has been resolved, the DSB keeps implementation under its surveillance; the Member concerned must provide a status report at each DSB meeting, and all WTO Members can follow developments and express their views.[10]

The DSU allows the parties to a dispute to agree on compensation as a temporary measure pending "full implementation of a recommendation to bring a measure into conformity with the covered agreement".[11] In practice, however, the parties to a dispute have more than once agreed on some form of definitive compensation in lieu of implementation, a choice that cannot be challenged under the DSU.[12] Retaliation (a term that the DSU does not utilize but is in common use) via the suspension of concessions or other obligations owed to the non-compliant party is referred to as a "last resort" under 3.7 DSU.[13] If compensation cannot be agreed upon, and compliance is not effected by the losing party, the complainant "may request authorisation from the DSB to suspend concessions or other obligations" under the WTO agreements. The DSB decides by reverse consensus (Article

8 As per Article 2.5 DSU, panel compliance proceedings should not exceed 90 days, but this deadline is as unrealistic and disrespected as the deadline for original panels (400 days has been the average). There have been instances in which more than one Article 21.5 proceeding was initiated due to a party alleging that the other party failed to comply with the recommendation of the previous compliance panel. In total, there have been 65 Article 21.5 compliance proceedings, 44 panel reports, and 21 AB reports circulated under Article 21.5, see *Van den Bossche* 309.

9 The Appellate Body has found that for a new measure to be deemed a measure taken to comply (and hence amenable to a compliance panel examination), regard must be had to the factual and legal background of its adoption. AB *US–Softwood Lumber IV* (Article 21.5) (DS 257-2005), 77.

10 Article 21.6 DSU.

11 Article 22.1 DSU.

12 Well-known disputes have been settled through agreed-upon compensation in the form of tariff reductions on products other than those involved in the dispute or by granting duty-free quotas on such products, notably in *US–Clove Cigarettes* (DS 406-2010), as well as in the *Hormones* disputes between the US and Canada on one side and the EU on the other side, *EC–Hormones* (DS 26, 48-1998) and *US/Canada-Continued Suspension* (DS 320, 321-2008). See A. Jara, S. Evenett, "Settling WTO Disputes Without Solving the Problem: Abusing Compensation" (CEPR, 9 December 2014), https://cepr.org/voxeu/columns/settling-wto-disputes-without-solving-problem-abusing-compensation accessed 26 July 2024.

13 In general, see C. Bown, J. Pauwelyn (eds) *The Law, Economics and Politics of Retaliation in WTO Dispute Settlement* (CUP 2010). The correct term under general international law is "countermeasures". They consist of "the non-performance for the time being of international obligations of the State taking the measures towards the responsible State … in order to induce that State to comply with its obligations" (Article 49 ARSIWA).

22.5), so that in practice the "winning" party can put in place countermeasures immediately after the expiration of the RPT, autonomously determining the level of concessions it intends to suspend.[14] This must, however, be in compliance with the paramount principle of Article 22.4 that "the level of concessions or other obligations authorized by the DSB shall be equivalent to the level of nullification or impairment".[15]

The economic impact on the losing party of the selective increase of import duties adopted as a countermeasure by the winning party is often higher than the prejudice that was caused to the winner by the other party's WTO-inconsistent measure. The party that faces suspension almost invariably objects to the level chosen by the other party and may refer the determination "whether the level of such suspension is equivalent to the level of nullification or impairment" to arbitration, preferably by the original panel, with no possibility to appeal the resulting award (Article 22.6).[16] When this occurs, concessions shall not be suspended during the arbitration but suspension can be applied thereafter, to be authorized by the DSB within the limits determined in the award (Article 22.7).

The DSU provides for a detailed order to be followed as to the type of obligations to be suspended, so as to avoid any unnecessary prejudice from countermeasures and respect the principles of proportionality and reciprocity. In suspending concessions, the complaining party shall therefore apply the principle that these should concern the same sector where the violation occurred (DSU 22.3(a)). Only when this is not practicable or effective, may the suspension of concessions be applied to other sectors within the same agreement. Finally, under Article 22.3(c), if also this is not practicable or effective and the circumstances are serious enough, the Member may consider suspending concessions under another WTO agreement.

The impact on a losing party may also be exacerbated where the retaliating Member engages in "carousel retaliation". This involves rotating the goods to which the suspension of concessions or other obligations applies, thus lowering legal certainty and impacting a wider range of sectors. This practice has been used by the US and Mexico.[17] Although formally legal, it appears to go against the principle that the countermeasures be equivalent to the level of nullification or impairment.[18]

14 If, however, the respondent initiates a compliance proceeding, the application of retaliation should be suspended. This requires however, and usually occurs through an ad hoc agreement between the parties, due to the lack of clarity of the DSU in this respect ("sequencing agreement"); see *Van den Bossche*, 308–309.

15 This provision conforms to Article 51 ARSIWA ("Proportionality"): "Countermeasures must be commensurate with the injury suffered, taking into account the gravity of the internationally wrongful act and the rights in question".

16 The lack of appeal underlines that arbitration under Article 22.6 involves an economic valuation rather than legal considerations.

17 L. Griffin, "Carousel Retaliation: Tariff Uncertainty on Another Ride", available on https://www.hinrichfoundation.com (18 August 2020), accessed 19 July 2024.

18 In a review of the DSU in the late 1990s, the EU proposed adding a footnote to Article 22.7 DSU in order to ban the rotating approach, while the US sought to introduce a footnote explicitly permit-

Practice concerning compliance with reports and retaliation in cases of non-implementation has declined after 2019. Following the paralysis of the AB, panel reports have only been adopted by the DSB (eleven times up to the end of 2023) when the losing party has not appealed into the void. [19] In some cases, the parties have reached a mutually agreed solution, as happened in 2023 in three disputes (DS 598, 585, 547). In all other cases (24), respondents have appealed unfavourable reports "into the void" to the non-functioning AB, thus suspending the finalization of the case and preventing compliance with such reports, consequently leading the other party in some cases to suspend concessions against non-compliance.[20]

2. *Implementation under RTAs*

WTO Members have tended to litigate at the WTO rather than under the dispute settlement mechanisms of RTAs for various reasons. These include the high levels of trust in the WTO dispute settlement system, the relative predictability of the system, the enforceability of WTO reports, and the reputational damage the offending Member may suffer if it is seen to be violating its WTO commitments.[21] It can also simply be that there are not so many disputes arising between trading partners under the RTA's preferential regimes, or that disputes are more easily settled by negotiations in a bilateral setting without going to formal proceedings although a surge of cases under RTAs has occurred recently. The question of whether this shows a shift towards dispute settlement under RTAs, also in view of the semi-paralysis of the WTO DSS, is examined in Chapter VII.[22]

CPTPP, USMCA, CETA, and RCEP are four major recent RTAs containing texts agreed to by several of the world's leading trading nations.[23] Each of these RTAs contains bilateral trade dispute settlement and enforcement provisions that can be described as building upon those found in Articles 19–23 DSU, with the

ting it. While there was "much wider support" for the EU position, the DSU review was de facto suspended altogether thereafter. See T. A. Zimmerman, *Negotiating the Review of the WTO Dispute Settlement Understanding* (Cameron May 2006) 101.

19 However, the EU asked for a compliance panel in DS 577, *US–Ripe Olives from Spain* (DS 577-2021), claiming that the US had not complied with the non-appealed adopted panel report, and the 21.5 panel found in favour of the EU (compliance report circulated on 20 February 2024).

20 Precisely to respond to such a situation, the EU has amended its "Enforcement Regulation" 654/2014 by Reg. 2021/167 to allow an immediate response with countermeasures against parties that would appeal unfavourable panel reports into the void in disputes with the EU.

21 See *Moran*, 24; V. Bleyer, "Dispute Settlement in Preferential Trade Agreements and the WTO: A Network Analysis of Idleness and Choice of Forum" 32 EJIL (2021) 433.

22 See Chapter VII.A.3 for more detail.

23 The CPTPP members are (end of 2024): Australia, Brunei Darussalam, Canada, Chile, Japan, Malaysia, Mexico, New Zealand, Peru, Singapore, the United Kingdom, and Viet Nam (China has applied for membership); USMCA members include the US, Mexico, and Canada; CETA Members include Canada, the EU, and its Member States; RCEP members are China, Japan, South Korea, Australia, New Zealand, and the ten members of ASEAN (Brunei, Cambodia, Indonesia, Laos, Malaysia, Myanmar, the Philippines, Singapore, Thailand, and Vietnam).

difference that there is neither appeal against panels' decisions, nor adoption of reports by a collective body such as the DSB.[24]

These agreements share certain key elements with the DSU concerning compliance and implementation, such as:

- if a breach has been ascertained, panels issue binding recommendations that the inconsistent measure be brought into conformity (CPTPP, CETA, and RCEP);
- an obligation of prompt compliance within a reasonable period of time (CPTPP, CETA, and RCEP);[25]
- in case of non-compliance, as a temporary remedy, the suspension of concessions or compensation by the complainant that is equivalent to the impairment caused by the breach;[26]
- the possibility of referring an objection to the level of suspension to arbitration or to a panel;[27]
- such suspensions of compensation are temporary (until the removal of the measure or some agreement is reached).

A key element of the DSU that does not feature in the enforcement provisions of any of these four RTAs is that of surveillance of implementation of the panels' recommendations. This is due to the fact that there is no structure in place similar to the DSB that may exercise analogous functions of keeping implementation of recommendations or rulings under surveillance.[28]

We recall that under the DSU, WTO Members have a reasonable period of time to comply with recommendations and rulings where immediate compliance is impracticable, as regulated in Article 21.3 of the DSU. The RPT is also dealt with under most recent RTAs. CETA, CPTPP, and RCEP each go into some detail on the RPT, while Chapter 31 USMCA makes no mention of it. CETA specifies that the arbitration panel may determine the RPT "within 30 days" of the request (Article 29.13.2). CPTPP provides that the chair shall determine the RPT "no later than 90 days" after the referral, while RCEP provides that this should take place "within 45 days". CPTPP and RCEP set out that, as a guideline the RPT should not exceed 15 months from the presentation of the final report, which is the same period provided by the DSU (see Articles 28.19.5 and 19.15.6, respectively).

24 See also the Gulf Cooperation Council – Singapore Free Trade Agreement (GSFTA), Article 9.8 (Compliance with the Award): "1. The arbitration panel award is final and binding from the date of its notification to the disputing parties". Annex X, Rule 14 deals with compliance with an award within a reasonable period of time.

25 As to USMCA, see n 29.

26 CPTPP (29.14.1), USMCA (31.19.1), CETA, and RCEP (19.17.3/7)

27 CPTPP (28.20.5 and 28.19.4), USMCA (31.19.3), CETA (29.14.5), and RCEP (19.17.8)

28 Article 21.6 DSU. CETA does, however, provide that "At any time after the midpoint in the reasonable period of time and at the request of the requesting Party, the responding Party shall make itself available to discuss the steps it is taking to comply with the final panel report" (Article 29.13.4).

Of the RTAs reviewed above, the enforcement provisions of the USMCA are more of an outlier, providing for an arrangement that is more diplomatic in nature than legal, at least by comparison. In particular, under the USMCA, a panel report is not binding; rather, where it finds an inconsistency with a party's treaty obligations, the disputing parties "shall endeavour to agree on the resolution of the dispute".[29]

It is too early to give a definitive evaluation of the effectiveness of implementation and rates of compliance under RTAs. In any case, it appears that the EU is satisfied with the results obtained where bilateral mechanisms have been triggered.[30]

B. The Investment Regime

1. Compliance and Enforcement of Investment Awards

As recalled in Chapter IV, there is a marked difference in the investment regime between ICSID awards, which are international decisions, and other awards, which are ultimately subject to some domestic legal systems.[31] In either regime, however, if a claimant investor prevails, the remedy that tribunals may grant under the relevant IIA consists of monetary compensation to make good the damages caused.[32] Specific performance, such as unwinding an illegal expropriation or reinstating a concession, has rarely been granted. It is in most cases not practicable and is not a remedy that can forcibly be imposed upon a sovereign state.[33]

The question of what constitutes compliance with awards under investment treaties is complex.[34] While compliance may ordinarily be understood to mean

29 Article 31.18 USMCA ("Implementation of Final Report") provides: "1. Within 45 days from receipt of a final report that contains findings that: (a) the measure at issue is inconsistent with a Party's obligations in this Agreement; (b) a Party has otherwise failed to carry out its obligations in this Agreement; or (c) the measure at issue is causing nullification or impairment within the meaning of Article 31.2 (Scope), the disputing Parties shall endeavor to agree on the resolution of the dispute. 2. Resolution of the dispute can comprise elimination of the non-conformity or the nullification or impairment, if possible, the provision of mutually acceptable compensation, or another remedy the disputing Parties may agree".

30 Report from the Commission on the Implementation and Enforcement of EU Trade Policy (COM(2023) 740 Final) of 15 November 2023.

31 This is also the case for awards under the ICSID Additional Facility and at the PCA, notwithstanding that these proceedings are administered by international organizations.

32 Article 14.D.13 USMCA provides that if a tribunal awards restitution of property, "the award shall provide that the respondent may pay monetary damages and any applicable interest in lieu of restitution". Moreover, "the tribunal may not order the respondent to take or not to take other actions, including the amendment, repeal, adoption, or implementation of a law or regulation". Under ARSIWA Article 35 (Restitution), states may pay monetary compensation for damages caused by a breach in lieu of re-establishing the status quo ante if such restitution is too burdensome.

33 For a review of the case law, see *Principles* 425. See in general G. Vidigal "Targeting Compliance: Prospective Remedies in International Law".6 JIDS (2015) 462.

34 On this issue in respect of commercial arbitration, see C. Rogers and others, "Compliance in the Shadow of the Award" Bocconi Legal Studies Research Paper No. 4757103 (March 2024), https://papers.ssrn.com/sol3/papers.cfm?abstract_id=4757103, YJIL (forthcoming).

enacting measures or paying the amount specified in an award, the aftermath of many investment disputes does not neatly fall into this category. Authors of recent empirical research on the subject adopt a "more inclusive" category of "resolved" in their dataset. "Resolved" is broader than what may be traditionally understood by compliance with an award and includes instances where "there is evidence of payment, or settlement, or if the award has been successfully annulled or set aside, or if the tribunal found liability but did not award compensation".[35] The authors examine rates of compliance for 236 awards issued by 31 December 2020 which entailed an obligation to compensate. In these disputes, compensation was received in 101 cases (43%), while 17 were annulled (7%), and the status of payment was unknown in 108 (46%). For the remaining ten awards, the state had clearly refused to pay (4%).[36]

This low rate of states refusing to pay a final adverse award may not, however, reflect the situation post-2020.[37] A recent study found that in 2024 various EU Member States alone had over 30 unpaid awards outstanding against them, which were worth approximately $3 billion, a threefold increase on the same 2022 Report both as to the number of awards and their value.[38] Most of these unpaid awards reflect ongoing challenges to awards in light of the *Achmea* and *Komstroy* decisions of the CJEU declaring awards in intra-EU disputes under BITs and the ECT contrary to EU law.[39] On the other hand, developing countries that are dependent on foreign assistance may be under pressure to comply due to the adverse financial consequences they could otherwise face.[40]

1.1. Compliance and Enforcement of ICSID Awards

Article 53.1 ICSID Convention is clear that awards "shall be binding on the parties and shall not be subject to any other remedy except those provided for in this Convention. Each party shall abide by and comply with the terms of the award".

35 N. Strain et al., "Compliance Politics and International Investment Disputes: A New Dataset", 27 JIEL (2024) 70 covering compliance in 595 resolved disputes for which awards were issued prior to 2021. Based on the significant number of awards that are not satisfied outright, T. St John and others, "Bargaining in the Shadow of Awards", 35 EJIL (2024) 603, conclude that monetary awards against states can be best defined as "endowments", on the basis of which successful claimants put in place a variety of strategies to get satisfaction (often not in the form of full payment). From a legal point of view, such awards represent, however, unconditional obligations of the respondent state.

36 N. Strain n 35, Appendix 1. Objecting respondents listed in this dataset include Burundi, Zimbabwe, Spain, Russia, DR Congo, Ecuador, and Argentina.

37 N. Lavranos, *Report on Compliance with Investment Treaty Arbitration Awards 2024* (3rd ed. 2024) 2, available onhttps://www.internationallawcompliance.com, accessed 8 January 2025.

38 Id. *Report on Compliance* (1st ed. 2022).

39 CJEU *Slovak Republic v Achmea*, C-284/16 (2018), 59–60 and *Republic of Moldova v Komstroy*, C-741/19 (2021), 61–66 on which see also n 46 *infra* and fn 71 of Chapter III.

40 See World Bank, *Disputes over Defaults on External debt, Expropriation, and Breach of Contract*, Operational Manual OP 7.40, para. 5, https://documents1.worldbank.org/curated/en/099606405052230407/pdf/IDU0f59cec8a0984e04f910a8090e70b077a4553.pdf accessed 26 July 2024.

If a respondent state does not voluntarily comply with an unfavourable award, enforcement of the pecuniary obligations imposed on it by the award may be sought in any contracting state, as if the award were a domestic final court judgment under Article 54 ICSID. Since awards are binding on both parties, a losing claimant investor is similarly under the obligation to pay any cost awarded against it.[41] Should this not happen voluntarily, the winning respondent state can enforce such pecuniary obligations (or any stemming from a successful counterclaim) in any ICSID member under the same provision.[42]

Most recent ICSID data show a very high rate of compliance with its awards.[43] Although ICSID awards are international in nature, there is no inter-state mechanism to enforce them, except for the possibility that the home state raises the issue of non-implementation diplomatically or through state-to-state arbitration provided in BITs.[44] Their recognition – as a necessary premise to render the pecuniary obligations enforceable – takes place within member states' legal systems. Article 54.1 ICSID reflects this situation by stipulating that "[e]ach Contracting State shall recognize an award rendered pursuant to this Convention as binding and enforce the pecuniary obligations imposed by that award within its territories as if it were a final judgment of a court in that State".

It is important to underline that an ICSID award is equated to a final domestic judicial decision, and not to a domestic or foreign award and that this is the case in all contracting states, not just in the state which was party to the proceedings and for which it is binding. This is an important feature that enhances the effectiveness of ICSID awards, of which claimants make extensive use against recalcitrant

41 ICSID AR 52 makes the awarding of costs, as a part of the final award, dependent on various criteria, the first of which is the outcome of the proceedings.

42 There is a risk that when a claimant loses and costs are awarded against it in favour of the respondent state, recovery by the latter might be difficult. This has been a reason for respondents to ask for security for costs under AR 53 (introduced in 2022), especially when a claimant has been financed by a third-party funder. See C. Titi and others, "Excessive Costs & Insufficient Recoverability of Cost Awards" Academic Forum on ISDS of 14 March 2019 <https://www.cids.ch/images/Documents/Academic-Forum/1_Costs_-_WG1.pdf> accessed 26 July 2024. Based on previously published research, the authors indicate that the median costs are around USD 3,600,000 for an ICSID arbitration both for claimants and respondents, with tribunals' median costs being around USD 850,000.

43 See ICSID, *Background Paper. Compliance with and Enforcement of ICSID Awards* (June 2024) 13, available athttps://icsid.worldbank.org/: "Notably, looking at all 151 Awards in the study that awarded damages to a party ('Damages Awards'), award creditors obtained satisfaction through voluntary compliance or post-award settlements in 66% of cases, while 31% went to enforcement and in 3% enforcement was not pursued. Excluding those Damages Awards for which the outcome of enforcement actions was unavailable at the time of the study (either because the enforcement was pending, not pursued or the outcome unavailable), satisfaction was obtained in 97% of Damages Awards".

44 See *a contrario* Article 27.1 ICSID precluding diplomatic protection for a national investor or the bringing of an international claim in respect of a dispute subject to ICSID "unless such other Contracting State shall have failed to abide by and comply with an award rendered in such dispute".

respondents.[45] The effect of this regime is that ICSID awards are not subject to the challenges that local awards may be subject to under domestic arbitration law, be they patterned after the UNCITRAL Model Law or not, or foreign awards under the NYC. An ICSID award is exempted from any review by domestic courts, including in respect of jurisdiction, content, or conformity to public policy, once its authenticity has been ascertained.[46]

The procedure to obtain recognition is reduced to a minimum since Article 54.2 provides that "A party seeking recognition or enforcement in the territories of a Contracting State shall furnish to a competent court or other authority which such State shall have designated for this purpose a copy of the award certified by the Secretary-General".[47] While in some countries adversarial proceedings may be required, in others an *ex parte* application may suffice to obtain recognition. Once recognised, the award provides a valid enforceable title allowing for the execution against the available assets of the non-complying defendant state in the forum, as far as they are not covered by immunity.[48]

However, even ICSID awards may face procedural hurdles not dissimilar to those other awards may face when respondent states oppose enforcement in court, before their own judiciary, or in a third country. Without prejudice to the defence of state immunity, which protects broad categories of foreign states' assets from execution,[49] according to Article 54.3 ICSID, execution of ICSID awards "shall be governed by the laws concerning the execution of judgments in force in the State in

45 The English Court of Appeals in *Micula v Romania* EWCA Civ. 1801 (27 July 2018), 121 went even further, ruling that the analogy of an ICSID award with a judgment of the High Court "is limited to defining the force and effect of a registered award for the purpose of execution. It does not give the High Court the power to refuse to enforce an award for a reason that would justify staying enforcement of an ordinary domestic judgment".

46 As to public policy, however, the CJEU has declared in its *Achmea* and *Komstroy* judgments of 2018 and 2021 (n 39) that intra-EU investment arbitration is contrary to EU law with the consequence that tribunals lack jurisdiction awards in such disputes are ineffective in the EU. Although the awards whose recognition has been denied in those cases were non-ICSID, the principle is also applicable to ICSID awards, as has implicitly been stated by the CJEU in *Commission v UK*, C-516/22 (2024), 69–80, notwithstanding the ensuing apparent breach of the ICSID Convention. For a critical view, see G. Sacerdoti "After Komstroy. Have the EU Member States Withdrawn by the Lisbon Treaty, as an Inter-se Agreement under Article 41 VCLT, their Consent to ICSID Jurisdiction on ECT Intra-EU Investment Disputes?" in *Arbitration as Balanced Administration of Justice. Essays in Honour of Piero Bernardini* (Brill 2024) 371; see also U. Kriebaum "The uneasy co-existence of EU Law and international investment law," Introductory Essay to a special issue on EU Law and Investment Law, 38 DCI (2024-3) 11.

47 The designations made by Member States to ICSID pursuant to Article 54.2 are published in doc. ICSID/8-E, https://icsid.worldbank.org/sites/default/files/documents/2022_Oct%2028_ICSID.ENG.pdf#page=14 accessed 26 July 2024.

48 For a review, see *ICSID Commentary* II, Article 54, 31 ff, specifically regarding the granting of recognition (*exequatur*) to ICSID awards in France, at 59–65. Regarding Italy, see the *ex parte* decision of the Court of Appeals of Milan of 21 September 2018 granting recognition to the ICSID award *Gavazzi v Romania*, Riv. Arbitrato 2019, 539, with comment by C. De Stefano.

49 Article 55 of the ICSID Convention specifies that "the law in force in any Contracting State relating to immunity of that State or any foreign State from execution" is thereby not derogated from.

whose territories such execution is sought" (Article 54.3). The applicable proceedings may be quite complex, as recent instances have evidenced, and may be equally applicable to ICSID and non-ICSID awards.[50]

1.2. Compliance and Enforcement of Non-ICSID Awards

In contrast to ICSID awards, awards issued under other arbitration frameworks – regardless of the rules or institution that governed the arbitration, such as the ICSID Additional Facility Rules,[51] the PCA established by a treaty, or the ICC and other comparable "private" arbitral institutions – are subject to local rules applicable in the seat of issuance in relation to challenges and enforcement. In other countries, their recognition and enforcement are subject, as discussed in Chapter V, to the provisions of the NYC as implemented in the relevant jurisdiction.

The grounds for annulment under the UNCITRAL Model Law (in the country of issuance) as well as the grounds for opposing recognition and enforcement as outlined in Article V of the NYC (in other countries) have been highlighted in Chapter V.

We examine here in more detail three grounds for denying recognition and enforcement of foreign awards that have been specifically raised in connection with attempts to enforce commercial and investment awards against foreign states or state-owned companies. The relevance of these grounds has been the subject of divergent decisions, including as to investment awards.

The first one concerns the application of Article V.1(e) NYC, according to which

> "Recognition and enforcement of the award may be refused, at the request of the party against whom it is invoked, only if that party furnishes to the competent authority where the recognition and enforcement is sought, proof that: … (e) The award … has been set aside or suspended by a competent authority of the country in which, or under the law of which, that award was made".

50 Thus, in the US conflicting decisions have been rendered as to whether the *ex parte* recognition of ICSID awards is admissible or whether ordinary proceedings are mandated under the US Foreign Sovereign Immunities Act (FSIA), as held by the US Court of Appeals for the Second Circuit in *Micula v Romania* (Summary Order, 27 October 2017) following *Mobil Cerro v Venezuela* (US Court of Appeals for the Second Circuit Decision, 11 July 2017, and US District Court Southern District of New York Decision, 22 January 2017). US proceedings for the recognition of the award *BG v Argentina*, an UNCITRAL award rendered in New York, went up to the US Supreme Court, see *BG Group v Argentina*, US Supreme Court 572 U.S 25 (2014).

51 ICSID Additional Facility awards are non-ICSID awards for the purpose of recognition and enforcement. However, since also "a-national or denationalized awards are covered by the New York Convention" (see *ICSID Commentary* II, Article 54, 18) in the US, these awards are among those considered as non-domestic US awards in conformity with Article I.1 NY Convention, even if they have been made at ICSID in Washington, DC.

This provision is generally considered and has been applied as a bar to enforcement when an award has been set aside by the courts of the country of origin.[52] It has been implemented in this way in many countries.[53] However, on a closer reading, this provision allows, but does not oblige, courts of other NYC parties to deny recognition to awards annulled in the country of the seat. This issue has mostly been raised in cases where an award that had ruled against the local government or a state-owned company has been annulled in the country of origin based on dubious, political grounds.[54] Courts in France and the US are known for having recognized and enforced foreign awards in these circumstances, notwithstanding their annulment in the country of origin.[55]

Unlike the annulment of an award in the country of origin, the refusal by a court of another country to enforce it for whatever reason under the NYC does not deprive the award of its legal force.[56] The decision is only applicable in that state, leaving the interested party the option of pursuing enforcement in other jurisdictions. Claimants often make parallel or multiple attempts to enforce investment awards against states, especially in view of the difficulty of locating assets not protected by sovereign immunity that can be attached to satisfy an award that has not been voluntarily complied with. These enforcement actions against foreign states may, however, create problems (such as diplomatic embarrassment to the local sovereign) that courts sometimes try to avoid.[57]

The second specific issue worth mentioning, because of its relevance to the enforcement of investment awards, concerns the presence of assets in the jurisdiction for an award to be recognized. Though this is not a requirement under Article III of the NY Convention, there have been instances of refusal of enforcement based on the lack of assets of the defendant in the forum.[58] Most recently, the Swiss

52 See the UNCTAD Guide, *Dispute Settlement. International Commercial Arbitration. 5.8 Court Measures* (2005) 27, available at <https://unctad.org/system/files/official-document/edmmisc232add42_en.pdf> accessed 26 July 2024. If an application to annul an award is pending in the country of origin, the authority before which the award is sought to be relied upon "may, if it considers it proper, adjourn the decision on the enforcement of the award" (Article VI NY Convention).

53 This is the case for Italy, where Article 840.5 of the Code of Civil Procedure explicitly denies recognition of foreign awards annulled in the country of origin.

54 For a review, see C. De Stefano, "The Recognition and Enforcement of Awards Annulled in the Country of Origin" 30 DCI (2016) 993; W. Park, "Annulled Arbitration Awards" in *Reflections on International Arbitration. Essays in Honour of Professor George Bermann* (Juris 2022) 641.

55 See the latest US case under the "Chromalloy doctrine" *Comissa v PEMEX* 832 F.3d 92 (US Ct Appeals 2nd Cir 2016) under Article 5.1(e) of the Inter-American Convention on International Commercial Arbitration, 1975 (identical to Article V.1(e) NY Convention). As to France, see the Court of Appeals Paris 17/19850 (2019), the most recent case applying the similar "Hilmarton doctrine".

56 See UNCTAD Guide, n 52, 28.

57 Thus in *Yukos Capital v OAO Tomskneft VNK*, EWCA Civ 799 (2007), the Irish High Court found that it would be inappropriate for it to assume jurisdiction over proceedings on the enforcement of an ICC New York award where the respondent had successfully resisted previous applications in Russia and France, and there was an ongoing application for enforcement in Singapore.

58 *Kammergericht [KG]* Berlin, 10 August 2006, 20 Sch 07/04. In *Tasarruf Mevduati Sigorta Fonu v Demirel and Anor*, the English Court of Appeal found that caution should be exercised before

Federal Tribunal has held that the enforcement of an ICSID award in Switzerland against a foreign sovereign state requires not only that the assets not be covered by immunity but also that a sufficient connection exists between the claim and Switzerland.[59]

Finally, another difference in approach has recently emerged across various jurisdictions of relevance when states are party to arbitration proceedings. The issue concerns the power of courts to deny recognition of an award if an opposing party submits that the tribunal failed to properly investigate allegations of corruption in the underlying transaction. Some jurisdictions consider the matter to be the exclusive competence of tribunals, while others have denied recognition based on the public policy exception, irrespective of the parties' burden of proof to raise and give evidence of such an allegation in the arbitral proceedings.[60]

1.3. Immunity from Execution in Respect of Claims Arising Out of Investment Awards

Once final, after all oppositions, if any, have been rejected, an award can be enforced in accordance with local rules concerning the payment of sums of money or other orders contained in the award. These rules are usually the same as those applicable to the enforcement of local judicial decisions and therefore also apply to ICSID awards under Article 54 ICSID.

If the party subject to enforcement is the local state, special provisions may apply as to execution against public assets. If execution is levied against the assets of a foreign state, immunity from execution protects their assets used for public purposes under customary international law and state legislation in the matter.[61] As to international law, the UN Convention on Jurisdictional Immunities of States and their Property (UNCSI) of 2004, though not yet in force, marked the culmination of a long process of codification of the rules of state immunity and reflects customary law in many provisions.[62]

"bringing a foreigner here" as a defendant "unless it can be shown that a 'solid practical benefit' would ensue". Thus, while it was found that there is no requirement to show that the respondent has assets in the jurisdiction, the claimant must ordinarily show that it can "reasonably expect a benefit" from the judgment. This "solid practical benefit" test was also applied by the Irish High Court in *Avobone NV v Aurelian Oil & Gas Limited* (IEHC 636-2016).

59 Judgment of the Federal Court/*Urteil des Bundesgerichts*, 5A_406/2022 of 17 March 2023.

60 Thus, the Paris Court of Appeal, by application of the public policy exception, has annulled awards (see RG 20/03242 of 5 April 2022) for failure of the arbitrators to investigate. Similarly, in England, in *Nigeria v Process & Industrial Developments Ltd*, High Court (2023) EWHC 2638 (Comm), in vacating a USD 13 billion commercial award against Nigeria, the court criticized the lack of proactive engagement by the arbitrators who had not investigated the matter ex officio. Swiss courts have instead stuck to a more deferential approach to arbitral tribunals, see Swiss Federal Tribunal decisions 4A_136/2016 and 4A_69/2022. On the issue, see also Chapter V, n 57.

61 See US Foreign Sovereign Immunities Act (FSIA) of 1976 as amended; as to the UK, see the State Immunity Act (SIA) of 1978.

62 See the *Commentary* to the UNCSI by R. O'Keefe, C. Tams (eds) (OUP 2013).

As well known, international law distinguishes immunity from suit (which is unavailable in respect of judicial actions stemming from *iure gestionis* operations) from immunity from execution, which protects property used by a foreign state for recognized public purposes from enforcement, irrespective of the origin or nature of the claim that a creditor seeks to enforce.

As to arbitration, Article 17 UNCSI (*Effect of an arbitration agreement*) provides that

> "If a State enters into an agreement in writing with a foreign natural or juridical person to submit to arbitration differences relating to a commercial transaction, that State cannot invoke immunity from jurisdiction before a court of another State which is otherwise competent in a proceeding which relates to: (a) the validity, interpretation or application of the arbitration agreement; (b) the arbitration procedure; or (c) *the confirmation or the setting aside of the award*".[63]

It is generally accepted that this provision reflects the current state of customary law and is applicable also in respect of ICSID awards.[64]

By accepting to submit to arbitration, based on a contract, domestic statute or an IIA, however, a state is not presumed to have renounced its prerogatives concerning immunity from execution of property used for recognized non-commercial purposes in respect of any liability arising out of that arbitration.[65] This is confirmed in respect of ICSID arbitration by Article 55 ICSID, according to which

> "Nothing in Article 54 [on the obligation of each contracting state to recognize ICSID awards and enforce the pecuniary obligations imposed by them] shall be construed as derogating from the law in force in any Contracting State relating to immunity of that State or of any foreign State from execution".[66]

Article 19 UNCSI ("*State immunity from post-judgment measures of constraint*") states, *inter alia*, that

63 Emphasis added. The "Understanding with respect to Article 17" annexed to the Convention specifies that the term "commercial transactions", which is defined at Article 2 (1)(c), includes "investment matters".

64 H. Fox, P. Webb, *The Law of State Immunity* (3rd ed OUP 2013). See *ICSID Commentary* II, Article 55, 7; dubitatively K. Parlett, "Commentary to Article 17 UNCSI", n 62, 285. As to the US, see section 1605(a)(6) FSIA (US), added in 1988, according to which a foreign state does not enjoy immunity from the jurisdiction of US courts regarding an action to enforce that agreement or a resulting award.

65 According to Article 20 UNCSI, "consent to the exercise of jurisdiction by a foreign court shall not imply consent to the taking of measures of constraint". However, a respondent state that relies on its sovereign immunity to avoid implementing an ICSID award would be in breach of its obligations to comply with the award under Article 53.1 ICSID.

66 See *ICSID Commentary* II, Article 55, 23.

> "No post-judgment measures of constraint, such as attachment, arrest or execution, against property of a State may be taken in connection with a proceeding before a court of another State unless and except to the extent that … (c) it has been established that the property is specifically in use or intended for use by the State for other than government non-commercial purposes and is in the territory of the State of the forum, provided that post-judgment measures of constraint may only be taken against property that has a connection with the entity against which the proceeding was directed".[67]

Under this approach (functional immunity), followed by most national jurisdictions, only assets of a foreign state which are not used for official state purposes are not covered by immunity against execution or other measures of constraint. States, however, do not commonly own such commercial property abroad. The pursuit of attachable assets in various jurisdictions by victorious claimants in ICSID disputes shows the difficulty of obtaining full satisfaction of a monetary claim from an unwilling sovereign.[68]

C. Comparative Evaluation

1. Commonalities

(a) The implementation of adjudicatory decisions in both the trade and investment regimes is a common objective, so that failure in compliance is of common concern in a way that extends beyond the obvious interest of the victorious party in a specific dispute. Non-compliance undermines confidence in both systems and encourages de facto self-help or the intervention of home states of affected traders or investors.

(b) Mechanisms have been set up within the DSU and at ICSID to encourage voluntary compliance and to involve all member states in post-decision compliance proceedings (multilateral surveillance by the DSB at the WTO,

67 Article 21 includes a non-exhaustive list of certain categories of property considered to be intended for government non-commercial purposes, such as "(a) property, including any bank account, which is used or intended for use in the performance of the functions of the diplomatic mission of the State … (c) property of the central bank or other monetary authority of the State".

68 See "Australia and UK Authorise Seizure of Spanish Assets over Non-Payment to Renewables Investors" https://thecorner.eu/ (13 April 2023). Assets attached in London include Spain's language and cultural centre, the Cervantes Institute. The claimants in the *Micula v Romania* "saga", having been blocked by the EU Commission and the CJEU in relation to the enforcement of ICSID award 05/20 (2013) (taken under the Sweden-Romania BIT), have turned to the UK and the US to enforce their award-based monetary claims. A similar saga has been that of the multiple arbitration proceedings against India, against its enforcement of retroactive taxation measures, whose favourable awards (granting in one case USD 1.2 billion as damages) claimants have proceeded to enforce in various jurisdictions until the disputes were settled. See K.A. Loya, V. Desai "The *Cairn Energy v. India* Saga: A Case of Retrospective Tax and Sovereign Resistance against Investor State Awards" (2 July 2021), https://arbitrationblog.kluwerarbitration.com, accessed 15 July 2024.

recognition of awards in all member states at ICSID), whose effectiveness, however, is subject to conflicting views.

(c) In both regimes, multilateral instruments have incomplete coverage (WTO/RTAs – ICSID/Non-ICSID awards). This fragmentation has been reinforced in the trade regime by the emergence of the MPIA, in force only within a subset of WTO Members, as a second-best alternative to remedy the absence of a functioning AB. The remedies available under RTAs or in respect of non-ICSID awards are, in any case, similar to those provided within the WTO or under ICSID respectively.

(d) In both systems, non-compliance with decisions, should it become widespread, would undermine trust in the respective DSS as instruments through which effective enforcement of parties' rights can be attained. Such a development would dissuade potential claimants from pursuing adjudicatory rule-based proceedings for the assertion of their rights, and encourage seeking alternative protections, including self-help.

2. *Differences*

The salient differences between the regimes may be summarized as follows in view of the fact that the models for enforcement of decisions are fundamentally different in the trade and investment regimes.

(a) In the *trade* regime, decisions are declaratory of a breach (if found) and focus on the obligation of the party not in compliance with its WTO obligations to remove the breach for the future (prospectively, *ex nunc* or *pro futuro*). This approach conforms to the customary regime on the consequences of the breach of international obligations (reparation for injury through restitution), except for the absence of an obligation to make good the consequences of a breach from the date it occurred.

(b) This is in stark contrast with the *investment* system, which is patterned after the methods for enforcement of judicial decisions and commercial awards in domestic law, based on the granting of pecuniary damages in case of breach and reliance on domestic enforcement systems to obtain payment. This approach is also in conformity with international principles on the consequences of the breach of international obligations, which admit reparation for injury through compensation.

(c) In *trade*, in the case of non-compliance by the losing party with a panel or AB report, the injured party may resort to countermeasures (retaliation) in the form of a temporary suspension of equivalent concessions until compliance is obtained (by withdrawal or appropriate modification of the measure challenged), or an agreement is reached on alternative compensation.

(d) In the *investment* regime, remedies are focused on ensuring effective monetary compensation for the injury (damages) caused by the breach, a remedy entailing full retroactive payment including interest from the date of the breach (*ex tunc*). If the party that is obliged does not comply with the award, the other party may enforce the (pecuniary obligations stemming from the) award in any national jurisdiction it chooses, or in several of them, until the judgment is satisfied.

(e) A key question concerning enforcement in the *trade* regime is the effectiveness of the multilateral surveillance of the DSB in order to obtain compliance. If this is not effective, alternative methods of resolving the dispute, such as unilateral measures or negotiated settlement, possibly on less favourable terms, are likely to become a necessity for the winning party.

(f) A key question concerning the implementation of *investment* awards against states is the difficulty of enforcing a monetary claim against a sovereign state. This is due to immunity from execution of property used for governmental functions, notwithstanding the status of ICSID and other final awards as binding.

Part II

From Success through Crisis to Reform.

7 From Success to Crisis

Table of Contents

Introduction

This chapter looks at the evolution of the WTO and investment law regimes, especially their dispute settlement systems (DSS), and how after several years of

DOI: 10.4324/9781003471509-10

successful operation they have entered a period of crisis. It charts the success of the WTO DSS over more than 20 years, the tensions it witnessed in its operations, up to the US unilaterally blocking the appointment of AB members, bringing about the suspension of its operations (2017–2020), and analyses the ensuing reactions. On the one hand, there is the semi-paralysis of the DSS due to the possibility of a party losing a case before a panel appealing the report "into the void" to the non-operational AB, thus blocking indefinitely the resolution of the dispute. On the other hand, the reaction of the EU and a sizeable number of other WTO Members aimed at remedying this blockage by agreeing inter se to an appeal mechanism of an arbitral type (the Multi-Party Interim Appeal Arbitration, or MPIA).

As to the investment regime, we review the widespread criticisms addressed to it from different sources (states, civil society groups, sections of academia) at the same time as recourse to investment arbitration was exploding. Some critics have called into question the overall legitimacy of such a system that empowers private investors to challenge host states' measures in a unique international forum, removing disputes from states' courts. A proposed solution on the table is that of replacing ISDS with an investment court system. Others have criticized specific features of the system, such as the methods of selecting adjudicators, the length and costs of proceedings, and the content and inconsistency of decisions. These critics have advocated specific reforms to improve ISDS that we also review.

Either type of criticism has not affected the carrying out of arbitral proceedings under the dispute settlement clauses of the relevant IIAs. Criticism has rather prompted changes in the text of the substantive and procedural provisions of recent IIAs, reducing their scope, clarifying their content, and amending arbitration rules (notably those of ICSID), while more comprehensive reforms are still at the discussion stage (as will be discussed in Chapter VIII).

A. Trade

1. *The Successful Record of the WTO DSS: 1995–2019*

Almost immediately upon the entry into force of the WTO agreements, recourse to the dispute settlement system became systematic and popular among its Members. Contrary to the expectations of the drafters, who thought that appeals would only occur occasionally, about two thirds of panel reports were appealed from 1995 to 2019, during the period when effective appeal was possible.[1]

The success of the WTO DSS as an effective instrument to settle trade disputes according to its design is evidenced by the following numbers. Since the DSS

1 WTO - Dispute Settlement Activity - Some Figures, https://www.wto.org/english/tratop_e/dispu_e/dispustats_e.htm, updated to the end of 2024, reports that panel reports were issued in 376 disputes leading to 297 panel reports (some covering multiple disputes) followed by appeal in 195 disputes (about 66%). As to the expectation of "occasional" appeals against "rogue" panel reports, see P. Van den Bossche, "The Making of the 'World Trade Court': The Origins and Development of the Appellate Body of the WTO" in *Key Issues*, 63, 65.

started functioning in 1995 up to the end of 2024, there had been 631 requests for consultations; 117 mutually agreed solutions notified to the DSB; and 286 panels composed covering 334 disputes. There have been 205 panel reports adopted by the DSB, together with the relevant AB report in cases of appeal, and 124 AB reports adopted, counting as one cases involving multiple complainants. There had been 37 compliance panels adopted (25 AB reports) under Article 21.5 of the DSU and 27 arbitrations on the level of suspension of concessions under Article 22.6 DSU. In most cases, at least some of the complaints against the respondent have been accepted.[2] This result is not surprising, taking into account that initiating a dispute involves complex internal decision-making processes, costs, and the risk of political tensions. Cases are therefore initiated when economic prejudice is material and the chances of success are reasonably high.[3]

In comparison with the limited number of interstate cases adjudicated by other international courts and tribunals, these figures show how the adjudication of international trade disputes has become a standard feature of the WTO system.[4] This is consistent with the statement in Article 3.10 DSU that "requests for conciliation and the use of the dispute settlement procedures should not be intended or considered as contentious acts".[5]

Practice has in several respects improved the functioning of the system in comparison with the blueprint enshrined in the DSU (which has never been formally amended[6]), making it more efficient, transparent, attentive to considerations of

2 According to *Mavroidis*, 185, Table 4.9, complainants have prevailed, at least by some accounts, in 70% of disputes submitted to panels.

3 The strategic filing of disputes as a response to another party's initiation of a dispute is discouraged by Article 3.10 DSU, which states that "complaints and counter-complaints in regard to distinct matters should not be linked".

4 In comparison, about 80 cases have been introduced at the ICJ between 1948 and 2023. The investment treaty regime shows a similar pattern to the WTO. Since the entry into force of ICSID in 1966, 1,000 cases have been registered as of February 2024 (with 329 cases pending). See, hereafter, Section B and UNCTAD, Investment Dispute Settlement Navigator available at https://investmentpolicy.unctad.org..

5 Not all protectionist measures affecting international trade are potentially WTO-inconsistent, and only a minority of those are brought to dispute settlement at the WTO. According to J. Kucik, L. Peritz, S. Puig, "Legalisation and Compliance: How Judicial Activity Undercuts the Global Trade Regime" 53 British Journal of Political Science (2023) 221, 228, "[t]here were over 12,000 protectionist policies around the world between 2009 and 2020. However, there were only 220 WTO disputes filed".

6 A decision taken at the end of the Uruguay Round envisaged "a full review of dispute settlement rules and procedures of the WTO within four years … and … a decision … whether to continue, modify or terminate such dispute settlement rules and procedures"; see WTO, *Decision on the Application and Review of the Understanding on Rules and Procedures Governing the Settlement of Disputes* available at http://www.wto.org/. Although the DSB initiated this review and its work went on beyond the four-year deadline, no agreement was reached on any of the several DSU modification proposals submitted and this work was finally abandoned, see D. Georgiev, K. Van der Borght (eds) *Reform and Development of the WTO Dispute Settlement System* (Cameron May 2006); V. Hughes, "The WTO dispute settlement system – from initiating proceedings to ensuing implementation: what needs improvement?" in *The WTO at Ten*, 193.

due process, and also responsive to the interests of stakeholders beyond WTO Members.[7]

Important developments have essentially been due to clarifications by the AB as to how proceedings should be conducted under the DSU. Thanks to the AB, parties have been authorized to be represented by private lawyers; *Amicus Curiae* briefs have been admitted; hearings have been opened to public viewing where the consent of the parties has been given; procedural due process principles have been made more stringent in respect of the use of experts and the burden of proof. These rulings have been met with broad support from the WTO membership and have helped placate criticism from civil society about the lack of transparency and accountability of the system towards stakeholders other than WTO Members.[8]

The most important contribution of the WTO DSS to international trading relations has been the successful resolution of the many disputes brought before it, thus satisfying the expectations of the negotiators, governments, and enterprises that effective remedies would be available to Members affected by non-compliance with the WTO Agreements by other Members. The flow of new disputes has been steady until the paralysis of the AB and there has been widespread participation of larger and smaller economies, industrialized countries, developing countries, and countries that have acceded to the WTO subsequent to its establishment, such as China and Russia.[9] About two thirds of WTO Members have participated in cases at least as a third party; 81 of the then 164 WTO Members participated in appeals in which AB reports were circulated between 1996 and 2020.[10] However, implementation has become more contentious in recent years, giving rise to an increasing number of compliance disputes under Article 21.5 DSU, and even to successive Article 21.5 proceedings in the same dispute.[11]

A notable qualitative evolution through the years has been the taking into account by the AB in its jurisprudence of non-trade values protected by international law as limits to the application of the trading system.[12] The best-known cases

7 See P. Van den Bossche, n 1 above, 69–79; D. Cass, *The Constitutionalization of the WTO: Legitimacy, Democracy and Community in the International Trading System* (OUP 2005); C. Joerges, E. Petersmann (eds) *Constitutionalism, Multilevel Trade Governance and International Economic Law* (Hart 2011); R. Howse, "The WTO 20 Years on: Global Governance by Judiciary" 27 EJIL (2016) 9.

8 For more details and references, see Chapter IV.A.1.7.

9 As of the end of 2023, 61 WTO Members had participated as respondents in disputes, with 53 Members having been complainants and 90 Members as third parties. Among the most active participants, the US has been involved in 198 disputes, the EU in 180, Japan in 105, China in 92, Canada in 86, Brazil in 71, and India in 69. As is natural, the most frequent users have been Members heavily engaged in trade relations, while a number of LDCs have never participated in any dispute (mainly countries whose trade is mostly subject to the GSP). For disaggregated data by groups of Members, see *Mavroidis*, 134.

10 See AB Annual Report for 2019–2020 (the last annual report of the AB), 157, www.wto.org/english/tratop_e/dispu_e/ab_anrep_2019_e.pdf

11 See *Mavroidis*, 252.

12 See R. Howse, "The WTO 20 Years on: Global Governance by the Judiciary" 27 EJIL (2016) 9, and the comment by H. Ruiz Fabri, "The WTO Appellate Body or Judicial Power Unleashed" 27 EJIL (2017) 1075.

have involved the application of the "General Exceptions" of Article XX GATT. Relevant cases are, chronologically, *US–Shrimp*[13] on the protection of endangered species as exhaustible natural resources, *EC–Asbestos*[14] *and EC–Hormones*[15] on the protection of human health, *Brazil–Retreated Tyres*[16] on the protection of the environment and sustainable development, and *EC–Seal Products* on the balance between competing non-trade values such as animal welfare and moral sensitivity, on the one hand, and the protection of the livelihood of indigenous populations on the other.[17] In this way, the Appellate Body helped assuage some of the concerns of those from outside governments and trade circles, such as environmental NGOs, who criticized the WTO as being solely focused on trade concerns.[18]

2. *The WTO DSS from Fatigue to Semi-Paralysis*

2.1. *Time Limits and Efficiency in DS Proceedings*

The dispute settlement system has, in a certain sense, been the victim of its own success, as a consequence of having gained unanticipated prominence within the WTO, compared with other branches of the organization (negotiations, surveillance of obligations). Sustained recourse to the DSS involving a number of complex disputes[19] has had the negative effect of putting strain on the system.[20] A paramount objective of the DSU is that, in stark contrast with the practice of most international courts and tribunals, proceedings are required to be expeditious, reflecting the needs of commerce and the aim of removing national barriers deemed to have been introduced in breach of WTO obligations.

Alas, panel proceedings have taken much longer than the 330 days envisaged by the DSU for consultations, panel and AB proceedings, even before the wave of cases that were initiated in the aftermath of the US restrictive trade measures

13 *US– Shrimp* (DS 58-2001).

14 *EC—Asbestos* (DS 135-2001).

15 *EC–Hormones* (DS 26-1998).

16 *Brazil—Retreaded Tyres* (DS 332-2007).

17 AB *EC–Seals* (DS 401-2014).

18 For example, protestors who blocked the Seattle WTO Ministerial Meeting in 1999. See L. Wallach, *The WTO: 5 Years of Reasons to Resist Corporate Globalization* (Seven Stories Press 1999); J. Stiglitz, *Globalisation and Its Discontents* (Norton 2002). See generally R. Howse, H. Ruiz Fabri, G. Ulfstein, M. Zang (eds) *The Legitimacy of International Trade Courts and Tribunals* (CUP 2016).

19 It has been suggested that the increase in disputes may have been encouraged by the lack of outcomes in WTO negotiations, such as the abandoned Doha Round. K. Pelc, "The Politics of Precedent in International Law: A Social Network Application" 108 American Political Science Review (2014) 547.

20 There were 17 new consultation requests registered in 2017; in 2018, the DSB established 31 panels (the highest number ever), see J. Pauwelyn and W. Zhang, 'Busier than Ever? A Data-Driven Assessment and Forecast of WTO Caseload' 21 JIEL (2018) 461 concluding that delays were due more to administrative bottlenecks and the complexity of cases than to their number.

and the countermeasures adopted by some of the countries affected in 2018.[21] Moreover, there have been substantial delays in the actual composition of panels, that is between the formal establishment of a panel by the DSB under Article 6 DSU and the appointment of panelists under Article 8.[22] This has been due both to the time it has taken for the parties to accept the names proposed by the DG (though such an acceptance is not formally required) and, at times, to a lack of available experienced legal staff in the Secretariat to assist panels, aside from the time actually thereafter required for panels to perform their task.[23]

The issue of these delays had become a major concern for the WTO membership as they increased to a level that appeared incompatible with the basic features of an efficient dispute settlement system for international trade.[24] However, having to choose between the quality of the decisions, speed of proceedings, and cost containment (the well-known "judicial trilemma" between these three valuable features in an adjudicatory system, only two of which can be attained at a time[25]) notwithstanding verbal complaints, WTO Members have *de facto* preferred the quality of the reports and budgetary discipline over the respect of the stringent deadlines of the DSU.[26]

21 Time limits are 180 days for panel work from its composition, a maximum of 60 days for filing an appeal, and 90 days for the appeal phase. In contrast, the actual data from panel composition to report circulation have been: DS 538: 20 months; DS 539: 26 months; DS 553: 22 months; DS 562: 22 months; DS 577: 25 months; DS 578: 16 months; DS 579: 25 months.

22 For example, in DS 598 it took three months to compose the panel after its establishment (28 May 2021/3 September 2021) and more than four months in DS 602 (26 October 2021/4 March 2022) as opposed to the requirement of Article 8 DSU that the DG should step in, at a party's request, if the parties have not been able to agree within 20 days.

23 In an address to the DSB on 28 October 2015, the DG at the time, Roberto Azevêdo, explained in detail the various administrative steps he had taken and was taking to mitigate delays, announcing that legal staff assigned to panels had nearly doubled – from 30 to 57 – since 2013. Delays may be caused by the parties: in DS 617, *US–AD Measure on OCTG (Argentina)*, the panel constituted on 4 January 2024 made it known (WT/DS/617/5) that "Both parties requested significantly more time to file their first written submissions than the time originally proposed by the Panel … which delayed the beginning of the Panel's substantive work. The Panel does not expect to be in a position to issue its final report to the parties before the first quarter of 2025", that is more than one year after it has been constituted.

24 Several complainants have lamented at DSB meetings the time required to complete a case. In 2015, Korea complained that a panel established on 18 March 2015 in DS 488 would not start its work before the end of 2016, while Canada complained that proceedings in the COOL dispute (DS 384), including under Article 21.3, 21.5, and 22.6 DSU, had not been concluded after four and a half years.

25 See J. Dunoff, M. Pollack, "The Judicial Trilemma" 111 AJIL (2017) 225.

26 The AB itself had warned the membership (to no avail) of the difficulties of dealing with the number of cases coming before it and the length of the parties' submissions in accordance with its procedural rules; see Communication from the Appellate Body, *The Workload of the Appellate Body* WTO Doc. No. JOB/AB/1 (30 May 2013) 46; WTO Appellate Body, *Annual Report for 2015* WTO Doc. No. WT/AB/26 (3 June 2016). See also C. Ehlermann (one of the first AB Members), "The Workload of the WTO Appellate Body: Problems and Remedies" 20 JIEL (2017) 705.

2.2. *The US Blocking of the AB*

The problems that affected the functioning of the WTO's DSS since 2014, in particular in relation to the length of proceedings, have been completely overshadowed by the demise of the AB, intentionally caused by the US due to the policy of Trump's first administration of obstructing the appointment and reappointment of its members by the DSB starting in 2017.

US administrations had already previously complained of unfavourable decisions by the AB, especially with respect of US trade remedies.[27] The US had signalled its dissatisfaction by not supporting the renewal of US nationals at the AB for a second term in 2007 (Merit Janow) and in 2011 (Jennifer Hillman).[28] The Obama administration had blocked the reappointment of AB Member Seung Wha Chang in 2016, claiming that he had ruled against the US in cases where he had been a member of the division.[29] This US initiative led to criticism from other countries at the DSB and to the unprecedented initiative of two public letters to the chairman of the DSB, one by Mr Chang's colleagues and the other by all former 13 living AB members, warning against interference with the independence and impartiality of the AB via the use of the reappointment process and the ensuing dangers for the credibility of the whole DSS.[30] The world press took notice and was highly critical of the US position.[31]

27 Especially the holding that the practice of zeroing followed by the US in calculating the dumping margins is contrary to the ADA has been criticized by the US; see AB *US–Zeroing (EC)* (DS 294-2006). In complaining because it had lost the zeroing cases, evidently, the US did not take into account the fact that in 2017 it had won a series of cases in a row before panels and the AB in high-profile disputes, both as complainant and respondent, notably against China, India, Mexico, and Indonesia. See J. Hillman, "A Reset of the World Trade Organization's Appellate Body" (Council of Foreign Relations 2020), available at https://www.cfr.org/report/reset-world-trade-organizations-appellate-body, according to whom the US had won 91% of the cases it brought against other Members.

28 The practice for renewal for a second term of outgoing AB Members had consistently been that no selection process would be launched if the outgoing AB Member had indicated a willingness to be reappointed and the delegations consulted by the selection committee had not raised objections, as had never been the case, see DSB *Annual Report* WTO Doc. No. WT/DSB/71 (24 November 2016) 2.2.

29 The accusation is curious because any decision of the AB is the result of the collective work of the Members of the division, while individual opinions are anonymous (there were, in any case none in the cases mentioned by the US at the DSB).

30 Available, respectively, at http//www.twn.my/title2/wto.info/2016/ti160516.htm and <http://worldtradelaw.typepad.com/files/abletter.pdf>, both accessed 29 July 2024. The US criticized both these letters at the DSB as "unfortunate".

31 See Financial Times, "Washington Threatens to Undermine the WTO – The US Is Wrong to Try to Manipulate the Dispute Settlement Process" (1 June 2016); M. Elsig, M. Pollack, G. Shaffer, "The U.S. Is Causing a Major Controversy in the WTO. Here's What's Happening" Washington Post (6 June 2016); and, later on, The Economist, "America Holds the WTO Hostage. The Rule-based System of Trade Faces Threat beyond Trump's Tariffs" (23 September 2017); South China Morning Post, "Donald Trump's Block on WTO Judges Creates 'Doomsday Scenario' for World Trade Disputes" (21 November 2019).

This uproar did not deter the Trump administration from taking the radical step of blocking the AB, seemingly for good, by alone preventing the necessary positive consensus for the launching of the appointment process under Article 2.4 DSU, starting in 2017. The result was a progressive decrease in the number of AB members in office. When in December 2019 the number was reduced to fewer than three, no division could be formed to decide cases. The AB ceased to be operational, with its members deciding to complete in early 2020 only the three cases in which hearings had already taken place.[32]

In order to justify its actions, the US has put forward a number of criticisms of the AB at DSB meetings, and the USTR collected these into a single document in 2020.[33] We summarize hereunder these criticisms, pointing out at the same time that any criticism, short of accusations of judicial impropriety, such as lack of independence, impartiality, or conflicts of interests (which the US has never raised), does not justify blocking the functioning of a key institution of an international organization, and is contrary to the duty to act in good faith.[34]

The US has claimed that the AB has improperly engaged in "judicial activism", such as by issuing "advisory opinions" and *obiter dicta* on issues not necessary for its decision (although the AB has always only decided cases submitted to it by Members as provided in the DSU).[35] The US has accused the AB (sometimes in unusually harsh terms) of improper "gap-filling" of provisions left vague by

32 The AB managed to go on working also thanks to resort to rule 15 of its Working Proceedings, which allows its members to complete cases to which they had been assigned before the expiration of their term. This practice was criticized by the US, although it had been resorted to in a number of cases in previous years without ever raising any criticism from WTO Members. See Minutes of the Meeting of the DSB of 22 November 2017, WTO Doc. WT/DSB/M/404 18. On the issue, see also former Appellate Body Member J. Hillman, "Independence at the Top of the Triangle: Best Resolution of the Judicial Trilemma" 111 AJIL Unbound (2017) 364–368.

33 USTR, *Report on the Appellate Body of the World Trade Organisation*, 2020, <https://ustr.gov/sites/default/files/Report_on_the_Appellate_Body_of_the_World_Trade_Organization.pdf> accessed 29 July 2024. For a rebuttal, see E. Petersmann, "How should WTO Members respond to the WTO Appellate Body crisis?" IELP Blog (13 December 2018), available at https://worldtradelaw.

34 See specifically Article 3.10 DSU that "if a dispute arises, all Members will engage in these procedures in good faith". For a critical comment, see I. Van Damme, "25 Years of Law and Practice at the WTO: Did the Appellate Body Dig its Own Grave?" 26 JIEL (2023) 124, at Section IV: "discontent with all or some of these decisions or the possibility of reasonable arguments supporting the availability of alternative decisions in respect of these matters is not a basis for any WTO Member to use the consensus rule as a means to effectively deny the rights that the WTO Agreement and the DSU guarantee to all WTO Members" and to cause the AB "becoming defunct". See in the same vein K. Reinert, "Steel, Security and the WTO Dispute Settlement Mechanism: A Trade Catastrophe in the Making" 47 The World Economy (2024) 2741: "[t]he arguments made by the United States in this regard are mostly spurious and reflect its status as a current bad faith actor within the WTO".

35 This criticism does not consider that the AB only decides, and must decide without any discretion, the cases which are appealed to it, addressing all the claims submitted by the parties as prescribed by Article 17.1 DSU ("The Appellate Body shall address each of the issues raised in accordance with paragraph 6 during the appellate proceeding"), without any possibility of refraining from deciding by a *non liquet* – which would automatically result in a respondent prevailing and being able to maintain the measures challenged as non-compliant with its WTO obligations. The AB has, how-

negotiators and of "overreach", by exercising functions beyond its mandate, notwithstanding that to the contrary the self-imposed interpretive restraint of the AB has generally been recognized.

The US has repeatedly objected to the AB's lack of compliance with the 90-day limit to issue its reports. It must be noted that delays have largely been due to the complexity of many cases, the limited human resources available to the AB to respect this short deadline, and a backlog of cases.[36] The US also objected to individual AB members remaining in office beyond their terms to complete appeals entrusted to them (although such extensions are provided for under Rule 15 of the AB Working Procedures, and this was the practice for more than 20 years). The US has advocated the use of greater judicial economy to avoid deciding issues raised on appeal but not strictly necessary to resolve the dispute.[37] The United States has contested that panels must – or more accurately, are expected to – follow the precedent set by the AB "absent cogent reasons", as the AB has stated, though the AB has always made clear that its reports bind only the parties and do not represent binding precedents.[38]

2.3. Developments in the AB Crisis since 2018

In general, other WTO Members have not shared most of these criticisms, though they have declared themselves to be open to amending and improving certain procedural rules through negotiations. In any case, they have mostly objected to the blocking of the appointments by the US, with a great majority of Members, lately more than 130, asking that the appointment process be restarted at every DSB meeting since 2018. By the end of 2024, this had occurred more than 70 times. They have, however, refrained from labelling the US attitude as abusive and contrary to good faith – a cardinal principle underlying dispute settlement that is spelt out in

ever, practiced "judicial economy" in order not to address issues that had become moot because of its decision on other claims. See S. Fries, "Judicial Economy" *MPEiPro* (2017).

36 Statistics show that the length of proceedings has been more pronounced at the panel level (average length compared to maximum prescribed length: 511 days v 180), than the appellate stage (112 days v 90), including the time for translation. These average delays are further reduced if one sets aside a few disputes where all the parties agreed that respecting the 90-day limit was impossible, such as the large civil aircraft ("Boeing/Airbus") disputes, the first one brought by the US: *EC and certain Member States–Large Civil Aircraft* (DS 316), and the second one brought by the EU: *US–Large Civil Aircraft* (DS 353). Panel proceedings in these two cases took from 2005 to 2011 and from 2006 to 2011, and AB proceedings 10 and 11 months respectively. The two disputes, considering subsequent compliance proceedings (panels and appeals), were pending for about 15 years each and have been only provisionally settled in 2021; see EU press release, "EU and US Take Decisive Step to End Aircraft Dispute" https://ec.europa.eu/commission/presscorner/detail/en/IP_21_3001, of 15 June 2021, accessed 30 July 2024. One wonders about the relevance of invoking the 90-day deadline of Article 17.5 DSU in such a context.

37 The US has labelled this as engaging in *obiter dicta* and "advisory opinions"; for a rejection of this criticism, see H. Gao, "*Dictum* on *Dicta: Obiter Dicta* in WTO Disputes" 17 World Trade Review (2018) 509.

38 See Chapter III.A.5.

Article 3.10 of the DSU. The Members have also refrained from resorting to majority voting for AB appointments as some voices deem legitimate.[39] Understandably, there has been a preference for dealing with the US position in diplomatic negotiating terms rather than confronting the US. Various groups of WTO Members tabled no fewer than 18 proposals to address the issues raised by the United States with a view to finding solutions and unblocking the appointment process before the disappearance of an operative AB at the end of 2019.[40] The US rejected those proposals, stating that they failed to address US concerns and that the proposals would rather "endorse the very practice the US has repeatedly complained of".[41]

For a long time, the US had refrained from tabling its own proposals for reform, notwithstanding repeated invitations to do so from other Members. The US claimed that the WTO membership must first clarify "why [the AB] has felt free to disregard the rules of the DSU", exceeding its authority and "straying from the role agreed for it by the WTO Members".[42] This is a hefty, unsupported accusation directed at 27 distinguished lawyers, diplomats, judges, academics, and senior national trade experts from 17 different countries whom the WTO Members have chosen by consensus over a 20-year period to settle their disputes, renewing their terms whenever they were available.[43]

39 See H. Gao, "Finding a Rule-Based Solution to the Appellate Body Crisis: Looking Beyond the Multiparty Interim Appeal Arbitration Arrangement" 24 JIEL (2021) 534.

40 A document meant to address the "concerns" of the US without undermining the key features of the rule-based two-tier dispute settlement system (Communication, tabled by the EU together with a wide range of diverse WTO Members including China, Canada, India, Norway, New Zealand, Switzerland, Australia, Korea, Iceland, Singapore, and Mexico), included proposals such as "Transitional Rules for Outgoing AB Members", "The meaning of municipal law as an issue of fact", "Findings unnecessary for the resolution of the dispute", and the "The issue of precedent" (see WTO, General Council, WTO Doc. No. WT/GC/W/752 (23 November 2018). The second Communication, tabled by the EU, China, and India, proposed "Additional Amendments" to the DSU to include one single longer term of office (six to eight years) for AB Members with a view to reinforcing their independence, and increasing their number from seven to nine with full-time appointments (see WTO, General Council, WTO Doc. No. WT/GC/W/753 (26 November 2018).

41 Statement of the US Ambassador at the GC meeting of 12–13 December 2018.

42 See US Mission to International Organisations in Geneva, "Statements delivered by Ambassador Dennis Shea – WTO General Council Meeting, July 23, 2019", available at https://geneva.usmission.gov/2019/07/23/statements-delivered-by-ambassador-dennis-shea-wto-general-council-meeting-july-23-2019/ accessed 29 July 2024.

43 As I. Van Damme concludes in her article "25 Years of Law and Practice at the WTO: Did the Appellate Body Dig its Own Grave?" 26 JIEL (2023) 124, notwithstanding its somewhat misleading title: "Undoubtedly, the Appellate Body could have decided differently on certain questions. However, asking whether or how the Appellate Body dug its own grave fails to acknowledge the role of WTO Members, collectively and individually, in preserving binding, compulsory WTO dispute settlement providing for appellate review". See also Y. Fukunaga, "Interpretative authority of the Appellate Body. Replies to the criticism of the US" in Cheng-fu Lo, J. Nakagawa, Tsai-fang Chen (eds) *The Appellate Body of the WTO and its Reform* (Springer 2022) 167, arguing that "the US wrongly or deliberately alters what the Appellate Body in fact stated past decisions in view to discrediting the Appellate Body".

In the meantime, appeals into the void to a non-operative AB have been numerous, thereby preventing the adoption of panel reports by the DSB and hence the final determination of non-compliance and the triggering of implementation obligations.

2.4 *The "Walker Proposals" of 2019*

In order to overcome the impasse, at the beginning of 2019 the General Council appointed New Zealand's ambassador to the WTO, David Walker, as a "Facilitator" to try to find a solution between the US' complaints and the other Members' proposals. Following extensive consultations, on 15 October 2019 Ambassador Walker came forward with a Report to the GC proposing a "Draft General Council Decision on Functioning of the Appellate Body", addressing the following issues:[44]

- transitional rules for outgoing AB Members (who could complete a case only if the hearing has taken place within their term);
- a 90-day deadline for AB reports (to be extended only with the consent of the litigants or in case of *force majeure*);
- municipal law (to be considered an issue of fact not reviewable on appeal);
- "advisory opinions" (the AB shall not address issues not raised by the parties or not necessary to resolve the dispute);
- precedent (dispute settlement proceedings do not create precedent, and previous reports should be taken into account to the extent they are relevant in a subsequent dispute); and
- "overreach", restating that panels and the AB cannot add to or diminish WTO Members' rights as stipulated in Articles 3.2 and 19.2 DSU and that panels and the AB shall interpret the Anti-Dumping Agreement in accordance with its Article 17.6(ii).

Academia has also engaged with this issue.[45] Even these modest "quick-fix" proposals have not, however, been considered by the US to be a meaningful basis for

44 WTO General Council, *Agenda Item 4 – Informal Process on Matters Related to the Functioning of the Appellate Body – Report by the Facilitator, H.E. Dr. David Walker (New Zealand),* WTO Doc. No JOB/GC/222 (15 October 2019).

45 It has been suggested that an authoritative interpretation of the DSU by unanimous decision of the General Council based on Article IX.2 of the WTO Agreement should be made; see T. Payosova, G. Hufbauer, J.J. Schott, "The Dispute Settlement Crisis in the World Trade Organisation: Causes and Cures" Peterson Institute Policy Brief (March 2018) available at https://www.piie.com On the issue, see J. Bacchus (the first US AB Member), "Saving the WTO's Appeals Process" CATO Blog (12 October 2018) available at https://www.cato.org; E. Petersmann, "Between 'Member-Driven' WTO Governance and 'Constitutional Justice': Judicial Dilemmas in GATT/WTO Dispute Settlement" 21 JIEL (2018) 103; G. Vidigal, "Living Without the Appellate Body: Multilateral, Bilateral and Plurilateral Solutions to the WTO Dispute Settlement Crisis" 20 JWIT (2019) 862 ff; C. Creamer, "From the WTO's Crown Jewel to Its Crown of Thorns" 113 AJIL Unbound (2019) 51 ff; E. Petersmann, "Between 'Member-Driven' WTO Governance and 'Constitutional Justice': Judicial Dilemmas in

the start of negotiations, showing a lack of interest in avoiding the demise of the AB.[46]

As highlighted and discussed in detail in chapter VIII, the matter of reform of the DSS was taken up by the WTO Members after MC12 in 2022 and has become more intensive, also with the participation of the US, after MC13 in 2024.

2.5. From the Suspension of the AB's Operations to the MPIA

With the AB having become inoperative at the end of 2019 (except for the completion of three pending cases in early 2020, leaving ten other appeals indefinitely suspended), the WTO was left lacking one of its fundamental pillars. The result has been a return to a GATT-style type of DSS, reintroducing a de facto veto by the losing party in sensitive cases.[47] The panel phase has also been impacted because panel reports appealed "into the void" by the losing party can neither be adopted by the DSB nor finally decided at the appellate stage. Disputes remain unresolved and breaches are not sanctioned. A frustrated winning party is tempted to react with countermeasures without first having recourse to the WTO DSS.[48] In brief, the whole WTO system of reciprocal rights and duties has been undermined.[49] At the end of 2024, 25 appeals "into the void" were pending, affecting the majority of panel reports issued after the blocking of the AB.

In order to avoid the paralysis of the appellate process, the consequent obstruction of effective panel proceedings, and indeed of the whole DSS, the EU announced in June 2019 the launch, in agreement with other Members, of the "Multi-Party Interim Appeal Arbitration Arrangement" (MPIA) as an "interim solution" to cope with the absence of the AB. The parties to this scheme agreed in advance that, should a dispute arise between two of them, they would resort in case of either

GATT/WTO Dispute Settlement" 21 JIEL (2018) 103; C. Haeberli, "Can Panels Save WTO?" WTI Working Paper No. 05/21..

46 See D. Ravi Kanth, *WTO: In a Radical Overhaul, US Proposes Single-Tier Dispute Settlement System* (TWN, 26 April 2023), https://www.twn.my/title2/wto.info/2023/ti230414.htm accessed 29 July 2024.

47 For an analysis, see J. Pauwelyn, "WTO Dispute Settlement Post 2019: What to Expect?" 22 JIEL (2019) 297 ff.

48 Following Indonesia's appeal into the void in *Indonesia–Raw Materials* (DS 592), in 2023, the EU has been considering activating immediate countermeasures under the EU Enforcement Regulation 2021/167 <https://eur-lex.europa.eu/legal-content/EN/TXT/PDF/?uri=CELEX:32021R0167> accessed 30 July 2024.

49 The paralysis of the binding WTO rules-based DSS appears to be coherent with the trade policy objectives of the first Trump administration (2016-2020) and its preference for unilateral protectionist measures and bilateral deals, a tendency that has not been repudiated by the Biden administration and that has been intensified by at the outset of Trump's second term. See R. Lighthizer (USTR during the Trump administration), *No Trade Is Free: Changing Course, Taking on China, and Helping America's Workers* (Harper Collins 2023); N. Boschiero, *US Trade Policy, China and the World Trade Organisation* (Routledge 2023). For observations as to the impact on the trading system, see G. Sacerdoti, "The Challenge of Countering Politicisation of Trade Relations and Revitalizing the Multilateral Rule-Based System" (Editorial) 22 JWIT (2021) 1–12.

intending to appeal to this alternative "appeal arbitration" under Article 25 DSU[50] (a provision that had hardly been used until then) for as long as the AB was inoperative. The MPIA was finalized in March 2020, with 24 WTO Members as participants (counting the EU and its Member States as one). Its details and usage are analysed in Chapter VIII. [51]

The MPIA alternative mitigates the damage caused by the dismantling of the AB, but nonetheless has several shortcomings. First, it is not applicable to all WTO Members, and aside from the US several of them (such as India and Indonesia) appear thus far to prefer the de facto resulting GATT-style type of DSS whereby losing a case does not result in an obligation to comply. The US is an obvious example in this regard, as it has enacted several WTO-incompatible measures since 2018, invoking the security exception and other justifications, which have been rejected by panels whose reports the US has appealed into the void.[52] A bifurcated regime is thus in place within the WTO, with some countries remaining subject to a binding dispute settlement system, and others escaping effective enforcement of its rules, inducing affected Members to resort to remedies outside the WTO DSS.[53]

The clear drop in activity at the DSB may be due to this situation. Four years into the AB crisis and the creation of the MPIA, WTO statistics show that, for new disputes, WTO Members tend to rely less and less on litigation as a form of dispute settlement. In 2023, only six requests for consultations were recorded compared to 20 in 2019 and an all-time high of 50 in 1997, when the difference between the number of requests for consultations and the number of panels composed and appeals notified was particularly high. In 2024, only two panels were composed, contrasting with a peak of 29 in 2018. In 2024, only four panel reports were adopted, while an all-time high of 15 panel reports being adopted was reached

50 Article 25 DSU *Arbitration*: "*1. Expeditious arbitration within the WTO as an alternative means of dispute settlement can facilitate the solution of certain disputes that concern issues that are clearly defined by both parties. 2. Except as otherwise provided in this Understanding, resort to arbitration shall be subject to mutual agreement of the parties which shall agree on the procedures to be followed. Agreements to resort to arbitration shall be notified to all Members sufficiently in advance of the actual commencement of the arbitration process. 3. Other Members may become party to an arbitration proceeding only upon the agreement of the parties which have agreed to have recourse to arbitration. The parties to the proceeding shall agree to abide by the arbitration award. Arbitration awards shall be notified to the DSB and the Council or Committee of any relevant agreement where any Member may raise any point relating thereto. 4. Articles 21 and 22 of this Understanding shall apply mutatis mutandis to arbitration awards*".

51 See EU, "WTO Multi-Party Interim Appeal Arbitration Arrangement" (24 January and 27 March 2020), available at https://www.consilium.europa.eu/en/press/press-releases/2020/04/15/council-approves-a-multi-party-interim-appeal-arbitration-arrangement-to-solve-trade-disputes/ accessed 29 July 2024 (with text attached). For a list of the Members, see Chapter VIII, n 31.

52 Appeals in DS 533, DS 539, DS 543, DS 544, DS 552, DS 556, DS 564, and DS 597.

53 The EU has announced that, in the event of a dispute between the EU and an opposing party that is not a party to the MPIA, the EU would immediately resort to countermeasures, relying on general international law principles in the area of state responsibility. See press release "Commission reinforces tools to ensure Europe's interests in international trade", available at https://ec.europa.eu (12 December 2019), Regulation (EU) 2021/167 ("Enforcement Regulation").

in 2000.[54] The impression is that the filing of new cases is discouraged by the absence of a functioning AB as the proper finalization of disputes is uncertain and has fundamentally been called into question.[55]

By 2024, appeals into the void have been filed by several WTO Members, as unsuccessful respondents before a panel, such as Russia, the United States, China, Indonesia, India, Morocco, Saudi Arabia, Korea, Pakistan, the Dominican Republic, Türkiye and the EU in disputes where one or both parties did not agree to use the MPIA.[56] Losing complainants have also exercised this option, hoping that on appeal, if and when it will occur, it may be that the measure they had unsuccessfully challenged before the panel will be found to be non-compliant.[57]

In 2020–2023, 36 panel reports were circulated. Of these reports, 24, that is 2/3, have been appealed into the void. If disputes between two MPIA Members are not considered, 24 reports out of 30 (80%) have been appealed.

Besides discouraging recourse to the DSS, the dysfunctional situation of the DSS pushes WTO Members to settle their disputes by negotiation.[58] This is not necessarily a negative result provided that such settlements are not driven by the impossibility of getting a rule-based solution within a reasonable timeframe and are not the result of pressure from the stronger party.[59]

54 See EU Briefing, "International Trade Dispute Settlement: WTO Appellate Body Crisis and the Multi-party Interim Appeal Arbitration Arrangement" (June 2024), https://www.europarl.europa.eu/thinktank/en/document/EPRS_BRI(2024)762342 accessed 29 July 2024.

55 Nine panel reports were issued in 2017 (compared with ten new panels established); eleven panel reports were issued in 2018 and 2019 each (compared to 28 and 11 new panels respectively established); five panel reports were issued in 2020 (compared to seven new panels that were established).

56 Besides the US (see n 52), appeals have been made by China in DS 558 and DS 562, Indonesia in DS 592, India in DS 584, Morocco in DS 578, Saudi Arabia in DS 567, Korea in DS 553, Pakistan in DS 538, and the Dominican Republic in DS 605. The EU appealed the panel report in *EU–Cost Adjustment Methodologies II (Russia)* (DS 494-2020), considering that Russia is not a party to the MPIA and did not agree to appeal arbitration. See Notification of an Appeal, WT/DS494/7, 1 September 2020.

57 See China's appeal on 16 September 2021 *US–Safeguard Measure on PV Products (China)* (DS 562).

58 Out of the four reports of 2023 that have not been appealed into the void, a mutually agreed solution was found in three of them (DS 598, DS 585, and DS 547). In the fourth dispute, *India–Tariffs on ICT Goods* (DS 588), the parties (Chinese Taipei and India) have repeatedly asked the DSB (as of the end of 2024) to postpone the adoption of the panel report that was issued on 17 April 2023 (which should have occurred within 60 days under Article 16.4 DSU), presumably while negotiations are pending between them (WTO Doc. No. WT/DS 588/15 of 16 April 2024).

59 See "EU and US Take Decisive Step to End Aircraft Dispute" (DS 316 and 353), available athttps://ec.europa.eu/commission/presscorner/detail/en/IP_21_3001 accessed 29 July 2024. The EU and US also agreed to suspend the application of the US steel and aluminium extra duties and the related EU related countermeasures until the end of 2024, suspending proceedings in DS 548 and 559. As a result of the visit of India's Prime Minister Modi to Washington in the US in June 2023, the two countries agreed to settle six pending disputes at the WTO. See USTR, *United States Announces Resolution of the Outstanding WTO Poultry Dispute with India* (8 September 2023), available at https://ustr.gov/about-us/policy-offices/press-office/press-releases/2023/september/united-states-announces-resolution-outstanding-wto-poultry-dispute-india accessed 29 July 2024.

The US has not merely exercised the option of appealing into the void; it has also more radically stated that it does not recognize the authority of WTO panels to "second-guess" Members' (US) measures that have allegedly been taken for security reasons, contrary to a stream of panel reports under the security exception of Article XXI GATT, thus further undermining the DSS.[60] In hindsight, the current semi-paralysis of the DSS serves the specific interests of the US in avoiding final unfavourable decisions in cases in which it invokes economic security reasons.

3. *Reacting to the WTO DSS Blockage. Has There Been a Shift to Regional Dispute Settlement Mechanisms?*

The lack of agreement at the WTO on the updating of substantive rules and the blocking of the DSS at the multilateral level have favoured a shift of priorities by a number of countries to the regional dimension. However, these "mega-regionals", in force or under negotiation, have also faced obstacles, mainly because of the divergence of interests within prospective parties and between them, especially when their coverage extends to areas beyond those covered in the WTO agreements such as labour standard, environment protection and digital trade.[61]

There has been an increase in the use of the dispute settlement mechanisms of RTAs in these areas. This includes disputes concerning subject matters that are absent from the WTO, such as TSD chapters and workers' protection chapters. This rise in disputes under these DSS has been noticeable since the AB has ceased to function. Procedural rules under RTAs are inspired by those of the DSU, but some include a number of innovations, such as in respect of transparency (including the making public of parties' filings, provisions on public hearings, and amicus curiae briefs). This points towards some decentralization in the trade regime, although major divergences tend to be avoided thanks to RTA trade provisions being patterned on those of the WTO, often directly incorporating or referring to WTO provisions, whose interpretations naturally serve as guiding precedent for RTA panels.[62] On the other hand, RTAs only govern a limited share of world trade and do not apply in the reciprocal trade relations between the largest trading WTO Members, the EU, US, and China.

From 2018 to 2021, there were ten formal disputes under various RTAs.[63] Seven of these disputes concerned trade remedies (Canada–US and EU–South Africa) and

60 See USTR, *Statement from USTR Spokesperson Adam Hodge* (9 December 2022), available at https://ustr.gov/about-us/policy-offices/press-office/press-releases/2022/december/statement-ustr-spokesperson-adam-hodge accessed 29 July 2024. For further details, see Chapter VIII.A.1.2.

61 For a critical view of the expansion of coverage of RTAs to non-trade areas, see G. Shaffer, "Package Treaties: Addressing the Negative Effects of Trade" (2024), <https://scholarship.law.georgetown.edu/facpub/2595> accessed 29 July 2024. For a positive view, see instead K. Claussen, "Trade Law Policing on the Factory Floor: Next Generation Agreements and Their Corporate Accountability Tools" 13 CJIL (2024) 6.

62 See Chapter II.A.2.3.

63 As to the EU, see the panel reports *Ukraine–Wood Export Ban* (2020) under the EU–Ukraine Association Agreement; *Korea–Labour Commitments*, Panel of Experts Proceeding Constituted under

general trade barriers (wood export restrictions in EU–Ukraine, imports of dairy in US–Canada relationships, restrictions on dairy products between New Zealand and Canada under the CPTPP, imports in general in EU–Algeria, and interpretations of rules of origin provisions in US–Canada).

Three other disputes concern matters where WTO rules do not establish obligations, such as environmental protection, labour standards, and competition. In these areas, RTAs often include different adjudicatory mechanisms, which do not always provide that the panel or expert report shall be binding, aiming more to ensure compliance in the future rather than to sanction breaches. These include disputes concerning environmental obligations (US–Korea)[64] labour rights obligations (EU–Korea), and competition law obligations (US–Korea). This variety in terms of subject matter and parties seems to indicate a (limited) increase in dispute settlement outside of the WTO system, including in matters that the WTO does not cover.[65]

This is not to say that recent disputes have primarily been taken under RTAs rather than at the WTO. In fact, since the AB stopped operating in early 2020, 31 disputes have been initiated at the WTO by the end of 2023 compared to ten disputes under RTAs during the same period.

B. Investment

1. The Development and Successful Functioning of ISDS

As is by now abundantly clear, ISDS is an integral element of BITs, which in turn have progressively become a fundamental feature of the international investment regime, even more so within economic globalization over the last 50 years. After

the EU–Korea Free Trade Agreement (2021); *SACU–Safeguards on Frozen Chicken Cuts* (2022) under the EU–SADC EPA, all three, available at https://policy.trade.ec.europa.eu/enforcement-and-protection/dispute-settlement/bilateral-disputes accessed 20 July 2024. An arbitration panel was also requested in relation to trade restrictive measures taken by Algeria in March 2021. A dispute settlement case was eventually launched under the EU–Algeria Association Agreement in June 2024 because of the failure to remove alleged breaches. As to the US, see the USMCA panel reports, *United States–Crystalline Silicon Photovoltaic Cells Safeguard Measure* (2021); *Canada–Tariff Rate Quotas (TRQ) Allocation Measures* (2021); and *US–Automotive Rules-of-Origin* (2022). The latest dispute was between New Zealand and Canada under the dispute resolution mechanism of the CPTPP., see CPTPP Panel Report, *Canada–Dairy Tariff Rate Quota Allocation Measures*, 5 September 2023.

64 Another environmental dispute arose under the United States–Peru Trade Promotion Agreement (PTPA). The matter raised by the US was referred to the PTPA's Environmental Affairs Council. See USTR press release "USTR Successfully Resolves Concerns Raised in First-Ever Environment Consultations Under the US–Peru Trade Promotion Agreement" 9 April 2019, available at https://ustr.gov/about-us/policy-offices/press-office/press-releases/2018/april/ustr-successfully-resolves-concerns# accessed 29 July 2024.

65 The EU Commission announced in June 2024 that it was starting formal proceedings against Algeria under the EU–Algeria AA of 2002 because of the EU's inability to remove otherwise certain alleged breaches, see news article "EU begins dispute settlement proceedings against Algeria to defend European companies" available at https://policy.trade.ec.europa.eu.

slow beginnings, a surge in ISDS claims has appeared to be unstoppable, at least until recently. With the addition of investment chapters in RTAs, ISDS has also found its place within regional economic liberalization agreements (FTIAs/PTIAs), such as NAFTA (1992) and thereafter USMCA (2020) as well as the CPTPP (2018) besides a number of bilateral agreements especially in Latin America.[66]

While the first BIT was signed in 1959 between Germany and Pakistan, the first BITs including treaty-based ISDS started to appear in BITs about ten years later. The first BITs to contain an unconditional offer of consent to submit disputes between a party and an investor of the other party to arbitration at ICSID were the 1968 BIT between Indonesia and the Netherlands, and, in clearer terms, the Italy–Chad BIT in 1969.[67] Disputes under BITs, however, only became prominent in the 1990s after the first reported investment award was issued by ICSID in 1990 under the UK–Sri Lanka BIT.[68]

BITs, followed by other IIAs, were then concluded in increasing numbers, with more than 2,200 in force as of 2024 (several replacing previous ones), although the pace of new agreements has slowed down in recent years.[69] They have not just been concluded between capital and investment exporting and importing countries but increasingly also within the South–South and North–North dimensions.

As a consequence, there has been a continuous increase in the number of proceedings. The accumulated total of just 57 in 2000 and over 400 in 2010 had by mid-2023 climbed to 1,303 known ISDS cases that had been initiated. Of these, 357 were pending, 924 had been concluded, while the status of 22 was unknown;[70] 133 states have been respondents in investment claims while claimants have come from 82 jurisdictions.[71] Data on the outcome of disputes show what can be defined as a balanced result: respondent states have prevailed in 344 cases, investors at least in part in 260, while 173 cases have been settled, and 124 discontinued.[72]

In parallel with the increase in the number of proceedings and awards, the limited annulment mechanism provided by Article 52 ICSID has been used more frequently in recent years, with 79% of such proceedings having been instituted since

66 ISDS moreover figures prominently in the ECT (1994), a sectoral agreement on energy that currently had more than 50 Members (before the withdrawal of many EU Members and the EU itself notwithstanding its "modernization" agreed in 2024).

67 Texts available at UNCTAD, IIA Navigator, https://investmentpolicy.unctad.org/international-investment-agreements/

68 *Asian Agricultural Products Ltd. v Republic of Sri Lanka* ICSID Case No. ARB/87/3 Award (1990)

69 At the end of 2024, there were 2,222 IIAs in force according to UNCTAD's International Investment Agreements Navigator, available at https://investmentpolicy.unctad.org/international-investment-agreements/ accessed 20 January 2025.

70 Ibid.

71 Ibid.

72 Ibid. They explain the classification as follows: "Decided in favour of State: the tribunal dismissed the case for lack of jurisdiction or found that the respondent State has not committed any breach of the applicable IIA. Decided in favour of the investor: the tribunal found that the respondent State committed one or more breaches of the applicable IIA and awarded monetary compensation or non-pecuniary relief to the claimant investor".

2011. As of the end of 2023, annulment has been sought against 189 awards but resulted in only 23 awards being annulled in whole or in part (5% of all awards).[73]

The above numbers show that ISDS has proved to be capable of handling and settling investment disputes between a variety of countries and in respect of all sorts of investments through the application of agreed rules of international law, thereby avoiding political conflicts and clashes between national jurisdictions.[74]

Compliance with awards has generally been high.[75] States that have been found to be in breach of their obligations and ordered to pay damages have mostly done so voluntarily, though some have been successful in avoiding full payment through negotiated post-award settlements.[76] Where this has not occurred, as discussed in Chapter VI, enforcement proceedings under domestic law in accordance with the ICSID and New York Convention have been both dissuasive and reasonably efficient instruments for ensuring compliance, taking into account the obstacle to enforcement against states due to sovereign immunity.[77]

ISDS as a method for solving disputes has thus become a standard feature in international economic relations on a global scale, to the point of being considered a "system", despite lacking centralized institutions and full uniformity of law.[78]

The structure and basic features of BITs, and subsequently of other IIAs, have changed over time. UNCTAD has divided the making of IIAs into several periods (initially only BITs) as follows:[79] an *Era of Infancy* (1950s–1964) with 37 new IIAs and no ISDS cases; a period of *Emergence of Dichotomy,* West–East/North–South (1965–1989) with 367 new IIAs and one case; an *Era of Proliferation* (1990–2007) with 2,663 new IIAs and 291 cases; an *Era of Re-orientation* (2008–2018) with

73 The ICSID *Background Paper on Annulment* (2024), available at https://icsid.worldbank.org indicates that there has been more than one annulment challenge in five cases, resulting in a total of 194 annulment proceedings. Challenges were rejected in 102 proceedings. Forty-two proceedings were discontinued, while (only) 23 awards have been annulled in full or in part.

74 See L. Poulsen, *Bounded Rationality and Economic Diplomacy: The Politics of Investment Treaties in Developing Countries* (CUP 2015); U. Kriebaum, "Evaluating Social Benefits and Costs of Investment Treaties: Depoliticization of Investment Disputes" 33 ICSID Rev (2018) 14; R. Polanco, *The Return of the Home State to Investor–State Disputes: Bringing Back Diplomatic Protection?* (CUP 2018) 230.

75 See E. Gaillard, I. Mitrev Penushliski, "State Compliance with Investment Awards" 35 ICSID Rev. (2020) 540.

76 See the detailed examination of compliance by N. Strain and others, "Compliance Politics and International Investment Disputes: A New Dataset" 27 JIEL (2024) 70, 74. Based on the review of 262 investment cases, the authors conclude that "disputes are commonly resolved through post-award dynamics rather than payment of the full amount ordered by the tribunal".

77 For updated information, see N. Lavranos, "Report on Compliance with Investment Treaty Arbitration, Awards 2024" (3rd ed. 2024), available at www.internationallawcompliance.com. The report lists Spain (in respect of intra-EU awards under the ECT, which the CJEU considers ineffective), Venezuela and Russia as the countries with the highest number of unpaid awards (in 2024, 24, 20 and 10, respectively, and unpaid total amounts of 1.6, 17.1 and 60.7 billion USD outstanding, respectively).

78 See S. Schill, *The Multilateralization of International Investment Law* (CUP 2009).

79 UNCTAD "Reform Package for the International Investment Regime", available at https://investmentpolicy.unctad.org. (2018) 15.

410 new IIAs (total new IIAs: 3,271) and 316 new cases (total 608). The structure, coverage, and details of ISDS provisions have also changed over time, moving to more elaborate regulation, incorporating more precise texts in light of arbitral practice.[80]

2. *Criticism of the Investment Regime in General*

While these numbers show the contribution of IIAs in establishing a stable investment framework and the effectiveness of ISDS in resolving disputes, the number of cases and the political and economic prominence of many disputes have led to an increased focus on the investment regime and considerable criticism of ISDS, particularly from a variety of civil society groups.

First, there is a lack of consensus that BITs actually attract foreign investment, with economic studies pointing in different directions.[81] Doubts have also been raised as to the additional advantage sometimes attributed to BITs, of promoting institutional reforms in host countries by inducing the extension to domestic investors of the treatment granted to foreign investors, and encouraging sound administrative and judicial processes through FET provisions.[82] Critics are of the view that since these positive effects are not demonstrated, the legal and political constraints that host developing countries accept in exchange for them are not justified.[83] In

80 See the comparative presentation of a first-generation (1996) BIT and a recent one (2022) in the table in Annex 1, Chapter II.

81 The economic research and literature are overwhelming. With special attention to legal features, see J. Salacuse, N. Sullivan, "Do BITs Really Work? An Evaluation of Bilateral Investment Treaties and Their Grand Bargain" 46 HILJ (2005) 67; J. Bonnitcha, "Assessing the Impacts of Investment Treaties: Overview of the Evidence" IISD Report (2017), available at https://www.iisd.org. Until recently, the discussion was focused on IIAs' contribution to the economy of the host country. Under the Trump first administration, the debate in the US has shifted to their alleged adverse effects on home countries by promoting capital outflows and the establishment in host countries (such as Mexico) of US-owned competitors to the US industry, thus endangering jobs in the US.

82 See also T. Ginsburg, "International Substitutes for Domestic Institutions: Bilateral Investment Treaties and Governance" 25 Int. Rev. Law and Economics (2005) 107; B.K. Guthrie, "Beyond Investment Protection: An Examination of the Potential Influence of Investment Treaties on Domestic Rule of Law" 45 NYU JILP (2013) 1152; BIICL, "Risk and Return – Foreign Direct Investment and the Rule of Law" (2015) 47, <www.biicl.org/documents/625_d4_fdi_main_report.pdf> accessed 10 July 2024; 83% of investors polled in this study stated that the absence of any investment protection treaty in force between their home state and a state in which they were considering investing affected their decision to invest while 14% stated it had no impact. See also J. Bonnitcha, L. Skvgaard Poulsen, M. Waibel, *The Political Economy of the Investment Treaty Regime* (OUP 2017); J. Bonnitcha, Z. Williams, "The Impact of Investment Treaties on Domestic Governance in Developing Countries" 46 Law & Policy (2024) 140.

83 See K. Sauvant, L. Sachs, *The Effect of Treaties on Foreign Direct Investment: Bilateral Investment Treaties, Double Taxation Treaties, and Investment Flows* (OUP 2009); J. Chaisse, C. Bellak, "Do Bilateral Investment Treaties Promote Foreign Direct Investment?" 3 Trans. Corp. Rev. (2011) 3; A. Berger and others, "Do Trade and Investment Agreements Lead to More FDI?" 10 IEEP (2013) 247; M. Sattorova, *The Impact of Investment Treaty Law on Host States: Enabling Good Governance?* (Hart 2018). See also D. Swenson, "Why Do Developing Countries Sign BITs?" 12 U.C. Davis Journal of International Law & Policy (2005) 131.

this connection, the fear has been expressed that an extensive interpretation of general terms by investment tribunals in favour of investors may dissuade governments (by inducing "regulatory chill") from adopting needed legitimate reforms.[84]

While the regime has flourished, criticism has sharpened.[85] The frequency of disputes and inclination for third-party adjudication is comparable to that of the trade regime, the other major pillar of treaty-based international economic regulation. However, in contrast to the WTO, criticism of the investment regime from civil society sectors, far from calming down over the years, has instead gathered pace.[86] In a certain sense, the most vocal critics of globalization have shifted their focus from the WTO to the investment regime.[87]

Criticism has centred around a "lack of legitimacy" of the regime, first because it would result in unwarranted limitations of states' sovereignty for the benefit of foreign private interests, constraining the exercise of their public powers to act in pursuit of the common good.[88] Hence, there have been calls for the "rebalancing" of rights and obligations so as to avoid the extension of broader rights to investors under international investment law than those available to investors in general under fair domestic standards.[89]

84 See K. Tienhaara, *The Expropriation of Environmental Governance: Protecting Foreign Investors at the Expense of Public Policy* (CUP 2009); L. Cotula, "Do Investment Treaties Unduly Constrain Regulatory Space?" 1 Questions of International Law (2014) 19–31.

85 For a review of the various criticisms, see K. Singh, B. Lee (eds) *Rethinking Bilateral Investment Treaties. Critical Issues and Policy Choices* (Both Ends, Madhyam, SOMO 2016).

86 See N. Klein, *No Logo* (Picador 2000); L. Wallach, *Whose Trade Organization? A Comprehensive Guide to the WTO* (The New Press, 2004); K. Jones, *Who's Afraid of the WTO?* (OUP 2004). Tellingly, the French magazine *L'Expansion* ("L'étrange tribunal du commerce mondial" July–August 2002, n 665, 149) had defined the WTO DSS as "un tribunal secret qui fait et défait l'économie de la planète".

87 See, for example, the website bilaterals.org, which presents itself as "a collaborative space to share information and support movements struggling against bilateral trade and investment deals which serve corporations, not people", accessed 30 June 2024.

88 On this issue see J. Kleinheisterkamp, "Investment Treaty Law and the Fear for Sovereignty" 78 Modern Law Review (2015) 793; M. Bronckers, "Is Investor–State Dispute Settlement (ISDS) Superior to Litigation before Domestic Courts? An EU View on Bilateral Trade Agreements" 18 JIEL (2015) 655; D. Behm, O. Fauchald, M. Langford (eds), *The Legitimacy of Investment Arbitration: Empirical Perspectives* (CUP 2020); N. Perrone, *Investment Treaties and the Legal Imagination. How Foreign Investors Play by their Own Rules* (OUP 2021); S. Schill (ed) *International Investment Law and Constitutional Law* (Elgar 2022).

89 As an example, some investment tribunals have found that Italy's "Spalma-incentivi" law (Law 116/2014), which reduced the fixed tariff set for a duration of 20 years by previous legislation for renewable energy operators, breached the legitimate expectations of the investors under the ECT. Meanwhile, the CJEU denied that the same reduction had breached their legitimate expectation as protected by EU law; see CJEU *ANIE and others v Ministero Sviluppo Economico*, C-798, 799/18 (2021), with comment by G. Dall'Agnola, "Italy's Spalma-Incentivi Decree and the ECT's FET Obligation: An Assessment of the Legitimacy of the Photovoltaic Cuts" 35 DCI (2021) 783. In general, see M. Potestà, "Legitimate Expectations in Investment Treaty Law: Understanding the Roots and the Limits of a Controversial Concept" 28 ICSID Review, 88 (2013).

Criticism of ISDS has been directed at it being a system of private justice, lacking the democratic basis and guarantees typical of states' judiciaries, open unidirectionally to claims by investors only, lacking transparency and accountability, administered mostly by practising lawyers subject to competing personal interests and conflicts.[90] This is amplified by its asymmetric nature, since it empowers foreign investors, and only them, to vindicate the rights granted to them by BITs through special international arbitral mechanisms, avoiding domestic courts.[91]

ISDS is also accused of being affected by a structural pro-business bias, thus favouring investors over states, and often resulting in excessive amounts of compensation to the charge of developing countries' budgets due to the vague undetermined criteria used for assessing damages.[92] A different criticism, also discussed below, is directed at the lack of consistency in the case law, resulting from different *ad hoc* arbitrators interpreting treaty clauses differently, thus generating unpredictability and uncertainty for states as to which regulations will pass the bar of an arbitral challenge.

Criticism has come from various constituencies, NGOs, certain academics, some developing countries, but also from the European Parliament and the US. Critics can be separated into those who attack the system with radical requests, up to the abolition of the regime, and those who seek incremental reforms to address the most evident dysfunctions of ISDS in order that it serves better its objectives. Among the former, there are anti-globalization movements and related NGOs,[93] as well as environmentalists who take the view that investment protection is an obstacle to the introduction of measures addressing climate change.[94]

The impact of widespread criticism from civil society directed at the policies of governments and institutions is exemplified by the developments that have characterized the EU post-2010. Hostility towards ISDS in sections of the public in several EU member states became particularly acute with respect to the potential inclusion of ISDS in the proposed TTIP between the EU and the US. This led the European and member states' parliaments, member states' governments, and the

90 See, for instance, G. Van Harten, *The Trouble with Foreign Investment Protection* (OUP 2020); D. Von Schneiderman (ed) *Rethinking Investment Law* (OUP 2023); K. Singh, B. Ilge (eds), *Rethinking Bilateral Investment Treaties* (Both Ends 2016).

91 See T. St John, *The Rise of Investor–State Arbitration* (OUP 2018). For a general overview of these concerns, see UNCITRAL, *Possible Reform of Investor–State Dispute Settlement (ISDS), Note by the Secretariat* Doc. No. A/CN.9/WG.III/WP.142 (18 September 2017) 19–45.

92 See, IISD Policy Brief with statistical data, J. Bonnitcha, S. Brewin, "Compensation Under Investment Treaties: What are the Problems and What Can Be Done?" (2020), available at https://www.iisd.org/system/files/2020-12/compensation-investment-treaties-en.pdf accessed 29 July 2024.

93 See L. Wallach, M. Sforza, *Whose Trade Organization* (Public Citizen Foundation 1999), Chapter 8.

94 A recent debate is on whether the long-term protection of existing investments in the energy sector under IIAs, notably the ECT, is an obstacle to the phasing out of fossil fuels. The introduction of carve-out clauses has been advocated to align investment treaties with the objectives of the Paris Agreement on climate change (2015), see, for example, OECD 9th Investment Treaty Conference "Supporting the global energy transition: Methods to align investment treaties with the Paris Agreement" <https://www.oecd-events.org/investment-treaty-conference> accessed 29 July 2024.

EU Commission to take action.[95] An EU Commission public consultation on ISDS in the TTIP in 2015 received over 150,000 responses.[96] The responses were generally negative, although over 97% of them were based on copy-and-paste templates "submitted through various online platforms of interest groups".[97]

This opposition contributed to TTIP negotiations being abandoned in 2019 as having become "obsolete and no longer relevant" due to the divergent positions of the US and the EU on key provisions. As a response to the specific criticism of ISDS, the EU Commission took the initiative, in agreement with Canada, to change the draft text of CETA, replacing ISDS with a two-tier investment court, as highlighted in chapter VIII.[98] The replacement of ISDS by international judicial bodies in new RTIAs is by now the firm policy of the EU,[99] with the Commission also having declared that for the EU "ISDS is dead".[100]

Criticism also persists in the US. Still in 2023, a group of prominent US academics, mostly economists, petitioned US senators and representatives to abrogate ISDS in US treaties, if needed unilaterally, claiming that ISDS is "a secretive arbitration system that allows multinational corporations to challenge local, state, and federal laws and regulations – often at the expense of climate protections, indigenous land rights, and local democracy".[101]

95 See, for instance, T. Bode, *TTIP. Die Freihandelslüge* (Deutsche Verlags-Anstalt 2015).

96 European Commission Press Release, "Consultation on Investment Protection in EU-US Trade" (13 January 2015), available at https://ec.europa.eu/commission/presscorner/detail/en/IP_15_3201 accessed 29 July 2024.

97 Drawing lessons from such quasi-automated responses to surveys should be interpreted cautiously. See F. Baetens, "Transatlantic Investment Treaty Protection – A Response to Poulsen, Bonnitcha and Yackee" Paper No. 4 in the CEPS-CTR project "TTIP in the Balance" and CEPS Special Reports, No. 103 (2005) 4, available at https://cdn.ceps.eu/wp-content/uploads/2015/03/SR103_ISDS_Baetens.pdf accessed 29 July 2024.

98 The EC proposal to replace ISDS with an ICS in the draft text of the TTIP did not deter criticism. Thus, in 2016, the German Judges Association (DRB) criticized the ICS as being without a legal basis and unnecessary in order to protect investors' rights in the EU. See translation at <https://www.bilaterals.org/?opinion-on-the-establishment-of-an/lang=en>, accessed 25 July 2024.

99 European Parliament resolution of 23 June 2022 on the future of EU international investment policy, EU Doc. No. 2021/2176(INI), available at http://www.europarl.europa.eu; Colin Brown (of the EU Commission), "The Contribution of the European Union to the Rule of Law in the Field of International Investment Law through the Creation of a Multilateral Investment Court" 27 Eur Law J. (2021) 96. The reasons for the EU's choice are set forth in the document "Possible Reform of ISDS: Submission from the European Union" (12 December 2017), available at https://undocs.org/en/, A/CN.9/WG.III/WP.145 (2017).

100 See European Commission, "A New EU Trade Agreement with Japan" July 2018, 6, available at <https://web.archive.org/web/20181225101454/http:/trade.ec.europa.eu/doclib/docs/2017/july/tradoc_1> accessed 29 July 2024. Since, on the other hand, Japan is in favour of maintaining ISDS, no investment dispute settlement mechanism has been included in the EU–Japan EPA of 2018.

101 "'Professors' Letter Opposing ISDS", available at https://forms.gle/hbi88dEnSY8zuUum8. See also the "White Paper" by D. Rangel, L. Wallach, "Turning the Tide: How to Harness the Americas Partnership for Economic Prosperity to Deliver an ISDS-Free Americas" *Rethink Trade* (2023), available at https://rethinktrade.org

3. *Critical Review and Responses to the Most Salient Criticisms of ISDS*

3.1. *Is Investment Arbitration Unbalanced?*

In the *first* place, investment arbitration is being criticized, as mentioned above, as a privileged derogation from the general jurisdiction of national courts to the benefit of foreign economic interests. This "private, secret justice" is furthermore perceived as being overly protective of corporate interests and unbalanced because the ability to submit claims only works in one direction, whereby investors can submit claims against governments. It is also criticized as being biased against the state because of its procedural features that may favour sophisticated investors in respect of ill-prepared governments. The vagueness of the substantive standards applied by arbitrators and instances of very large amounts awarded as damages against states because of actions aimed at pursuing general interests are cited as evidence of arbitrariness, bias, and a general lack of legitimacy.

The response to this criticism is that arbitration, a basic feature of ISDS, represents a derogation from national jurisdiction as a natural consequence of the system being international.[102] The unidirectional nature of the right to submit claims against host states given to foreign investors is due to the fact that states do not need to resort to international arbitration to enforce their laws, regulations, and measures against foreign investors in their territories. Their administrative authority and police powers allow them to do so. The risk of domestic courts in many countries being biased against foreign investors and ill-equipped to adjudicate complex disputes under international law and redress their own government's arbitrary actions is the very reason for BITs granting foreign investors access to international arbitration.[103] Removing the pressure of diplomatic protection by powerful home countries is an additional reason and advantage for submitting disputes to independent arbitration outside the court systems of both BIT parties.[104]

The detailed examination of the features of ISDS, which we have carried out in previous chapters, shows, in our opinion, that many of these perceptions are ill-conceived. Reasonable concerns as to the independence, competence, impartiality,

102 See K. Miles, *The Origin of International Investment Law* (CUP 2013). The CJEU has held that ISDS and ICS represent such a derogation that exceeds the exclusive competence of the EU in trade matters and must therefore be approved by EU Member States, Opinion 2/15 of 2017 (ECLI:EU:C:2017:376) on the then proposed EU–Singapore FTA. Following that Opinion, the investment chapter of the draft agreement was deleted and dealt with in a separate investment agreement. For more detail, see Chapter VIII n 99–101.

103 See C. Brower, S. Schill, "Is Arbitration a Threat or a Boon to the Legitimacy of International Investment Law?" 9 Chicago J Int L (2009) 5; G. Kaufmann-Kohler, M. Potestà, "Why Investment Arbitration and Not Domestic Courts? The Origins of the Modern Investment Dispute Resolution System, Criticism, and Future Outlook" in *Investor–State Dispute Settlement and National Courts: Current Framework and Reform Options,* EYIEL, Special issue (Springer 2020) 7.

104 A recent empirical study shows that the accusation of bias towards investment tribunals is unsupported by evidence; see A. Stone Sweet, M. Yunsuck Chung, A. Salzmann, "Arbitral Law Making and State Power: An Empirical Analysis of Investor–State Arbitration" 8 Journal of International Dispute Settlement (2017) 579.

transparency, equality of arms, as far as they are substantiated in practice, can be addressed and have been addressed. Appropriate changes to the set-up of ISDS and its functioning have been introduced under the rules and supervision of well-equipped, treaty-based (and hence legitimate) institutions, ICSID in the first place, as well as by the initiative to replace ISDS with investment courts.

Investment courts would eliminate the private *ad hoc* arbitral system that ISDS has "inherited" from and shares with commercial arbitration, and would better reflect the public nature of investment disputes.[105] This transformation is, however, not universally supported since the flexibility and responsiveness to the users' needs and preferences that the current system prominently features would thereby get lost. On the other hand, in a context where cases become more political, the sums of money involved grow exponentially, and tribunals are called upon to rule on sensitive areas falling in the area of sovereign discretion, concerns about the legitimacy of *ad hoc* tribunals to adjudicate will not be resolved by technical improvements to ISDS.

3.2. The Selection and Qualifications of Arbitrators

A *second* criticism focuses on the selection, impartiality, independence, and qualifications of ISDS arbitrators. In this respect, criticism has focused on the lack of diversity of arbitrators, concerning national and ethnic origin, gender, and background, potentially affecting the impartiality of the process, the fairness of the outcome, and the quality of the decisions.[106] There has been criticism of most of the arbitrators coming from a small, similarly-minded "Western" group, with frequent re-appointments.[107]

Arbitrators, directly or indirectly chosen by the parties, tend to come from the legal profession, often associated with and *de facto* selected by large international law firms, rather than from academia or courts.[108] It is alleged that commercial arbitrators acting in investment disputes, as is often the case, lack expertise in public international law, including customary law rules on the interpretation of treaties,

105 See generally G. Van Harten, *Investment Treaty Arbitration and Public Law* (OUP 2009); S. Schill, "International Investment Law and Comparative Public Law. An Introduction" in S. Schill (ed) *International Investment Law and Comparative Public Law* (OUP 2010), 3; A. Kulick, *Global Public Interest in International Investment Law* (CUP 2012); A. Roberts, "Clash of Paradigms: Actors and Analogies Shaping the Investment System" 107 AJIL (2013) 45; J. Arato, "The Private Law Critique of International Investment Law" 113 AJIL (2019) 1.

106 See T. St John, D. Behn, M. Langford, R. Lie, "Glass Ceilings and Arbitral Dealings: Explaining the Gender Gap in International Investment Arbitration" PluriCourts Research Paper (2017), available at https://ssrn.com/abstract=3782593

107 See S. Franck and others, "The Diversity Challenge: Exploring the 'Invisible College' of International Arbitration" 53 CJTL (2015) 429.

108 In 2018, the ICJ decided however that its sitting judges could not be appointed to investment tribunals. This terminated the traditional practice of ICJ judges being called to chair investment tribunals, thereby enhancing their standing, although raising concerns as to its compatibility with their judicial function. See iisd.org, Investment Treaties News of 21 December 2018.

and in the area of State responsibility.[109] A further criticism concerns the practice of "double-hatting" (arbitrators also being practising lawyers in the field), thus increasing the possibility of bias and conflicts of interests.[110]

Some of the above criticisms seem unwarranted or immaterial in view of the scarcity of upheld accusations of partiality and the high quality and reputation generally enjoyed by awards, as confirmed by references to them by tribunals and scholarly works. Efforts by institutions to increase diversity are yielding results, which must be welcomed because diversity undoubtedly increases the legitimacy of arbitration in the eyes of stakeholders and is a must in view of the worldwide coverage of IIAs.[111] At the same time, experience and reputation are fundamental factors that parties take into account when selecting arbitrators. Professional arbitrators and institutions are most interested in maintaining the highest competence and ethical standards. The data on the outcomes of cases at ICSID showing that states tend to prevail undermine the opinion that the system is tilted in favour of investors.[112] The small percentage of annulments granted against ICSID awards, and the paucity of challenges against arbitrators that are accepted, belies the accusation of incompetence and conflicts in international arbitration.[113]

The repeated appointment of well-known, experienced practitioners (often also academics) who have specialized in the field of investment law as arbitrators reflects the advantage of specialization and the trust of parties in recognized experts in the field to decide their disputes. While some of these experts are considered to be "pro-business" (and are repeatedly appointed by claimants), several reputed arbitrators are systematically appointed by defendant states, being considered more responsive to the protection of state interests. The same can be said for law firms specializing in investment law, where some tend to represent claimants, that is investors, while others tend to represent host states as respondents.

In any case, in order to remedy the concerns about the professionalism and independence of arbitrators, UNCITRAL WG III (made up of state representatives) has drafted in cooperation with ICSID, Codes of Conduct for Investment Arbitrators and Judges of a future judicial body, which were approved by the UNCITRAL

109 A well-known example is the award in *CMS Gas v Argentina* ICSID ARB/01/8 (2005), which was heavily criticized in the annulment decision because of the "manifest errors of law" it included. The Annulment Committee held, however, that its limited mandate under Article 52 ICSID did not allow it to annul the award.

110 Double-hatting has been limited under the UNCITRAL Code of Conduct for arbitrators, which was adopted in 2023; see Chapter VIII.B.5.2.2(b).

111 Thus, as of 28 June 2024, the current list of 20 names on the roster of arbitrators and conciliators designated by the Chairman pursuant to Article 13.2 ICSID includes 11 women (five arbitrators and six conciliators).

112 See n 72 above.

113 As to annulment, see above n 73. At ICSID, of about 100 disqualification proposals that have ever been made pursuant to AR 22 and its predecessor, only six have been upheld; see https://icsid.worldbank.org/cases/content/tables-of-decisions/disqualification accessed 29 July 2024.

Commission and the UNGA in 2023.[114] The double-hatting of arbitrators, whereby they also act as counsel – a situation that raises justified concerns as to their independence – has been regulated in both codes. Moreover, recent EU treaties provide that ICS tribunal members must be eligible for appointment to the "highest judicial offices" as is the case at the ICJ and the CJEU.[115] They shall not be affiliated with any government or take instructions from any government with regard to matters related to the dispute.[116]

Some criticisms that are shared with commercial arbitration, such as those concerning the length and cost of proceedings, conflicts of interest, and third-party funding, have also been dealt with by bodies and arbitral institutions such as the IBA and the ICC, by revising their arbitration rules and issuing guidelines as to the conduct of proceedings.[117]

3.3. The Inconsistency of Decisions and the Lack of Appeal.

Another area in ISDS that has been the subject of criticism is the lack of a centralized check for legal correctness, coherence, and consistency, an issue amplified by the growing number of cases. The decentralized model of decision-making in investment disputes, by different *ad hoc* arbitrators in respect of different treaties, inevitably gives rise to inconsistency in the jurisprudence, though parties systematically invoke previous decisions as precedent and tribunals refer to them.[118] This cannot be said to be objectionable and harmful per se in a fragmented investment landscape, where the treaties under scrutiny are rarely identical and bind different states. Parties in a dispute may even find comfort from the fact that the relevant case law has not crystallized one way or the other.[119]

Lack of consistency has characterized the interpretation and application of provisions such as umbrella clauses, most-favoured-nation clauses in respect of dispute

114 UNCITRAL, *Code of conduct for arbitrators in international investment dispute resolution and commentary* Doc. No. A/CN.9/1148 (21 April 2023); UNCITRAL, *Draft Code of conduct for judges in international investment dispute resolution and commentary* Doc. No. A/CN.9/1149, see chapter VIII.B.5.2. See also the IBA "Guidelines on Conflicts of Interest in International Arbitration" (updated in 2024). The purview of these Guidelines is broader as they are also applicable to commercial arbitration; they include obligations of disclosure upon the parties besides than upon arbitrators, lay down detailed procedural requirements, and distinguish between different types of actual or potential conflicts (red, orange, green lists, waivable and non-waivable situations).

115 See, e.g. EUSIPA Article 3.10.4.

116 EUSIPA Article 3.11 provides that: "In addition, [Members of the Tribunals] upon appointment shall refrain from acting as counsel, party-appointed expert or party-appointed witness in any pending or new investment protection dispute under this or any other agreement or domestic law".

117 Stricter deadlines have been introduced for the issuance of awards by ICSID AR 58 (2022) and by Article 31 ICC (2021). As to the time-line of ISDS cases compared with WTO panel proceedings see J. Alvarez Zarate and others, "Duration of ISDS Proceedings" 21 JWIT (2020) 300 (special issue n 2-3 on "UNCITRAL and Investment Arbitration Reform").

118 See Chapter III.B.5. on "Applicable Law and the Role of Precedent".

119 See G. Zarra, "The Issue of Incoherence in Investment Arbitration: Is There Need for a Systemic Reform?" 17 Chinese Journal of International Law (2018) 137.

settlement, and the customary and treaty law defence of necessity. Similarly, this has been the case as to whether financial instruments and security entitlements related to sovereign debt qualify as protected investments under BITs.[120]

The failure to ensure legal certainty and avoid contradictory awards may be to the detriment of both investors and respondent states, depending on the context.[121] This would be avoided if the regime had a centralized appellate mechanism to check for legal correctness on the merits (a function which goes beyond the task of annulment committees at ICSID). It would serve as an authoritative guide for future tribunals through a "jurisprudence constante", even if the differing provisions of BITs that would come before any centralized appellate body would make binding precedent impossible.[122] The call for mechanisms ensuring consistency appears especially convincing where case law has been inconsistent in respect of the same BIT provision applied to the same host state measure in different disputes.[123]

An appeal review could moreover favour judicial economy if the appeal body were endowed with the power to issue a new decision on the merits in case it quashes the award appealed. Currently, in case of annulment of an award at ICSID

120 See *SGS v Pakistan* ICSID Case No. ARB/01/13, Decision on Jurisdiction (2003) and *SGS v Philippines* ICSID Case No. ARB/02/6, Decision on Jurisdiction (2004). The former decision construed the umbrella clause narrowly, rejecting the notion that it transformed contractual breaches into treaty breaches (at 167 and 172). The latter decision found the opposite (at 126). Divergences have occurred as to whether the MFN clause covers dispute settlement clauses in BITs (this was found to be the case in *Maffezzini v Spain* ICSID Case No. ARB/97/7, Decision on Jurisdiction (2000), and *Plama v Bulgaria* ICSID Case No. ARB/03/24 Decision on Jurisdiction (2005); this was found not to be the case in *Tecmed v Mexico* ICSID Case No. ARB(AF)/00/2, Award (2005), and *Wintershall v Argentina* ICSID Case No. ARB/04/14, Award (2008)). Similarly, as to whether state bonds issued abroad are covered by BITs: this was found to be the case in *Abaclat et al v Argentina,* ICSID Case No. ARB/07/5 Decision on Jurisdiction (2011); but found not in *Poštová v Greece,* ICSID Case No. ARB/13/8 Final Award (2015). These contrasting outcomes have led the drafters of later BITs to clarify that foreign bonds are not covered and that jurisdictional clauses are not subject to the application of MFN clauses. See Z. Douglas, "The MFN Clause in Investment Arbitration: Treaty Interpretation Off the Rails" 2 JIDS (2011) 97.

121 A well-known example is that of the two awards *Ronald S. Lauder v Czech Republic*, Award (2001), available at https://www.italaw.com/cases/610 accessed 29 July 2024, and *CME v Czech Republic*, Award (2001), https://www.italaw.com/cases/281 accessed 29 July 2024. In the first case, the claim of the controlling shareholder of CME under the US–Czech BIT was rejected. In the second case, a few days later, under the Netherlands–Czech BIT, CME was awarded damages of USD 250 million for the same breach.

122 See generally A. Bjorklund, "Investment Treaty Arbitral Decisions as Jurisprudence Constante" UC Davis Legal Studies Research Paper No. 158, available at https://papers.ssrn.com/sol3/papers.cfm?abstract_id=1319834. On the precedential value of ICSID decisions, see G. Kaufmann-Kohler, "Arbitral Precedent: Dream, Necessity or Excuse? The 2006 Freshfields Lecture" 23 Arbitration International (2007) 368. See also K. Diel-Gligor, *Towards Consistency in International Investment Jurisprudence: A Preliminary Ruling System for ICSID Arbitration* (Brill 2017).

123 Contradictory awards also characterize the case law involving Italy and Spain regarding the conformity of the reduction in their respective long-term renewable energy subsidies with the FET standard in Article 10 ECT. See, respectively, G. Dall'Agnola, n 89; F. Balcerzak, *Renewable Energy Arbitration – Quo Vadis? Implications of the Spanish Saga for International Investment Law* (Brill 2023).

or by a domestic court, the investor has to commence fresh proceedings if it intends to pursue its rights further, as has happened more than once at ICSID.[124] On the other hand, appeal would make proceedings even lengthier than they are presently and would add to the costs.[125]

Proponents of appellate review have looked to the WTO AB as a model, ironically about the same time that US opposition has rendered it no longer operative. The lack of centralized second-tier review is thus now common to both regimes. The lack of appeal in the investment regime is, however, less damaging than at the WTO. While WTO adjudicators interpret and apply a uniform and limited set of rules (the WTO Agreements) for the benefit of the WTO Members at large and not merely the litigants, investment arbitration in most cases concerns different states, different investors, and the application of different, albeit often similar, provisions.

3.4. The Termination of BITs and Sunset Clauses

Finally, the investment regime has faced criticism for the difficulty of terminating IIAs and the burden this places on future lawmakers and policymakers intending to terminate or replace a BIT.[126] Criticism has been addressed at "sunset clauses" that ensure the provisions protecting investments continue to apply after the termination of an IIA, usually for a considerable number of years, up to 20 in the ECT.[127] These clauses are economically valuable because they ensure stability for investors who can rely on the terms of the agreement in force when an investment is made. This represents an important guarantee for large, long-term investments, such as in the extractive industries, oil and gas exploration and exploitation, utility concessions, and energy projects where a major part of the investment costs are incurred upfront and recovered over the years of the concession. On the other hand, they make treaty exit and changes to outdated treaty provisions with no further post-termination obligations difficult.

124 See Chapter V.B.2.

125 As to the issue of costs (the greatest part of which reflects lawyers' fees rather than arbitrators' compensation), see S. Franck, *Arbitration Costs, Myths and Realities in Investment Treaty Arbitration* (OUP 2019).

126 See European Parliament, Study requested by the JURI Committee, A. Kouroutakis, *Sunset Clauses in International Law and their Consequences for EU Law* (2022) 37, available at https://www.europarl.europa.eu. For a more radical criticism, see L. Johnson and others, "Clearing the Path: Withdrawal of Consent and Termination as Next Steps for Reforming International Investment Law" Columbia Center on Sustainable Development Policy Paper (2018), available at https://scholarship.law.columbia.edu

127 Article 47.3 ECT, whose application or abrogation in the context of the EU decision to withdraw from the ECT in 2023–2024, has been contentious; see T. Morgandi, L. Bartels, "Exiting the Energy Charter Treaty Under the Law of Treaties" 34 King's Law Journal (2023) 145; N. Braoudakis, R. Craveia, C. Baldon, "Neutralising the ECT Sunset Clause *Inter Se*" 39 ICSID Rev (2024) 347.

The options for exiting or terminating IIAs are those available to parties for all treaties.[128] Depending upon the terms of the relevant final clause, IIAs may remain in force for a specific, usually tacitly renewable period of time[129] or for an indefinite period.[130] In the latter case, either party can terminate the treaty by notice in writing to the other party at any time or after an initial period. Thanks to sunset clauses, however, existing investments will continue enjoying the treaty's protection (including access to ISDS) for the duration provided for in the relevant clause. Treaty parties can agree to modify the sunset clause, such as by shortening its duration or cancelling it upon termination. This, however, requires a specific agreement on which the parties may have divergent views.

4. *From Criticism to Reform*

All matters considered, the number of IIAs in force, as updated, evidence that investment treaties, including ISDS, continue to enjoy the support of a large majority of states, business interests, practitioners, and a number of academics and commentators.[131]

While sharing the criticism of certain features and specific substantive provisions of BITs, many, if not most observers believe in the merits of the system, also comparing it with alternatives. They believe, as the present authors do, that its shortcomings are curable through appropriate reforms, both in terms of its substantive standards (specifying them better and reducing their scope) and procedural provisions, such as those that most recent IIAs and other instruments have been implementing in order to enhance their benefits to the development of host countries.[132]

128 See Article 54–64 VCLT, C. McLachlan, "The Assault on International Adjudication and the Limits of Withdrawal" 68 ICLQ (2019) 499.

129 See typically Article 18 of the China–Uzbekistan BIT (2011): "1. This Agreement shall remain in force for a period of ten (10) years. 2. Either Contracting Party may give a written notice to the other Contracting Party to terminate this Agreement after the expiration of the initial ten years" effective six months after the notice was given.

130 For example, Article XV.8 of the Canada–Czech Republic BIT (2009): "This Agreement shall remain in force unless either Contracting Party notifies in writing the other Contracting Party of its intention to terminate it. The termination of this Agreement shall become effective one year after notice of termination has been received by the other Contracting Party. In respect of investments made prior to the date when the termination of this Agreement becomes effective, the provisions of Articles I to XIV inclusive of this Agreement shall remain in force for a period of 15 years".

131 See J. Pauwelyn, "At the Edge of Chaos? Foreign Investment Law as a Complex Adaptive System, How It Emerged and How it Can Be Reformed" 29 ICSID Rev (2014) 372. Talk of a backlash against ISDS (as against international courts in general) was probably premature in 2010, see M. Waibel, A. Kaushal, L. Chung, K-H. Balchin (eds), *The Backlash against Investment Arbitration* (Wolters Kluwer 2010).

132 See C. Brower, "What's in a Meme? The Truth about Investor–State Arbitration: Why It Need Not, and Must Not, Be Repossessed by States" 52 CJTL (2014) 690 ff; G. Kaufmann-Kohler, M. Potestà n 103.

Criticisms of the indeterminate definition of certain key substantive standards in first-generation BITs, and of certain features of ISDS, have brought their supporters and policymakers more generally to acknowledge that more detailed and balanced provisions are justified, first in order to balance standards of protection with other societal values, and secondly to more rigorously ensure fairness and impartiality in arbitral proceedings. IIAs should not only focus on the protection of investors. Hence the calls for the addition of duties and obligations upon investors in respect of social and environmental obligations as a way of rebalancing their traditional approach, ensuring the policy space of host countries in these areas.[133]

International organizations such as UNCTAD have been active in promoting new standards, accountability of investors, and transparency.[134] Reaffirming the policy space of the state parties as well as their "right to regulate" is pursued by rearticulating the scope of what were vague criteria, such as fair and equitable treatment, indirect expropriation, and the legitimate expectations of investors. An aim is to thereby limit the discretion of tribunals in determining their content.[135] Reaffirming state control in investment law is intended to redress the balance between investors' rights and states' prerogatives and responsibilities.[136]

133 This reflects the evolution of other fields of international economic law (such as the UN Guiding Principles on Business and Human Rights of 2011 and the OECD Guidelines on Multinational Enterprises and Responsible Business Conduct, rev 2023) as well as the Paris Agreement on Climate Change (2015) and its follow-up.

134 UNCTAD, whose Investment and Enterprise Division ("the focal point in the United Nations System for investment and enterprise development") has consistently advocated substantial revisions of existing IIAs models, although it has softened its criticism over the years, submitting a number of reform proposals. UNCTAD's comprehensive document *Reform Package for the International Investment Regime* (2018), available at https://investmentpolicy.unctad.org is presented as a "coherent, sequenced and user-friendly set of options for countries engaging in IIA reform at a time when IIA reform has entered the mainstream of international investment policymaking". At UNCITRAL, WG III was mandated in 2017 with addressing procedural issues concerning ISDS reform, including drafting the blueprint for a "permanent mechanism" such as the EU proposal for a MIC, leaving aside the reform of substantive treatment provisions; see Chapter VIII.B.5.2.

135 A connected development has been the addition of provisions granting parties more control over the functioning of investment adjudication. This has been added to treaties by providing that joint committees may issue interpretations of treaty provisions, declaring them as binding on tribunals. For a review see C. Côté, S. Hamamoto, M. Menkes, X. Qian, "The Growing Interest for Joint Interpretations of Investment Treaties by State Parties" Columbia FDI Perspective No 386 (2024), available at: https://ccsi.columbia.edu. See also Chapter VIII.B.5.3.

136 On the issue, see generally G. Sacerdoti, P. Acconci, M. Valenti, A. De Luca (eds), *General Interests of Host States in International Investment Law* (CUP 2014); M. Paparinskis, "Masters and Guardians of International Investment Law: How to Play the Game of Reassertion" in A. Kulick (ed) *Reassertion of Control over the Investment Treaty Regime* (CUP 2016); S. Puig, G. Shaffer, "Imperfect Alternatives: Institutional Choice and the Reform of Investment Law" 112 AJIL (2018) 361; C. Baltag, R. Joshi, K. Duggal, "Recent Trends in Investment Arbitration on the Right to Regulate, Environment, Health and Corporate Social Responsibility: Too Much or Too Little?" 38 ICSID Rev. (2023) 381. For recent treaty texts addressing these concerns, see Chapter VIII n 85, 168.

Criticism of the investment system has thus not led to its rejection and demise. A number of states have updated their model BITs and have been successful in replacing existing BITs.[137] Very few countries have exited the system, while the case of Brazil, which, like South Africa, is not a party to ICSID and has not signed BITs with ISDS, has remained isolated.[138] The EU has negotiated several RTIAs (with Canada, Mexico, Chile, Viet Nam, and Singapore[139]) with innovative substantive and procedural investment chapters.[140]

The current, more nationalistic, protectionist, and unilateralist mood prevailing in many countries has also made home states more attentive to the constraints rather than the benefits of IIAs and has impacted some texts. This mood has led, as to the US, to the replacement of some treaties, such as the NAFTA by USMCA in 2020 (which includes more limited investment protection and reduced availability of ISDS),[141] the withdrawal from finalized or not finalized negotiations (e.g. the US rejecting the TPP in 2017 and abandoning the TTIP negotiations in 2018), and

137 See, for instance, the model BIT of Norway (2015), https://edit.wti.org/document/show/3b8bd5cf-2a4c-438c-a8cf-21ebdc1cce91; of India (Model Text of 2016), <www.iisd.org/toolkits/sustainability-toolkit-for-trade-negotiators/wp-content/uploads/2016/06/Model-Text-for-the-Indian-Bilateral-Investment-Treaty.pdf> which retains the ISDS mechanism to settle disputes with foreign investors though it adds a number of conditions that an investor needs to meet before accessing ISDS; the model BIT of the Netherlands (2019), <https://investmentpolicy.unctad.org/international-investment-agreements/treaty-files/5832/download>, and Canada's model of 2021, available at https://www.international.gc.ca/trade-commerce/trade-agreements-accords-commerciaux/agr-acc/fipa-apie/2021_model_fipa-2021_modele_apie.aspx?lang=eng all accessed 29 July 2024. See also the Reciprocal Investment Promotion and Protection Agreement between Morocco and Nigeria (2016) and the draft investment protocol of the AfCFTA (2023). On South Africa, which terminated most of its BITs and is not an ICSID Member, see E. Schlemmer, "An Overview of South Africa's BITs and Investment Policy" 31 ICSID Rev. (2016) 167. As to the policy of India, see K. Singh, "An Analysis of India's New Model BIT" and P. Ranjan, "India's BIT Programme – Past, Present and Future", both in K. Singh and B. Ilge (eds) *Rethinking BITs supra* n 90, at 81, 101. See also M. Misra, "Investment Facilitation and India: A Closer Look" Columbia FDI Perspectives, No. 301 (2021), available at https://www.econstor.eu.

138 Bolivia (2007) and Venezuela (2012) have exited ICSID, but cases against the two countries have been ongoing for alleged breaches in the past. Ecuador, which had withdrawn in 2009, reentered ICSID in 2021. Honduras announced its withdrawal in 2023. As to Brazil, see the Agreement for Cooperation and Investment Facilitation with Mozambique (2015). It provides a mechanism for the prevention and resolution of disputes through the activities of national "Focal Points" and a Joint Committee, with inter-state arbitration, in a format to be defined, should an investment dispute not be resolved. See G. Vidigal, B. Stevens, "Brazil's New Model of Dispute Settlement for Investment: Return to the Past or Alternative for the Future?" 19 JWIT (2018) 475.

139 Though originally negotiated as a single trade and investment agreement, following Opinion 2/15 of the CJEU, the EU–Vietnam FTA and EU–Singapore FTA were split to create separate Investment Protection Agreements (IPA). See Chapter VIII.B.3.

140 Once these provisions enter in force, they will replace EU Member States' BITs with those countries, based on EU competence in international investment matters under Article 207 TFEU as amended by the Lisbon Treaty (2007). See F. Montanaro, *The EU and International Investment Law* (Hart 2023) 97.

141 See J. Galbraith, "NAFTA is Renegotiated and Signed by the United States" 113 AJIL (2019) 150.

persistent requests to delete ISDS from US BITs.[142] Opposition to CETA's ratification in several EU Member States persists, notwithstanding the innovations that it presents compared with previous RTIAs of the EU and BITs.[143]

C. Comparative Evaluation

There are commonalities to be underlined but also distinctions to be made as to the type, origin, seriousness, and effects of the criticism directed at the two regimes, as well as in respect of responses to them.

1. Commonalities

(a) In both regimes, substantive provisions (trade rules and investment rules) have been criticized but most criticism has focused on their DSS;

(b) Criticism has been widespread, notwithstanding and in part because of the successes of both DSS in settling disputes in a manner that is binding, law-based, and impartial. This has led to objections and obstruction by parties who have lost cases that are sensitive for them, attempting to block the process.[144]

(c) Criticism has led to calls for reform, in part with a view to loosening the binding nature of the DSS or reducing their coverage. The prevailing tendency has, however, been in the opposite direction, towards improving their functioning, such as in respect of the qualifications of the adjudicators, conflicts of interest, transparency of proceedings, length and costs, also in order to overcome the legitimacy crisis of the DSS in the eyes of the wider public;

(d) In both systems, there is a tendency by states to "reassert control" concerning the adjudicators. In trade, this is illustrated by criticism of the de facto precedential effect of the AB's case law, which has made changes in the case

142 The US had been among the first proponents of treaties geared towards the protection of American investments abroad, from FCN treaties to BITs with ISDS. See K.J. Vandevelde, *U.S. International Investment Agreements* (2009). However, in the context of the recent NAFTA re-negotiations, USTR stated that the US Government was "skeptical about ISDS", *inter alia* because investor–state arbitration grants to foreigners "more rights than Americans have in the American court system". USTR suggested that investors should rather resort to state-to-state dispute settlement or negotiate arbitration clauses in their contracts, Robert Lighthizer (USTR at the time) at a hearing before the US Congress Ways and Means Committee, 21 March 2018 (transcript available on the IELP Blog, available at https://worldtradelaw.typepad.com/ielpblog/2018/03/brady-lighthizer-isds-exchange.html accessed 29 July 2024. See also n 101 above; as to policy statements against ISDS by the Biden administration, see Chapter VIII, n 96. In the same vein, on 16 January 2025 USTR announced a Decision of the US-Colombia FTA (Trade Promotion Agreement) interpreting restrictively the standards of investment protection under the investment chapter of the TPA.

143 The Parliament of Cyprus (in 2020) and the French Senate (in 2024) have voted against ratification. The Irish Supreme Court in 2022 has conditioned ratification on amendments to the Irish Arbitration Act.

144 Compare the US blocking of the appellate stage of the WTO DSS with EU Member States invoking EU law and the intervention of the EU Commission and the CJEU to avoid intra-EU investment arbitration under the ECT. For more information, see Chapter VI n 39, 46.

law more difficult. While this criticism, which undermines the stability and predictability of the even-handed application of the WTO agreements, has essentially come from the US, current reform projects ("the Molina proposals") favour loosening the authority of past cases. The proposal also envisages increased engagement from parties concerning decisions laid down by adjudicators.[145] In investment, control by the parties over the functioning of investment adjudication has been increased by empowering joint committees to interpret agreements with binding effects upon tribunals;

(e) Exit from ISDS (which only a handful of countries have committed to cancel from their BITs) has been limited to a few countries, while the de facto exit of the US from the appellate stage of the WTO has had a paralyzing effect on the whole system and all Members;

(f) The moving away from the multilateral trade DSS due to its semi-paralysis may invigorate bilateral DSS under RTAs, thus approximating the trade DSS to the fragmented, non-multilateral setting of bilateral and regional investment DSS.[146]

2. *Differences*

(a) Recent criticism of the WTO DSS has mainly come from within the system, namely from the US, while criticism of the investment DSS has mostly originated from outside;

(b) Since the WTO DSS is more centralized, it has been substantially affected by the US' actions of blocking the functioning of the AB, leading to a partial paralysis and to a double regime of dispute settlement (MPIA/non-MPIA). The investment regime's DSS has been more resilient thanks to being decentralized. It has only been marginally affected by radical internal opposition (such as exits and resistance to compliance and enforcement). Criticism both from states and from outside has rather stimulated reform initiatives by participants, bilaterally as well as multilaterally at UNCITRAL and ICSID. This process has resulted in the updating of traditional provisions in new BITs and RTIAs, both as to substantive protection and DSS (to the point of the EU replacing ISDS with the ICS);

(c) Global, multilateral reforms remain elusive in the two systems (DSU/MIC). Investment dispute settlement provisions and underlying standards of protection have been amended in a number of IIAs, inevitably leading to increased fragmentation. The multilateral WTO system has not proved conducive to

145 For more detail, see Chapter VIII.A.3.1.

146 See V. Beyer, "Dispute Settlement in Preferential Trade Agreements and the WTO: A Network Analysis of Idleness and Choice of Forum" 32 JIEL (2021) 433.

amendments or the adding of plurilateral agreements, as these actions require the consensus of all Members;[147]

(d) There is a curious inversion of approaches in the two regimes: while the AB was taken as a model for a hypothetical appellate review of investment decisions with a view to extending review beyond annulment, at the WTO there is a strand of opinion in favour of reducing the scope of appeal, advocating a more limited second-tier of review, or even abrogating the appellate stage altogether.

147 See, however, the signing of a plurilateral e-commerce agreement in July 2024 by 92 WTO Members (not including among others the US and India) after five years of negotiations within a "joint statement initiative". See Borderlex, "WTO Members Seal Plurilateral E-Commerce Deal – US Opts Out", https://borderlex.net/2024/07/26/wto-members-seal-plurilateral-e-commerce-deal-us-opts-out/. An open question is whether non-participants will agree to the addition of this agreement to the WTO plurilateral agreements (part IV of the WTO agreement), thus making it part of the WTO rule book.

8 Reforming the Trade and Investment Dispute Settlement Systems

Approaches, Results, and Work in Progress

Table of Contents

DOI: 10.4324/9781003471509-11

Introduction

This chapter sets out, from a comparative perspective, current reform initiatives that have been underway at the WTO and in the investment law regime in recent years. The criticisms that have been directed at the two systems, both as to their substantive and procedural rules, which we examined in Chapter VII, have recently resulted in several reform proposals of their procedural rules (more so than their substantive rules). Few of them have, however, been finally agreed upon and are in operation as of March 2025. Discussions on other reforms (such as on appellate review at the WTO) are far from concluded. We therefore also review the possible outcomes of the current work in progress.

In this final chapter, concerning *trade*, we look at the initiatives of WTO Members to overcome the blocking of the AB by the US, reviewing in detail the alternative appeal system of the MPIA. We further look at proposed revisions of the DSS that were drafted in informal discussions among WTO Members from 2022–2024 and were submitted, but not examined, at MC13 (Abu Dhabi, February 2024) following the mandate of MC12 in June 2022. The work has resumed thereafter, focusing on the accessibility of the DSS to all Members and on appellate review, with a view to reaching a shared result by the end of 2024. Though the project is still far from completion and was paused at the beginning of 2025 we evaluate the type of reform that may emerge and the future role of dispute settlement within the WTO. Notwithstanding the engagement of the membership, a speedy exit from the present semi-paralysis does not appear likely. This is especially the case since the current climate of geopolitical and economic fragmentation and confrontation, exacerbated by the Trump Administration's protectionist trade policy and unilateral tariffs increases since March 2025, is not conducive to relaunching multilateralism with the WTO at its core.

Regional systems do not appear to represent real alternatives notwithstanding the variety of dispute settlement mechanisms that they offer, which extends to non-typical trade disputes such as in respect of labour relations.[1] First, major trade flows, such as between the EU, US, and China, are not covered and between the EU and the US, are not covered by RTAs. Second, the conclusion and the entry into force, if at all concluded, of new regional agreements, extended or not to social or environmental issues and which may also cover investment, are encountering growing resistance.[2]

1 As to North America, see R. Howse, "Developments in USMCA Dispute Settlement" *USMCA Forward 2024* (Report of the Brookings Institution, 2024).

2 See for example the current difficulties in ratifying CETA within the European Union (with only 17 EU Member States' ratifications having been completed out of the 27 required after seven years), the latest development being its rejection by the French Senate on 25 March 2024. The reluctance to enter into trade agreements that include binding liberalization and market access commitments has prompted the US to promote economic cooperation agreements focused rather on economic policy cooperation in selected areas. This is the case of the 2022 US-led Indo-Pacific Economic Framework for Prosperity (partnering with 14 countries in the area), which, in view of its content and nature, does not include any dispute settlement mechanism. The Framework does, however, provide for a

As to *investment*, we first take stock of the reforms that have been put in place: the Codes of Conduct for Investment Arbitrators and Adjudicators by UNCITRAL WG III and the new (2022) ICSID Arbitration Rules, as well as the recent approval, in principle, by the UNCITRAL Commission of an Advisory Centre on International Investment Law. We then look at what is currently the central effort towards reform, the work of WG III to reform procedural features of the investment regime by elaborating rules that could be used to amend existing IIAs and inserted in or serve as guidelines for future ones.

We also examine the innovations that have been made in respect of ISDS on a bilateral and regional basis, with an emphasis on the EU's Investment Court System, which is present in some recent EU RTIAs (though none of their investment DSS are yet in force) and is a model for the proposed Multilateral Investment Court (MIC), whose project is also under discussion at UNCITRAL. The final section of this chapter looks at perspectives and lessons that can be drawn from the reform processes of the two regimes to date, also taking into account the broader framework of current attitudes towards the adjudication of international disputes.

A. Trade

1. The WTO in Crisis

1.1. The WTO Facing the Challenge of Unilateralism

Negotiations of new agreements have been stalled since the comprehensive Doha Development Round, launched in 2001, failed to achieve its objectives and was *de facto* abandoned in 2016. Only two additional multilateral agreements have been concluded since the establishment of the WTO, namely the Trade Facilitation Agreement in 2013 at MC9 in Bali and a partial agreement on Fisheries Subsidies in 2022 at MC12 in Geneva. Plurilateral deals have proved difficult to conclude despite protracted negotiations.[3] Furthermore, surveillance of the implementation of the agreements currently in place and notifications on implementation and

reporting mechanism for labour rights inconsistencies and a Supply Chain Crisis Response Network (Articles 9 and 7 of IPEF's Supply Chain Agreement, respectively).

3 At MC13, an agreement was reached in substance on plurilateral agreements on Investment Facilitation for Development (among 123 Members) and on the Domestic Regulation of Domestic Services (71 Members). Their formal addition to the WTO package as plurilaterals in Annex 4 of the Marrakesh Agreement was, however, blocked under the consensus rule due to the opposition of India and South Africa. See P. Ungphakorn, *Objections Dropped on Services Regulation Say Nothing About Other Plurilaterals* (28 February 2024), available athttps://tradebetablog.wordpress.com/. On this issue see: J. Bacchus, "The Future of the WTO: Multilateral or Plurilateral?" Cato Institute Policy Analysis No 947, (25 May 2023), available athttps://www.cato.org/. Recourse to plurilateral agreements has been advocated for years, see B. Hoekman, P. Mavroidis, "WTO 'à la carte' or 'menu du jour'? Assessing the Case for More Plurilateral Agreements" 26 EJIL (2014) 319.

measures taken by individual WTO Members are also widely considered to be unsatisfactory.[4]

Respect for multilateral rules and obligations has been undermined since the "Trade War" that the US initiated against China in 2018, accusing it of abusing the multilateral system and generating growing bilateral trade surpluses. The US introduced a consistent unilateral increase in customs duties on imports of Chinese products (to which China responded with its own increases).[5] The imposition by the US of additional duties on steel and aluminium imports from all sources followed, with the US invoking the security exception found in GATT Article XXI.[6] The "phase one" agreement between the US and China in 2020 reduced the parties' reciprocal increases in duties but did not terminate the conflict, which on the contrary has been characterized by further trade and investment restrictions up to today.[7] On the other side, there is China's dubious record of complying with the fundamentals of a market economy (while insisting on its developing Member status despite being the world's largest trading nation), as evidenced by accusations of over-production which depresses world prices, and extensive trade-distorting opaque support to its SOEs.[8]

The first Trump administration's policy objectives were the protection of US domestic enterprises and "bringing back" manufacturing jobs to the US (by the way inspiring the Republican program for the November 2024 presidential elections).[9] The Biden administration softened the tone of disdain for the WTO, but did not

4 Information on notifications is published on the WTO Notifications Portal; see https://notifications.wto.org/en

5 These measures and countermeasures resulted in the filing of DS 543 by China, and DS 558 by the US. The extra duties of both parties were found by the duly established panels to be contrary to the enacting Members' WTO obligations. Both panel reports have been appealed into the void and have thus not been adopted by the DSB.

6 The countries affected responded by filing a series of cases (DS544, 547, 548, 550, 551, 552, 554, 556, 557, 564, 566). Some of these countries also enacted immediate countermeasures invoking the Safeguard Agreement to which the US responded by filing DS 557, 558, 559, 561, see n 23.

7 See https://ustr.gov/phase-one and more generally, P. Navarro (an economic advisor to the Trump administration), *The Coming China Wars: Where They Will Be Fought and How They Can Be Won* (FT Press 2008); and for an opposite view, P. Mavroidis, A. Sapir, *China and the WTO: Why Multilateralism Still Matters* (Princeton 2021). See also P. Blustein, *Schism: China and America and the Fracturing of the Global Trading System* (CIGI 2019).

8 See the EU Commission Report on *Significant Distortions in the Economy of the People's Republic of China for the Purposes of Trade Defence Investigations* (10 April 2024), available at https://policy.trade.ec.europa.eu/news/commission-updates-report-state-induced-distortions-chinas-economy-2024-04-10_en accessed 24 July 2024. In general, see L. Borlini, "When the Leviathan Goes to the Market: A Critical Evaluation of the Rules Governing State-Owned Enterprises in Trade Agreements" 33 LJIL (2020) 313.

9 The "President's 2018 Trade Policy Agenda" of February 2018 envisaged "a new era in American trade policy", available at <https://ustr.gov/sites/default/files/files/Press/Reports/2018/AR/2018%20Annual%20Report%20FINAL.PDF> accessed 27 February 2024. As to the electoral programmes for the 2024 US election, see "The Trade Section of the GOP 2024 Platform", IELP Blog (15 July 2024), available at <https://ielp.worldtradelaw.net/2024/07/the-trade-section-of-the-gop-2024-platform.html> accessed 24 July 2024.

reverse its trade policies nor did it cease blocking the AB.[10] Indeed in May 2024, the Biden Administration announced tariffs of up to 100% on a series of imports from China, adopting a selective "small yard and high fence" approach.[11]

On the other hand, in a number of official statements, within and outside the WTO, the EU and the generality of other Members, including China, have repeatedly restated their confidence in multilateralism as a method and a framework, and in the WTO as a forum for negotiation, implementation, and dispute resolution.[12]

The introduction by the Trump administration in March-April 2025 of sweeping unilateral, general or "reciprocal" tariffs as a key instrument of its protectionist trade policy is at odds with the foundations of the multilateral trading system. The WTO faces sliding into irrelevance if its rulebook is not respected and enforced and a number of major economies prioritize geoeconomic concerns over a commitment to open trade.[13] What is being pursued by major economies is "(strategic) autonomy" through unilateral trade and industrial policy measures in key advanced sectors and more generally "economic security". These policies also intend to reduce reliance on international supply chains, which are based on the absence of barriers to free trade, in favour of "near-shoring", "re-shoring" and "friend shoring", thus impacting on enterprises' efficient choices of their suppliers and cost-effectiveness.[14] Notwithstanding its official stance in support of the multilateral system, the EU has followed the US in developing its own (more modest) industrial policy, loosening anti-trust regulation, and competing with the subsidies offered by the Biden's Inflation Reduction Act (IRA).[15] The EU has also progressively put in place unilateral "autonomous" measures, including export and import restrictions

10 On the Biden administration's trade policy see J. Bacchus, "Biden and Trade at Year One, The Reign of Polite Protectionism" Cato Policy Analysis 926 (16 April 2022), available at <https://www.cato.org/policy-analysis/biden-trade-year-one> accessed 24 July 2024.

11 White House, "Fact Sheet: President Biden Takes Action to Protect American Workers and Businesses from China's Unfair Trade Practices" 14 May 2024. For a critical comment on the tariff increase incompatibility with the WTO, see the "Comment" by S. Charnovitz, *Comments on the Biden Administration's Proposed New Tariffs on Imports from China* (6 June 2024), available ath-ttps://ielp.worldtradelaw.net/.

12 See the communiqué of a meeting in Ottawa in October 2018 by 12 active WTO Members (not including the US and China), available at https://www.canada.ca/en/global-affairs/news/2018/10/joint-communique-of-the-ottawa-ministerial-on-wto-reform.html accessed 24 July 2024.

13 See the statement of 3 April 2025 by DG Okonjo-Iweala at www.wto.org/english/news_e/spno_e/spno57_e.htm; P.Stoll, : Reciprocity in Trade?: The Recent Initiative of the US President on "Reciprocal Trade and Tariffs", VerfBlog, 2025/2/28,- https://verfassungsblog.de/reciprocity-in-trade/, -DOI: 10.59704/dc4fd99d64da494b. Previously, see G. Schaffer, *Emerging Powers and the World Trading System. The Past and Future of International Economic Law* (CUP 2021); J. Bacchus, *Trade Links: New Rules for a New World* (CUP 2022); R. Howse, J. Langille, "Continuity and Change in the World Trade Organization: Pluralism Past, Present, and Future" 117 AJIL (2023) 1.

14 See B. Javorcik and others, "Economic Costs of Friend-Shoring", CESifo Working Paper No 10869 (2024), available at <https://papers.ssrn.com/sol3/papers.cfm?abstract_id=4696010> accessed 24 July 2024.

15 See for example, European Commission Press Release, "Commission Approves €5 billion German State Aid Measure to Support TSMC in Setting Up a New Semiconductor Manufacturing Facility (20 August 2024), available at https://ec.europa.eu/commission/presscorner/detail/en/ip_24_4287

and the subsidization of entire sectors in order to support technological innovation and face the challenge of climate change.[16] Some of these measures intend to respond to domestic public opinion and concerns over respect for human rights and the protection of the environment in the production of imported products, but meet objections from developing producing countries that will be affected by them.[17]

These policies are being pursued without much attention to WTO commitments.[18] A robust DSS is all the more necessary in such a context, but its current semi-paralysis may accommodate Members that enact measures of dubious compatibility with their WTO obligations, making challenges against them ineffective.[19]

At the same time, no Member has ever expressed a desire to leave the WTO; on the contrary, membership increased to 166 at MC13 and several accession negotiations are pending. Whatever criticisms there may be of the WTO, governments still believe there is value in membership.[20]

16 The latest contentious issue concerning import restrictions and climate change is that of the compatibility of the EU CBAM scheme, under which importers of carbon-intensive selected products into the EU will be subject to specific charges to match the EU internal production standards. See I. Espa, J. Francois, H. van Asselt, "The EU Proposal for a Carbon Border Adjustment Mechanism (CBAM): An Analysis under WTO and Climate Change Law" WTI Working Paper No 06/2022 (2022), available at https://www.wti.org

17 See the US *Uyghur Forced Labour Prevention Act* of 2021. As to the EU, see the *Deforestation Regulation* (2023/1115/EU), which will impose due diligence obligations on importers aimed at tackling deforestation and forest degradation. See also the *Directive on Corporate Sustainability Due Diligence*, adopted by the Council on 24 May 2024. See generally N. Moran, *Reviewing "Open Strategic Autonomy" on the Eve of the EU Elections* (2024), available at <https://dcubrexitinstitute.eu/2024/05/reviewing-open-strategic-autonomy-on-the-eve-of-eu-elections/> accessed 24 July 2024. As to developing countries' reactions, see A. Beattie, "Why Brussels Can't See the Deforestation for the Trees" (18 July 2024), available at https://www.ft.com/content/03ce886b-c110-45fd-bc56-0254daa75969 accessed 24 July 2024.

18 See the concerns expressed in the various contributions collected in IMF, *Finance & Development* (June 2023), "Trade, Disrupted". As to the EU, see European Commission Press Release, "Commission Proposes New Initiatives to Strengthen Economic Security" (24 January 2024), available at <https://ec.europa.eu/commission/presscorner/detail/en/IP_24_363> accessed 24 July 2024: "The Commission adopted five initiatives to strengthen the EU's economic security at a time of growing geopolitical tensions and profound technological shifts. The package aims to enhance the EU's economic security while upholding the openness of trade, investment, and research for the EU's economy, in line with the June 2023 European Economic Security Strategy".

19 See, however, *US–IRA (China)* (DS 623), where China has requested the establishment of a panel in July 2024 in respect of certain tax credits granted by the US under the IRA as being inconsistent with the SCM Agreement. In December 2022, China had requested consultations with the US in respect of the widely-publicized US restrictions on the exports to China of semiconductors and machinery to produce them (*US–Semiconductors (China)* DS 615).

20 See MC13 Ministerial Declaration, WTO Doc. No WT/MIN (24)/W/12/Rev.1 (19 February 2024), para 5, restating that WTO Members "resolve to preserve and strengthen the ability of the multilateral trading system, with the WTO at its core, to provide meaningful impetus to respond to current trade challenges, take advantage of available opportunities, and ensure the WTO's proper functioning". See also F. Stucker, C. Gammage, *Why Developing Countries Must Unite to Protect the WTO's Dispute Settlement System* (28 February 2024), available at https://theconversation.com

1.2. Revising Substantive Provisions: The Issue of the Security Exception

Reviving the role of the WTO requires not only revamping its DSS but also addressing the need to reform key substantive provisions.[21] First and foremost is the issue of the application of the security exception of GATT Article XXI. This provision, which had remained dormant during the GATT and the first 20 years of the WTO, has become contentious due to recent geopolitical and armed conflicts and the extension of the concept of security from the military to the economic dimension.

The national security exception to the GATT found in Article XXI came before a panel for the first time in a dispute initiated by Ukraine in *Russia–Traffic in Transit* (DS 512-2019). This is the only report on the matter that has been adopted by the DSB since it was not appealed by the parties, while later panel reports (though by and large following DS 512) in disputes concerning the security exception were appealed into the void and thus have not become part of the WTO *acquis*. The panel found that the existence of a situation of "war or other emergency in international relations" is required by subparagraph (b)(iii) and that whether this is the case is not self-judging. The existence of such a situation has to be evaluated objectively by a panel, contrary to the position taken by Russia and supported by the US as a third party.[22]

The US thereafter invoked GATT Article XXI to defend its additional duties on steel and aluminium in 2018 and other import restrictions subsequently. All panel reports (appealed by the US into the void) have rejected the US claim that the exception provided for measures "taken in time of war or other emergency in international relations" is fully self-judging and non-reviewable by a panel.[23] The US has in turn successfully challenged the countermeasures that some of the counterparties had immediately enacted considering the US duties to be safeguard

21 Besides addressing the security exception, this involves notably the subsidy disciplines. See J. Hillman, I. Manak, "Rethinking International Rules on Subsidies" (Council on Foreign Relations 2023), available at www.cfr.org/report/rethinking-international-rules-subsidies

22 The panel was chaired by former AB Member Professor G. Abi-Saab; see generally J. Bacchus, "The Black Hole of National Security: Striking the Right Balance for the National Security Exception in International Trade", CATO Policy Analysis No 936 (2022).

23 See the *US–Steel and Aluminium Products* complaints filed by China (DS 544), India (DS 547), the EU (DS 548, suspended by mutual agreement together with the US case against the EU countermeasures, DS 559), Norway (DS 552), Russia (DS 554), and Switzerland (DS 556), Türkiye (DS 564). Cases challenging the US steel and aluminium tariffs brought by Canada (DS 550) and Mexico (DS 551) were settled and DS 554 later terminated. In addition, the security exception has been raised in cases involving Qatar as a complainant/respondent against neighbouring countries, which has since been settled (DS 567, panel report of 16 June 2020, and related cases 526, 527, 528, and 576), and in four disputes between Russia and Ukraine (DS 499, 512, 525, and 532). Panel reports rejecting the US defence have been issued in DS 544, 552, 556, and 564 in respect of the steel and aluminium extra-duties, as well as in DS 597, *US–Origin Marking (Hong Kong)*. Introducing safeguard measures under Article XIX GATT, as had been done by the US to protect the domestic steel industry under the Bush administration in 2002 (DS 248), would have been more appropriate and WTO-compliant in order to shield US industries concerned from foreign competitors, as was the aim of the US.

measures, countervailable under Article 8.1 of the Safeguards Agreement.[24] It is difficult to imagine that the US would accept being bound by a compulsory DSS again in the absence of this politically sensitive issue having been resolved.[25] On the other hand, in the absence of a system that resolves international trade disputes and upholds those rules independently and impartially, "WTO rules will cease to have practical meaning and the WTO as an institution will wither away".[26] A possible way out of this dilemma could be a negotiated solution that might extend the coverage of the national security exception to certain matters involving economic security.[27] Such an enlargement of the exception based on economic reasons should be balanced by the right of Members hit by the restriction to re-establish the previous balance of rights and obligations through proportionate countermeasures as is provided for in the case of safeguards under the Agreement on Safeguards, or by resorting to a non-violation complaint as suggested recently by the US.[28]

2. *The Hobbling Functioning of the DSS in the Current Crisis*

As set out in previous chapters, US criticism of the AB's activity led to the US blocking the appointment of AB members starting in 2017,[29] bringing about the cessation of its operations in 2020. As a consequence, the adoption of a panel report by the DSB can be blocked by the losing party by appealing it into the void,

24 US complaints against Canada, China, the EU, Mexico, and Turkey (DS 557, 558, 559, 560, and 561, respectively).

25 See the statement by the US at the DSB meeting of 27 January 2023: "For over 70 years, the United States has held the clear and unequivocal position that issues of national security cannot be reviewed in WTO dispute settlement and the WTO has no authority to second-guess the ability of a WTO Member to respond to a wide range of threats to its security". For a contrary view on the original purpose of Article XXI as drafted in 1947, based on extensive archival research, see M. Paulsen, "Trade Multilateralism and U.S. National Security: The Making of the GATT Security Exceptions", 41 Mich. J. Int'l L. (2020) 109. The similar security exception included in US BITs was not meant to be self-judging either until a change of the US model BIT in 2004; see *Continental Casualty v Argentina* ICSID/ARB/03/9, Award (2008) 182–188, relying on ICJ *Nicaragua v United States of America*, Merits (1986), 222.

26 J. Bacchus, *Trade Links*, *supra* n 13. As to the concerns on the issue of the security exception, see I. Dreyer, *WTO at 30: Director-General Calls for National Security Exception Fix*, reporting on a speech from WTO Director-General Ngozi Okonjo-Iweala at the Peterson Institute in Washington, DC (15 April 2024), available at https://borderlex.net/2024/04/16/

27 Should the current text be interpreted as self-judging, it has been suggested that any affected Member could initiate a "non-violation" complaint under Article XXIII.1(b) GATT. However, this approach would shift the burden to the respondent which would be prevented from adopting equivalent countermeasures until a decision in the case.

28 See *Reflections from the United States on the handling of disputes involving essential security measures*, WTO/JOB/DSB/10 of 13 December 2024. If the defence would be self-judging, the response could also be considered to be in this vein, although the equivalence of the countermeasures could be justiciable under Article 22.6 DSU.

29 See minutes of the DSB at WTO Doc. No WT/DSB/M/400 (31 August 2017). See generally M. Wagner, *The Impending Demise othe WTO Appellate Body: from Centerpiece to Historic Relic?* https://ssrn.com/sol3/papers.cfm?abstract_id=3399300 (5 June 2019)

as has happened about 25 times since this became a possibility.[30] The result is that disputes in which the panel report is not accepted by the parties, and as a consequence adopted by the DSB, or which are not otherwise settled between them, are not resolved so that a non-compliant respondent may keep WTO-inconsistent measures in place.

2.1. The Multi-Party Interim Appeal Arbitration (MPIA)

By devising and adopting the MPIA, a group currently of 27 willing WTO Members (54 counting the EU Member States individually) has shown their desire to maintain an appellate stage, as well as legal certainty in WTO proceedings.[31] The fact that some WTO Members have joined later, after initially taking a "wait and see" approach, may hint at a future increase in the number of participants once they will be involved in an actual dispute.[32]

The MPIA works as follows.[33] Participants have undertaken by a framework agreement (MPIA) that, in case of a dispute between any of them reaching the panel stage, they will follow the MPIA procedure annexed to their agreement. This essentially involves committing beforehand to arbitration under Article 25 of the DSU in case either party decides to appeal the panel report.[34] The MPIA text provides more specifically the following:

- Members of the MPIA undertake, should a dispute arise between them, to use the MPIA if either decides to appeal;
- In such a case, before the circulation of the panel's report, the parties ask that the panel's proceedings be suspended;

30 As to the latest developments, see G. Sacerdoti, C. De Stefano," The WTO Dispute Settlement System in 2023-2024" 34 IYIL (2024) forthcoming, https://ssrn.com/abstract=5176727, 4 April 2025, See Chapter VII.A.2.5 for more detail. Information on the MPIA is available at https://wtoplurilaterals.info/plural_initiative/the-mpia/

31 For the text, see WTO Doc. No JOB/DSB/1/Add.12, communication of 30 April 2020. The MPIA participants were, as of December 2024, Australia; Benin; Brazil; Canada; China; Chile; Colombia; Costa Rica; Ecuador; European Union; Guatemala; Hong Kong; Iceland; Japan; Macao; Mexico; Montenegro; New Zealand; Nicaragua; Norway; Pakistan; Peru; the Philippines; Singapore; Switzerland; Ukraine; and Uruguay. Conspicuously absent are India, Indonesia, the UK, besides of course the US, among others.

32 Japan joined in 2023 in anticipation of an appeal in a dispute with China (DS 601-2013), which, however, neither party thereafter filed. Other countries may similarly consider joining (opt-in) if and when they are involved in an actual dispute.

33 The MPIA has been notified to the WTO; see WTO website, "Statement on a Mechanism for Developing, Documenting and Sharing Practices and Procedures in the Conduct of WTO Disputes", WTO Doc. No JOB/DSB/1/Add.12 (30 April 2020). For more details on the MPIA set-up, see G. Tereposky, D. Hohnstein, "Multi-Party Interim Appeal Arbitration Arrangement (MPIA)" *MPEiPro* (2022).

34 In legal terms, such an agreement to enter into a future binding undertaking can be defined as a *pactum de contrahendo*. See the text of Article 25 DSU at Chapter VII n 50.

- Under the agreed procedure annexed to the MPIA, appeals should be initiated by filing a notice of appeal, as required in appellate proceedings under the DSU;
- Each appeal will be heard by three Members of the pool of ten arbitrators which the parties to the MPIA have initially established, randomly selected by the WTO DG.[35] Consultations among all arbitrators shall take place, a practice inspired by the consultations (exchange of views) provided for among all AB Members in the WP, to ensure every arbitrator's involvement and maintain a unified approach within the pool;
- The arbitrators have the same powers as the AB to uphold, modify or reverse the legal findings of the panel. They will address only "the issues that are necessary for the resolution of the dispute";
- The arbitrators must issue their award within 90 days following the same procedural rules applicable to the AB, including the right of participation of third parties. Any extension to the 90-day period must be agreed with the parties;
- The parties agree to abide by the arbitration award which shall be final and which shall be notified but not adopted by the DSB as provided for in Article 25.3 DSU.

As is clear from the above, most of the procedural features are patterned after the rules applicable to AB proceedings. Some provisions have built on recent practice, such as requesting the arbitrators to take "appropriate organizational measures to streamline the proceedings", including decisions on "page limits, time limits and deadlines as well as on the length and number of hearings required".[36] Other rules are more innovative, reflecting suggestions made in reform discussions and in the Walker proposals, such as the provision discouraging appeals based on Article 11 DSU and avoiding dealing with irrelevant issues.[37]

2.2. Experience and Lessons from the MPIA

The MPIA has, up to the end of 2024, only been used once (*Colombia–Frozen Fries (EU)* (DS 591-2022)), while another MPIA appeal has started in April 2025, although a previous appeal arbitration *Türkiye–Pharmaceutical Products (EU)* (DS 583-2022) (initiated by Türkiye) was based on a discrete agreement by the

35 See MPIA, Annex, 8: "The arbitrators may discuss their decisions relating to the appeal with all of the other members of the pool of arbitrators, without prejudice to the exclusive responsibility and freedom of the arbitrators with respect to such decisions and their quality". This follows the practice of collegiality ("exchange of views") adopted by the AB (Rule 4.3 of its Working Procedures, WTO Doc. No WT/AB/WP/6 (16 August 2010)).

36 MPIA, Annex 1, paragraph 12.

37 MPIA, Annex 1, paragraph 13: "If necessary in order to issue the award within the 90 day time-period, the arbitrators may also propose appropriate arrangements to the parties, such as an exclusion of claims based on the alleged lack of an objective assessment of the facts pursuant to Article 11 of the DSU". See also J. Pauwelyn, "MPIA: What's New?" 22 WTR (2022) 693.

two parties that had the MPIA as a model since Türkiye is not a MPIA member.[38] In other disputes, the parties had agreed to resort to the MPIA in case of appeal, but no appeal was thereafter filed, and the panel reports were adopted by the DSB.[39] The fact that an appeal was agreed upon based on the MPIA model in a case not involving an MPIA party is significant as an example that might be followed in other disputes. This is even more pertinent considering that of the 166 WTO Members after MC13 (counting the EU Members individually), of which more than 130 regularly plead for the reinstatement of a functioning AB at each DSB meeting, just 54 (27 counting the EU as one) have subscribed to the MPIA.[40] In fact, such an appellate review entrusted to *ad hoc* arbitrators chosen by the parties on a case-by-case basis might even accommodate the US preference that appellate review not be carried out by a permanent body of adjudicators such as the AB, whose case law becomes *de facto* authoritative as a precedent for the interpretation of the WTO agreements in subsequent disputes.[41]

The appeal arbitral report in DS 583 (which confirmed the panel's finding that Türkiye had breached certain GATT provisions) is interesting due to some of its procedural innovations compared to the practice of the AB. The report was first issued only in English to avoid the delays associated with translating it into the other official WTO languages. The report is only 49 pages long and was issued 79 days from the appointment of the arbitrators by agreement of the parties.[42] This is well within the 90-day time limit set in Article 17.5 DSU (one of the US objections

38 See WTO Doc. No WT/DS 583/ARB 25 (25 July 2022). The EU and Türkiye had entered into a similar connected appeal arbitration agreement on 25 March 2022 in *EU–Safeguard Measures on Steel (Turkey)* (DS 595-2022), but thereafter neither party appealed the panel report. An appeal under the MPIA has been initiated by the EU in DS 611(*EU-China*) in April 2025, WT/DS611/10.

39 An MPIA agreement has been concluded in several other cases that thereafter were not appealed or were settled: DS 524 (Mexico–Costa Rica), DS 537 (Australia–Canada), DS 589 (Canada–China), DS 595 (EU–Türkiye), DS 598 (Australia–China), DS 602 (Australia–China), DS 603 (China–Australia); DS 601 (Japan–China). In DS 524, concerning sanitary requirements imposed by Costa Rica on the importation of avocados from Mexico, which could have been the first MPIA dispute, the panel report is more than 400 pages long (!) and proceedings lasted almost three years.

40 See at the DSB meeting of 25 January 2022 the statement of Canada in respect of DS 579, 580 and 581 (*India–Sugar*), appealed into the void by India on 24 December 2021, that "A Member acting in good faith should find no comfort in an unfair – and short term – advantage that has arisen because of the absence of a functioning Appellate Body. In addition, Canada reiterated its invitation to India to consider joining the MPIA in order to safeguard binding dispute settlement with access to appellate review in disputes with other participants", WTO Doc. No WT/DSB/M/460 (7 March 2022), para. 6.19 and 7.4. Canada stated similarly at the DSB of 20 December 2022 (WTO Doc. No WT/DSB/M/474 (15 February 2023)) in respect of Indonesia's appeal into the void of the panel report in *Indonesia–Raw Materials (EU)* (DS 592-2022).

41 At the DSB meeting in which the arbitration report in *Türkiye–Pharmaceutical Products* (DS 583-2022) was notified to the DSB, the US applauded the choice of the parties to resort to appeal arbitration to resolve the dispute. See WTO Doc. No WT/DSB/M/469 (10 October 2022), 5–6.

42 The three arbitrators were chosen by agreement of the parties outside the roster of the MPIA and included a former AB Member as the chairman.

against the AB is due to it exceeding this deadline).[43] On the merits, the arbitrators referred extensively to and followed the AB position on the evidentiary burden in cases involving protection from risks to health or human life under Article XX(b) GATT.[44]

The first appeal between MPIA parties occurred in *Colombia–Frozen Fries (EU)* (DS 591-2022). This resulted in an award of just 39 pages issued a mere 74 days after the notice of appeal was lodged. This was also due to some procedural innovations that may be a model for the future.[45] This is a significant reduction from the average duration of the last 20 appeals filed before the Appellate Body, which was 360 days. A caveat must however be expressed, that the delays in the latter days of the AB were mainly due to the complexity and number of appeals before it, including a significant backlog of disputes (not to mention the reduced number of ABMs still in office), a problem that did not affect the disposal of the appeal in the first MPIA arbitration.[46]

The appeal panel confirmed the findings of the panel that Colombia's anti-dumping investigation had been flawed in several respects.[47] On the merits, this award has been noted for its innovative analysis and interpretation of Article 17.6 ADA, whose interpretation by the AB has in the past drawn fierce criticism from

43 The press release of the EU Commission, *EU Wins in WTO Appeal About Colombian Anti-dumping Duties on Frozen Fries* (21 December 2022), available at <https://ec.europa.eu/commission/presscorner/detail/en/ip_22_7858> accessed 24 July 2024, contains the following comment which is also applicable in respect of the appeal in DS 583: "The swift issuance of a high-quality appeal award confirms that appeal proceedings at the WTO can be managed in a focused and efficient way while fully respecting parties' rights. This speed was helped by some of the innovations embedded in MPIA procedures, such as the requirement to address solely issues that are necessary to resolve the dispute and the possibility, availed of by the arbitrators here, to take or suggest measures streamlining the proceedings". The EU has complained thereafter of the lack of compliance by Colombia with the appeal report and has initiated compliance proceedings under Article 21.5 DSU, see WTO, *European Union Initiates Compliance Proceedings over Colombian Duties on Frozen Fries*, available at www.wto.org/english/news_e/news24_e/ds591oth_04jun24_e.htm accessed 24 July 2024.

44 Article 25 DSU Arbitration award, *Türkiye–Pharmaceutical Products (EU)*, 6.117–6.123. As to the merits, it has been argued that the arbitrators did not follow the AB case law in interpreting the scope of the public procurement derogations of Article III.8(a) GATT; see S. Pahis, "Appeals after the Appellate Body" 23 *World Trade Review* (2024) 296 .

45 For the text of the award, see WTO Doc. No WT/DS591/ARB25 (21 December 2022). This short timeframe was also due to special "Additional Procedures" that were agreed with the parties to streamline proceedings. These included: a limitation on the number of pages of the submissions; a virtual pre-hearing conference to identify "those issues that are necessary for the resolution of the dispute", so to avoid those "not necessary for the resolution of this dispute"; the transmission from the arbitrators to the parties ahead of the hearing of a list of questions to be answered at the hearing, see paras 1.11 and 1.12 and Annex 2A, WTO Doc. No WT/DS/591/ARB25/Add.1 (21 December 2022). In the practice of the AB, by contrast, questions have been read orally to the parties at the hearing.

46 See https://worldtradelaw.net/databases/abtiming.php. As a comparison, the first AB appeal (*US–Gasoline* (DS 2-1996)) took 68 days from the date of lodging of the appeal to the issuance of the award.

47 Award 4.31.

the US, especially as to the AB conclusion that the US practice of "zeroing" is not admissible under the ADA agreement.[48] Contrary to the holdings of the AB, the arbitrators concluded that Article 17.6(i) and (ii) allow more than just one "permissible" interpretation of Article 5 ADA. The arbitrators confirmed, however, the panel's conclusion that the interpretation adopted by Colombian authorities was impermissible.[49]

The approach of the award to distance itself from the AB, not relying on its past case law, and specifically to admit that Article 17.6 ADA permits more than one interpretation of Article 5 ADA (as the US had pleaded in the zeroing cases), was unsurprisingly praised by the US at the DSB meeting in which it was discussed.[50] It will be interesting to see whether (a) the reasoning in MPIA awards will be deemed to be of authority (precedential value) and followed by future panels faced with the same issues and (b) future arbitration appeal awards will similarly distance themselves from previous AB interpretations.[51]

3. *Reforming the WTO DSS*

3.1. The Ongoing Process of Dispute Settlement Reform at the WTO (2022–2024)

A. The "Molina Proposal" on Panel's Upgrading and Related Reforms

The final MC12 document in June 2022 recorded WTO Members' commitment, "to conduct discussions with the view to have a fully and well-functioning dispute settlement system accessible to all Members by 2024".[52] Instead of the typical structured negotiations, an informal process was preferred to carry out this commitment which was entrusted to the then Deputy Permanent Representative of Guatemala, Marco Molina, as yet another "Facilitator" (after Ambassador Walker in 2019–2020 and to be followed by Ambassador Usha Dwarka-Canabady of Mauritius after MC13 in respect of appellate review). In the course of his work, he collected confidentially more than 70 proposals from Members in which they set forth their interests and concerns, keeping the WTO membership informed by periodically reporting to the DSB.

Within this process, the US finally disclosed its position, which skipped over the role and reform of the appellate stage and focused on negotiations and the panel

48 See especially *US–Hot Rolled Steel (Japan)* (DS 184-2001), *US–Zeroing (EC)* (DS 294-2009), *US–Zeroing (Japan)* (DS 322-2007), *US–Continued Zeroing (EC)* (DS 350-2009).

49 Award para. 4.14–4.22. For comments see G. Sacerdoti, "The WTO and its Dispute Settlement System in 2022", 32 IYIL 2022 (Brill 2023) 399; S. Pahis, *supra* n 44.

50 DSB, WTO Doc. No WT/DSB/M/475 (27 January 2023).

51 It has been highlighted, on the other hand, that panels continue to rely strictly on the case law of the AB; see R. Howse, "Unappealable but not Unappealing: WTO dispute settlement without the Appellate Body" IISD (17 July 2023), available at http://www.iisd.org/ accessed 15 July 2024.

52 Outcome Document, WTO Doc. No WT/MIN/(22)/24 (22 June 2022) 4. On the perspective of a reform that would safeguard the essential features of the DSS compulsory and binding settlement of disputes, see A. Wolff, "Restoring Binding Dispute Settlement" PIIE Working Paper (April 2022), available at https://www.piie.com.

stage. The US proposed preserving the "policy space" of the Members, respecting their "essential security interests" and stressing that the WTO DSS "cannot be a means to change the commitments and rules of the WTO agreements without the consent of all members". The US communication did not contain any specific proposal. It supported "a system that delivers quality, consistent, and efficient adjudication through the fair application of treaty interpretation according to the terms of the agreements as agreed by Members, while leaving to Members to further develop their commitments and rules through negotiation".[53]

Just before the opening of MC13 in February 2024, the result of this process was disclosed and presented to a special meeting of the General Council, in the form of a consolidated text of a draft Ministerial Decision, comprising no fewer than 36 pages of a fully articulated proposal, though notably not covering appeal.[54]

At MC13 in February 2024, there was no substantial discussion of these proposals. WTO Members agreed that the "Molina process" be furthered, instructing officials to "accelerate discussions in an inclusive and transparent manner, build on the progress already made, and work on unresolved issues, including issues regarding appeal/review and accessibility to achieve the objective by 2024 as we set forth at MC12". On 18 April 2024, a new phase of the dispute settlement reform process was formalized with the appointment of Ambassador Usha Dwarka-Canabady of Mauritius as the new facilitator. Negotiations should focus on the accessibility of the DSS to all Members (facilitating the participation of LDCs) and appellate review, and should be concluded by the end of 2024 as per the MC12 and MC13 mandates. This deadline was, however, missed, although a comprehensive collection of participants' positions was circulated shortly before the year's end.

The format that the text resulting from the reform process might take remains completely open: options include a GC decision, an amendment to the DSU, an authoritative interpretation under Article IX.2 of the WTO Agreement, or a combination thereof.

We now highlight the main aspects of the Molina proposals submitted to MC13, which seem to be widely (but not universally) supported within the membership, with the caveat that until an agreement is reached on all issues, prominently on appeal, nothing can be considered definitive:

1. Reinforcing non-adjudicatory, non-contentious mechanisms to settle disputes, adding to consultations and good offices two further alternatives: formal mediation and conciliation;
2. Making the selection of panellists more transparent by having them chosen following new procedural rules from the roster submitted by WTO Members

53 See "US Objectives for a Reformed Dispute Settlement System" WTO Doc. No JOB/DSB 4 (5 July 2023).

54 WTO Doc. No JOB/GC/385 (16 February 2024). The Molina report's approach has been criticized by a group of developing countries (Bangladesh, Egypt, India, Indonesia and South Africa) as undermining their interest in the DSS reform, Communication JOB/DSB/8 of 12 February 2024.

under Article 8.4 DSU. Nominations to the roster would, moreover, be for a defined term, subject to scrutiny and vetting to ensure competence, availability, and diversity;

3. Making panel proceedings more transparent and rigorous, adding the option of pursuing "simplified arbitration proceedings", according to annexed model rules pursuant to Article 25 DSU. Stricter limits on the length of submissions would apply, especially if a case is not considered "complex";
4. Adding mechanisms and bodies in order to facilitate WTO Members' oversight of the functioning of the DSS as well as corrections or amendments by the membership in light of the experience gathered. The document proposes that reports and awards be transmitted to relevant WTO bodies for discussion of the "technical and policy implications of the provisions interpreted in adopted panel reports". Moreover, a new plenary "Advisory Working Group" should be established in order "to discuss, build consensus and provide guidance on legal interpretations developed by adjudicators";[55]
5. All phases of the various types of proceedings – good offices, conciliation, mediation, arbitration, and the panel stage – are to be pursued under strict timeframes;
6. A specific Title (V) of the proposal includes "guidelines" (though with seemingly binding language) on treaty interpretation for adjudicators, on the burden of proof in relation to challenged measures, and guidance on focusing "on what is necessary to resolve the dispute". A specific paragraph stresses that past reports have no precedential value, but that "Each adjudicator bears the responsibility to develop its own interpretation of a provision of the covered agreements applying customary rules of interpretation of public international law as required by Article 3.2 of the DSU";
7. Compliance would be facilitated by providing for conciliation, mediation, and good offices at this stage.

We consider that most elements of the "Molina proposal" (which comprises a great many details for each procedural element) are noteworthy and positive, especially those reinforcing the qualifications and responsibilities of panelists. It remains, of course, to be seen whether, if and once the proposal is adopted, the parties to disputes will actually make use of the various ADR options offered to resolve them through the newly provided alternative means.

The innovative proposed establishment of the Advisory Working Group can also be considered positively, since it gives a say to WTO Members on the interpretation

55 This body "which is expected to be used rarely", could be convened by the DSB or by Members and "shall not relitigate disputes nor function as an [appeal/review] mechanism". The outcome of its discussions could be (a) a draft recommendation for adoption of an authoritative interpretation in accordance with Article IX of the WTO agreement, (b) a recommendation to the DSB "to agree that the interpretation at issue shall not be considered persuasive"; or (c) record Members' diverging views about interpretation (Annex, Title VI, Chapter II).

of provisions by the adjudicators and allows them to exercise some "party control" over the evolution of the case law. They would thus be able to intervene collectively, if they reach consensus, to rectify any such interpretation in respect of future cases. Of course, Article IX:2 of the WTO Agreement has always provided for the possibility that the WTO Members adopt (binding) interpretations of the WTO Agreements at Ministerial Conferences or at the General Council, though this possibility has never been used in the 30 years of existence of the WTO.

Serious perplexities are raised instead by the emphasis on the lack of precedential effect of reports, especially should this be applicable to the reports of a reinstated AB, under the heading of "Guidelines for Adjudicators, Chapter III "No precedential values of past Reports":

> Adjudicative reports shall have no precedential effect … An adjudicator may use a previous report in developing and explaining its own interpretation only to the extent the adjudicator determines the report to be relevant to a provision at issue in the dispute and to contain persuasive analysis of that provision under customary rules of interpretation of public international law, or to distinguish its interpretation from a previous report. Neither Members nor adjudicators may presume that an interpretation of the covered agreements contained in a WTO dispute settlement report is persuasive.

Although the statement that "Adjudicative reports shall have no precedential effect" in itself conforms to the current situation at the WTO and generally in international tribunals, the added specifications and emphasis above, if adopted, would discourage consistency in interpretation and therefore undermine the effectiveness of the DSS. Further, it would raise perplexities making outcomes less predictable, and the uniform application of WTO law among the Members less certain, besides raising perplexities as to its conformity with the role of adjudication as a subsidiary source of international law.[56]

56 Annex 1, Consolidated Text Referred to in Mr. Molina's Report (n 54), Title V, Chapter III, "No Precedential Value of Past Reports". See on this issue, Chapter III.A.5. A harsh criticism of this position has been expressed by P. Van den Bossche, *The Uncertain Future of WTO Dispute Settlement. An Appraisal of the February 2024 Consolidated Text Resulting from the Molina Process on Dispute Settlement Reform*, WTI Working Paper Series No. 2/2024, p.10–11. He considers "deliberate and quite unfortunate" the omission of any reference in the text "of the ultimate purpose of the WTO DSS", namely "to bring security and predictability of the international trading system and that therefore there is a legitimate expectation of WTO members that the same legal issue will be decided in the same way in subsequent cases". In his view, the statement that an adjudicator may not presume an interpretation in a previous report to be persuasive runs counter to the principle of taking into due account previous decisions on the same legal issue, which is central in the work of international adjudicators; this instruction "is thus misguided if not foolish".

B. The Post-MC13 Reform Process on Appellate Review

After MC 13 work on issues of "appeal/review" and accessibility (capacity building and technical assistance) has advanced with ambassador Usha Dwarka-Canabady of Mauritius appointed as Facilitator. The result of this work that has involved a majority of the WTO Members with the assistance of six "Co-Convenors to lead technical discussions" has resulted in "significant progress" set forth in the 50-page "Progress Report" annexed to the statement made at the General Council of 16-17 December 2024 by its Chairperson ("draft negotiating text").[57]

Potential reforms discussed focus on (i) narrowing the claims reviewable on appeal/review to those that would have a material impact on the respondent's implementation obligations; (ii) clarifying adjudicator's role with respect to reviewing the panel's objective assessment of the facts of the case; (iii) making changes to the existing interim review stage of the panel process such that it may provide a more meaningful opportunity for the panel to correct factual and legal errors; and clarifying Members' expectations with respect to adherence to timeframes.[58]

In more detail, the Annex resumes and sets forth the often divergent positions of the participants focusing on (A) *Scope of review* ("focus appeal/review on the issues necessary to resolve the parties' dispute; and to avoid the perception of "law making" by the adjudicators; to ensure adjudicators do not make advisory opinions or provide unnecessary reasoning"); (B) *Standard of Review* ("A high or limited standard of review that gives some deference to the panel" or that "an appellant must establish that the panel was guilty of gross misconduct, bias or serious conflict of interest...or manifestly exceeded its power, authority or jurisdiction"); (C) *Form of the mechanism* ("To address a concern that an institutionalized standing body (with a limited number of adjudicators) may be perceived as having a greater authority and legitimacy than other adjudicators, which leads to "rule-making" and *de facto* precedent, and does not guarantee correct decisions", while, however, "Most Members consider that a standing body of highly-qualified experts support their interests, which include correctness, predicatability, consistency, coherence, legitimacy, transparency, accountability, fairness and efficiency"; *(D) Reducing/changing incentives to appeal* ("To reduce responding Members'

57 JOB/GC/DSR/5 of 18 December 2024, Statement on the Dispute Dettlement Reforn Process by Ambassador Peter Ølberg. For the previous phase, see "Facilitator, Co-Convenors Update Members on Dispute Settlement Reform Work" (18 July 2024), available athttps://www.wto.org/english/news_e/news24_e/disp_18jul24_e.htm accessed 24 July 2024. For an initial comment see Appeal/Review Proposals under Consideration in the WTO Dispute Settlement Reform Process", IELP Blog by S. Lester, 22 Dec. 2024, https://ielp.worldtradelaw.net/2024/12/appealreview-proposals-under-consideration-in-the-wto-dispute-settlement-reform-process.html.

58 Statement n 57, 7. For previous documents on the process see WTO, Minutes of the Heads of Delegation Meeting (30 May 2024). WT/GC/DSR/M/1, 4 June 2024, available at https://docs.wto.org/dol2fe/Pages/SS/directdoc.aspx?filename=q:/WT/GCDSR/M1.pdf/Open=True ; IELP Blog (24 July 2024), "WTO Members Statements on Appeal/Review in the DS Reform Process", available at https://ielp.worldtradelaw.net/2024/07/wto-member-statements-on-appealreview-in-ds-reform-process.html accessed 29 July 2024.

incentive to file tactical appeals to gain additional time to comply"); (E) *Clarifying Members' expectations of adjudicators* ("To ensure the prompt resolution of disputes; to ensure that parties and adjudicators remain focussed only on those issues necessary to resolve the dispute, and to ensure that Members' directions regarding timeframes are met"); (F) Access to the mechanism ("The majority of Members consider that the right of appeal must be guaranteed and therefore should not be contingent on the agreement of the other party. There is broad support for the current system under which any party may seek appeal/ review (compulsory jurisdiction) to correct legal errors)".

A review shows a strong preference for retaining an independent, impartial, two-tier dispute settlement system as a central element in providing security and predictability to the multilateral trading system, as currently enshrined in the DSU, for the final and binding resolution of trade disputes. Thus, *China* shares "the value of a 'filter and focus' approach to explore a more focused and efficient appeal review mechanism". It agrees that the focus of discussion should be on interim review, the material impact of decisions on implementation, admissibility check, order of analysis, streamlined process, output of appeal, and incentives to reduce frivolous appeals.[59]

For the *UK*, decisions should be timely, focused on what is necessary to resolve disputes, and without gap-filling. The system should promote a coherent and predictable set of rules and therefore secure a predictable and stable trading environment for businesses and the Members who represent them. According to the UK, an appeal review mechanism should "not have an overweighted influence on the substantive rules themselves, i.e. there should be no gap filling".[60]

For the *EU*, the dispute settlement system must guarantee a degree of consistency, security, and predictability, and therefore the right to review legal errors on appeal must be preserved. At the same time, "the concern with lawmaking and overreaching by adjudicators" should be addressed. Conclusively, "The EU will continue its constructive engagement and openness to reform. We will seek to preserve the right to appeal review, the adjudicators' ability to review and correct legal errors, and a standing adjudicative body. We believe it is possible to reconcile these characteristics with the interests of all Members, including the interests in avoiding law-making by adjudicators and in focusing the dispute settlement function on resolving disputes".[61]

According to *Norway*, "There is broad agreement that the dispute settlement system is a fundamental element of a vital and well-functioning WTO. The system has in our view served us all well throughout the years, and it is a top priority for Norway to get it fully back up and running. A key interest for Norway is having

59 China, Minutes n 58, 2.18.

60 UK, ibid 2.15.

61 EU, ibid 2.3.

disputes settled with binding effect, by this we mean an obligation for the losing party to put the WTO inconsistency to an end".[62]

A number of developing countries and LDCs have stressed the importance to them of appeal/review and "the full restoration of a binding two-tier dispute settlement system in the WTO. Recourse to appeal/review of panel decisions should be automatic. Rather than diminishing the role of such a mechanism, our reform efforts should strengthen it".[63] *Djibouti*, on behalf of the LDCs, declared their full support for the two-tier system and the reconstitution of the AB as "an issue that must be resolved soon".[64] *India* stressed "the legitimacy and stability based on the adherence to the foundational principles, primacy of a two-tier adjudicative process with a permanent appeal mechanism which is multilateral, rules-based, based on automaticity and consensus, and special and differential treatment for developing and LDC Members".[65] *Nigeria*, on behalf of the African Group, recalled that the "African Group has proposed that we revert to a two-tier dispute settlement system and therefore call for the immediate restoration of the system".[66] *Brazil* supports "the possibility of review to correct legal errors; the binding nature of decisions that bring closure and effectiveness to disputes; the consistency of decisions; independence and impartiality of appeal adjudicator and strengthening the interim review stage".[67]

South Africa seeks "a multilateral, rules-based, dispute settlement system whose decisions have automatic effect". Basic features should include

> (a) A two-tier Appellate Body to guarantee correction of possible legal errors and preserve the coherence and effectiveness of the system. We do not want a pre-WTO GATT dispute settlement, a system without a functioning Appellate Body being brought back in terms of the degree of its enforceability. (b) Legal rulings must push toward compliance. We cannot afford to have a system that enables Members to take unilateral trade actions without any international legal constraint. Being allowed to sidestep rulings would further marginalize developing and LDC Members, undermining the WTO's mission to foster equal competitive conditions, and risks leaving less economically developed Members unable to challenge trade rule violations and seek remedies against unfair trade practices. (c) A standing appeal body to provide predictability, legitimacy, stability, and consistency.

The *US* is on record with the following statement: "The United States has an interest in a dispute settlement system that supports parties in the resolution of their disputes and that has legitimacy, not just here but also at home. In that context, we

62 Norway, ibid 2.28.
63 Antigua and Barbuda on behalf of the ACP countries, ibid 2.4.
64 Djibouti on behalf of the LDCs, ibid 2.12.
65 India, Minutes 2.13.
66 Nigeria, Minutes 2.35.
67 Brazil, ibid 2.23.

would like to explore further with delegations whether appeal/review is a necessary feature of a system that supports parties in resolving their disputes. We have heard points made about the need for consistency and the ability to correct legal errors. We do not view a standing Appellate Body as the only way of achieving those objectives. Consistency, if wrong, does not serve anyone's interests. In addition, you can have a binding system without having a second tier – and by 'binding', we mean finality in the dispute".[68]

3.2. Evaluating Reform Proposals

As evidenced by the above overview, the form of the (most likely standing) appeal/review body has not yet been decided. Notwithstanding the widespread appreciation of a system akin to the present one in its operation and results, support can be detected in favour of discouraging appeals, a more limited review, more party-control over, and involvement in the process, enhancing the role of panels, possibly making them the centerpiece of the DSS, and loosening the status and authority of those in charge of deciding appeals. This entails the risk that the rigour of the current appeal system will be weakened and that the AB may be replaced by a "super-panel" patterned after the MPIA arbitrators, with less authority and less of a guarantee of consistency in its case law, thus providing less security and predictability and less of a guarantee of equal treatment for all Members in disputes. A renewed appellate body should ideally build upon, rather than weaken, 25 years of successful experience in providing independent, final, consistent, law-based decisions on trade disputes between WTO Members. Instead of apparently starting from scratch and attempting to "reinvent the wheel", negotiators would be well-advised to focus on revitalizing the existing system and addressing any perceived shortcomings, taking into account the experience of the many courts and tribunals currently operating internationally. It is difficult to see how the objectives shared by most Members, based on their statements, could be attained in a manner other than reinstating an appeal stage, patterned after the one devised during the Uruguay Round negotiations (1986–94). The US appears to be the main stumbling block in this respect.

The paralysis of the AB shows the fragility of international dispute settlement systems, even one as sophisticated as that of the WTO when they are fundamentally

68 US, ibid 2.41. Additionally, the US repeated its past criticism of the AB: "We have seen how an appeal/review mechanism – and by extension the dispute settlement system – can stray from this foundational purpose". encouraging delegations to look at the USTR report on the AB of 2020 (see Chapter VII.A.2.2) "that identified several U.S. concerns with that appeal mechanism". The US concludes that "Notwithstanding these concerns, we have made clear our commitment to work towards a system that meets the interests of all delegations". See also in the same critical vein the USTR *2025 Trade Policy Agenda and 2024 Annual Report* of February 2025, 190, available at the the USTR website (https//ustr.gov), stating i.a. "The US remains committed to working towards a *fundamentally reformed* and improved system (emphasis added).

challenged by a powerful Member and the rules do not prevent such unilateral action. It also demonstrates that the "judicialization" of international trade disputes is not universally accepted, in any case not for all kinds of disputes.[69] This contrasts with the current trend of litigation before international courts, which has witnessed a substantial increase in the number of cases, including systematic requests for provisional measures.[70] Some of those disputes have been, however, so politicized as to justify the criticism that international justice risks being "weaponized".[71] At the WTO, disputes concern real contrasts of interests. The expansive role of its DSS and its judicialization is based on the DSU and reflects a deliberate choice of the WTO Members to delegate future contentious issues to adjudicators, entrusting them with deciding specific disputes on the basis of objective legal criteria. This need has not disappeared. The effectiveness of proposed alternative non-contentious mechanisms (conciliation, mediation, arbitration) is open to doubt.[72]

The inability of WTO Members to agree up until now upon a solution to the paralysis of appellate review is telling of the rift between two positions. On the one hand, the bulk of, or possibly all, WTO Members except the US support an appellate review such as that performed by the AB under the DSU. This does not exclude being open to improvements that may make dispute settlement proceedings more efficient, speedy, flexible, and transparent. Most Members have appreciated the AB's contribution to safeguarding the rights and obligations of all Members in a secure and predictable manner when disputes arise.

On the other hand, the US currently appears to be critical of a quasi-judicial system of binding appellate review, such as the one that has been operating from 1995 to 2019.[73] Recent disputes on the national security exception have reinforced US objections. The US appears to favour some kind of extraordinary review, akin to

69 The US, in its communication of 2023 (n 53), criticized the WTO DSS because it "has become synonymous with litigation, leading to increased judicialization of the system". Notwithstanding the US invocation of the security exception (see DS/635/3), the US additional tariffs of March-April 2025 have been the object of several immediate challenges, though ultimately ineffective, by affected Members under the DSU (DS/633,634,635,637, 638).

70 The docket of the ICJ at the beginning of 2024 included more than 40 pending cases, compared with 14 cases which were pending at the beginning of 2014. See "Report of the International Court of Justice (1 August 2014–31 July 2015), Chapter V. Pending contentious proceedings during the period under review"; see also generally J. Crawford, "The Current Political Discourse Concerning International Law" 81 The Modern Law Review (2018) 12.

71 As stated by Sir Daniel Bethlehem in his keynote speech for the 125th Anniversary of the PCA on 12 June 2024 (available at www.pca.org): "There is a growing docket of international cases that are less self-evidently driven by an imperative to resolve disputes than by a political purpose of holding a respondent to account".

72 See the case of the dispute between Thailand and the Philippines (*Thailand–Cigarettes* (DS 371): after an AB report of 2011 and two compliance panel reports, the dispute was still pending in 2024 notwithstanding the appointment of a Facilitator in 2022. For more detail, see S. Pahis "Appeals after the Appellate Body", *supra* n 44. See generally on ADR C. Tomutschat, M. Kohen (eds) *Flexibility in International Dispute Settlement: Conciliation Revisited* (Brill 2020).

73 In view of the US position, according to K. Rockwell, "Six Takeaways from WTO MC13" (5 March 2024), available at https://www.hinrichfoundation.com, "It is unclear how a new Appellate Body

annulment, limited to correcting serious procedural and substantive errors on an *ad hoc* basis and without any precedential effect.[74] It appears from the texts of recent FTAs concluded by the US that its preference is for non-binding panel decisions, on the basis of which the parties will negotiate a settlement.[75]

The current situation of panel reports not becoming binding if the losing party appeals into the void has the additional shortcoming of exempting the party facing compliance with an adverse decision from the obligation to do so if it has not subscribed to the MPIA. Reverting to a system akin to that of the GATT, where *ad hoc* panel reports did not establish consistent jurisprudence and were little more than advisory opinions or non-binding conciliation proposals, would grossly undermine the current multilateral system.[76] Such an approach is not consistent with the carrying out of international trade under a legally predictable framework. It would signal the return to the "power-oriented approach" to trade relations, which relies on unilateral trade restrictions and bilateral deals with, or imposed on, weaker countries. Such a "transactional" approach to dispute settlement, as currently pursued by the US, is at odds with the spirit and rules underpinning the current multilateral rule-based system based on non-discrimination.[77] As mentioned above, the positions expressed by the generality of the WTO Members until now are against such an

would look but it is inconceivable that there will be a return to a powerful WTO 'court'. A pared-down and less heavy-handed mechanism is inevitable".

74 See P. Van den Bossche, "Can the WTO Dispute Settlement System Be Revived?" in E.U. Petersmann, A. Steinbach (eds) *Constitutionalism and Transnational Governance Failures* (Brill 2024) 308; D. Chow, "Why the US wants and needs a permanently crippled WTO https://papers.ssrn.com/sol3/papers.cfm?abstract_id=4865896, JWT (forthcoming 2025). The US distrust towards international justice dates back in time, see C. Romano (ed), *The Sword and the Scales. The US and International Courts and Tribunals* (CUP 2009).

75 According to Article 31.18 USMCA: *Implementation of Final Report:* "1. Within 45 days from receipt of a final report that contains findings that: (a) the measure at issue is inconsistent with a Party's obligations in this Agreement … the disputing Parties shall endeavor to agree on the resolution of the dispute. 2. Resolution of the dispute can comprise elimination of the non-conformity or the nullification or impairment, if possible, the provision of mutually acceptable compensation, or another remedy the disputing Parties may agree". Under Article 31.19: "If the disputing Parties are unable to agree on a resolution to the dispute … the complaining Party may suspend the application to the responding Party of benefits of equivalent effect to the non-conformity or the nullification or impairment until the disputing Parties agree on a resolution to the dispute".

76 Already in 2003, C. Ehlermann (one of the first AB Members) reflected on the Appellate Body of the WTO in "Reflections on the Appellate Body of the WTO" 6 JIEL (2003) 695, 706, opposing "all suggestions that tend to turn the wheel of history back, in reintroducing elements of the original 'diplomatic' model of dispute settlement".

77 Voluntary Export Restrictions (VER) and similar arrangements, which had spread in the final period of GATT in breach of the MFN principle, were deliberately prohibited under the WTO by Article 22.1 and 23 DSU ("Strengthening of the Multilateral System"). They have, however, made their comeback between the US and China and the US and the EU, though officially as solutions to freeze pending disputes on a temporary basis. A recent research paper of the WTO (available at wto.org/Data Blog of 25 January 2025) documents that more than 80% (before April 2025) of world trade is carried out under the MFN non-discrimination standard of Article I GATT (53% MFN duty-free) while preferential treatment under RTAs governs about 17%.

involution. The trend in the current appeal/review discussions is not geared to such a radical overhaul of the present system but may still endanger it by diminishing the effectiveness of appeal in law for the WTO membership at large.

We are sceptical that empowering panellists and increasing their status and the required qualifications for this role (which is *per se* welcome), without maintaining a review by a central body of legal experts such as the AB acting in a manner typical of an international court, would resolve all problems of correctness, consistency, and coherence required for the effectiveness of the WTO DSS. To the contrary, more divergent interpretations can be expected from the operation of more panels issuing final decisions subject to limited review.[78] Reducing at the same time the value of adopted reports would encourage further "self-interpretation" of their obligations by WTO Members and increase divergence in the application of the multilateral trade agreements, to the detriment of the security and predictability of multilateral trade rules.[79]

B. Investment

1. Effects of Criticism on ISDS Reform

As outlined in Chapter VII, in recent years, investment arbitration has become the object of growing criticism from several viewpoints, leading to new approaches and reform proposals concerning dispute settlement in the investment regime.[80] Criticism has led to an in-depth re-examination of the content of IIAs and of ISDS in particular, also in light of how certain provisions have been interpreted by tribu-

78 A few specialists have indeed envisaged ways of replacing the appellate stage by reinforcing the panel level, e.g. by establishing a roster of full-time appointees. See B. Hoekman, P. Mavroidis, "To AB or not AB? Dispute Settlement in WTO Reform" 23 JIEL (2020) 1; T. Cottier, "Recalibrating the WTO Dispute Settlement System: Towards New Standards of Appellate Review" 24 JIEL (2021) 515 (suggesting that appeal be limited to "constitutional issues"). See also A. Sykes, "The Utility of Appellate Review at the WTO and Its Optimal Structure" (18 April 2024), available at SSRN. https://ssrn.com/abstract=4799758, who argues that "the WTO does not present a compelling economic case for a two-stage judicial process … if some form of appellate review is to be retained in the WTO, a discretionary 'certiorari-like' mechanism is the best option, which dominates alternative proposals such as those for a more deferential standard of review or the elimination of de facto 'precedent'" (also referring to the review enshrined in Article 52 ICSID limited to "annulment an exceptional remedy, available only in egregious cases" as a valuable example for the WTO). As we say in the text, such a limited review would be clearly a second best in a centralized multilateral system such as the WTO, while a certiorari-like filter would increase the discretion of the appellate reviewers, contrary to the preference of the author. In favour of fixing the impasse along the lines of the Walker proposals, see instead former AB Member J. Hillman, "A Reset of the WTO Appellate Body" (Council of Foreign Relations 2020), available at https://www.cfr.org/report/reset-world-trade-organizations-appellate-body

79 As stated by I. Van Damme (Chapter VII, n 34), "exterminating a court or tribunal that almost all WTO Members wish to maintain and contribute to delivering the WTO promise of a stable and certain framework within which international trade takes place undermines the effectiveness of the WTO as an organization and the rule of law in the regulation of international trade".

80 See Chapter VII.B.4.

nals, bringing substantial changes over time to the succinct "first generation" BITs and their ISDS clauses.[81]

Besides interested governments, intergovernmental organizations, the business world, and the "investment community", the debate has involved civil society and NGOs as well as legal experts in various capacities, with the active participation of engaged academics.[82] Changes to the investment regime's legal framework have been the result of unusually open discussions and reflections, as highlighted in Chapter VII. Investment law is thus not just the product of a closed group of interests (where investors and host states represent divergent positions) but reflects and is open to cross-border societal values and concerns, such as in respect of accountability and legitimacy, the environment and climate change, sustainable development, the protection of human rights and labour conditions.[83]

This process has affected the drafting of new BITs, as well as trade agreements that include investment provisions (RTIAs). Their basic objectives, however, remain the same: they are *ad hoc* agreements or chapters of RTAs meant to protect foreign investments in a bilateral or regional framework, entrusting disputes to ISDS. They aim thereby also at improving the "investment climate" in host countries. The addition of obligations for investors and new provisions aimed at reconciling their protection with the safeguard of broader societal concerns in the host state, inserting in the texts obligations upon them, has, however, substantially impacted the format and content of new model BITs and actual texts.[84] Recent agreements tip the balance between investors' and host states' rights by proclaiming the right of states to regulate in the public interest.[85] As to dispute settlement,

81 See the comparative table annexed in Chapter III.

82 Notwithstanding recent criticism (see W. Byrne, "The Influence of Legal Scholars on the Development of International Investment Law" 27 JIEL (2024) 278), international law academics have traditionally been a feature in the international legal landscape exercising multiple roles as teachers, arbitrators and judges, advisors, consultants, and in authoring publications. These functions accord with the role attributed by Article 38.1(d) of the ICJ Statute to "the teachings of the most highly qualified publicists of the various nations, as subsidiary means for the determination of rules of law".

83 See P. Muchlinski, "Negotiating New Generation International Investment Agreements. New Sustainable Development Oriented Initiatives" in S. Hindelang and M. Krajewski (eds) *Shifting Paradigms in International Investment Law* (OUP 2015) 41. For a skeptical view, see N. Perrone, *Investment Treaties and the Legal Imagination. How Foreign Investors Play by Their Own Rules* (OUP 2021). For an up-to-date critical presentation, see M. Sornarajah, *The International Law on Foreign Investment* (5th ed. CUP 2021).

84 Model BITs can be found on the UNCTAD IIA Navigator, <https://investmentpolicy.unctad.org/international-investment-agreements/model-agreements> accessed 24 July 2024. See also L. Achtouk-Spivak, R. Garden, "The Revised OECD Guidelines: A Strengthened Forum for Resolving ESG Disputes?" Columbia FDI Perspectives, n 382 (2024).

85 See AfCFTA Protocol on Investment (2023, not yet in force), Article 24. (Right to Regulate): "1. In accordance with customary international law and other general principles of international law, each State Party has the right to regulate, including to take measures to ensure that investment in its territory is consistent with the goals and principles of sustainable development, and with other national environmental, health, climate action, social and economic policy objectives and essential security interests. 2. For greater certainty, measures taken by a State Party to comply with its international

the replacement of traditional arbitral ISDS by permanent tribunals in EU agreements is the most marked change.

As highlighted in Chapter VII, very few countries (Bolivia, Venezuela, Honduras) have chosen to exit the system altogether by withdrawing from ICSID and/or unilaterally terminating their BITs. A few others, such as India and South Africa, have terminated their older BITs with a view to negotiating more "modern" treaties of this type.[86] Some recent RTAs, on the other hand, do not contain investment chapters (which the EU includes in separate agreements for internal constitutional reasons since 2018) or do not include ISDS.[87]

ISDS has not been replaced in BITs by state-to-state dispute settlement.[88] Rather new investment protection provisions feature longer texts that address new issues and go into traditional issues in more detail. For example, the UK–Azerbaijan BIT (1996) featured 14 articles over seven pages, while the investment chapter of the UK–New Zealand FTA (2022) includes 19 articles across 17 pages.[89] Typically, the new terrain covered by the investment chapter of this FTA includes "Corporate Social Responsibility" (Article 14.19) and "Investment and Environmental, Health, and Other Regulatory Objectives" (Article 14.18). In terms of standard protections, the treaty from 1996 merely states that investments "shall at all times be accorded fair and equitable treatment". The UK–New Zealand FTA fleshes out the nuance of this provision in considerably more detail over five paragraphs.

Recent BITs include provisions on the promotion and facilitation of investments, address new concerns, and feature better-defined exceptions, patterned after Article XX GATT and in case of balance-of-payments difficulties.[90] In CETA,

obligations under other relevant treaties shall not constitute a breach of this Protocol. 3. For avoidance of doubt, the exercise of the right to regulate under Paragraphs 1 and 2 cannot give rise to any claim by an investor for compensation".

86 See Chapter VII n 137, 138. Thus, India retained ISDS in its the 2016 Model BIT "though in a much-diluted form", see P. Ranjan "The 2016 Model Indian Bilateral Investment Treaty: A Critical Deconstruction" 38 Nw. J. Int'l L. & Bus. (2017) 16.

87 See A. Lugg and others, "Why Is There No Investor-State Dispute Settlement in RCEP? Bargaining and Contestation in the Investment Regime" Business and Politics (2024) 1. The investment chapter of the India–EFTA Trade and Economic Partnership Agreement (2024) includes neither standards of protection nor ISDS. See, however, the typical ISDS provisions that were included in the bespoke 2009 ASEAN Comprehensive Investment Agreement (in force since 2012).

88 K. Gordon, J. Pohl, "Investment Treaties over Time–Treaty Practice and Interpretation in a Changing World" OECD Working Papers on International Investment 2015/02 (2015), available at https://ssrn.com/abstract=2555606, As to the EU policy, see Regulation 1219/2012 establishing transitional arrangements for bilateral investment agreements between Member States and third countries (Grandfathering Regulation) under which Member States' old BITs remain in force and even new ones can be concluded by them with third states upon authorization of the EU Commission. See F. Montanaro, *The European Union and International Investment Law* (Hart 2023) and the contributions published in the special issue 38(1) of DCI "The EU in International Investment Law: Perspectives and Challenges" (G. Minervini, L. Mola, F. Ortino, F. Palombino, G. Zarra eds 2024).

89 For a comparison between first-generation and recent BIT provisions on dispute settlement, see the table annexed in Chapter III.

90 See T. Ishikawa, *Corporate Environmental Responsibility in Investor–State Dispute Settlement* (CUP 2022).

the EU and Canada have included precise definitions of the contours of "fair and equitable treatment" under the agreement.[91] The parties' joint committee also issued in 2024, even before its entering into force, a draft interpretation of several provisions to clarify that "the Parties can regulate in the framework of climate, energy, and health policies to achieve legitimate public objectives".[92]

Recent ISDS clauses that could be described as innovative include more rigorous obligations to pursue ADR, including waiting periods to encourage amicable settlement before an investor can initiate arbitration, a defined role for the other treaty party/parties in proceedings ("non-disputing parties"), transparency requirements (including in respect of third-party funding), amicus curiae rights for interested private third parties, time limits to initiate a dispute, procedural deadlines, and limitations on the power of tribunals to award remedies. The public nature of investment arbitration is thereby taken into account, distancing it from typical commercial arbitration proceedings.[93]

2. *US Reaction to Criticism: From NAFTA to USMCA*

Even the United States, traditionally a supporter of ISDS as an instrument to protect its investments abroad, has reduced the scope of investment arbitration in recent trade agreements. Investment protection and ISDS between the three parties to NAFTA were drastically curtailed in the 2018 negotiation which led to its replacement with the USMCA. ISDS was abolished between the US and Canada, the latter having become disenchanted with the previous system in light of the many disputes brought against it by US investors under NAFTA Chapter 11. Under USMCA, between the US and Mexico most investors will only be able to file ISDS claims for breach of national or most-favoured-nation treatment or in cases of direct expropriation in certain sectors, while protection against indirect expropriation and breaches for fair and equitable treatment have been eliminated. Moreover, ISDS shall only be available after recourse to domestic courts for 30 months unless

91 See CETA, 8.10.2: "2. A Party breaches the obligation of fair and equitable treatment referenced in paragraph 1 where a measure or series of measures constitutes: (a) denial of justice in criminal, civil or administrative proceedings; (b) fundamental breach of due process, including a fundamental breach of transparency, in judicial and administrative proceedings; (c) manifest arbitrariness; (d) targeted discrimination on manifestly wrongful grounds, such as gender, race or religious belief; (e) abusive treatment of investors, such as coercion, duress and harassment; or (f) a breach of any further elements of the fair and equitable treatment obligation adopted by the Parties in accordance with paragraph 3 of this Article".

92 Draft Interpretation of 9 February 2024 regarding Article 8.10, Annex 8-A, Article 8.9, and Article 8.39, available at <https://policy.trade.ec.europa.eu/news/joint-statement-sustainable-economic-growth-eu-and-canada-through-comprehensive-economic-and-trade-2024-02-09_en> accessed 24 July 2024.

93 See C. Titi, "Investment Treaty Arbitration Caught in the Public-Private Law Divide" 45 Michigan J. Int. L. (2024).

such recourse is obviously futile.[94] The "spaghetti-bowl" situation due to the existence of a multiplicity of RTIAs between the same parties sometimes leads to curious results. Thus, while ISDS was cancelled between Canada and Mexico under the USMCA, it has re-emerged under the CPTPP of which the two countries are Members.[95] Depending on the attitude that the Trump 2025 administration will take in respect of investments of US multinationals abroad, the US may refrain from inserting ISDS in future IIAs and RTIAs altogether. Most recently, the US has been pursuing a policy of restricting investors' rights under existing RTIAs by promoting a more rigorous understanding of treaty standards by way of interpretation by Joint Commissions under those treaties.[96]

3. *The Investment Court System: Bilateral Tribunals in the EU's FTIAs*

3.1. Concluded Agreements

The EU's new approach in its FTAs with an investment chapter (FTIAs), or in separate BITs, has been to negotiate the replacement of investment arbitral tribunals with a so-called Investment Court System.[97] This step represents the most radical

94 See USMCA, Annex 14-D, Mexico-United States Investment Disputes, Article 14.D.5, "Conditions and Limitations on Consent", available at <https://ustr.gov/sites/default/files/files/agreements/FTA/USMCA/Text/14-Investment.pdf> accessed 24 July 2024. See commentary by A. Lopez, *ISDS Under the USMCA: The First Three Years at a Glance* (25 November 2023), available at https://arbitrationblog.kluwerarbitration.com

95 Following UK accession to the CPTPP as its 12th Member in 2023, ISDS will also be available between the UK and Canada. The first case by a Canadian investor against Mexico under the CPTPP was filed in 2024; see News Release, *Almaden to Pursue International Arbitration under the CPTPP Against Mexico* (11 June 2024), available at www.transnational-dispute-management.com

96 In an official letter of 25 May 2023 USTR Katherine Tai stated: "President Biden does not believe corporations should receive special tribunals in trade agreements that are not available to other organizations, and he opposes the ability of private corporations to attack labor, health, and environmental policies through ISDS. I share these views, and the United States is not currently pursuing any trade or investment agreements that would establish ISDS", available at https://www.uschamber.com/assets/documents/USTR-Warren-FY24-Release-Partly-Redacted.pdf accessed 24 July 2024. As to interpretation by Joint Commissions see the USTR Press Release of 20 January 2025 "The US and Colombia issue FTC Decision interpreting standards of Investment protection under the US-Colombia TPA" adressing its chapters on NT, MFN and minimum treatment standards, expropriation and compensation, investment and environment, submission of a claim to arbitration, governing law and definitions. The Press Release states that "The decision reflects the longstanding US understanding of the standards of investment protection under the TPA...This decision with Colombia demonstrates our willingness to use tools under existing agreements to ensure arbitrators adhere to the US understanding of its commitments and seek to address concerns about ISDS", though the decision falls short of renegotiation (which apparently was under consideration).

97 Periodically, the idea has been floated in the past of introducing an appeal stage in ISDS as an alternative to a two-tier ICS/MIC, replacing annulment and thus reinforcing legal control over awards and consistency of decisions, to the point of being envisaged as a possible future option in US BITs at the end of the 1990s, see B. Legum, J. Paulsson, A. Qureshi, S. Gulzar Khan, "Critical Views on an Appellate Mechanism in Investment Disputes" in K. Sauvant (ed) *Appeal Mechanisms in International Investment Disputes* (OUP 2008). A feasibility analysis was made by ICSID in 2005

reform of the traditional format of ISDS to date, while maintaining a functioning DSS between investors and states. The European shift from investment arbitration to a permanent court system, moreover characterized by two tiers, including a tribunal of first instance and an appellate tribunal, responds to a variety of criticisms and concerns expressed towards investment arbitration. These range, as highlighted in Chapter VII, from a perceived lack of legitimacy, which dominated the public consultation held by the Commission on the proposed TTIP in 2015, to more technical concerns related to the *ad hoc* nature of the arbitral system.[98] The results of that consultation prompted the EU and Canada to renegotiate CETA's already agreed draft text, replacing ISDS with ICS in its investment chapter.[99]

EU internal requirements have moreover resulted in dropping investment chapters from other bilateral trade agreements that would have included ICS.[100] The investment chapters of the Vietnam and Singapore FTIAs were separated from the main trade agreement.[101] Once in force, these Investment Protection Agreements (IPA) are due to replace the existing BITs of EU member states with these two countries. The most recent EU FTIAs, the one agreed "in principle" with Mexico in 2018, whose negotiations were finalized in January 2025, and the EU-Chile Advanced Framework Agreement of 2023, also feature ICS.[102]

but this option was never pursued; see ICSID Background Paper, *Suggested Changes to the ICSID Rules and Regulations* (2005), available at https://icsid.worldbank.org. The idea is back now among those on the table to revise ISDS at UNCITRAL WG III; see *infra* n 129.

98 See Chapter VII.B.2.

99 For an overview, see L. Puccio, R. Harte, "From Arbitration to the Investment Court System (ICS): The Evolution of CETA Rules" (European Parliament Research Service,2017), available at <https://www.europarl.europa.eu/thinktank/en/document/EPRS_IDA(2017)607251> accessed 24 July 2024.

100 In Opinion 2/15 (16 May 2017) (on the EU–Singapore FTA), available at <https://curia.europa.eu/juris/document/document.jsf?docid=190727&doclang=en> accessed 24 January 2025, the CJEU held that FTAs are "mixed agreements" on which the competence is shared between the EU and its Member States. Therefore, trade provisions of FTAs are within the purview of the exclusive competence of the EU (Article 3.1.(e) TFEU), while investment-state dispute provisions require the ratification of all Member States. All the FTAs mentioned, including CETA, have provisionally entered into force in accordance with Article 218.5 TFEU as to the trade chapters, while investment chapters are waiting for the (slow) process of national ratifications required for the whole treaty to enter into force. See Council Decision (EU) 2017/38 (28 October 2016) on the provisional application of the CETA, available at http://eur-lex.europa.eu

101 This resulted in separate BIT-like agreements: the EU–Singapore Investment Protection Agreement in 2018 and the EU–Vietnam IPA in 2019. The EU-Mercosur Partnership Agreement, politically agreed in December 2024 (which may also be subject to being divided into several treaties for the reasons explained in n 100) also envisages a two-tier ICS.

102 See *Negotiators conclude on [sic] modernized Global Agreement with Mexico*, www.ec.europ.eu, Press Release 17 January 2025; and *Towards and EU–Chile Advanced Framework Agreement*, available at <https://policy.trade.ec.europa.eu/eu-trade-relationships-country-and-region/countries-and-regions/chile/eu-chile-agreement_en>, (accessed 24 July 2024). The EU–Japan Economic Partnership Agreement of 2018, in force since 2019, has no investment chapter because Japan did not agree on the ICS proposed as a *sine qua non* by the EU for the settlement of investment disputes. Likewise, the EU–New Zealand Trade Agreement which entered into force on 1 May 2024 does not contain an ICS.

3.2. *Main Features*

Taking the CETA as a model, the ICS is made up of a tribunal of first instance and an appeal tribunal. In the CETA, the jurisdiction of the ICS is limited to breaches by contracting parties of the obligations under the agreement, "where the investor claims to have suffered loss or damage as a result of the alleged breach" (Article 8.18.1).[103] Market access and admission obligations are, as a rule, not enforceable by investors before the tribunal under EU treaties,[104] in line with the BIT practice of EU member states.[105]

The CETA tribunal of first instance shall be made up of 15 members, five of them nationals of the EU member states, five nationals of Canada, and five nationals of third countries, all to be appointed by the CETA Joint Committee (Article 8.27.2).[106] They will be appointed for a five-year term, renewable once, and will decide cases in divisions of three members, of whom one is a national of a member state, one a national of the other contracting party, and one a third-country national, acting as chair of the division.

Members of the tribunal will serve "hearing the case on a rotation basis, ensuring that the composition of the divisions is random and unpredictable, while giving equal opportunity to all Members of the Tribunal to serve" (Article 8.27.7). The disputing parties' power to appoint their arbitrators in a given dispute, a power typically provided for in all forms of arbitration, will thereby be eliminated.

The treaty requires the judges to possess specific qualifications: above all, expertise in public international law, including, as "desirable", expertise in international investment law and international trade law and in the resolution of disputes arising under international investment or trade agreements (Article 8.27.4). The CETA explicitly requires the tribunal to apply "the Agreement as interpreted in accordance with the Vienna Convention on the Law of Treaties and other rules and principles of international law applicable between the Parties" (Article 8.31.1). The same article clarifies in paragraph 2 that, on the one hand, the tribunal does not "have jurisdiction to determine the legality of a measure, alleged to constitute a breach of this Agreement, under the domestic law of the disputing Party"; on the other it

103 For a detailed comparative analysis, see M. Keller (ed) *EU Investment Protection Law: Chapter Eight of CETA, the Vietnam and Singapore Free Trade Agreements and EU Regulations 1219/2012, 912/214, and 2019/452. Article-by-Article Commentary* (Beck, Hart and Nomos 2023).

104 See, for instance, Article 8.18.2 CETA, providing that investors' claims of breach of treaty obligations "with respect to the expansion of a covered investment may be submitted only to the extent the measure relates to the existing business operations of a covered investment and the investor has, as a result, incurred loss or damage with respect to the covered investment".

105 On the practice of EU Member States including in their BITs just post-establishment protection standards, see A. De Luca, "New Developments on the Scope of the EU Common Commercial Policy under the Lisbon Treaty, Investment Liberalisation vs. Investment Protection?" in K. Sauvant (ed.) *Yearbook on International Investment Law and Policy 2010/2011* (OUP 2012) 165.

106 The tribunal under the EU–Vietnam IPA will have nine judges (Article 3.38), the EU–Singapore IPA provides for six judges (Article 3.9) while the EU-Mercosur tribunal would comprise 15 judges.

specifies that "in determining the consistency of a measure with this Agreement, the tribunal may consider, as appropriate, the domestic law of the disputing Party as a matter of fact".[107] In doing so, the tribunal shall follow the prevailing interpretation given to the domestic law by the courts or authorities of that Party, and any meaning given to domestic law by the tribunal shall not be binding upon the courts or the authorities of that Party.[108]

Judges are subject to strict conflict of interest rules, initially those of the IBA Guidelines on Conflicts of Interest in international arbitration.[109] They are prohibited from acting as counsel, party-appointed expert, or witness in any pending or new dispute under the agreement, and also in any dispute under any other investment agreement (Article 8.30.1 CETA), including third countries' agreements completely unconnected with the CETA or other agreements of the EU or Canada.[110] The conflict of interest rules are even stricter in the EU–Vietnam FTA, where the prohibition is extended to disputes under domestic law.[111] CETA and the EU–Singapore IPA tribunals shall be assisted by the ICSID Secretariat, while tribunals under the EU–Vietnam IPA may be assisted alternatively by the PCA.[112]

These agreements also create appellate tribunals with a broad mandate to review awards. For example, CETA provides that "[t]he Appellate Tribunal may uphold, modify or reverse a Tribunal's award based on: (a) errors in the application or interpretation of applicable law; (b) manifest errors in the appreciation of the facts, including the appreciation of relevant domestic law; and (c) the grounds set out in

107 This innovative provision was clearly inserted in order to comply with the holding in this respect of the CJEU in its Opinion 1/17 of 30 April 2019, 118, on the compatibility of the CETA tribunals with the EU treaties: "since those Tribunals stand outside the EU judicial system, they cannot have the power to interpret or apply provisions of EU law other than those of the CETA or to make awards that might have the effect of preventing the EU institutions from operating in accordance with the EU constitutional framework".

108 Moreover, according to Article 8.31.3: "Where serious concerns arise as regards matters of interpretation that may affect investment, the Committee on Services and Investment may, pursuant to Article 8.44.3(a), recommend to the CETA Joint Committee the adoption of interpretations of this agreement. An interpretation adopted by the CETA Joint Committee shall be binding on a Tribunal established under this Section. The CETA Joint Committee may decide that an interpretation shall have binding effect from a specific date". Cf. Article 31.3 VCLT according to which in interpreting a treaty "There shall be taken into account, together with the context: (a) any subsequent agreement between the parties regarding the interpretation of the treaty or the application of its provisions".

109 Judges are entitled to a monthly retainer and to a *per diem* fee when they are actually hearing cases (as is the case for Members of the AB at the WTO), to be calculated as for ICSID panellists (Article 8.27.12 CETA).

110 Challenges against a judge are to be decided by the President of the ICJ (Article 8.30.3 CETA).

111 Similar restrictions to ensure the avoidance of conflicts of interest are spelled out in the UNCITRAL Code of Conduct for judges in international investment dispute resolution (on which see *infra* Chapter VIII.B.5.2.2(b)) approved on 7 December 2023 by UNGA Res. A/78/105, Article 4: "He or she shall not engage in any other occupation of a professional nature which is incompatible with his or her obligation of independence and impartiality or with the demands of the terms of office. In particular, a Judge shall not act as a legal representative or an expert witness in any other proceeding".

112 Article 8.27.16 of the CETA and EU–Singapore IPA Article 3.10.14.

Article 52.1(a) through (e) of the ICSID Convention, insofar as they are not covered by paragraphs (a) and (b)".[113] As compared with the grounds for appeal under the DSU and annulment under Article 52 ICSID, the extension of the grounds for appeals also to "manifest errors of facts" is noteworthy. Further matters have been left (and postponed) to a future decision of the Joint Committee of the Contracting Parties (Article 8.28.7 CETA), including: the number of members of the Appellate Tribunal, administrative support (including the institution of a permanent secretariat), procedures for the initiation and conduct of appeals and for referring issues back (remand) to the tribunal for "adjustment" of the award, term of office, vacancies, remuneration, costs, and other elements necessary for the effective functioning of the appellate tribunal.

3.3. ICS: Judicial Courts or Arbitral Tribunals?

The relevant provisions are ambiguous as to the nature of the system, whether it is judicial or arbitral, considering that the set-up is judicial but there are many references to ICSID procedural rules.

A permanent adjudicative mechanism, with judges appointed by the contracting states to hear disputes between private parties and states (such as the ICS), need not necessarily be considered to be a court rather than a form of arbitration. A good example of such a mechanism that has been considered to be arbitral in nature, also in respect of the recognition of its decisions, is the Iran–United States Claims Tribunal, as highlighted in Chapter I.B.4.[114]

In the investment dispute section of recent EU agreements, there are several references to ICSID. Thus, Article 8.23.2 CETA provides that an investor may submit treaty claims either in accordance with the ICSID Convention and Arbitration Rules, or the ICSID Additional Facility Rules if the Convention does not apply;[115] the UNCITRAL Arbitration Rules; or any other rules on the agreement of the disputing parties. According to Article 8.25.2 CETA, the respondent's consent to the settlement of investment disputes by the tribunal in accordance with the procedures set out in the section on investment protection and the submission of a claim by an investor "shall satisfy the requirements of: (a) Article 25 of the ICSID Convention and Chapter II of the ICSID Additional Facility Rules regarding the written consent of the disputing parties; and, (b) Article II of the New York Convention for an agreement in writing". Similarly, a decision of the tribunal qualifies as an ICSID award if the claimant had recourse to ICSID, and "as an arbitral award that is deemed to relate to claims arising out of a commercial relationship or transaction

113 See Article 8.28.2 CETA.

114 See Iran–United States Claims Tribunal, available at https://iusct.com/about/ accessed 24 July 2024, explaining that "The Tribunal conducts its business in accordance with the arbitration rules of UNCITRAL, as modified by the Governments and the Tribunal".

115 Canada became a party to ICSID in 2013, while Poland is the only EU Member that is not a party to ICSID.

for the purposes of Article I of the New York Convention", if the claimant submitted the claim to UNCITRAL arbitration (Article 8.41 CETA).

Other EU FTIAs also include innovative procedural mechanisms. Thus, the investment protection chapter of the "modernized" EU–Chile Advanced Framework Agreement (2023) establishes a right of intervention for "any natural or legal person which can establish a direct and present interest in the specific circumstances of the dispute". This arrangement is designed to expand the amicus curiae system. If granted, the intervention also entails the right to access case documents, submit a written statement, and to make an oral statement at the hearings. However, the intervention is "limited to supporting, in whole or in part, the legal position of one of the disputing parties".[116]

3.4. The Enforceability of ICS Decisions

The ICS is an original experiment meant to respond to a number of the criticisms addressed to ISDS, especially in the EU, regarding the selection, independence, and impartiality of the adjudicators, and balance, transparency, and accountability towards the member states and the public.[117] Its set-up, however, presents several drawbacks, including the enforcement of its decisions, notwithstanding the efforts of the EU Commission to ensure the effectiveness of the new system. On the one hand, the ICSID Convention and Arbitration Rules are referred to as possible sources of applicable procedural rules; on the other, the modifications to the ICSID Convention introduced by the ICS, namely the complete elimination of the right of disputing parties to appoint tribunal members and the replacement of annulment by appeal, call into question the compatibility of this new system with the ICSID Convention. As pointed out above in Chapter II.B.2.1, the ICSID Convention establishes a special form of investor–state arbitration on a multilateral basis as a self-contained system. Moreover, it provides that ICSID awards "shall not be subject to any appeal or any other remedy except those provided for" in the Convention itself (Article 53.1 ICSID Convention). We are therefore in the presence of a modification to a multilateral treaty between some of its parties only, as permitted by Article 41 VCLT, provided, however, the modification "does not relate to a provision, derogation from which is incompatible with the effective execution of the object and purpose of the treaty".

Notwithstanding the precedent of the Iran–US Claims Tribunal mentioned above, a permanent tribunal, the members of which are all appointed only by the state parties (such as the CETA ICS), completely removing the appointing power of private parties, is substantially and intentionally different from traditional

116 Article 10.48 of the Chile–EU Advanced Framework Agreement, which is not yet in force.

117 As to the remedies that can be granted, CETA Article 8.39 specifies, "If the Tribunal makes a final award against the respondent, the Tribunal may only award, separately or in combination: (a) monetary damages and any applicable interest; (b) restitution of property, in which case the award shall provide that the respondent may pay monetary damages representing the fair market value of the property at the time immediately before the expropriation".

arbitration (ICSID arbitration included). It is doubtful whether decisions of the ICS, albeit qualified as ICSID awards in the EU agreements mentioned,[118] will be able to benefit from the ICSID or NY Convention recognition and enforcement mechanisms in third states. This is because the modification introduced by ICS treaty provisions *inter se* between the parties, even if permitted under Aticle 41 VCLT, would remain *res inter alios acta* and, as such would not be binding for third parties to the modifying agreement.[119]

Consequently, it is uncertain whether the decisions of a European bilateral ICS, albeit qualified as ICSID awards, would enjoy the treatment that other ICSID parties are bound to grant to other ICSID awards under Article 54.1 ICSID. Should they be considered as foreign judicial decisions by domestic courts of third states, they would be subject to review there under the same conditions as any other foreign judgment. If not considered ICSID awards, it appears more likely that ICS decisions may qualify as foreign awards pursuant to the NY Convention, and as such they would be subject to recognition proceedings (*exequatur)* before domestic courts of third states for the purpose of enforcement there. This depends, however, on the interpretation of Article I.2 of the NY Convention, which provides that "The term 'arbitral awards' shall include not only awards made by arbitrators appointed for each case but also those made by permanent arbitral bodies to which the parties have submitted". In this respect, a favourable precedent is that of judgments of the Iran–US Claims Tribunal having been recognized and enforced as awards under the New York Convention.[120]

In any case, the parties to CETA (and the other agreements) have been careful to envisage the broadest possible recognition of these decisions. Article 8.41 ("Enforcement of awards") provides first that "1. An award issued pursuant to this Section shall be binding between the disputing parties and in respect of that particular case. 2. Subject to paragraph 3, a disputing party shall recognise and comply with an award without delay". Moreover, The following paragraphs are also relevant:

> 5. A final award issued pursuant to this Section is an arbitral award that is deemed to relate to claims arising out of a commercial relationship or transaction for the purposes of Article I of the New York Convention. 6. For greater certainty, if a claim has been submitted pursuant to Article 8.23.2(a), a final award issued pursuant to this Section shall qualify as an award under Chapter IV, Section 6 of the ICSID Convention.

118 See Articles 8.39 and 8.41 CETA, which envisage that the award may be issued under the ICSID Convention or the Additional Facility, or the UNCITRAL Arbitration Rules.

119 See A. Reinisch, "Will the EU's Proposal Concerning an Investment Court System for CETA and TTIP Lead to Enforceable Awards? – The Limits of Modifying the ICSID Convention and the Nature of Investment Arbitration" 19 JIEL (2016) 22, 25.

120 See P. Bernardini, "Reforming Investor–State Dispute Settlement: The Need to Balance Both Parties' Interests" 32 ICSID Review (2017) 38, concluding that the New York Convention would not be applicable. For the opposite view, see A. Reinisch, n 119.

In our view, the issue is mostly theoretical, at least for the time being. While there are enforcement issues in the EU in relation to awards under intra-EU BITs after the CJEU has held that they are contrary to EU law, it seems unlikely that a party to one of the EU RTIAs featuring ICS (or to one of the self-standing bilateral IPAs of the EU), be it a member of the EU or the other party, would not comply with an unfavourable decision and have no assets within the territory of the EU or the other party to the treaty.[121]

4. The Multilateral Investment Court (MIC) Proposal

Besides successfully inserting ICS into recent IIAs to replace ISDS, the EU has been promoting the establishment of a self-standing multilateral investment court as a radical departure from the traditional ISDS system at a global level.[122] In March 2018, the EU Council gave the EU Commission the mandate to negotiate such a MIC.[123] Prior to this, the EU had already been active within UNCITRAL WG III in promoting it as one of the options for ISDS reform that WG III has been examining since 2017.[124]

Although the MIC replicates the model of other international courts, it would be unique in that it would have jurisdiction over claims of private foreign investors

121 Even in the case of non-compliance, it seems unlikely that a party's assets would not be located within either the EU or Canada, available to satisfy the award.

122 See Colin Brown (of the EU Commission), "The Contribution of the European Union to the Rule of Law in the Field of International Investment Law through the Creation of a Multilateral Investment Court" 29 Eur Law J. (2022) 1. This choice has been reinforced by the CJEU Opinion 1/17 (30 April 2019), available at https://curia.europa.eu which has upheld the compatibility of the CETA ICS with the basic principles of EU law. Article 8.29 CETA (and corresponding provisions of similar IIAs of the EU) already envisages the MIC by providing that "[t]he Parties shall pursue with other trading partners the establishment of a multilateral investment tribunal and appellate mechanism for the resolution of investment disputes".

123 Council of the European Union, *Negotiating Directives for a Convention Establishing a Multilateral Court for the Settlement of Investment Disputes*, EU Doc. No 12981/17 (20 March 2018), available at <https://data.consilium.europa.eu/doc/document/ST-12981-2017-ADD-1-DCL-1/en/pdf> accessed 24 July 2024. This Council document sets out the basic features that the court should have.

124 The reasons for the EU choice are set forth in the document *Submissions from the European Union*, UN Doc. No A/CN.9/WG.III/WP.145 (12 December 2017), available at https://documents.un.org/doc/undoc/ltd/v17/088/32/pdf/v1708832.pdf?token=nXUEsUvHcnN6YKEQIs&fe=true accessed 24 July 2024. See generally G. Kaufmann-Kohler, M. Potestà, "The Composition of a Multilateral Investment Court and of an Appeal Mechanism for investment awards" CIDS Supplemental Report (2017), <https://archive-ouverte.unige.ch/unige:147563> accessed 24 July 2024; M. Bungenberg, A. Reinisch, *From Bilateral Arbitral Tribunals and Investment Courts to a Multilateral Investment Court. Options Regarding the Institutionalisation of Investor–State Dispute Settlement* (Springer 2020). The need to strike a balance between competing objectives is stressed by S. Puig, G Shaffer, "Imperfect Alternatives: Institutional Choices and the Reform of Investment Law" 112 AJIL (2018) 361.

against states.[125] The experience of ICSID and the PCA, besides the model of the ICS and of the AB, has also been taken into account in drafting a "MIC Treaty".[126] According to the draft statute (treaty) being discussed by WG III, the MIC - for the time being defined as a "standing mechanism"- would have an institutional structure with a plenary body of its member States (the Conference of the Parties), which would be responsible for drafting appropriate regulations, appointing qualified judges for a non-renewable term possibly of nine years (following the recommendations of a selection committee) among candidates submitted by the member states or also pursuant to an open call, setting the budget, and providing a secretariat headed by an executive director.[127] The MIC would have a bench of judges (distinct for the tribunal and the appellate court), to be elected in a way that ensures diversity in respect of gender, regional representation, and legal background, ensuring at the same time that each member has the necessary expertise. The adoption of a code of ethics for the judges (the one already approved by UNCITRAL), the jurisdiction of the MIC, basic procedural features, and deciding the applicable law to a dispute would also be covered.

Two sensitive issues that a MIC treaty–statute must deal with are subject matter/consent jurisdiction and the enforceability of its decisions. As to the first issue, the MIC treaty should have an annex listing all IIAs whose ISDS would be replaced by the jurisdiction of the MIC if all the parties to such IIAs would be members of the MIC treaty. The treaty would thus amend existing BITs'/IIAs' ISDS provisions, replacing or adding to the reference to exisiting mechanisms, such as ICSID, the jurisdiction of the MIC. An additional feature might be that states may opt to accept the jurisdiction of both the first-tier and appeal tribunal or just that of the latter. As to recognition and enforcement, the treaty would provide for the obligation of all member states to recognize and enforce MIC decisions as if they were domestic judgments.

Establishing a MIC represents a challenge, also as to its relation with annulment mechanisms of investment awards provided for in the instruments referred to in existing BITs. On the one hand, it would resolve a number of shortcomings in the current arbitral ISDS, such as in respect of organization and consistency, which the institution of several bilateral ICSs, such as in CETA, could only solve in part.[128] On the other hand, setting up the MIC requires facing questions of political

125 The MIC would also be competent in respect of state-to-state disputes on the interpretation and application of the treaty.

126 See H. Lenk, 'The EU Investment Court System and its Resemblance to the WTO Appellate Body' in G. Gáspár-Szilágyi, D. Behn, M. Langford (eds), *Adjudicating Trade and Investment Disputes Convergence or Divergence?* (CUP 2020) 62.

127 The drafting of a complete statute of the MIC, based upon the set-up of other international courts, has recently been the object also of an academic project. See M. Bungenberg, A. Reinisch, *Draft Statute of the Multilateral Investment Court* (Nomos 2021).

128 For reflections and criticism, see J. Calamita, "The challenge of establishing a Multilateral Investment Tribunal at ICSID" 32 ICSID Rev (2017) 611; C. Brower, J. Ahmad, "From the Two-headed Nightingale to the fifteen-headed Hydra: the many follies of the proposed International Investment Court" 41 Fordham Int. Law J. (2018) 791.

equilibrium and costs, and would also add rigidity to the system.[129] As with ICS, a significant, possibly problematic, difference from ISDS is that investors, who would be the claimants, would not be entitled to appoint an adjudicator to the tribunal.[130]

The contribution of a MIC to the resolution of the various problems and concerns discussed in Chapter VII would be contingent on the proposal attracting the support of a "critical mass" of developed, developing, and emerging economies in a relatively short time, so that the new mechanism would be authentically multilateral and the judges would reflect its geographical makeup.[131] Developing countries that are critical of the current ISDS system may be interested in the MIC proposal. On the other hand, a number of typically home countries, such as the US and Japan, have indicated their opposition to the multilateral proposal as being unnecessary, or in any case inadequate, to overcome the concerns raised by investment arbitration.[132] At WG III work on a MIC, cautiously for the time being named "standing mechanism" has been progressing but without addressing for the time being fundamental issues concerning the conditions for the entry into force of the mechanism (and its name). In 2024, the complete text of a draft statute comprising 44 articles and commentaries thereto, providing for a two-tier tribunal, was released by the Secretariat and is the basis for the ongoing (2025) work at WG III on the matter.[133]

129 On the MIC, see also *Standing Multilateral Mechanism: Selection and Appointment of ISDS Tribunal Members and Related Matters*, UN Doc. No A/CN.9/WG.III/WP.213 (8 December 2021); *Appellate and Multilateral Court Mechanisms*, UN Doc. No A/CN.9/WG.III/WP.185 (29 November 2019). For current work at WGIII see n 133.

130 See R. Gulati, N. Lavranos, *Guaranteeing the independence of the judges of a MIC. A must for building the Court's credibility,* Columbia FDI Perspectives No 262, 7 October 2019, *https://ccsi.columbia.edu/columbia-fdi-perspectives.* A partial remedy to this situation could be that the home country of a claimant be entitled to appoint an *ad hoc* judge, as is the case at the ICJ, where either party may appoint a judge *ad hoc* if the ICJ does not include a judge of its nationality (Article 31.2 of the ICJ statute).

131 An approach such as that of the Mauritius Convention would not be advisable. The Mauritius Convention required only three ratifications to enter into force, which was reached in 2017, but ten years on from its signature it has not yet reached ten ratifications, notwithstanding so many public statements on the importance of transparency in investment arbitration. See https://treaties.un.org/Pages/ViewDetails.aspx?src=IND&mtdsg_no=XXII-3&chapter=22&clang=_en accessed 24 July 2024. In chronological order, these include Mauritius, Canada, Switzerland, Cameroon, Gambia, Benin, Australia, Bolivia, and Iraq. The EU and its member states have decided to become a party of the Mauritius Convention in June 2024 and the EU has signed it on 2 July 2024, see Chapter IV n 78. See *Council Approves EU Signature of Convention on Transparency for Dispute Settlement* (25 June 2024), https://policy.trade.ec.europa.eu/news/council-approves-eu-signature-convention-transparency-dispute-settlement-2024-06-25_en accessed 24 July 2024 and the EU has signed it on 2 July 2024.

132 For references, see M. Bungenberg and A. Reinisch, "Draft Statute" n 127.

133 See *Possible Reform of Investor–State Dispute Settlement (ISDS): Draft Statute of a Standing Mechanism for the Resolution of International Investment Disputes*, UN Doc. No A/CN.9/WG.III/WP.239 (8 February 2024) and its *Annotations*, UN Doc. No A/CN.9/WG.III/WP.240 (5 February 2024) which is currently being (2024-2025) discussed at WG III..

5. *Multilateral Reform Initiatives*

5.1. *The ICSID revised Arbitration Rules (2022)*

Criticism of existing procedural rules, as being insufficient to deal with new developments and concerns (such as relating to transparency, delays, and third-party funding), has led to substantial amendments of the 2006 ICSID Arbitration Rules with the approval of a revised text in 2022. These Rules represent the common procedural law for ICSID disputes, which may be supplemented or derogated from by specific provisions of applicable IIAs in disputes under those treaties. This is the case with pre-arbitration friendly settlement attempts, ADR and cooling-off periods which are increasingly required in IIAs, while ICSID does not contain any provision in this respect.

The 2022 amendments were agreed to without opposition by the ICSID Administrative Council, where all Member States are represented, however after a six-year process of elaboration. The new text can, therefore, be said to reflect the common understanding of the international community on the appropriate means of ensuring due process and efficiency in the conduct of ISDS cases.[134] The 2022 amendments lay down stricter time limits, and provide in more detail or *ex novo* on matters such as preliminary objections and bifurcation of proceedings, early dismissal of claims in case of "manifest lack of legal merit", the publication of awards and decisions (at a minimum in redacted form), disclosure of third-party funding, provisional measures, expedited arbitration, non-disputing treaty parties' submissions, amicus curiae briefs, consolidation and coordination of proceedings, electronic filing, and costs.[135] While some amendments deal with technical issues, making proceedings more responsive to the needs of the users and more efficient, others, such as those just mentioned, address matters raised by various stakeholders in recent years as being of concern in respect of the legitimacy of ISDS in the eyes of the public.[136] These are issues that UNCITRAL WG III addresses in a broader framework, but the expectations that normative results may be reached there in the short term are much lower.[137]

134 With the 2022 edition, ICSID Arbitration Rules differentiate themselves more markedly from those of international commercial arbitration. See O. Armas, N. Searle (eds) *Comparison of International Arbitration Rules* (6th ed. Juris Publishing 2022).

135 For more detail, see Chapter IV.B.1. The rules and guidance are available at the ICSID website https://icsid.worldbank.org/procedures/arbitration/convention/overview/2022 accessed 24 July 2024.

136 See I. Torterola, F. Sharipov, "The 2022 ICSID Arbitration Rules: Modernizing International Investment Dispute Resolution" 39 ICSID Rev (2024) 314.

137 See J. Marcoux and others, "Discourses of ISDS Reform: A Comparison of UNCITRAL Working Group III and ICSID Processes" 27 JIEL (2024) 314 ff. The ICSID Secretariat has also contributed to the work of WG III by addressing the difficult issue of modifying the ICSID Convention between only those parties that would agree on appeal as an alternative to annulment (also in light of the constraints in Article 41 VCLT), see ICSID, *Note on a Potential "inter se" Modification of the ICSID Convention*, April 1, 2025, available on the WGIII website.

5.2. *ISDS reform at UNCITRAL WG III*

5.2.1. *The Mandate*

UNCITRAL entrusted WG III with a broad mandate to work on the reform of ISDS in July 2017.[138] The Working Group's role was to: 1) identify and consider concerns regarding ISDS; 2) consider whether reform was desirable; and 3) develop any relevant solutions to be recommended to the Commission. The process, which has been correctly labelled government-led, consensus-based, and fully transparent, has become the focal multilateral initiative for the reform of ISDS worldwide.[139] Most of the current 70 members of UNCITRAL participate regularly in sessions, which are also open to observers from the EU, international organizations, and non-governmental entities, including arbitral institutions, which follow closely its work. They thereby have the possibility to supply participants with information and advice based on their experience in the field. WG III has injected a much-needed multilateral approach into the process of ISDS reform and is helping avoid the otherwise inevitable increase in fragmentation. At the same time, the consensual approach of its work makes reaching agreement a slow process.[140]

WG III started its work on the possible reform of ISDS in November 2017 (including the alternative of a permanent dispute settlement mechanism alongside ISDS, which we have dealt with in the preceding section), supported by the remarkable research and assistance work of the Secretariat. The Group is supposed to focus only on the procedural aspects of ISDS reform, although the distinction between procedure and matters of substance is uncertain and is a constant element of friction between members in the discussions. The WG III mandate is to "(i) first, identify and consider concerns regarding ISDS; (ii) second, consider whether reform was desirable in light of any identified concerns; and (iii) third, if the Working Group were to conclude that reform was desirable (as it has done), develop any relevant solutions to be recommended to the Commission".[141] In respect of "procedural and cross-cutting issues" WG III has been discussing provisions addressing a broad range of concerns with the current system, covering several areas. These include conditions for and limitations on the submission of claims, state-to-state disputes, recourse to local remedies, limitation periods, shareholder (derivative) claims, counterclaims, the right of states to regulate, the conduct of proceedings, costs and security for costs, third-party funding, the assessment of damages and

138 All materials and documents of WG III are published at the WGIII website, at https://uncitral.un.org/en/working_groups/3/investor-state. WG III meets three-four times per year for one-week sessions alternatively in Vienna and New York.

139 UNCITRAL press release, *UNCITRAL to Consider Possible Reform of Investor–State Dispute Settlement*, Doc. No UNIS/L/250 (14 July 2017) available at https://unis.unvienna.org/unis/en/pressrels/2017/unisl250.html accessed 24 July 2024.

140 See A. Roberts, "Incremental, Systemic, and Paradigmatic Reform of Investor-State Arbitration" 112 AJIL (2018) 410.

141 UNCITRAL, *Possible Reform of Investor–State Dispute Settlement (ISDS), Note by the Secretariat*, UN Doc. No A/CN.9/WG.III/WP.142, para. 3 (18 September 2017).

compensation, and the duration of proceedings.[142] Transparency, coherence and consistency, as well as questions on the independence and impartiality of arbitrators (conflict of interest), have also been discussed.

A not unexpected rift soon appeared between most developing countries and industrialized states as to the desirable outcome. The former group aimed at a multilateral binding instrument that would also modify existing BITs, while the latter envisaged that provisions agreed upon would be guidelines or model clauses from which states could pick and choose when negotiating new BITs or amending existing ones.

5.2.2. Results

(a) Model Provisions and Guidelines on Mediation

The first concluded result of WG III's work has been the finalization of Model Provisions and Guidelines on Mediation, which were approved by the UNCITRAL Commission at its 56th session in July 2023.[143] The aim of this work was to provide an optional instrument for resolving investor–state disputes in a more cost-effective and time-efficient manner. Its provisions may be included by states in bilateral or multilateral investment treaties, domestic legislation governing the use of mediation, investment contracts, or agreed on an *ad hoc* basis. These provisions are not the first ones that have been drafted to encourage ADR in investment relations. Other examples of specific rules in this area are the ICSID Mediation Rules of 2022 and the IBA Rules for Investor–State Mediation of 2012.[144] There is, however, a substantial difference between the availability of mediation models and actual recourse to them in a given dispute.[145]

(b) Codes of Conduct for Judges and Arbitrators

In 2023, WG III finalized two parallel Codes of Conduct: one for judges of any future "permanent mechanism" (MIC) to settle investment disputes, and the other for arbitrators and their assistants.[146] The latter has been established in coopera-

142 See *Possible Reform of Investor–State Dispute Settlement (ISDS): Draft Provisions on Procedural and Cross-Cutting Issues*, UN Doc. No A/CN.9/WG.III/WP.231 (26 July 2023) updated in doc. 244 (and its *Annotations* UN Doc. No A/CN.9/WG.III/WP.245 (8 July 2024) which is the current working document of WG III. The WG reports to the UNCITRAL Commission.

143 Draft *UNCITRAL Guidelines on Investment Mediation*, UN Doc. No A/CN.9/1151 (21 April 2023). See UNCITRAL Commission Sessions <https://uncitral.un.org/en/commission> accessed 24 July 2024, approved by UNGA 79/104 (7 December 2023).

144 The ICSID paper *Overview of Investment Treaty Clauses on Mediation* (2021), available at https://icsid.worldbank.org shows that only about 600 IIAs contain specific mediation clauses.

145 See M. Gotsiridze, "Challenges of Mediating Investor-State Disputes" 37 ICSID Rev (2024).

146 See UNCITRAL, *Draft Code of Conduct for Arbitrators in International Investment Dispute Resolution and Commentary*, UN Doc. No A/CN.9/1148 (28 April 2023); *Code of Conduct for Judges in International Investment Dispute Resolution and Commentary* UN Doc. No A/CN.9/1149 (28 April 2023), both adopted by the Commission in July 2023 and approved by UNGA Res. A/78/105 (7 December 2023).

tion with the ICSID Secretariat, and both were approved in summer 2023 by the UNCITRAL Commission.

The adoption of the codes is voluntary, but it is expected that they will be adopted at ICSID and other arbitral institutions and that they will be considered to be the general standard and best practice in the field. The texts of the two Codes deal with similar matters.[147] The Code for Arbitrators covers: independence and impartiality, limits to multiple roles, the duty of due diligence, integrity and competence, prohibition of ex parte communications of arbitrators with parties, confidentiality, fees and expenses, assistants, disclosure obligations, and compliance with the Code.[148]

The Code for Arbitrators is more detailed as a consequence of the *ad hoc* position of arbitrators (as opposed to members of permanent courts). Arbitrators have other activities besides arbitrating and may thus more easily run into conflicts that may impair their independence and impartiality. Another difference between the two texts is that the Code for Judges imposes on them broader obligations to maintain independence and impartiality compared to those of arbitrators. The Code also prohibits them from having any parallel role as a party representative or expert and requires them not to publicly discuss or comment on any decision for three years following the end of their term in office. A code for arbitrators to unify or harmonize provisions in this area is also warranted given the diversity in terms of the background, geographical origin, and legal education of arbitrators. There may also be differences in national, ethical, and professional standards, resulting in different expectations in terms of their conduct and their obligations.

A detailed regulation in the Code for Arbitrators, which is innovative compared to the prevailing practice, is found in Article 11 on the information that a prospective arbitrator has to disclose to the parties and the governing institution when contacted for appointment, to be updated during the proceedings. The basic provision is that of Article 11.1: "A Candidate and an Arbitrator shall disclose any circumstances likely to give rise to justifiable doubts as to his or her independence or impartiality". A list follows of circumstances to be disclosed "Regardless of whether required under paragraph 1", to be read in conjunction with two caveats: first, "A Candidate and an Arbitrator shall err in favour of disclosure if he or she has any doubt as to whether a disclosure shall be made", and, second, "The fact of non-disclosure does not in itself necessarily establish a lack of independence or impartiality" (paras. 5 and 7). The list of matters to be disclosed includes any financial, business, professional, or close personal relationship in the past five years with the parties, their legal representatives, other arbitrators or experts; and any direct or indirect financial interest in the outcome of the case. It is a fairly broad obligation to require arbitrators to disclose their appointments as an arbitrator or party

147 Articles 1–12 of the Draft Code of Conduct for Arbitrators are exactly mirrored in the code for judges except for Articles 9 (fees and expenses) and 10 (assistant), which do not feature in the code for judges.

148 Decision-making functions cannot be delegated, including to tribunal secretaries, according to Article 6(c) as explained in para. 48 of the Commentary.

representative (that is, counsel) over the previous five years in any international investment dispute, including proceedings where the parties to the current proceedings were not involved. The duty to disclose these circumstances, although they are not likely to be a cause of conflict, shows that the approach has been that of favouring full knowledge by the parties of an arbitrator's profile so that their choice of the adjudicators is fully informed, and challenges are consequently less likely.

A hotly debated issue has been that of regulating and limiting the "double-hatting" of arbitrators, which refers to those who also act as counsel in other investment proceedings. This practice has raised justified concerns about potentially affecting their independence. The compromise solution adopted has been recorded in Article 4 of the Code of Conduct for Arbitrators.

> "Article 4 – *Limit on multiple roles*. 1. Unless the disputing parties agree otherwise, an Arbitrator shall not act concurrently as a legal representative or an expert witness in any other proceeding involving: (a) The same measure(s); (b) The same or related party (parties); or (c) The same provision(s) of the same instrument of consent.
>
> 2. For a period of three years, a former Arbitrator shall not act as a legal representative or an expert witness in any other IID or related proceeding involving the same measure(s) unless the disputing parties agree otherwise.
>
> 3. For a period of three years, a former Arbitrator shall not act as a legal representative or an expert witness in any other IID or related proceeding involving the same or related party (parties) unless the disputing parties agree otherwise.
>
> 4. For a period of one year, a former Arbitrator shall not act as a legal representative or an expert witness in any other IID or related proceeding involving the same provision(s) of the same instrument of consent unless the disputing parties agree otherwise."

The above quoted final text shows that "issue conflicts" (an arbitrator having decided a dispute raising the same issues or having expressed his or her views as an author) have not been considered to be relevant as circumstances giving rise to actual, potential, or perceived conflicts of interests. The Codes appear to have been well received by arbitral institutions and the community of adjudicators, though warnings have been expressed against "due process paranoia" that might be used by a party raising challenges in bad faith to derail proceedings.

(c) The Advisory Centre on International Investment Dispute Resolution

Recent WG III work has also focused on the establishment of an Advisory Centre on International Investment Law. A draft statute, in the form of an annex to a draft treaty covering these matters, was agreed to by the Working Group at its 48th session in April 2024, which was approved "in principle" by the Commission in

July 2024.[149] The model for this Centre has been the Advisory Centre on WTO Law, established in Geneva as a self-standing organization in 2001. The ACWL provides legal advice on international trade law issues and provides assistance and representation in respect of disputes involving developing members and LDCs on concessional terms.[150]

Developing countries and LDCs have shown strong interest in WG III in favour of establishing a similar Centre on investment law, specifically to assist them in case of disputes with investors in lieu of, or in conjunction with specialized law firms (and on less onerous terms). WG III has discussed in detail the various issues involved in the Centre's set-up (preferably within UNCTAD for cost and efficiency reasons), participation/membership, the services that the Centre would provide (including to whom and on what financial terms), and the ways of financing it (members' scaled annual fees, voluntary contributions and service fees).

Beneficiaries of the Centre's services will be all its Members (any state or regional economic organization) but the Centre shall, in principle, give priority to Members included in the list of LDCs, followed by members listed as developing countries.[151] According to Article 6, the Advisory Centre shall provide technical assistance to its Members and engage in capacity-building activities with regard to international investment dispute resolution, including by: "(a) advising on issues pertaining to dispute prevention; (b) providing tailored training with regard to possible means of preventing and resolving disputes", among other activities.

As to the key issue of the provision of legal services by the Centre in relation to disputes, according to Article 7: "Upon the request by a Member, the Advisory Centre shall provide legal support and advice with regard to an international investment dispute proceeding prior to and after its initiation, including by: (a) Providing a preliminary assessment of the case, including the appropriate means to resolve the dispute; (b) Assisting in the selection of mediators, arbitrators or other types of adjudicators (including any challenge) as well as experts, taking into account geographical diversity and gender balance; (c) Supporting the preparation of statements, pleadings and evidence as well as other aspects of the proceeding; (d) Representing the Member in the proceeding, including in a hearing, at the instruction of and in conjunction with a team of that Member; (e) Facilitating the appointment of an external legal representative". Further preparatory work is currently being conducted (specifically as to its financial coverage) to operationalize the Centre in view of its actual establishment.

149 *Draft Statute of an Advisory Centre on International Investment Dispute Resolution*, UN Doc. No A/CN.9/1184 (25 April 2024).

150 See Chapter IV.B.3 and the website of the Advisory Centre on WTO Law <https://www.acwl.ch/>.

151 Article 7.3.

5.3. A Work in Progress

Since 2023, the work of WG III on procedural and "cross-cutting issues" has focused on drafting provisions that are being examined, re-examined, and re-drafted at each session.[152]

The list and title of the draft provisions are more telling than a summary. They include: "A. *Submission of a claim – conditions and limitations* 1. Consultation and negotiation 2. Mediation 3. Dispute resolution proceedings 4. State-to-State dispute settlement 5. Period for amicable settlement 6. Recourse to local remedies 7. Waiver of rights to initiate dispute resolution proceeding 8. Limitation period 9. Denial of benefits 10. Shareholder claims 11. Counterclaims 12. Right to regulate B. *Conduct of the proceedings* 13. Evidence 14. Bifurcation 15. Consolidation of proceedings 16. Interim/provisional measures 17. Code of Conduct 18. Transparency 19. Early dismissal 20. Security for costs 21. Third-party funding 22. Suspension and termination of the proceeding C. *Decisions by the Tribunal* 23. Assessment of damages and compensation 24. Period of time for making the final decision 25. Allocation of costs." All major issues that are currently being debated and whose satisfactory regulation would be a step towards enhancing the legitimacy of ISDS are thus being addressed by WG III members.

On the substance, as to the general structure and function of the future text and the content of several key provisions, there is a divide between two groups of countries. On the one side, those whose aim is to limit access to ISDS by investors and enhance the rights of respondent host states; on the other hand, those opposing reforms that would restrict access by investors to ISDS, such as through the obligation of prior recourse to local courts, preventing shareholders' claims, or by limiting the amount of damages that a tribunal may grant. A further divide is between those who aim at a multilateral treaty that would, in one go modify existing treaties that participating states would list,[153] and those who consider that the exercise should lead to guidelines for IIA negotiations or model clauses, from which states could pick and choose texts to be inserted into their IIAs. These divergent views have not deterred WG III from engaging in the drafting of such a multilateral treaty starting in 2024.[154]

152 See *Possible Reform of Investor–State Dispute Settlement (ISDS): Draft Provisions on Procedural and Cross-Cutting Issues*, UN Doc. No A/CN.9/WG.III/WP.244 (8 July 2024) and its *Annotations* UN Doc. No A/CN.9/WG.III/WP.245 (8 July 2024).

153 A precedent often referred to is the Multilateral Convention to Implement Tax Treaty Related Measures to Prevent Base Erosion and Profit Shifting (BEPS MLI) negotiated at the OECD, signed by more than 100 tax jurisdictions, and which entered into force on 1 July 2018. The MLI modifies specific clauses of double taxation treaties covered by it where both parties to such a treaty so notify the OECD, see OECD, BEPS Multilateral Instrument <https://www.oecd.org/tax/treaties/multilateral-convention-to-implement-tax-treaty-related-measures-to-prevent-beps.htm> accessed 24 July 2024.

154 *Possible Reform of Investor–State Dispute Settlement (ISDS): Draft Multilateral Instrument on ISDS Reform – Note by the Secretariat*, UN Doc. No A/CN.9/WG.III/WP.246 (8 July 2024).

Countries that have an extensive network of IIAs in place and consolidated experience in this respect (both industrialized and developing countries) are not in favour of any UNCTAD text that would constrain their treaty-making power. On this issue, a choice, if one is needed (since the various options are not incompatible), may only be forthcoming at the end of the work. A solution, not necessarily supported by universal acceptance, could favour those who would only accept a non-binding instrument as a lowest common denominator or a framework treaty with various protocols annexed to it, leaving several options open *à la carte* to individual states as to which instrument or provisions to accept.

C. Comparative Evaluation

We have until now outlined the origin, as well as the results, of the push for reform of both DSS. This was propelled by the dissatisfaction voiced by various participants and other stakeholders with both systems and the widespread desire to improve their functioning by making them more efficient and responsive to a broader platform of stakeholders.[155] We will now sum up commonalities and differences in the reform processes and possible outcomes that are currently taking shape, with the caveat that it is impossible to predict future solutions with any certainty. While engagement towards reform has increased lately, one cannot rule out that stumbling blocks, for instance due to increased geopolitical confrontation, may appear that will block the two processes, bringing about, if not the collapse, in any case further debilitation of the two systems.[156]

For the time being, the absence of a functioning appellate review at the WTO (with its consequence of partially paralyzing the functioning of the whole DSS and making the WTO less functional) and the replacement of ISDS with investment tribunals in some (not yet in force) EU agreements are the most relevant changes that have materialized (though the dismissal of the AB is the result of a crisis, not of reform).

Looming in the background is the backlash against globalization, now originating from some of the biggest players, including the US and some quarters of the EU, notwithstanding the benefits of trade (and investment[157]) as highlighted by the WTO DG Ngozi Okonjo-Iweala in June 2024: "One of the most remarkable changes since 1995 is that trade-enabled growth has lifted over 1.5 billion people

155 See the section on Comparative Evaluation at the end of Chapter VII.

156 For such a perspective, see The Economist "The Liberal International Order is Slowly Coming Apart. Its Collapse Could Be Sudden and Irreversible" (11 May 2024), available at https://www.economist.com. But see, to the contrary FT, The Editorial Board, "Fears of Destructive Protectionism are Overdone. An Aversion to Trade in the US is Not Widely Shared Elsewhere" (24 April 2024), available at https://www.ft.com.

157 As highlighted in the UNCTAD *World Investment Report 2024* available at <https://unctad.org/wir2024> accessed 24 July 2024, summary: "In 2023, global foreign direct investment decreased by 2% to $1.3 trillion, with inflows to Africa dropping by 3% to $53 billion amid an economic slowdown and rising geopolitical tensions".

out of extreme poverty", she said. This period also saw low- and middle-income economies nearly double their share in global exports from 16.5% to 32.2%, while the percentage of their populations living on less than $2.15 per day has dropped from 40% to under 11%.

Despite these advances, the current global trade landscape faces several challenges. "We are now in troubled times. We see increasing protectionism, the return of industrial policy, and the shaping of a narrative about trade that casts it as anti-people and anti-planet. We see signs of fragmentation in the trade data, with like-minded countries beginning to trade more with each other than with others that are not so like-minded".[158] America, on the other hand, "is now in the grip of a dangerous bipartisan consensus that threatens to return the world to the trade and currency wars of the 20th century".[159] As DG Ngozi Okonjo-Iweala further puts it: "Just as poor countries left behind during the recent wave of globalization look to benefit from the open, predictable multilateral trading system, they are being told that globalization is over, and presumably that they should find another way to fend for themselves. At the same time notwithstanding the dramatic increase in unilateral barriers to trade, flows have shown to be remarkably sustained and resilient".[160]

1. Commonalities

(a) A novelty is that states have recently engaged in multilateral reform negotiations in respect of both DSS. The current confrontational climate in international economic relations makes the prospect of successful comprehensive reforms less likely, although discussions on DSS reforms have somehow been shielded from the broader conflicts.

(b) Commonalities characterize the process, since both the WTO and UNCITRAL, where reforms are being discussed, are multilateral fora open to all member states, as well as observers in the case of UNCITRAL. While the discussions at the WTO are restricted to its Members, UNCITRAL is also more open to the

158 See the inaugural speech of DG Ngozi Okonjo-Iweala at the 9th Global Review of Aid for Trade, available at www.wto.org/english/news_e/news24_e/aid_26jun24_e.htm accessed 24 July 2024.

159 Both sides "believe that the global trading system is rigged against the US and want tariffs to protect specific favoured industries, especially autos and steel", see FT, "America's No-Good Tai-Lighthizer Consensus" (24 June 2024), https://www.ft.com/content/0515cdc5-6164-4af6-8b64-71b8be55a8d3 accessed 24 July 2024. Economists believe that tariffs such as those imposed on imports from China by the first Trump administration, and again in 2024 by the Biden administration, raise domestic prices and decrease the purchasing power of US consumers. The same is widely believed to be the case for the tariffs that President Trump has imposed at the start of his second term.

160 Speech cit. *supra* fn 158. An ICC Study of April 2024 ("The impact on developing economies of WTO dissolution") shows that WTO collapse could slash exports of developing countries by as much as 33% and cause them a permanent GDP loss of over 5%, https://iccwbo.org/news-publications/policies-reports/study-shows-wto-collapse-could-slash-exports-of-developing-countries-by-33-percent/. See also "Increase in trade restrictions against backdrop of unilateral policies," Annual Report 11 December 2024, available at tmdb.wto.org (accessed 25 January 2025).

input of other stakeholders, such as NGOs and experts. This is to be expected in view of the broad interest raised by ISDS and the direct participation in it of private (mostly corporate) interests.

(c) A common feature is that both reform processes are focused on procedural features of the DSS and do not aim at overhauling or dissolving either system. Rule-based binding adjudication of disputes between the participants in the trade and investment regimes remains the basic feature that characterizes these two sectors of international economic law and distinguishes them from all others.[161]

(d) In both regimes, reform is a slow and cumbersome process. Results, if measured by the adoption of new rules to date, have been limited. Most work is still in progress, and its outcomes are uncertain because the necessary overall consensus on multilateral solutions looks difficult to reach due to the divergent positions of various key actors and groups.

(e) Until now, reforms in both regimes have been fragmented and partial (see the MPIA/ICS). Partial reforms have been put in place to ensure the functioning of the respective DSS (MPIA/ISDS Codes of Conduct and updated Arbitration Rules), though with shortcomings in effectively and efficiently attaining the aim of settling disputes under their rules.

(f) A commonality that characterizes reform is that initiatives are also developed beyond the multilateral framework. Quite a few recent RTIAs/IIAs have incorporated improvements in both trade and investment DSS, adopting proposals in matters of proceedings that have not yet been incorporated at the multilateral level (transparency, deadlines, codes of conduct, selection methods, and party control through decisions of Joint Commissions).

(g) At the same time, this uncoordinated movement increases internal fragmentation, rather than making the two systems more coherent. Should WTO Members prioritize trade regionalization over the centralized WTO system? Will a critical mass of parties agree upon the establishment of a multilateral investment court? New solutions are not accepted by all parties, not even by a sizeable share of them under the same terms, contributing to making multilateral reforms elusive and possibly out of reach.

(h) Introducing an appeal stage for ISDS, applicable to a number of different IIAs, thus increasing engagement between the two systems, has not been considered a priority until recently but the outlook may change within UNCITRAL WG III. There is no systemic reason why appellate mechanisms ought not to be introduced in the investment regime, although adding a second layer would increase delays and costs. The rationale for introducing an appeal in ISDS is

161 See A. Bjorklund, "The Road(s) Not Taken – the Past, Present, and Future of International Investment Law Reform" 39 Arbitration International (2023) 455. Also their judicialization is a common feature, see Hong Zao (a former AB Member), " From "Contractual" to "Quasi-judicial" - The Progressive Appraoch of International Dispute Settlement and Mechanism Reform of the WTO Dispute Settlement" 14(2) J. of WTO and China (2024) 3.

that of increasing correctness, consistency, and predictability of decisions. The EU, however, is pushing for a more radical change, that of replacing ISDS arbitration with a (two-tier) ICS and MIC, while at the WTO the appellate stage is inoperative and participation in the MPIA (whose features are arbitral, not judicial) and usage of it remains limited. Potential convergence between the two systems may or may not happen at different levels of centralization.

(i) If ISDS does not move towards appeal, and if a functioning centralized system of appeal is not reinstated soon at the WTO and the membership of the MPIA decisions remains limited, the two systems may somehow converge on a lower level of review rather than vice versa. The "standing mechanism" to resolve investment disputes under discussion at WG III, in parallel with its work on reforming ISDS, however, provides, for a "Dispute Tribunal" and an "Appeal tribunal" inspired by the DSU model.[162]

(j) Commonality characterizes the effort to promote ADR as a preliminary stage of dispute settlement or as an alternative. Mediation and conciliation have always been possible in both systems, but the emphasis on structured, compulsory proceedings is new. However, even if ADR instruments are encouraged and made more reliable through formal mechanisms, more extensive recourse to them depends, as in the past, on the parties' interest and willingness, which cannot be taken for granted.

(k) Another area where there is commonality of approaches concerns reinforcing the independence and impartiality of adjudicators, as well as their professional qualifications. In this respect, requirements are being increased, including disclosure obligations to avoid potential conflicts, both for ISDS adjudicators and WTO panelists. The aim is not just to reinforce the impartiality of proceedings and confidence in decisions but also to thereby increase trust in the two systems and thus bolster their legitimacy.[163]

(l) A common orientation underlying reform work in both areas, shared by participants across the board, is at the same time increasing party control over the selection of adjudicators and that of reducing their margins of appreciation in exercising their powers (jurisdiction) and in interpreting the agreements that are to be applied. The mantra is to increase (reassert) party control as well as regulatory space and discretion concerning the exercise of the functions delegated to the adjudicators. This is implemented both by revising the substantive provisions to make the texts more precise (FET, indirect expropriation clauses in IIAs), thereby reducing judicial discretion, and by introducing or advocating carve-outs (public interest matters, Article XX GATT-type exceptions in IIAs, making security exceptions fully self-judging). As to proceedings, this involves opposing references to precedent, emphasizing the arbitral

162 See n 133.

163 See above Chapters VIII.A.3.1 and VIII.B.5.2.2(b), respectively, on the Molina proposals for the selection of panelists and the codes of conduct approved at UNCITRAL for investment judges and arbitrators.

rather than the judicial function of panels, the AB, and investment tribunals, introducing and making use of binding joint interpretations of IIAs, and the engagement of Members with the case law at the WTO DSS.[164] While this approach could lead to adjudicatory systems that are less rule-based (at the expense of adjudicators' independence), such state involvement and control may even increase trust in the binding adjudication of trade and investment disputes.

(m) Recalling our description in Chapter I of the WTO system as being top-down, in view of its multilateral character and centralized DSS, and ISDS as being bottom-up in view of the fragmentation of IIAs and their ISDS (with corresponding effects on the respective jurisprudence), we conclude that the WTO DSS is tending to become or risks becoming less so, while through the work of UNCITRAL WG III more uniformity and coherence may be injected into ISDS, somehow bringing the two systems closer together.

2. *Differences*

(a) There is a marked difference in the origin of criticisms that have led to the reform processes of the two regimes. In trade, dissatisfaction with the existing system has come from a major participant, the US, while criticism from those outside the system has rather been directed towards the system's substantive rules. This has occurred both from Members (such as on the adequacy of the existing regime for subsidies and SOEs) and from other stakeholders accusing these rules of endangering non-trade values (such as the protection of human health or the environment).

(b) The bulk of criticism of the investment regime, both of substantive standards and ISDS, has instead been voiced by non-business circles, including some academics, to the point of advocating for its elimination from BITs.[165] These radical proposals have not been successful up to now. Criticism has rather led to more practical, incremental changes of ISDS in the direction of improving transparency, integrity and accountability, as well as efficiency, and hence the legitimacy of investment arbitration, while retaining its basic features. Only the MIC initiative of the EU would mark a fundamental change in ISDS, but it is still far from enjoying support from a significant number of countries. In any case such a development would enhance rather than dismantle the current system whereby foreign investors can bring their complaints against host states to international justice.

(c) There are also differences in the reform efforts themselves. UNCITRAL is working on centralizing the reform of proceedings in the investment regime, which until now has been fragmented across thousands

164 See Chapter VII n 135, 136.

165 See Chapter VII.B.2–3.

of different IIAs. The level of progress that has been achieved at WG III, though far from concluded, has not been matched at the WTO, a venue where the need for procedural reform (in particular the need to find a remedy for appeals into the void) is all the more compelling. This is because the pressure for treaty change at the WTO requires consensus by all Members and mainly centres around its biennial Ministerial Conference (MC). On the other hand, reforms at WG III also mostly remain a "work in progress" whose outcome is uncertain.

(d) The introduction of regional or plurilateral ICSs that include an appeal stage, as has been characteristic of recent IIAs of the EU, does not seem to represent an area of commonality between the regimes as mentioned above. The adjudicators in ICS are all appointed by the states, but commonalities with the semi-arbitral panel system of the WTO stops here. Even more divergence is apparent comparing ICS (or the proposed MIC) to the MPIA which is arbitral in its set-up.

(e) An area where action has not followed words and differences still prevail is that of transparency. In fact, transparency is greater in the WTO DSS and in recent FTAs than in ISDS.[166] Both states and investors have shown a marked reluctance to accept more transparency in proceedings, as well as the full publication of ISDS awards. This is confirmed by the low number of ratifications of the Mauritius Convention and the limited progress made on full publication of awards in the 2022 reform of the ICSID Rules. On the other hand, there are specific IIAs (such as NAFTA/USMCA and CETA) where the level of transparency is much higher.

(f) Finally, an evolution is taking place as to the substantive standards of the two regimes, both being geared in this respect to reaffirm state control. In the investment regime the evolution in new IIAs points to a reduction of the protection of investors as compared with the recognition of the role of (host) states, also as a reaction to interpretations by arbitrators that were considered to be too broad. As to the investment system, new IIAs in many respects reduce the protection afforded to investors, in an attempt to rebalance investment promotion and protection with other public policy or regulatory objectives.[167] The spelling out of the

166 See Chapters IV.1.A.8 and IV.1.B.8.

167 In a sample of 120 IIAs concluded between 2005–2019, 78 (65%) of their preambles recognized the need to balance the promotion and protection of investment with the pursuit of other public policy objectives. See *Moran*, 55. For a plea in favour of increasing states' control over ISDS decisions, see J. Webb Yackee, "Controlling the International Investment Agency" 53 Harvard JIL (2012) 392; see also N. Perrone, "Bridging the Gap between Foreign Investor Rights and Obligations: Towards Reimagining the International Law on Foreign Investment" 7 Business and Human Rights J (2022) 375; A. Küçüksu, G. Ünüvar, "Vulnerability Theory as a Paradigm Shift in International Investment Law: Reimagining the Role of the State", 8 Business and Human Rights J (2023) 1.

paramount right to regulate of the state is typical of such "rebalancing" that goes in the direction of accommodating criticism of the alleged pro-investor bias of the investment regime.[168] There has been a concern that investment adjudicators have at times given overly expansive interpretations of the fair and equitable treatment (FET) standard with reference to the succinct provisions of first generation BITs.[169] This concern has been specifically directed at the concept of "legitimate expectations" as part of FET, or where measures have affected the "stability of the legal or business framework" in which a company operated. Such readings of this standard have been criticized as being too "open-ended".[170] In order to get rid of the vagueness surrounding what might constitute "fair and equitable" treatment, EU treaties (and others) now clearly list a narrow set of instances where this standard may be breached.[171] The evolution (or involution) of the wordings of FET provisions could not be clearer.

(g) Such updating of the treaties is more difficult to enact in the trade system due to the difficulty of reaching a consensus on amending the WTO texts.[172] No such development is in sight in respect of trade relations

168 See typically (besides AfCFTA Protocol on Investment (2023), Article 24 (*Right to Regulate*), text *supra* n 85), Article 29 *Right to regulate and levels of protection* of the Sustainable Investment Facilitation Agreement between the EU and Angola (2023): "1. The Parties recognise the right of each Party to determine its sustainable development policies and priorities, to establish the levels of domestic environmental and labour protection it deems appropriate and to adopt or modify its relevant laws and policies. Such protection levels, laws and policies shall be consistent with each Party's commitments to the internationally recognised standards and agreements referred to in this Chapter. 2. Each Party shall strive to ensure that its relevant laws and policies provide for, and encourage, high levels of environmental and labour protection, and shall strive to improve such levels, laws and policies. 3. A Party shall not weaken or reduce the levels of protection afforded in its environmental or labour laws in order to encourage investment. 4. A Party shall not waive or otherwise derogate from, or offer to waive or otherwise derogate from, its environmental or labour laws in order to encourage investment. 5. A Party shall not, through a sustained or recurring course of action or inaction, fail to effectively enforce its environmental or labour laws in order to encourage investment".

169 For example, Article 9.1 of the Japan–Vietnam BIT (2003): "Each Contracting Party shall accord to investments in its Area of investors of the other Contracting Party fair and equitable treatment and full and constant protection and security". A more detailed but still very broad definition of FET, which was originally meant to protect investors in the uncertain legal frameworks of former Asian Soviet Republics, is that of Article 10.1 ECT (1994). This provision has been at issue in most of the disputes involving Spain with reference to its reduction of incentives to RE operators.

170 G. Van Harten, "Leaders in the Expansive and Restrictive Interpretation of Investment Treaties: A Descriptive Study of ISDS Awards to 2010" 29 EJIL (2018) 507, 518; J. Hepburn, "The Legal Justification for the Doctrine of Legitimate Expectations in International Investment Law" 36 EJIL (2025) https://doi.org/10.1093/ejil/chaf017.

171 See the text of Article 8.10 CETA in n 91 above.

172 Certain WTO Members have made their dissatisfaction with the interpretation of a particular term by WTO adjudicators known, but no discussion has followed on possible reforms. See, for example, *Joint Statement of the Trilateral Meeting of the Trade Ministers of Japan, the US, and the EU* (2020) 6, available at USTR <https://ustr.gov/about-us/policy-offices/press-office/press-releases/2020/january/joint-statement-trilateral-meeting-trade-ministers-japan-united-states-and-european

especially in respect of contentious issues that have the potential to further stall a return to a fully functioning DSS (SOEs and subsidies, the national security exception).[173] First of all, the context is different: in IIAs states grant rights to private parties limiting their own governing powers; at the WTO states exercise their treaty rights under the DSU towards other states, both being in a position of parity. However, the reduction of the role of adjudicators' reports denying them precedential effect, as envisaged in the Molina report, hints at a restriction in the role of adjudication to the resolution of specific disputes, and therefore the recognition of broader policy space for states, also at the WTO.[174] While more consistency is sought in ISDS, less consistency in adjudication and hence less predictability of the law may result at the WTO.

-union> accessed 24 July 2024: "The Ministers observed that many subsidies are granted through State Enterprises and discussed the importance of ensuring that these subsidizing entities are captured by the term 'public body'". Other WTO Members may, of course have an opposing view. See generally R. Howse, J. Langille, "Continuity and Change in the WTO: Pluralism Past, Present and Future" 117 AJIL (2023) 1.

173 See above Chapter VIII.A.1.2.

174 See above, Chapter VIIIA.3.1(a).

Author Index

Subject Index

Made in the USA
Las Vegas, NV
20 September 2026

421b6d58-fce2-4642-8c34-bff3419b8981R02